American Scary

Conversations with the Kings, Queens and Jesters of Late-Night Horror TV

by Michael Monahan

Midnight Marquee Press, Inc.
Baltimore, Maryland, USA

All Chiller Theatert ads courtesy of chillertheatermemories.com and used with their permission

Copyright © 2006 POOB Productions and © 2011 Michael Monahan
Interior Layout: Gary J. Svehla
Cover Design: Susan Svehla

Without limiting the rights under copyright reserved above, no part of this publication may be reproduced, stored in or introduced into a retrieval system, or transmitted, in any form, or by any means (electronic, mechanical, photocopying, recording or otherwise), without the prior written permission of the copyright owner or the publishers of the book.

ISBN 978-1-936168-25-5
Library of Congress Catalog Card Number 2011945082
Manufactured in the United States of America
First Printing by Midnight Marquee Press, Inc., December 2011

Dedication
This book is dedicated to
every kid who tuned into their local
monster movie show to watch the host.

Table of Contents

Acknowledgments	5
Some People Call Us Horror Hosts	6
Scaring is Caring	7
Preface: From the Carnival to the Couch	8

Interviews:

1.	Vampira: Maila Nurmi	10
2.	Zacherley: John Zacherle	25
3.	Dr. E. Nick Witty: Alan Milair	40
4.	Baron Daemon: Mike Price	48
5.	Big Chuck: Chuck Schodowski	56
6.	Tim Conway	76
7.	Lil' John: John Rinaldi	82
8.	Christopher Coffin: Reed Farrell	87
9.	Chilly Billy: Bill Cardille	98
10.	Bob Wilkins and Bob Shaw	109
11.	Count Gore De Vol: Dick Dyzel	115
12.	Svengoolie: Jerry G. Bishop	123
13.	The Ghoul: Ron Sweed	130
14.	Dr. Creep: Barry Hobart	142
15.	Fritz the Nite Owl: Frank Peerenboom	151
16.	Son of Svengoolie: Rich Koz	163
17.	Crematia Mortem: Roberta Solomon	175
18.	Stella: Karen Scioli	186
19.	Commander USA: Jim Hendricks	194
20.	Son of Ghoul: Keven Scarpino	201
21.	Joe Bob Briggs: John Bloom	215
22.	Zomboo: Frank Leto	224
23.	Balrok: Brian Hall	231

Acknowlegments

No project like this is the creation of a single person. A finished work reflects the contributions of many. Sometimes all it takes is to be the friend who sits across the table while you spit out your ideas, smiles warmly as you finish, claps a hand on your shoulder and says, "I've heard worse."

Frank Sheridan as the immortal Asmodeus, host of KEMO-TV 20's *Shock It To Me Theater*, circa 1970.

First and foremost, I want to recognize the important women in my life.

My mother, Virginia, opened the door to the weird and wonderful world of horror hosts when she brought home a UHF-enabled television set in 1970. Within 24 hours, I had discovered *Shock It To Me Theater* on KEMO-TV 20. She took me to see *Thunderball* (1965) and *Fahrenheit 451* (1966) in the theaters, and she joined me for a screening of *Faster, Pussycat! Kill! Kill!* (1965) at my home in the late 1980s. Seriously, is that some kind of Mom, or what? She nurtured my passion for films and books from childhood and forever remained a champion for my artistic endeavors.

Dee Plunkett is my absurdly indulgent wife and best friend, always intensely supportive, but firmly practical. I learn something from her every day, whether I want to or not. Her smile brings light to the morning and comfort to the night. I love you, sweetie.

I can't think of this book without thinking of my dog, Stella, our beautiful girl. She watched me writing every day and always made sure I got out for walks. She passed away at the age of 11 in March 2011, just as I was wrapping up the bulk of this manuscript. She is loved, remembered and missed.

For the rest of you clowns, sincere thanks go out for all your support over the years. The following barely scratches the surface: Dave and Debbie Billman, Richard von Busack, Nicolas Caesar, Joseph Capuana, George "Egor" Chastain and his invaluable horror host website, John Cork, Kent Daluga, Jim Fetters, Gabrielle and Magoo Gelehrter, Jeff "The Sickie" Hall, John and Kelly Hlucky, Lon Huber, Chuck Jarman, Brian and Sarah Karas, Tim Lones, Bob Paulin, Steve Sherman and ak smith. And if I didn't mention my brothers, Frank and Jim, I would get clobbered.

A special thanks goes to Frank Sheridan, who portrayed horror host Asmodeus on *Shock It To Me Theater*. You never forget your first. Thanks for the inspiration, Frank. You were the best.

Sandy Clark and John Hudgens: Thank you for inviting me into your project.

And finally, sincere thanks and appreciation to a nation of local TV horror hosts, the women and men who wove cherished memories from the stuff of which nightmares are made.

Some People Call Us Horror Hosts

We have gnat-like cultural memories that are awash in distractions from *Angry Birds* to *Dancing with the Stars*. We are too busy learning the next thing to remember the last.

There are not just new distractions, but new screens for new distractions. Most of us carry around enough electronics to make Dick Tracy look like a Luddite. Make no mistake; all of these new technologies are draining the old media empires that guided television up to this point. Your iPads and YouTubes force the head back and the fangs are in. Viewers are trickling away.

That is one reason the 2002 Wondercon in Oakland, California was so baffling for me. I was selling a comic book, trying to slip it under the door of the media machine. I struck up a nice conversation with a guy named Bob Wilkins, who used to host KTVU's *Creature Features* throughout the 1970s.

What in the world a guy who had been off the air for 22 years was going to do at a comic book convention, I couldn't say, but I enjoy talking to old broadcasters. They remember a time when your local programming decisions were made a lot closer to home. They remember when your television used to respond to you. Kids could send in photos to the kiddie shows and Bob Wilkins would read your letter on the air.

Still, that was more than 20 years before, and I was clueless.

The doors opened and the stampede of people started. I hustled funny books. In the down times, I glanced over at Bob. The line went around the hall and out the door. When I broke for lunch, the line was still there. When they began to shut the show down, the line was still there. I realized that I was missing some crucial understanding of horror movies, Bob Wilkins or the obsessive nature of fans.

"Well, I don't know," Bob said. "People really loved us. Some people call us "horror hosts," but I just tried to give people a good show."

He used the word "us." That implied a twilight fraternity of similar guys out there. I got curious. I hadn't had a horror host growing up in the hills of Tennessee. The closest I came was Commander USA. Now, here was a world of collective experience that played out locally on a national scale. How had I missed this? I couldn't let that idea go.

So that's how *American Scary* was born, and it barely scratches the surface. There are so many more hosts, and so much material we had to leave on the floor that I sometimes despair at the impossibility of telling a comprehensive tale.

The great thing about this moment in time, though, is that it is all becoming available again. We live in the age of availability. Netflix will bring *American Scary* to one of your screens, even if you don't want Amazon to bring a hard copy for your shelf.

It seems that every one of these hosts has someone willing to digitize their clips and bring them back. If they don't, then maybe you should. The technology gets cheaper every day.

That's the other great force at work, the democratizing of media. Right at this time when the quality of mainstream offerings claws at being inoffensive enough to lick the last drop of blood off the corpse, new life springs from the corpse itself.

Now you have the ability to open the door so others can see your childhood hero. Remind people of an age when they knew the people talking to them on the TV. Make media personal again. Maybe decide to become a horror host, or something like it, yourself.

This book is a collection of just those kinds of stories. People who became unexpected stars or just thought it would be a hoot to play at becoming a monster for a while. You can read it as history. You can read it for fun. I'd like to invite you to read it as inspiration.

This is the time. You can make a show. Maybe, some people will call you a horror host.

—Sandy Clark, December 2010

Sandy Clark (right) with cameraman Trey Stokes

Scaring Is Caring

At the time Sandy Clark first approached me in 2003 for information on the history of TV horror hosts, I had been researching the genre for about five years. I grew up in the San Francisco Bay Area, where we enjoyed a particularly rich and varied mix of hosts, beginning with Terrence (Russ Coglin) in 1957. Being a zygote at the time, I never got to enjoy Terrence. But when I discovered Asmodeus and *Shock It To Me Theater* in 1970, I knew my world had been fundamentally and irrevocably changed.

Bob Wilkins followed in 1971 with *Creature Features*. The Ghoul was imported from Cleveland on our local Kaiser station, KBHK-TV 44, in 1973. An ex-Marine named Tom Stone donned a Dracula cape to host *Saturday Nite Dead* as Tom B. Stone, military issue crew cut intact. John Stanley attempted to fill the void left by Bob Wilkins' departure from *Creature Features* in 1979. But by that time hormones had superseded horror in my world and I was no longer paying attention. The Son of Svengoolie arrived from Chicago in 1982 just in time to stir nascent nostalgia, he being the seed brought to bloom by cable host Commander USA in 1985.

In the late 1990s, Bob Wilkins released a multi-volume set of *Creature Features* highlights on VHS, reigniting a childhood passion for classic monster movies and the people who presented them. I was trading tapes with fellow collectors across the country and started asking for any old programs featuring a horror host.

The first example to arrive was Indiana's Sammy Terry. The show struck a shockingly familiar chord. All the traditional elements I had grown up were on colorful display. At the same time, the show generated a sort of regional vibration that marked it as the creation of a specific time and place. This experience was repeated as other hosted shows came in from Cleveland, Florida and Missouri, leading me to view horror hosting as a form of American folk art worthy of serious study.

That was the pitch I gave Sandy when we first got together. Sandy had recently seen lines snaking out the door at a comic book convention leading to a table occupied by Bob Wilkins and marveled at the idea of crowds swarming a local personality, whose show had been off the air for a quarter of a century. The joyful and passionate atmosphere of the moment suggested this was ripe material for some sort of documentary.

As I laid out the materials I'd gathered in my research and explained the national scope of the phenomenon, he started grinning like a kid. "When I came here, I wasn't sure there was enough for a short," he said at the time. "But, damn, this is a feature!" And that's how I got involved in making the film documentary, *American Scary* (2006).

Author Michael Monahan conking coconuts with Maila Nurmi (Vampira) in 2004

The film was a celebration of local TV personalities and their intimate, inspirational connection to the community. With corporate ownership of media poised to snuff the last struggling ember of local broadcast identity, it's more important than ever to remember a time when the person on that television screen was a neighbor, someone who said your name on the air, read your letter, showed your artwork, announced your birthday, made you laugh and showed you really cool monster movies.

The opportunity to expand the conversations we had with these unique celebrities is something I treasure, because, in full, they present a sweeping oral history of radio and television in America. If you can't remember a time when TV was fun, you will by the time you're done reading.
—Michael Monahan, May 2011

Editors note: Some of these interviews were conducted in the early-to-mid 2000s and regrettably several of the interviewees have passed away since that time.

Preface:
From the Carnival to the Couch

TV horror movie hosts were the last popular purveyors of a show biz style that pre-dates the birth of the movies themselves. The footprints of the genre can be found in the sawdust of the traveling carnivals, where midway barkers called crowds into the tents, promising forbidden delights and freakish horrors.

The Spook Shows of the late '20s and 1930s brought these dark attractions out from behind the canvas flaps and onto the stage, mixing blatant ballyhoo with a potent blend of magic and spiritualism to create a uniquely American form of Grand Guignol. These highly theatrical presentations, presided over by showmen with names like Dr. Silkini, Ray-Mond and Kara Kan, usually ended in a blackout, wherein all of the lights in the house were extinguished. In total darkness, strings from the balcony and from under their seats would tickle audiences, while glow-in-the-dark "ghosts" and skeletons swirled over their heads.

By the mid-1930s, the revival of cinematic horror led to the slightly tweaked Midnight Horror Show. Monsters—often running right through the audience—were added to the mix, as was an element that would tie it directly to the TV horror host of the 1950s. The midnight show, hosted by an elegantly dressed figure, aided by mad scientists and monsters, punctuated by screams and ghoulish humor, climaxed with the presentation of a mystery or horror feature. It was a ritual that audiences a generation removed would come to know intimately.

Vampira offered a tantalizing glimpse of things both past and future in 1954. But it wasn't until 1957, with the release of Universal studio's *Shock* movie package, that TV horror movie hosts would explode into popular culture. In October of that year, the grim, lurching, classic monsters of Hollywood's premiere horror factory spilled out onto America's hearth, ushered into living rooms across the country by an army of comically spooky sideshow barkers.

These hosts served a variety of functions. At a time when most markets were limited to three or four competitive channels, a station's family of local personalities inspired the same sort of brand loyalty as network TV households, like The Cleavers, The Nelsons and The Flintstones. On a practical level, they were highly adaptable time fillers. The average film running times varied anywhere from 60 to 75 minutes, and the host could stretch or contract their air time as needed to fit the show into a 90-minute time slot.

The horror host went through various cycles of popularity and influence. The initial wave ignited the Monster Kid boom, ushering in an era of *Famous Monsters of Filmland* on the newsstands, Boris Karloff's *Thriller*, *The Munsters* and *The Addams Family* on TV and Aurora monster model kits on bedroom shelves.

Gothic horror was usurped in the mid-1960s by space-age adventure as

Dr. Evil (Phillip Morris) toured the country with his on-stage Spook Show for two decades, transitioned to television as the host of *Horror Theater* on WBTV-TV 3 in Charlotte, North Carolina. He is equally famous for owning Morris Costumes, a Halloween and prop company.

James Bond 007—personified by the brutishly elegant Sean Connery—created a fanatical global superspy mania. By 1965, kids had shifted their allegiance from man-made monsters to *The Man from U.N.C.L.E.*—though horror stars like Vincent Price and Boris Karloff popped up on the *Man* and *Girl from U.N.C.L.E.* shows, and Martin Landau would rehearse for his Oscar-winning role as Bela Lugosi in *Ed Wood* (1994) by appearing as THRUSH agent, Count Zark, in "The Bat Cave Affair."

The Beatles, Batman, surfing and psychedelia competed for attention throughout the decade. And while horror movies remained a staple, their cultural power was diluted by the overwhelming bounty of '60s popular culture. These distractions were on the wane within a few years. A pudgy, embittered Sean Connery hung up his rocket pack and tossed away his license to kill after *You Only Live Twice* in 1967. The Beatles were famously imploding in recording studios and courtrooms across England and nobody gave a crap about Batman by 1968.

With the proliferation of UHF stations in the latter part of the decade, local television once again found itself with a lot of time to fill, and many station owners eyed cheaply produced monster movie shows as a fun and potentially profitable way to fill the space in between the endless off-network reruns. And so the early 1970s saw another significant wave of horror hosts. Some, like Cleveland native The Ghoul, even attracted national recognition, thanks to sister station affiliation on the Kaiser network.

The party was largely over by the mid-1980s. A few new hosts, like Chicago's Son of Svengoolie and Northeast Ohio's The Son of Ghoul, established long-term careers. But local stations were disappearing under a steamroller of corporate ownership. The whole concept of local programming was becoming quaintly old-fashioned. Even Elvira's nationally syndicated *Movie Macabre*—which began on local Los Angeles station KHJ-TV 9 in 1981—was gone by the middle of the decade.

Commander USA and Joe Bob Briggs appeared on cable in the '80s and '90s. Fondly remembered local hosts across the country enjoyed brief revivals or seasonal Halloween specials. Zacherley, a pioneer of the original *Shock Theater* days, was making television appearances as late as 2008. And generations of fans, both old and new, were carrying the early TV traditions to the Internet. But as a popular mainstream force, the time of the horror host had passed.

As the world approached the new millennium, a few feisty independent stations began to reassert themselves. The Son of Svengoolie had returned to television on WCIU-TV 26 in 1995. But as the son becomes the father, so The Son of Svengoolie became simply Svengoolie. His resurrection proved strong and lasting, eventually leading to limited national syndication in 2011.

In 1999, KOLO-TV 8 in Reno, Nevada launched a new host in Zomboo, who also showed continued strength after more than a decade on the air. KOFY-TV 20 in the San Francisco Bay Area began an aggressive campaign of locally produced programming, following an extended period as the market's WB affiliate. One of the first new in-house shows to go on the air was *Creepy KOFY Movie Time*, debuting at midnight, January 1 in 2009. Co-hosted by a demon named Balrok and a foul-mouthed zombie called No Name, it quickly established itself as one of the station's highest rated shows.

Elvira returned with a syndicated movie program in 2011, and suddenly everything old was new again.

By the time horror hosts first appeared on television in the 1950s, the formula had been so perfectly refined that any changes to it after the first big wave were purely cosmetic, dictated by trends in the popular culture or enhancements in technology. Through it all, the TV horror hosts continued to ply the same strain of grotesque burlesque popularized by their forebears in radio, the comics, Spook Shows and carnivals. They remained capering cornball crypt keepers, friendly phantoms with a rotted skull in one hand and a rubber chicken in the other.

Grave Looted Of Skull For Boys' Show

JERSEY CITY, N. J.—(A)—Police nabbed seven boys—ranging in age from 6 to 12—and said they had looted a graveyard of a human skull to hold their own version of a television horror show.

The boys were caught yesterday after police had found the skull, a candle stuck in it, in the basement of an unfinished housing project. Police picked them up when they returned to the basement for a horror session.

They were released in custody of their parents pending juvenile action.

Article from the *Tucson Daily Citizen* July 9, 1959

The Vampira Monologues
Vampira (Maila Nurmi)
Interviewed by Sandy Clark and Michael Monahan (2003)

On May 1, 1954, unsuspecting late-night viewers in Los Angeles tuned into KTLA-TV 5 to find a strange and unnatural figure bleeding out of the darkness from the end of a long hallway. Tightly swathed in black—highlighting a distressingly tiny waist—she resembled a hornet nightmarishly reared up on its back legs, skittering forward on a roiling carpet of smoke. In one thudding heartbeat her face, glamorous and kabuki white, filled the screen, abruptly seized into a rictal mask and issued a nerve-shredding shriek. Spent, she melted into a kittenish pose. "Screaming relaxes me so," she purrs; a coy come-hither from the crypt.

The mysterious woman was Vampira, created and played by stage performer and pin-up model Maila Nurmi, who debuted not only television's first horror host, but also a uniquely disturbing marriage of ancient terror and modern technology, the first newly minted mythological creature of the atomic age. Her body was an unsettling union of the voluptuous and the cadaverous, the softly rounded invitation of the bosom swelling over the desiccated cradle of birth. She was death, the irrepressible flirt.

The physical image, coupled with a disdainfully cosmopolitan sophistication, introduced early TV viewers to something genuinely radical—in a medium already developing a reputation for playing it safe.

The effect was immediate and beyond all expectations. Within weeks Vampira, the star of a local Southern California television show, became a worldwide phenomenon. The very scope of her popularity led to her downfall, as the station—already concerned about her tendency to challenge propriety—pressed for controlling interest in the character. The strong-willed Nurmi refused and quickly found herself evicted from her studio haunt (blacklisted is the term she uses).

She reappeared briefly on rival station KHJ in May 1956, but was off the air by the end of the year. She survived for a time on work in low-budget exploitation fare, like *The Beat Generation* (1959), *Sex Kittens Go to College* (1960) and, most memorably, Ed Wood's wigged-out masterpiece, *Plan 9 from Outer Space* (1959).

Maila Nurmi kept herself creatively active throughout her life, making jewelry, selling Vampira art, and fronting a punk band in the 1980s. She briefly reclaimed media attention when she once again fought for control of her character by filing a lawsuit against Cassandra Peterson, who was finding fame as the ersatz-Vampira clone, Elvira.

The case was dismissed by court in 1989.

Maila Nurmi passed away on January 10, 2008.

Sandy Clark: The image of Vampira is iconic and powerful.

Oh yeah, there's that one still of her from *Plan 9 (from Outer Space)* that they always use where she's in alpha state. Lots of people use it for tee shirts and such. She scared lots of little boys when they were growing up. She was in alpha state. I was in an alpha state, literally, on camera. People say they don't know what they're looking at and it scares them. Because when we see something we don't understand it's frightening, especially to little kids. So it wasn't just someone being spooky. It was someone in another state of mind, in another state of being.

SC: Tell us about the genesis of Vampira. I know it started with the costume, so start with that. What were you thinking when you put the costume together?

Back in 1953, I needed $20,000, which was a lot in those days, because I wanted to sponsor myself as an evangelist. And I figured the best way to do it was with this new business, television. They pay me lots of money, and all I have to do is stand up and be me. I had been a monologist for 15 years, and so audiences were mine for the grabbing, you know? I thought I'd get their money. But what do they like? What's everybody watching on TV? So I checked it, and they were watching a show called ... I think it was called *The Websters (she is likely referring to* Father Knows Best, *which premiered in 1954)*. It was the most popular thing, and it was a most mundane portrait of family happenings. And I thought, well, that's what they're watching. I guess I should do this. And then I thought, no, that's too pedestrian. I can't be so bourgeois. Well, I'll satirize it. And then I thought, oop, Charles Addams already did just that. And then I thought I'd do Charles Addams! We'll get Charles Addams. So I proceeded to make the Charles Addams dress, thinking to put it on TV.

I did the dress. And then there was this great masquerade ball that 2,000 people used to attend. And they were sophisticated people, because Lester Horton hosted.

It was *The Lester Horton Ball Caribe*. I thought these are the readers of the *New Yorker*, they would recognize this character. Nobody else would know who she was. So I went there. And I practiced my Victorian curtsey, because I expected to win. The character didn't have a name. But I had lavender make-up. You know, powdered with a little lavender, looking as though I had risen from the grave. Turning a little blue, you know? Barefooted, like that lady was … Flat chested, but otherwise wan and wonderful.

I won the first prize. I chose a radio, rather than dance lessons. And then I went away. They didn't know who I was. But a TV programmer had been there, from KABC, a local station. He couldn't use me for anything, because he didn't have a spot for me. But he was transfixed by the visual. Everybody was talking about me all night, asking about my husband, my family, you know? Morticia (*the Charles Addams character*) didn't have a name yet. Now this was a housewife, I was being a housewife. I wasn't Vampira yet.

So Huntz Stromberg, the program director, finally found me after five months. He asked Rudy Gumwright, who had been one of the judges, who said, "Oh, I know Maila Nurmi. She was the first person in California to wear backless shoes."

"Well, where can I find her?"

"You can find her in the phone book. She's listed as Mrs. Dean Roddesdam."

Come back, Little Shiva! The Goddess of Death strikes a kittenish pose.

So they found me and asked me to come in. He said, "Come in costume." And I came in, during the Ides of March, wearing a great cape. And the winds, the winds of the Ides of March were flapping it. People were coming out of their little bungalows saying, "Oh, there's Huntz's vampire!" I had no hair. I had just lost it in a beauty parlor accident. You just didn't see ladies with crew cuts in those days. But I had all sorts of things women didn't see in those days.

He wanted me. But the seniors at the station didn't, because it was too expensive to do *The Addams Family*. So they said, "We're going to steal this one little character. We're going to do it." I said I don't do that, I don't steal from artists I admire. I don't steal from anyone. But, I said, give me a few days. I'll think of something. So then I saw a book by John Willie, *Bondage and Discipline*. I said, aha, that's it! I had been a pin-up model. I had done cheesecake right at that time. So I took the cheesecake and the bondage and the discipline, and I cinched up her waist. And I got some phallic symbols going, like a long cigarette holder, you know, black. And I put on the fishnet hose. I slit the dress. I changed Morticia's statement, right?

Now Vampira is supposed to be the grand mommy of the Goths, but I'm not really the first one. Theda Bara, I think, was the first one. A Gothic lady today must wear skull and crossbones. She must be raised from the grave. She's got to be a vamp. She's got to be somber, and she's got to be very pin-uppy provocative. She's got to be those three things: death-related, a pin-up, and a dominatrix. She can't be a submissive, like Bettie Page. She's got to be a dominatrix like Theda Bara. She's got to be strong, and that's what she (*Vampira*) is. Of course there are Goths with a touch of everything. There are little Gothic girls with touches of this and touches of that. But the pure, pure Goth has got to be all three of those things. Vampira was, in spades.

Michael Monahan: So essentially, sex, death and control.

Yes, sex, death and control. I gave her Hollywood make-up and the bedraggled former glamour haircut with the disarray. I took on an attitude. I kept the cheesecake mood, but remembering there too was something a little like Greta Garbo in there, and something a little Dos-

11

Vampira on the Couch. A captured moment in pencil, drawn by Maila Nurmi, 1998.

toyevsky. And something a wee bit spooky, like Norma Desmond, who had just turned me on big in *Sunset Blvd.* (1950), too big. Now when you see it, I look like I'm imitating Norma Desmond … that I was. But not consciously, it was subliminal. So they said, "Okay, come in and show yourself to the producers again," which I did. I persuaded them to go for $75 a week; I would do it. My take-home was $59.60 a week. It all went to taxis and body make-up.

SC: What was different about America that was feeding into this? You must have been surprising and shocking to people.

Horrifying to people, dazzling and horrifying. When I'd do a show like *Playhouse 90*, we would rehearse for a week. I would know everybody and chat with the people and everything. Now it's show day and I would retire to my dressing room. I'd do my own make-up and come out three hours later. People were afraid of me, people I'd worked with all week. (*Laughs*) I really terrified them. The illusion was something real, I guess, because I tried to make her believable. Not like someone in a costume, but a demented woman who believed who she was…A sort of semi-surreal entity—and semi-human. I tried to make her believable that way, and it did spook people.

SC: And there wasn't that style of acting on television at that time. There was still a very presentational style of acting. People didn't come on as characters.

No, they didn't. Everything was very staid, the whole world. The whole world we lived in was very conventional and very conservative. And Vampira was a complete bombshell, a complete bombshell. It terrified and fascinated people. That's why we got so much press. We didn't have to hire a press agent. I had a fellow drive me from place to place, but we didn't have to advertise.

SC: Were you ever afraid that you might have pushed it too far? Did you ever look at something and think, "You know, this might be pushing it over the top?"

Twice. I did a live show at the Pan Pacific, and little teenage girls came and said, "Oh, we have a fan club," and I had so many fan clubs all over the world. And they said, "Oh, the terrible things we have to do to get into the club!" And I suddenly realized I was inspiring young people to do bad things. I wanted to quit. I didn't, but I struggled with myself and worried about it.

And then about a year later, I was doing a glamour shoot in a cemetery, you know, cemetery cheesecake. And the photographers had set up by an open grave already dug for a funeral. They had set up a lot of chairs. The photographer had me sit there and said, "You're the only person who came to your own funeral, and you're mourning yourself." I'm sitting there mourning myself, but then the people who were going to bury an Asian man, a daddy, came. Little children came, and they were supposed to attend their father's funeral. But instead they came to me. They wanted to be with Vampira for the autographs. They wanted to see Vampira. They didn't even care about their daddy who was going away forever. It was awful. And that's about when … I was blacklisted anyway. I might have quit if they hadn't blacklisted me then. I might have laid it down for a while anyway.

SC: Do you think you could get away with anything like that on TV today?

Oh, you couldn't do anything like that. But there were things you couldn't do then. I couldn't say once, "My sister was arrested for raping a snake." We were cut off the air, because you couldn't say "rape." But today you can get away with all sorts of things. I don't know what the essences were in Vampira that wouldn't be allowable today.

SC: It's just occurring to me as we're talking about it that, in many ways, Vampira was 50 years ahead of her time. You look at the Goth kids today and you would fit right in.

Well, I'm the grandmommy of Goth, they say. And I look at those kids, with their rags and their skeletons and their drug habits, and I'm mortified. I don't like them. I think they're very physically beautiful. I love the illusion. Some of them are great make-up artists. But their moral outlook is vacant. But that's today's civilization, that's what they're reared in. It's not their fault, and it's not really my fault. But I do blame myself. I wouldn't want a child who behaved that way.

SC: So what are the other threads that have changed in America from the time you were on till now? I think Vampira was able to stand out because she was so unique. There was a quiet and stillness around where she could be heard. Do you have any thoughts about the changes that happened from that time till now?

No, actually. I have pretty much withdrawn from the world, withdrawn from society. I used to live inside the walls when I was a child at home. I was always hiding, or inside the wall bed. I've always withdrawn to some degree. But this society has changed and I haven't kept up with it. I'm not really aware. I'll read newspapers occasionally and watch a little TV. But I'm not aware how the world is changing. And like so many elderly people, I'm living my elderly life, which is a whole different thing. A sort of divorce from the whole general theme, you know. So I really don't know. I just live in my little world, my little cocoon. I know my way to the doughnut shop and the way to the laundry mat and so on.

SC: You mentioned your childhood. What were the influences in your childhood that led you into a character like Vampira, which gave her that visual sense?

Oh, very much, very calculated.

SC: Where did that come from? Was there a moment in your childhood where you remember having this sense of the visual world and how things could be put together to be more attractive or more enticing?

Well, no. What happened was I was terrified once I popped out of the womb. I was terrified because people were so big, noises were so loud and I wasn't able to communicate. So I hid in the closet, anyway, then. And I found a mouse; that was my first friend, someone who was not bigger than me, someone who was a good friend, who understood me, who was as meek as I was. And in the dark, we bonded. I was, like, 18 months old. That was in Finland. But then my mother found out and she pulled me out of the closet and shut the latch. She didn't want the rat to eat the baby. I remembered it 35 years later. She said, "I can't believe you remembered that, you were 18 months old." But it was a trauma for me, because I couldn't get to my friend anymore. I couldn't reach the latch.

So that was the beginning. I had already, for some reason, rejected the world and feared it. I had crawled into my own world. After that, wherever we lived, I usually did find a crawlspace somewhere to go into and hide. I just had low self-esteem—I was a great, great introvert. I was a nerd, a real creep as far as the world was concerned, you know? But then I saw people who weren't. I saw them in the comic books. I saw The Dragon Lady in *Terry and the Pirates*, who was cool and invincible, and very, very beautiful. I was hideously ugly, and she was very, very beautiful. My mother told me it was a pity I was homely. I had to figure out how to become less homely. By the time I was 12 … it was a lot of work. And I kept studying and figuring how to become less homely. My identity was building and building.

And then into the movies came the Evil Queen in *Snow White* (1937). She was the black-haired lady who was powerful and invincible. She's probably been around since the era of the caveman. Who knows? But that impressed me. That made a big impression on me, the Evil Queen. She again was cool and imperious and nobody could harm her. That's what I wanted. I didn't want to be evil, but I did want to be invincible and free from harm. And I wanted to be cool and beautiful. I wanted to be cool and beautiful because I was so ugly and torn. And then I saw Theda Bara, and of course that made a big, big impression on me. I liked that Russian melodrama, because all of that was in my blood anyway. I thought, oh yeah, I can make that statement. Oh yes, yes, yes! That was it.

Then along came *Sunset Blvd*. Norma Desmond really struck a note with me and sent me into action. I think I saw that in 1950? I think that's when it was released. And within a year, I was doing Vampira. I didn't know why I was doing it, but I'm sure that was why, that was the final impetus. Because I was way, way too much of an impersonation of her, you know, of the character. Because it suited everything else I had figured out. Of course, I did a lot of body sculpting, too. I wanted her to have a tiny little waist. I wanted her to have that perfect hourglass figure. And I created a Wonder Bra, before they were created, and a spot reducer that whittled my waist away. I'm still in the *Guinness Book of Records* for smallest waist in the world. But I'm not showing it today (*laughs*).

SC: What must this sudden fame have been like for an introvert, for someone who had crafted the layers of another self to go out into the world?

It's the other side of the coin. I had been a monologist. On stage I was always at home, before an audience. I was only at home then, when I was not Maila Nurmi. When I'm on stage and I'm not Maila Nurmi, its fine. It's fine, I can take on the world.

MM: I've read many articles about you and Vampira, but never really heard or read anything about the actual production of your show or the other people who worked on it.

Nobody has asked. Nobody cares. Well, you care. But nobody seems to have cared till now. The director was Hap Wyman. You know, Hap for happy? (*Laughs*) He probably should have been directing *Snow White and the Seven Dwarfs*. And we had a brilliant scriptwriter, Peter Robinson, who had been with the Bob and Ray show in Chicago. He arrived here without a job; a family and no job. He saw the show, the first show we had, which was very bad because the writer was actually a piano player who wanted to write, and they said okay. And it was an embarrassment what I had to say. The first two weeks were very bad. But Peter Robinson saw the show and wrote a script. He said, "That's a character without a script, and here's the script I'm suggesting." So he came on board, and he was a brilliant writer. That was so lucky. He did the third show for us right away.

The lighting man was an 18-year-old boy who had apprenticed with a very old man who was still using flash powder. This was his first job where he was in control of the camera himself, and the lighting. We filmed—this is the most amazing thing that no one mentions—in the same studio where they filmed *The Jazz Singer* (1927). That was our studio. Now that's a big one for you, no one knows that. My then father-in-law, Chuck Riesner, said, "Oh, so you have a job, you have a TV show. Where are you filming?" And I said, at Prospect and Talmidge at KABC. And he said, "Oh, that's where we filmed *The Jazz Singer*." He was the assistant director. The studio at that time had these little bungalows and this one big barn-shaped building with rafters upstairs, like a hayloft.

That's where my first pin-up layout was taken, in that hayloft. And that's where we filmed the show.

SC: Tell me about the routine for the show. You had a writer. So he'd write scripts and you'd rehearse?

No. They liked his writing so much they had him writing 11 shows a week. I'd get my script when I arrived at the studio. The director would say, "Use your marks" and "… a little guillotine, don't cut your fingers off" and "this light here." And I'm doing that, and then there's the teleprompter… I was named the best female teleprompter reader in America. Bob Montgomery was the best male. But I was really doing cold readings. You have to have someone who senses your timing, the one who runs the teleprompter. And of course Vampira could lounge and glance at the script. And then she would muse some more … and then slowly say it. Because of the tempo, she could take her time, you know, to do a cold reading and not make it look like a cold reading.

SC: So it was bit like improv for you. Because the physical business you had to come up with on the fly had to match what you were reading.

And I had to make my own props. I'd get a notice about the middle of the week from the studio: "We're going to need this, that and that." I modeled hats one time and I had a bandaged head with an arrow through it. Bauer and Bauer made it. Suitable for archery matches. (*Laughs*) Things like that. I was a one-woman *Saturday Night Live*, that kind of comedy.

SC: Was there ever any input or collaboration on your part in terms of scripts? Did you come up with any ideas?

Peter Robinson said, "If there's anything you want to say, just go right ahead and slip it in." I rarely did, but occasionally I did. But my husband, Dean Riesner, sometimes wrote special material for me, like when I went to the Miss Rheingold contest (*a beauty pageant sponsored by Rheingold's Beer*). You know, they used these Irish colleens and one—they all looked alike—would win. Very wholesome, they looked about 17 or 18, and they looked very Irish, just little colleens.

So I went in full drag, with the vulture hat and carried a gold-headed stick. I was at the tail end; all the ladies had passed in their bathing suits. Then I passed the judges and I said—my husband had written this for me—"Gentlemen, I seem to be suffering under a grave misapprehension. I had thought Rheingold's Beer would be at the center of a Wagnerian funeral." Well, they were stunned. They didn't know what to make of it. It was early on and nobody really knew who Vampira was. So my husband wrote that little piece for me. Our producer was also pretty bright, Huntz Stromberg. He was good about press agentry. He wanted me to jump out of a helicopter with a black parachute, but I wasn't going to risk my life.

SC: What people came and went on the show? Did you have guests?

Couldn't afford them. They came by telephone and mail. I had Jimmy (*James*) Dean on one day, but that was just because he had come with me and was sitting there. They said, "Hey kid!"—one of the crew said—"Put this jacket on." He was unkempt looking, uncombed, and I was being a librarian. Pulled the hair back—a nasty librarian—and I had to rap the knuckles of a nasty student who was too noisy. So I rapped his knuckles with my ruler. They showed his back and shoulders. They didn't pay him. They didn't know he was a movie star.

SC: Do you think any of that footage still exists at KABC? Do they have anything still?

They threw it all away when they boycotted me. But there were nine shows on one big disc, and they gave that to UCLA. And then, two years or three years ago, they were going to have a few minutes of me on the news. So they sent for the thing and looked at it, let's say on a Tuesday, and the next day they were going to air it. When tomorrow came, it was missing. It has been missing ever since, as far as I know. Nine shows. But some people say they have seen them. I think they may have just seen the couple of minutes that are on the newsreel. There was also an eight-minute piece that was made as a sample that was sent back East to show what had been done here. That's without sound effects, without the dry ice, and so without a lot of the visuals. It was not a true rendition of the show. The shows themselves do exist ... somewhere.

I wasn't on a political blacklist. It was just that I offended one man with a lot of clout and a big ego. He didn't want me to work, and he decided to take what I did and make it bigger to make money for himself and really punish me. He called me into his office and said, "There are $60,000's worth of work offers for you and I've refused them all. You don't get to know who they're from." And I couldn't pay my rent that month. So it was one man with a lot of clout. They blacklisted me; that was it. My contract had nine months to run out. They paid me this pittance for the nine months, but kept me out of work. It was illegal. They tried to do it to Walt Disney. But he said, "Wait a minute!"

But I didn't know about lawyers or anything. They just kept me off, hoping that people would forget about

An evocative abstract representation of Vampira, drawn by Maila Nurmi, 2002

me. And they did forget about me after nine months, and then they moved in with *The Addams Family* (The Addams Family *TV series aired on ABC in 1964*), which is what ABC wanted to do.

SC: Throwing out the films is not uncommon. They may have had a grudge against you, or were blacklisting you, but they did this to everyone eventually. They threw everything away. Do feel something lost when these shows were tossed out? Do you feel that, nationwide, they threw away a piece of history at that moment? I know for you personally there was a sense of loss, but did you have a sense of a greater loss around that?

I'm not sure I'm that impressed by the idea of cultural hallmarks or that kind of thing. I don't care much about culture. But I've always loved fashion. When I was five years old, I was already making movie star dresses for

Vampira—an icon is born!

the dollies, little white satin evening gowns for them to wear to premieres. They were two for a nickel. That was in Cleveland. We were living in Cleveland and my girlfriends had celluloid dollies. They were little pot-bellied Clara Bow dolls. You know, with the little hairdos. And I made little tiaras for them and glued them on with gum. And the evening wrap, the little ermine wrap, they could get for 10 cents. But I was always making things for premieres. By then, I was Hollywood-struck. I didn't speak English then. But I saw the magazines; I saw the pictures.

SC: I can see where that worked for you, too. It was a project you could do in your isolation, and then present it. And people would be wowed.

Well, the Vampira dress, everything she wore, is now highly, highly fashionable. In *Harper's Bazaar*, you see the tattered dress everywhere, the tattered hemline. You see the clothing with holes in it. I was the first person, I think, to wear tatters as a fashion statement. I wore them very proudly, as if they were beautiful ... and mine. And models today wear platform shoes for height, and Vampira wore that. Models wear Wonder Bras, and she wore a Wonder Bra. I wore a waist cincher, but they wear the bustier to cinch their waist. And they wear the fishnet hose. Those are commonplace now in fashion, commonplace. There's not a designer that doesn't use them.

SC: Let's talk a little about the national Vampira hysteria.

We started the show at KABC in, I think, March of 1954. Within three weeks *Life* magazine telephoned the studio. A photographer phoned KABC and said, "I would like to shoot a layout of Vampira for *Life*." So the studio called me. Well, I had already called *Life* magazine, because I'd had a precognition. I had three precognitions about Vampira before she came to be, but one was profound. I was making a Victorian bathing suit, for no reason, when I was in pin-up, which hid way too much. You couldn't use it for cheesecake. I woke up my sleeping husband and I said I just had a flash. I saw myself wearing this bathing suit on the cover of *Life* magazine. And I'm wearing a black wig, and I don't know why.

I had hand sewn it, I didn't have a sewing machine. It had a tattered hemline. When I finished it, I put it away. So when Vampira happened, I thought, so that's why I made that bathing suit, for this character! So I call *Life* magazine, thinking they need me, they're going to be looking for me. So I called them, and they said, "Don't call us, we'll call you. Thank you." They thought I was some lunatic calling. Here a voice came out of nowhere saying, you want to photograph me. So after that phone call, the studio called and said, "When you come to the studio, look extra nice, because *Life* wants to photograph you." I said, oh, so they answered my call after all.

It was Dennis Stock, wanting to freelance, who was responsible for this spread. He was 18 years old, too ... a lot of 18-year-olds buzzing around at that time. He had seen me on *Cinerama* and said, "Oh god, what is she doing here? She belongs in New York." High fashion, you know? So he watched the show and he decided he needed to film. And sure enough, he sold it to *Life*. So we were in *Life* magazine after only three weeks (*June 14, 1954*), which was quite a thing, especially since it was a local show with no great money behind it.

Then of course, fan clubs formed all over the world, which I don't think has happened since for a local show.

Maybe they do, but ... not many. Local fan clubs started all over the world. And when the *Funk and Wagnall's* came out in '55, and they covered what had happened in '54, I was the most outstanding female entertainer in America that year. Danny Kaye was the most outstanding male. They didn't say talented or anything. They just said outstanding. Maybe they meant the Wonder Bra, I don't know.

And I was the most photographed person, besides the President, in America. That's because people like that visual. Photographers wanted to do it. And most photographers did not throw away their Vampira negatives, even when they did away with their others. They've saved their Vampira negatives, and they keep turning up and turning up. And the archivists steal them and hide them. Lots and lots of pictures now belonging to archivists. And the libraries are full of Vampira. They all have files, all over the country.

SC: There was something you mentioned early on about that form in black and white over color, and why you would never do Vampira in color.

Oh, because color photography heightens things like bright eyes, lovely skin and luxurious hair that catches highlights. That's the sort of thing color is good for. But those are details. Form is best in black and white, because as soon as you add color, it detracts from the form. Your eye is distracted looking elsewhere. But if it's black and white, the form makes a very dramatic statement. Vampira was mainly form, and vampires are form. Visually they're primarily form to begin with. That's the first striking thing that gets the hold on you. So I thought when Vampira is photographed in color, it diminishes her.

SC: Can we talk a little about James Dean and your relationship with him? How did you meet him and what was going on culturally out here that you would bump into him?

Well, when the Vampira phenomenon happened, suddenly I was the golden girl and I could have met anybody in town. For the moment, I had the key to the city. So I thought I'd go to a premiere. I thought naively that everybody who was anybody would be at a movie premiere. I wasn't very bright. So I went as a movie viewer, with a little camera around my neck and sat in the bleachers outside of the Paramount Theater, I think. It was an Audrey Hepburn movie called *Roman Holiday* (1953), a big premiere. I looked at all the people and there was nobody that I wanted to know, especially Martha Hyer. She was in all of the movies in those days. She was a typical leading lady and the mistress of the head of Paramount, Hal Wallis.

I was looking, wondering, who do I want to meet? Hmmmm ... I wanted to meet the little boy who came with Terry Moore. He was wearing a tuxedo and seemed to hate it. His hair was uncombed and he was ... furious. He was filled with just fury. And I watched him and he didn't talk, he didn't seem to communicate with her or anyone. He was just fury, and that was who I wanted to meet, Terry Moore's date. So 12 hours later, he came into the coffee shop I was sitting in, Googie's. He drove up on a motorcycle. And it was the same kid. I didn't know who it was.

So I jumped up and hit my knees under the side of the table. You know crazy bones? When I saw him, I muttered, Jesus Christ, and I wasn't given to swearing. But suddenly, I swore. I guess an evil spirit got into me. I was saying, Jesus Christ, and I was just hissing the words out. And I stopped halfway up and halfway down, because I was stunned from the shock—the physical as well as the psychic shock. My friend's thought I'd had a stroke. And I said, that's the one who was with Terry-Moore. I've got to meet him.

Well, the fella who was sitting with me said, "Naw, naw ... You can meet anyone you want, you don't want to meet him." I said, yes, I do! "No, believe me. You don't want to meet him." I said, why do you say that? He said, "I just finished making a movie with him." That fella sitting with me was Jonathan Haze, who was later in *Little Shop of Horrors* (1960). He had watched Jimmy behaving and being hated and despised by all the other actors, and torn apart. Jimmy was always misconstrued, and they all misconstrued him during the filming of *East of Eden* (1955). Nobody liked him, as was true on all his sets. But it was the worst on *Giant*, of course. That's what he meant.

"No, you don't want to meet him." But I sent Jonathan in search of him. Jonathan went away and didn't come back. He just didn't want to affect the introduction. So when I started to leave, I was waiting at the cigarette machine, waiting for my friend to pay the bill, Jimmy came over. He left the counter where he was sitting and pretended to buy cigarettes, but it was to arrange an introduction, which he got. It was karmic. We were meant to meet.

SC: It sounds like you had some similarities, too. You saw the outsider in him and were attracted to that.

Well, we're both from other planets and didn't know our way around on Earth, you know. We realized that, and

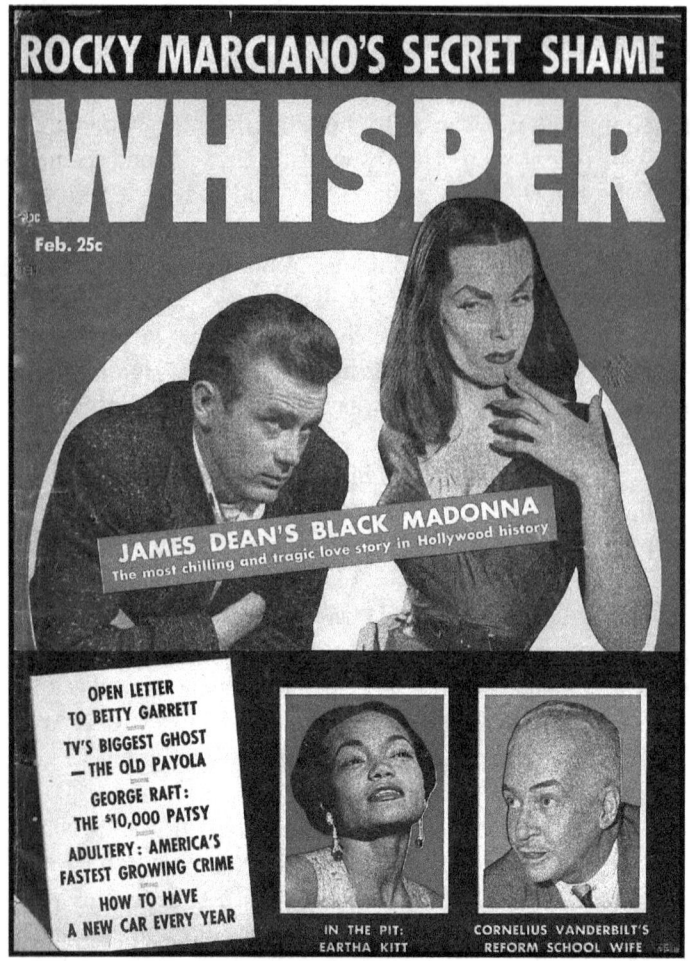

A tabloid treatment of Maila Nurmi's relationship with James Dean. The enclosed article gave a great deal of play to Vampira's graveside photo sent to Dean shortly before his death, inscribed by Nurmi: "Darling, come and join me!"

saw that in one another. We saw that comradeship. And we were both named after poets. His mamma named him after James Byron, and my father named me after Maila Talvio, the Finnish poet laureate. And when you're raised like a hothouse flower, then thrown out among the barracudas, it's just pretty hard to function. We could compare notes.

SC: What kinds of things did you guys do together?

We hung out, just like teenagers. I was living the adolescence I never had. And he was just a perpetual adolescent. I guess he had always been one. But we did pranks. You know, climbed up on rooftops, threw bottles, foolish things that teenagers do. Went to a lot of bongo sessions. He played the drums and I danced Bop. And we sat in Googie's. There were about five all-night restaurants we sat in all the time: The Hamburger Hamlet, Barney's Beanery, Up's, and Tiny Naylor's (aka the midget carpenters), but mostly we connected at Googie's.

MM: "Tiny Naylor's, the midget carpenters." I'd never heard that one before.

That's what my then-husband, Dean Riesner, used to call it. Dean wrote *Dirty Harry* (1971). A lot of guys like that. They say, "Dean Riesner, a man's man!" When he was a young boy, he was Dinky Dean; he was a Chaplin-esque star.

MM: I saw a brief clip of you dancing with Liberace in a jester's costume, which is pretty surreal. There's no way I would put you two together. Were you doing work in Las Vegas at the time?

Most people don't know that's Liberace, because he's in that funny costume and they don't recognize him. He wrote a show for Bela Lugosi as a co-host, starring himself in a history of music, going back to the caveman day. And then he found Bela was too old to do it. And then he thought, "Oh gee, I've already spent $60,000 and I don't have a co-host. There's no one else I can get." And somebody said to him, "How about Vampira?" I was already blacklisted, boycotted, whatever. He didn't mind about that, so he approached me. And I said sure, swell. It was in the beginning, when I could still do a little, before no one would hire me. But he hired me.

MM: How was that show? Did you have a good time?

Maybe, yes. But it was only a short run, maybe 15 days in Vegas. But that's when I met Elvis. I wouldn't have met Elvis otherwise. He was opening at the New Frontier.

MM: Wow. What was that meeting like?

The night before we opened our show, Lee (*Liberace*) and his mother were there, and so was his brother, along with his entourage, and we went around to see as many of the shows as we could see while we were still free. We went to the New Frontier and this band in the lobby was playing some music. It sounded really good. They were older musicians, sounded really good. Then we sat at the table in the dinner theater. When the curtain went up, a kid came out, and the kid had the real talent. Played the same way, but the kid was amazing.

There was a big band, the one who used to play at the Coconut Grove, Freddy Martin I think it was, a 22-piece orchestra with older players, and they were playing. And then the one kid came out with a guitar. He had a lot of eye make-up and no one had seen a man with eye make-up. He started to play and act like a stripper, spinning his hips. He was so gifted. I was so stunned. I said to Liberace, the people out in the lounge are imitating this boy. And

Lee said, "Well, in the lounge, that's Chuck Berry. He's been doing that for fifty years." So it was Elvis and Chuck Berry (*Laughs*). I thought Chuck Berry was ripping off Elvis (*Laughs*).

When Elvis did that, people were appalled. The theater was full and people were appalled. And the orchestra, one by one, they put their instruments down and crossed their arms like this behind him. Finally, he was playing alone. He continued to sing and play without the orchestra. Then when Elvis finally stopped playing, there was a big silence. Then they booed, they all booed. Then I excused myself from Liberace. I said I had a headache. We were staying at a hotel adjacent, the old Frontier. I said I'll walk home. He said, "I'll walk you." I said no. I'll walk home, it's just right here.

So I went around to the back. I deduced that the stage door was out around there somewhere near the swimming pool. So I went out there. It was dark, just the blue lights from the swimming pool providing illumination. There were two big golden doors leading to the casino, and then I saw a silhouette coming out of the doors with a canary yellow jacket on. A voice had told me he'd be out there with a canary yellow jacket.

The kid came out, looking into the dark, and I said, I'm over here. It was Elvis, and we had a long talk. I said, don't worry, *Life* magazine will cover you and they'll say that you're so wonderful. And then everybody will kiss your shoes, any minute. He's says (*Elvis impression*), "Comin' out Thursday." (*Laughs*) I said, they just booed, 'cause they didn't know what to do. He said, "Every night before I go out, I pray. I pray to God. Every night I'm in the wings and he always answers me." And he said, "Tonight, he didn't answer me. And when I saw all those gray hairs and glasses, I knew why."

He went in to do a second show. I walked him to the stage door. He was going to do a second show, which to me was phenomenal, to walk back into that, unheard of. How could a human do that, especially a sensitive artist? And he said to me ... Now let's see, I was 33 years old. He was 19. He said, "I know you're getting old and all, ma'am. But if you'd care to come back after the show, I'd be proud to take you to my bungalow." (*Laughs*). He turned me on, but I wasn't into young boys. I didn't think that would have been nice. I was a little too prudish for that.

MM: What was your most satisfying work outside of Vampira: dancing, painting?

Must I confine it to the arts? The most satisfying thing was being a cigarette girl. I would design my own make-up, write my own dialogue, pick out my own phone numbers, flirt with the greatest guys in the place, and hear music all night and hide tips in my bra. I loved it. I was a cigarette girl in New York City, inhaling all that smoke for free (*Laughs*). I loved that.

MM: That's great. And it underscores a certain New York style of sophistication you brought to Vampira. You mentioned earlier the "New Yorker crowd." There was a genuine East Coast sophistication in Vampira, as well as real darkness. She did not always seem to be playful.

Well, I didn't go to finishing school. I was a pauper during the Great Depression, an immigrant, an immigrant pauper and a child with low self-esteem. But I aspired to appear genteel and well read. So this is what I did. When I first got to the big city, I went to work in hotels where wealthy people lived, so I could learn their demeanor by association. That was my finishing school.

I was the first female bellhop in New York City, photographed on the front page of the old *New York Sun*. That was in the New Western Hotel. And I met the Roosevelts, and I met the Rockefellers. I worked in a private club for the social register, as a cigarette girl. That was on the East Side, the Upper East Side. There they wanted the girls who were actresses and could put on the proper Mid-Atlantic accent, as they sold wealthy people tobacco.

MM: Did you feel more at home on the East Coast than the West? There's a real difference, culturally, between New York and Los Angeles, in terms of theater and such. Did you have a preference?

Yes, when I was young, I certainly did. I didn't read, but I looked at the pictures, and I aspired to the elite and the effete. As a young adult, I just aspired to be very glamorous and very grand, everything I wasn't. We sometimes do that. But then as I matured, I preferred the earthiness of the West Coast. I liked the reality of being a beach bunny. When I first went to New York, I was an existentialist, that's what we were called. Then I was a Bohemian and then I became a Beatnik and then I became a punk rocker (*Laughs*). Helen Heaven, the punk rocker.

MM: Do you hear from that crowd these days?

Those are the kind of people with whom I associate, when I associate with people. I'm pretty reclusive. Yeah, I still know folks from the underground.

SC: You were DIY before that phrase was coined—that whole 1970s DIY movement in punk. Just build it yourself, just make it yourself, you don't need a record label. And

Nurmi attends the Los Angeles premiere of *The Tomb of Ligeia* (1964) with Vincent Price, Carol Borland, L.A. horror host Jeepers' Keeper and Elsa Lanchester.

just what you were saying about assembling your own props. You were very much ahead of your time.

I was a pioneer in so many things I did, apparently, like being the first female bellhop. That was during the Second World War, when women had not done those jobs that were always customarily given to men. We had the first female bartender then, the first shoeshine woman. I was neither of those, but I was the first bellhop. I carried the Roosevelts' baggage, Franklin, Jr.'s and Eleanor's. They paged me from the desk and I went up to the residential part of the hotel to get a bag, and it was he and his mom. And he had a two-suitor, this one two-suitor, with nothing in it. I could carry two overnight things full of stuff, 'cause I was very strong. I picked up this little two-suitor and he took it away from my hands. And mother said, "Franklin, allow the young woman to earn her livelihood." And so he did, he let me carry it all the way to the elevator. Then he took it away again, he couldn't bear it (*Laughs*). I remember that. We are prone to remember things that impress us, and I was very impressed by Eleanor. She was my heroine.

SC: Did you ever meet her again, or was that the only time?

That was the only time. But I heard a wonderful speech she made from Hawaii shortly before she died. And I didn't even know who it was. I said, who is that wonderful person saying all of those wonderful things that nobody has said before? And it was Eleanor. I was such a fan of Eleanor that I didn't do my teeth for a while. And now the gay boys, when they get together, say, "Oh yeah, I know Maila Nurmi. I knew her before teeth and after teeth." (*Laughs*)

MM: As the seminal character in horror host history, I'm curious if you met any other hosts over the years.

When I was in *Ken Murray's Blackouts* as a chorus girl, there were two very beautiful twin girls who were also in the chorus with me. There were only five of us altogether. But these two were identical twins. They had pale skin and long dark hair, very beautiful. And they were the Rohmer Twins, Lynn and her sister. And years later, when I got all done up as Vampira, I said, this is the third Rohmer twin, they're triplets. Later on, when Vampira was not functioning on local television, Channel 9 decided to put a lady like that on. So they hired Lynn Rohmer (*aka Lisa Clark*) and she was Moona Lisa. Very nice lady, but she was too soft and romantic to be compared to Vampira in any way, other than visually. But she naturally looked the way that I made myself up. She still functions, I think, in San Diego. But I don't think I knew any other horror hosts.

MM: You did meet L.A. horror host Jeepers' Keeper.

Oh, that one. That's right, I did encounter him.

MM: It was a promotional event for a horror film.

Elsa Lanchester was there. And the other star there was that lady who was with the *Dracula* movie in 1931, what was her name?

MM: Carol Borland. She wasn't in Dracula, *but she co-starred with Lugosi in* Mark of the Vampire (1935).

That's it. She was there. And Vincent Price, those three people were there. Forry Ackerman arranged the whole thing. It was quite an affair.

MM: What was your relationship with Forry Ackerman and Famous Monsters?

Oh nothing, he never wanted to do me. I think I was in *Famous Monsters* once, as Vampira. And he didn't have me at the Ackermansion. He pretended I didn't exist. When people would ask about me, he pretended he'd never heard of me, though I knew him very well. But he did all of my clones. He had lots of Elvira around and lots of Vampirella around, but he never had Vampira. I think maybe because he felt he'd created Vampirella. He took it and sold it for $25,000. Now he and I are friends and now he admits I exist. But there's still no Vampira in his collection. A tracing of me produced Vampirella. I have a picture Frazetta used to trace for Vampirella.

MM: The popularity of the horror host has gone through a number of cycles. Was there ever any temptation on your part to return to the genre at some point in the 1960s or 1970s?

No. I had intended to recreate Vampira when I was ready for retirement and I wanted to make some money. I thought by that time the blacklist would have been forgotten, the people would all be dead who hated me. I took the blacklisting very seriously. I believed I must have done something wrong, because everybody hates me. I didn't understand the nature of it, that it was just somebody else's greed. I just thought it was somehow my fault, and I recoiled and hid for many years. But finally I thought, I own Vampira; I kept the control. Now I can bring it back and syndicate it in 1980 and start it over again. I took it to KHJ and they stole it. And hired somebody I don't approve of.

I didn't want to do it myself. I wanted to find a person and train a new girl, because I want Vampira always to be beautiful, never older than her mid-1930s. I can see something contemporary about Vampira. They've painted her on toilet seat covers and put it on eBay, and now I've been asked to pose with the Dalai Lama. So everything from toilet seat covers to the Dalai Lama, and everything in between (*Laughs*).

MM: You said you maintained control of Vampira.

Maintained control. Not to the extent that Disney controls Mickey Mouse. I have never leased anything, other than a few short leases, which were carefully abided by. There's so much piracy that I can't control. But I do own all the rights, nobody else. Any poster that you see is illegal, except the one I sell. And any tee shirt is illegal. All the stills from *Plan 9 from Outer Space,* that's illegal. They have no merchandising rights. That fellow from St. Louis, what's his name, W.W. that everybody hates?

MM: Wade Williams.

He's so hateful. When an artist named Tom Coonts made a sculpture of me, Williams said if he so much as looked at a still from *Plan 9.* I would own him royalties. And we signed no merchandising rights with *Plan 9*, there are none. The merchandising belongs to us. And besides that, Vampira was created before I went into *Plan 9*.

MM: Of course, years before Plan 9 *was made.*

So I never signed away pieces. And I copyrighted her, the visual character, before she was named in '53, and then reestablished her as I went along, every year and a half.

SC: What about now, if someone came to you. Would you revisit Vampira and train up another girl?

Oh no, because they'd do it all wrong. I wouldn't allow it. I worked very hard to keep her intrinsic statement intact. I've been horrified by clones that have done it, have been recognizable, and still taken great departures. That horrified me.

MM: Do you think, in that regard, that Vampira was something very specific to her time and place and may not translate to another era?

Oh no, no, no! She's like Tarzan. She strikes a chord in the human psyche that existed before Vampira came into being, and will always exist. She's endless.

MM: There are some current Vampira pieces that you're creating, paintings and sketches. Was it interesting to revisit that, to revisit the style that you had put into Vampira?

Yeah. I want to get into fashion. I just love fashion. I just want to get into that so badly, and I guess I'm not going to. I'm running out of steam. But I love fashion. And so much of Vampira is already in fashion. It's been overdone and market's milked … what's left to do? But I would still like to do accessories or something, have merchandising rights and some say in the designing of "Poison Perfume," and some nice little things.

I see right now, for example, a see-through bra, a very soft flesh-colored net that appears not to be there, and have beaded spiders crawling around all over it. I resent women with big bosoms; I had to fake mine! And today, they're getting them all inserted. There are so many ways you could go with Vampira-style accessories that would be sellable today. Of course they've done almost everything anyway. But to give it that label, to give it that name.

MM: What other areas of fantasy interest you?

I adore Ray Harryhausen. I met him once, in the early 1990s when I attended a huge gathering of fantasy personalities here in Los Angeles. I'm not sure what it was. But I was with some people, and a bunch of us were going down some wide stairs, and others were coming up.

MM: The 1994 Famous Monsters convention?

Was that what it was? I guess so. But coming up the stairs was one of the most beautiful people I've ever seen.

A light moment with Maila during her 2004 *American Scary* interview

He was with a woman, but never mind, and I said, oh, there you are or something like that. And he proposed marriage right then and there. And it was Harryhausen. I didn't know. Then he made a speech and I thought, no wonder. I saw his genius. I just saw this genius, this light, and I fell in love with it, you know? I saw the essence of the man. He saw something too. Maybe he responded to my admiration. But I saw his speech that evening, and then I examined his work afterwards. I found the work after I found the man. What a great artist.

MM: Working in various areas of the arts yourself, what did you find to be the most satisfying medium?

The most satisfaction was in the sixth grade, when I was drawing movie star pictures. In the movie magazines, they would have these gorgeously done portraits of the beautiful movie people, classically beautiful. And I would draw renderings of them. If I had a two-hour class, I would just sit there at my drafting table and be lost until the bell rang and woke me up. I was in heaven, trying to recreate this beauty. I wasn't a trained artist, but I just loved doing it. And of course those things don't even sell now. I started out on eBay with renderings of Greta Garbo, and Humphrey Bogart—not that he's so beautiful. They sold a little, but fans of those people were dying out. They're old and dying out, the people who can afford them, who remember who they are. You have to do things that the geeks want. I don't want to cater to the geeks. I try a little and I'm not gifted. I can't do cartoons. I don't have natural sense of perspective. It doesn't flow through my hands.

Dana Gould came into my art studio and I was showing him some things. I don't draw and paint like everybody else. I don't have a style. I do a Hirschfield here, and do a Picasso there, and an Olivia here. So I was saying to Dana, this is a that-and-that and that. And I had done a sign for a friend of mine who had a shop, and she wanted a sign that said "Nail Hitting" (*adding studs to clothes*), because she did nail hitting back in the 1960s. I drew her with a faded blue jacket and little cap and some studs and that '60s lettering that said she did studding. But I did it Picasso, a little abstract. So I said to Dana, that's the Picasso. And he said, "In his blue denim period." (*Laughs*) He's one of those quick wits.

I love drawing and I really, really like making the pins. I made little sculptured pins, using findings. I prided myself in using non-precious materials. Sometimes I'd use a thing like a camel's tooth, but nothing precious. They were just form and color and I just enjoyed doing it.

MM: What sort of organic materials are used in your work?

Well, I use natural stones, but only semi-precious and uncut. I would go to thrift shops and swap meets and buy vintage jewelry, and then break it up. I did necklaces for a while; I was successful with those, too. I'd find a lady's color for the season, what color she was working in, and find a lot of beads and end things in those colors. And sometimes I would make necklaces out of little thread holders and knee-high stockings. I'd cut them up and stretch them and use them for string. And when the Japanese period was in with fashion, I did things a woman would find in an open [hair] roller, but were still decorative, bones from a capon; bleached in Purex and strung through with pieces of nylon stocking. And cornrow beads, I liked those because I could string them through with the nylon stocking.

MM: And you said you used dog hair?

I was a decorator at one period, and of course as a decorator, you've got to make it nice. The point is to make it nice, make people think it's nice. And now I've got a landlord, an Armenian and very meticulous, and I've got to make it nice. So I thought, wouldn't it be nice if I made a room that was un-nice? So I did a collage of a dirty, scary room (*Laughs*), really dirty and scary, a room with no windows. But it has a furnace in the living room, like all good living rooms, roaring hot and red. What he's cooking in there we don't know. But he's invited you to have a bite. It's a dirty, dirty room ... And I enjoyed it.

MM: When you were hosting films as Vampira, were there any that stood out for you, any favorites?

I'm not a moviegoer, never have been. But I like to see black and white; don't like to see color at all. I don't even like to view color films. I don't like to lose form. I have a heightened sense of form, apparently.

MM: How about any of the old horror films, the Universal Frankenstein series and such?

Yes, I like the old ones. I guess they were not English, I guess they were American, in the 1930s. Although I was not a theatergoer, the few that stood out in my mind were those classics. Those I savored, and to this day. I loved seeing Tim Burton's *Ed Wood* (1994). It was black and white, and I liked that. And the other one, *I Woke Up Early the Day I Died (1998)*, Ed Wood wrote with no dialogue. That was one of the best movies I've seen. It has gotten great, great reviews. It's supposed to be a really good movie. I thought it was, but I don't understand films, so I'm no judge of that.

MM: What were your feelings of Burton's Ed Wood (1994) *film in terms of accuracy and presentation?*

He never intended to be accurate. It wasn't a documentary; it was a docudrama. So he was taking liberties as he saw fit, which he's entitled to do in that media. But I just liked the way he did it altogether. I don't mind the fact that he had Maila Nurmi saying things that she wouldn't have said in those days. But she might say them today. I'm an old bag; I can say anything I want! (*Laughs*) But I was a genteel young lady in my earlier times.

MM: So, you don't see films, really. How do you take in the visual arts?

Oh, I love Erte. Erte was one of those early French set decorators, and I just love those high, high decorating art—very, very chic. I mean, it out-Decos Deco. I mean, Deco itself has become so plebian. But Erte, his minimalism was so beautiful to me. I loved him. I could have met him too, because he came here and appeared on La Cieniga when he was 100 and something. One hundred and two, I think, just before he died. I wanted to go and just didn't get around to it. Another one I loved was *The Listing Addict* by Edward Gorey. I love his work; I love his drawing.

MM: Do you do much reading of poetry or novels?

Camus, I love Camus. My husband at the time—I keep referring to him again—he was a great reader from the time he was born. He would read easily seven or eight books every day of his life for 80 years. I had never read a book. I was just doing bikinis and seeing if the stitching was right. And he said, "There's a book I want you to read." And I said, a book!? And he had this high IQ, like 182. And you want me to read a book? I don't want to sit still and train my eyes to a page. Life is out there; the world is out there. I don't want to glue my eyes onto a page. Why do you want me to read this? "I want you to explain it to me." It was *The Stranger* by Albert Camus.

And I read it, and I thought, what's to explain? It's so obvious, why did he bother to write it down? It was too obvious to even put pen to paper—to me. But to him it was a mystery, a great mystery. Because he didn't understand that kind of psyche. And he was right. Because it was the kind of psyche that I was, I was able to slowly explain it to him, to some degree at least. It's in what we view, right? At one point, I was so disappointed in life. There was nothing left in the world that interested me, and no one. I could walk in a crowd and I could see everyone. I knew how they decorated their homes, what they ate for breakfast, who they were. And there was no mystery left. I was so jaded. And there was only one thing left, and that was for me to get on a freighter, go to Europe and find Camus. But he died. I didn't go, and he did die shortly after. But that's something I felt very at home with, that psyche.

And then there was a playwright, and I was discovered to play in one of his shows. Rachel Rosenthal cast me—when I wasn't even looking for work—in a play by Ionesco, *Jacques ou la Submission (Jack or the Submission)*. She cast me as my husband's mother. She cast him, but he'd only get the part if I played the other role. He wanted the part; he was one of those *act*-ors. So we rehearsed it for a long while, but it never came into being. We never did it with an audience. Working with her was a nightmare, but I loved him, the playwright. I love to read his plays and I love to see his plays. But I don't think she has a right to direct them. She does other things well. I don't think she does him well.

My husband worked at Warner Bros., and he said. "One of the story editors is writing a story about us. It's called *Laurel Canyon*." My husband was a yuppie, a yuppie young man raised with a lot of money, very shel-

The magnetic gaze as powerful as it was when Vampira bent the airwaves to her will in 1954.

tered and protected. He had a kind of a plastic view on life. Bright, but he was a yuppie. Then I was this weird Scandinavian psychic young woman, who was his wife. And we had five cats. We lived in one room, very poor, with five cats. But I was very, very psychic, abnormally psychic, in that period. And it spooked him, because that was a foreign thing to him. But he'd see it. He'd see I wasn't just talking some bullshit. I evidenced lots of things. I had a lot of "preferred knowledge," they call it.

And my mother was a real witch. Not a practicing witch, but she just knew everything. There was noting she couldn't see. She could see through everyone, she knew everything. We had no money, and I was upset because the rent was due. And she said, "Don't worry, there's $213.64 coming in the mail today." I said, from where? She said, "The tax return. I saw it in a dream. I saw the mailman carrying a letter." And he did come with that check that she saw in her dream. That's the kind of witch my mother was. She could see everything.

So my husband would go to work and he'd talk about this wife of his. And now a story editor's writing about us. The yuppie married to the girl, and his mother-in-law's a witch, and the cats and everything. And they changed the title to *Bewitched*. Then they hired a girl who looked like I used to look—and sound—Elizabeth Montgomery. I sounded very much like Elizabeth Montgomery in my genteel days. But that's what that started out as, *Bewitched*.

But anyway, I was so psychic. We were at Norm's on Vine St. and my husband was trying to get to the bottom of this psychic phenomenon thing. How could I know these things that people don't know? How does one get this kind of information? I said, I don't know. You just get it, like you hear it in you ear, or get the picture like you're watching television. You see it or you hear it.

SC: What sort of advice would you give to anyone trying to do a hosted horror show today, because they're swimming against the tide of corporate media? What sort of artistic advice would you give?

Unless there's something that you really, really care about—with your gut—if you don't feel that, don't waste you time. But if you do feel that, stick with it. Stay as true, as true as you can to that feeling and just do it, no matter what anyone says. Just do it. Hone in on it, think about it from all aspects, feel it, live it and just do it—real truthfully. And then it will sell, because truth always sells. Even through all the plastic bullshit. Truth will eventually tell. Stick by your own truth. Each man has his own truth. We all have, you know, our basic truths that have come home to us. Things that live within us, you know? And if you can find that core, and stay with it, and play that tune, you're home free. It may take awhile, but it'll come around.

SC: If you had a chance to write a syllabus for childhood artistic education, are there certain things you would make sure a child saw at certain ages, art that you would expose them to? What do you think should be seen that's not being shown in a child's school these days?

I think that the main thing is something that may be impossible to do today, and that is to have the courage of your convictions. Find out who you are and be who you are, and don't try to be somebody else. But of course teenagers need to go through a period in which they are feeling themselves in relation to society. They have to clone a little and try different suits on. But find out the real core of your being and just stick with being who you are—and you'll make a statement. It's hard, maybe even impossible in today's world. I don't know today's world, how hard it is to be an individual and survive. They try to kill you, because they don't like individuality—the boys that run the world.

> Maila Nurmi, Vampira
> passed away January 10, 2008.

Zacherley At Large
Zacherley (John Zacherle)
Interviewed by Sandy Clark (2004)

John Zacherle began his horror-hosting career in Philadelphia, where he was hired to introduce the Universal monsters on WCAU-TV 10's *Shock Theater* in 1957. In the guise of "Roland," Zacherle's comic crypt keeper was hugely popular. By fall of 1958, he was lured to New York by WABC-TV 7 to usher Frankenstein and Dracula into the Big Apple. The New York program was similarly titled *Shock Theater*. But to keep ownership issues clear, his character's name was changed from Roland to Zacherley. Within a year *Shock Theater* itself was rechristened *Zacherley At Large*.

Success in a major television market raised his profile considerably, and Zacherley was soon racking up impressive pop cultural credentials. His ghoulish features twice adorned the cover of *Famous Monsters of Filmland* and he was prominently featured in the *Saturday Evening Post*'s coverage of the horror host phenomenon (*"TV's Midnight Madness," August 16, 1958*). To promote the release of his new 45 record, "Dinner with Drac," in 1958, he appeared on *American Bandstand* with Dick Clark, securing his place as the first nationally popular monster movie host of the *SHOCK!* era.

He became the most recognizable and quintessential representative of the genre, appearing over the years on the Mike Douglas and Tom Snyder programs, as well as *Saturday Night Live*. He invaded bookshelves in 1960 with *Zacherley for President*, a photo book with humorous captions. He even lent his name to a pair of paperback horror collections: *Zacherley's Vulture Stew* and *Zacherley's Midnight Snacks*.

He is easily the most prolific horror host recording artist, with a clutch of popular singles, as well as the albums *Spook Along With Zacherley, Zacherley's Monster Mash, Scary Tales, Zacherley's Monster Gallery, Dead Man's Ball* and *Internment for Two*. As the turn of the century approached, Zacherley reestablished his bona fides with a guest appearance on Rob Zombie's 1998 CD *Halloween Hootenanny*.

His feature film work includes *Brain Damage* (1998), *Geek Maggot Bingo (1983), and Frankenhooker* (1990). He was also involved in the video projects *Zacherley's Horrible Horrors* (1986), *The Zacherley Archives* (1998), and the documentary *Aurora Models: the Model Craze That Gripped the World* (2010).

For generations, his ghoulish exuberance has made him the genre's most recognizable ambassador—the jolliest man in the graveyard, the Santa Claus of the sepulcher.

So when and how did you start?

I'd been in Philadelphia doing a thing we called Roland, introducing the late-night movies. I've had a great experience in TV, because I was doing it just when television went from live to tape. So I experienced both things, and it was kind of a shock when I realized, whoa, the guy says we can't keep the engineers here late at night anymore. You've got tape now, and we're going to tape the show Thursday afternoon at four o'clock. You got about an hour and half to do an hour and a half show. Bang! I was there on a Thursday afternoon and nobody was there seeing it except for the engineers and the guy behind the camera. It was a very strange feeling. A lot of people who were in the early days of television also experienced this shift after working maybe 20 years of live—and suddenly it's tape. They had great stories to tell.

How did it change the way you approached the show? How did it affect your performance?

It was a funny feeling, a very strange feeling. The audience in the studio was the same, and sometimes the cameraman would break up or something, but you couldn't hear what was going on in the control room. Broadcasting live you really had the feeling you were talking to people out there. That was missing now and I don't know how to describe that in some psychological way. It just was very different. The fact that I wasn't doing it late at night was different also. I don't know … there was something very nice about doing a late-night scary show at *night*. Suddenly it wasn't that way anymore. It never kept me awake; I didn't lose any sleep over it. But it was a very different experience.

Any of us on TV in those days were not trying to scare anybody. We were just having a lot of fun. In Philadelphia, the owner of the station there, the general manager, whatever he was, Charlie Vanda, saw our first couple of shows. I would come down the stairway with a basket in my arms, and it was dripping—chocolate syrup, of course. And he said, "Damn it, if there's a head in that basket, I want to see it!" He wanted it more horrible, not funny.

John Zacherle faces off with his alter-ego Roland on a 1957 fan club card. Roland hosted Philadelphia's *Shock Theater* from October 1957 through September 1958, when Zach took his act to New York.

We didn't pay a lot of attention to that, or maybe we did for a show or two. I think the way we solved that was we lifted the head out of the basket—we didn't lift out all the way—up about this far. And we gave it a haircut, then let it drop down. That seemed to please him. Mostly we were having fun, we were kidding around. Everybody in the country—they weren't being scary, they were being funny.

What was your sense of your audience? Did you sense you were connecting with people, that there was an intimacy there? Even before you started getting mail?

Yeah. The guy who wanted it more horrible looking, he decided we needed to find out how many people were watching. We were getting a lot of mail. We asked people to send in a hair from their head so we could make a pillow for my dear wife who lived in a box. You never saw her, because we couldn't afford to have anyone else on the show. So she was always in the box. And we got all this hair from barbershops and everywhere else, some of it not especially from people's heads. So that was very impressive. We received *a lot* of mail.

That wasn't enough for him, I guess. The next thing he wanted was to have an open house, to see physically how many people would come. Well, thousands of people showed up. Stopped the traffic on the main street where the station was. The newspapers said there were like 20,000 and the cops said there were 12,000. If only 1,000 people had shown up, I'd have been happy. But it was a freaking mob scene!

The real beginning, if I can go back to it, had been on a cowboy show (*Action in the Afternoon*) in Philadelphia: live television, five days a week. I became a player who changed beards and coats and hats and all this stuff. They tried very hard to sell that to a breakfast food company. They didn't quite pull it off. They claimed at that time it was because we were opposite Kate Smith in the afternoon, which is big time ratings, and we beat her. But they were never able to sell the show. I don't know why.

It was very awkward in the beginning. We had everybody dressed as cowboys in 1880, in a town called Harborlee, Montana. They built false fronts out in the back behind the studio: a lot of trees, a little stream, everything there. Now it's all high buildings, you couldn't do it. We would come into town on our horse, you know, and get off and tie up. And you had to go somewhere near the hitching post, because that was where the microphone was hidden, and talk about something. "Well, I'm gonna have a drink, boy!" So you turn around and go through this door. Then as soon as you've gone through, you turn around and run like crazy around the side to get inside the building, where the set was for a particular scene. It was very confusing for a lot of people.

We had actors coming from New York to take over the lead role of the villain or whatever Monday, and by Friday, he was either dead, chased out of town or married the daughter of the preacher or something like that. Then another strange guy would come in to keep the story going. I played an undertaker one time. It ran for a year. And I think within a year or two the *Shock Theater* thing came out from California, with all the movies. Cities all around the country had stations that made deals, and they would take this package and it was theirs to play with. They called me up and said, "Do you want to do this?"

They remembered I wore a big black coat. I was some sort of undertaker (*a character named "Grimy Jones"*) in this particular episode. I would go around the countryside making coffins, a year's supply of coffins, and then I would move on to some other town. It was kind of a fishy story, but they remembered that. So I got the job of doing these horror movies, which I had never seen in my life. I eventually saw all the Dracula and Frankenstein films on a small screen, like everybody else did. I never saw them in a movie house. My parents got a little listing of films that were coming out and whether they were good or not, like a rating system for parents. So I never saw a horror movie in a movie house.

Let's talk a little more about that, about what your parents allowed you to see and not see. Also radio ... Did you listen much to radio?

Oh yes, a lot of radio. When I was a kid, my parents weren't terribly strict. Radio wasn't strict. There was no Howard Stern on the radio. You know, can you imagine? (*Laughs*) There was *Jack Armstrong*, *Fibber McGee and Molly* and all these things I grew up with. One of the great things was all this big band music. Boy, late at night you could tune in, and you got live music from all over the country. Here in New York City, "From the top of the Kaufman Hotel, this is Guy Lombardo." Or whoever is was, Jimmy Dorsey, whatever. And you could follow it all across the country. Your radio at night could reach New Orleans from New York City and Philadelphia. It was great. But there were also scary mystery theaters and things like that.

And the movies ... during the late 1920s and early 1930s, a lot of the stars started leaving their bras home. So you got a lot of jiggle movies, and that upset a lot of people. And so they eventually formed the Hays Office, whose production code said married couples had to sleep in twin beds and all those restrictions were added to Hollywood movies. A guy came over to a woman; he had to keep his feet on the floor. He couldn't sit on the bed with her, that kind of stuff. (*Laughs*) Can you imagine? It's ridiculous. Anyway, these little catalogs that came out on films kept me from a lot of Saturday afternoons. The kid up the street and I had to suffer through that. But we didn't know any different, so it was okay. So like I say, I never saw any horror films till I saw them in the late '50s on a little screen.

How old were you when you started doing Roland?

I was older than a lot of people thought. I just finished serving in World War II. I was in World War II, isn't that exciting? It's a wonder we won that war, to tell the truth, considering the people I worked with. We were always behind the lines in supply. It was like having a nine-to-five job. And yet 50 miles away, particularly in Italy, people were killing each other. But we were going home every night and having the good meals and stuff. I think we took Sunday off. It was crazy, crazy ... insane.

How important was radio to you during the war?

Radio was great in the war. We used to get a lot of stuff direct from English radio. The U.S.O. used to send these big transcription discs. Have you ever seen them? Big ones, they were bigger than 12 inches, complete shows. And we officers ... I was an officer, do you believe that? We would hog this machine and listen to all our favorite shows. And then we would let the grunts, you know, the GIs, listen to them. All our favorite radio shows were transcriptions. It was great. I'm sorry someone didn't just hang onto those things.

Let's talk about some of your early shows.

In Philadelphia, the station had no way of saving, duplicating, kinescoping their shows. In the early days of television, Philadelphia and I guess Chicago and New York, as they were developing the networks, were all feeding into coaxial cables, and the microwaves they had for a while. Now they send it to the moon and back. It's astonishing what's happened in my lifetime, yours too. But anyway, somebody knew there was a chiropractor downtown in Philadelphia, who was a nut for television and stuff. He was very excited about it. He knew you could make a kinescope by aiming a camera at a television tube, basically. And then pick up the sound, however you do that. He made a kinescope of one of our shows. It's pretty crude, but it shows what we were doing.

When I got to New York, a guy named Ellis Sard was producing the show. He loved it; he was just great. He had a lot of experience on TV before I got here. One of the things he used to do was *The Lucky Strike Hit Parade*. Music, you know, he was very much into music. He knew all about the ins and outs. About halfway through the season he got one of the engineers who knew all about kinescoping to copy some shows. They had all the equipment, and they used to go out in the street with a 16mm camera, you know, and shoot fires, accidents and various ceremonies ... current happenings. And they'd run back in and develop it and show it on the evening news. That was the best they could do to cover exciting events. And because they had that equipment, they were also saving some shows by aiming at the tube. Ellis Sard said to the engineers, "Hey can you make a kinescope?" And we have kinescopes of the intermissions of three shows. What he did was go into the newsroom and steal some raw stock of 16mm film. And he made kinescopes on Sunday afternoon, when he was off duty.

Then halfway through that first season, they suddenly said, "Hey, we've got two video tape machines now." Great big suckers, you know? The tape was *that* wide. "You have to do your show on tape from now on." But the trick was those reels cost $300 a piece. In those days that money was like a $1,000 today. And we didn't think we could afford to do that—as far as saving things for the future. We weren't thinking about the future either. I wish we had been. So that's all they got for the first show.

The next experience I had was when I went to Channel 9, which was a Warner Bros. network, I think. I'm not sure who owned it. Anyway, that's WOR Channel 9 in New York City. They were so cheap they only used tapes other people had used. Used tapes, there was a market for used tapes. Every time you used the tape, you'd mark down the name of the show on it and they'd degauss it on the next day and use the tape over again. And when they'd used it so many times, they'd sell it. And WOR used these tapes. So they started taping the show. They taped every one of them. And then they tried to show them at their sister station in L.A. It ran for six or eight weeks and then something happened. It wasn't too good, we lost a lot of the local humor about New York City, and we couldn't kid around with the commercials, because we didn't know what the commercials would be. It didn't make sense. But the interesting thing is that they kept all those tapes and played them all over again in New York City before they degaussed them. And it never occurred to me to go in there and save them. There must have been a couple of really good shows out of all the whole season. But eventually, they were gone.

Not just your own show, but all these kinds of shows in general—what do you think we lost by not keeping them?

We lost a lot, because the local entertainment situation has just kind of disappeared. All the kid shows that used to exist are gone. We had lots of them here and I guess every city had them. When I was a kid in Philadelphia, we thought Philadelphia was a big town, you know. Big enough, though, not like New York. Even they had all kinds of people doing local shows. Ernie Kovacs started down there, and there were some other guys who were on my station, who came up here eventually and worked on the technical side of things.

Were you a fan of Ernie Kovacs?

Oh yeah! I remember sitting in his studio. They had a grandstand kind of built. He and his wife, they were both carrying on there. It's amazing. And I forget, but I think he started before the horror thing started. We were just talking yesterday about the Nairobi Trio. At one time, Jack Parr and a couple of guys got in the masks and did the thing, an imitation. Oh, god!

What do you think was the essence that horror hosts took from Kovacs?

I don't know. I'd never seen him, because we didn't have a TV in my house. We had a hard time getting television in our house. My brothers and sisters tried to convince my parents that they should have a TV, you know? I was the last one living at home, and finally we decided we'll get a really ugly one that they won't like. And it worked. We got this great thing; it was like a monster sitting here. So we said, we'll get a smaller one. And we did and they accepted that. Anyway, I didn't really see him until later when I got to New York. In fact, when I was living in New York, I was living in a hotel up here and all I had was a radio. I didn't see him at all. I went back to Philadelphia on the weekends, until my parents finally passed on, or passed over, however you say it. Or kicked the bucket. Remember that great movie with Jimmy Durante, and he goes "Kick the bucket!"

Yes! It's a Mad, Mad, Mad, Mad World, *I love that movie!*

When I finally settled down up here, I had TV. But I didn't see a lot of Kovacs. I think I was doing two shows a week here, and it was a lot of work to put it together. Not that I did it all myself. But we'd have to be in the studio, in the screening room, to check out the movies, to find out where we could have some fun.

I was talking with a friend just yesterday saying, why didn't we have the goddamn brains to get Boris Karloff? He was here in a play. He was doing Captain Hook on stage in *Peter Pan*. Another friend of mine was saying, "You know, he lives right around the corner." I never saw him on the street. "He goes into that bank over there." But I think I must of thought he'd think it was a big imposition to do this. We had a girl come down from Columbia to help us with the mail. And she said years later she met him at some kind of affair and she introduced herself. She said, "I used to work on the Zacherley show, showing your old movies." And she said, "I hope you didn't mind what we did." And he said, "Not at all, my dear. You brought me back to life." But we should have reached out to some of these guys. We never had any guests on the show. In the first place, we would have had to pay them. In those days, you'd have to pay anytime they stuck their face in front of a camera.

An early promotional portrait of horror film's iconic Roland

What else do you think has been lost because now there is no local TV?

You mentioned earlier about an audience. I go around to conventions now, meeting people in their mid-50s who used to watch me. But when I was doing the show, I never really ran into these people. I did a tour, like a Saturday afternoon tour to movie houses. But there was no such thing as a convention. I think the radio disc jockeys had big followings, and they would go out and do record hops and meet kids every Friday and Saturday night. Even Dick Clark, who was on national TV, was doing it in Philadelphia. He would make a lot of money, going to two or three record hops a night. He'd jump in his car and go to another one.

Was that part of the appeal of music for you? You did deejay music and hosted Disc-O-Teen, *right?*

That was just a lucky break. But then that's the best break I ever had in my life, I think. Always been lucky. Anyway, I did the horror host at three stations here, used up all their movies. The best were the ones in the *Shock Theater* package. The other stations had things like *King Kong* (1933) and *Mighty Joe Young* (1949). And then the last station I worked at had some pretty feeble mystery movies that really didn't fit too well. And they also had the *Attack of the 50 Ft. Woman* (1958) and things of that

Zacherley poses with Disc-O-Rama guests Age of Reason

ilk. Never had *The Blob* (1958); wish we'd had *The Blob* When was *The Blob* made? A good friend of mine played Lt. Dave in *The Blob*. "Don't go in there! It's the most horrible thing I've ever seen!"

The Blob, released in 1958, was made possible in part by what you were doing. The popularity of the Shock *package led to a whole new generation of horror movies.*

Yeah. So, after doing the three horror movie things— at different channels—one of the guys I worked with at Channel 11, the last place I worked with movies, he was aware of the fact they were going to be dropping some people, including him. I was involved with a kiddy show in the afternoon. We had a guy showing *Popeye*, Captain Jack. And then we had Officer Joe showing the Three Stooges, and Fireman Bill and Beachcomber Bob, a whole bunch of people. And then there's me. They were trying to beat the competition. We had three stations here in New York, independent stations that were after the kiddy market for advertisers. And of course they had Soupy Sales on Channel 5. I can't remember all the guys. It's all gone, like you just mentioned. It's all disappeared. I don't know if that's good or bad.

But this guy, Barry Landers, said he was getting a job at this new TV station across the river in Newark. Three guys we had worked with here in public broadcasting had invested in a station. It was a UHF station, before cable. And he was proposing to them that they do a dance show. They had to do counter programming. They couldn't get any movies. The stations in New York City signed up all the movies. So they had bullfights and live wrestling, foreign language and English language, interviews and stuff and a dance show. Nobody was doing a dance show in New York City at that time. So I did a dance show. It was crazy, like a Transylvania Dick Clark show. That's where I really got into the music a little bit, because they were playing 45s. He and I used to throw them to each other—catch them like this. It was a great game we had, catching 45s. He was instrumental in getting me the job. That lasted about three years. Finally they decided to let go of the station and turn it entirely into a foreign language station.

A friend of mine who was responsible for the *First Family* comedy album, Earl Dowd, he used to listen with the earphones. Earphones—boy, all the things that came in that era! You had AM radio, you know, mono. Mono ... wow! Have you listened to mono lately? It's terrible, those old records? Not too thrilling. He'd sit there and listen to these things, and I'd come home after the dancing show and have dinner with him. We're playing all this stuff and he said, "What you should do is go on down to WNEW there." They had just started FM radio. Wow, all this stuff happening in the late '50s, early '60s, I guess. So everybody's running out and buying a stereo, you know. "Sit here! You get stereo, man!" And LPs; no more 45s. You couldn't get your finger through the hole in the LP! Oh god, you couldn't do it!

I went down there and I got interviews. And all I could tell them was that I had been listening to all these 45s, especially the British Invasion that was happening. It wasn't totally British. The Doors and everybody else were coming out, and even they had 45s. There were two fairly young guys running the station, and the one went home and asked his son, "What would you think of Zacherley as a deejay?" And the kid says, "Zacherley!?" He remembered me from TV, you know? So I got a job. And it was the greatest job in the world, because you had total freedom of what to play.

So how has that changed these days? There's no freedom. That's one of the things several hosts who have been deejays talked about. You go into a station today; it's programmed on a computer. What changed about society too, from then to now? You had fans writing you, letters coming in. Nobody writes to shows anymore.

That's right. That's true. I don't know how it happened, but I guess the marketplace drove everything. I go to these conventions now and it's like going to an electronics convention. I see people coming in with cameras. But I don't see any films anymore. I say, wow, where'd you get that camera? They're the most elaborate things, I'll tell ya. The most elaborate camera you have, you know, there's some guy back in the research department. He's building something even better. I think that's what's driving this whole thing.

Do you think it's a good opportunity now for people to create their own entertainment?

Oh yeah. I was involved with a guy who works at NBC in the Master Control. He's a whiz. Every time a new piece of equipment comes in—like High Definition TV is the current rave—they tell him, "You do this." And he reads the catalog instruction book and picks it up very quickly. He's an expert. He's like that guy I described who made the kinescopes. He just uses their equipment! When he's off duty, he makes his own movie.

So let's see, you've got the fan that made a kinescope in Philadelphia, you've got a fan that got you a job as a deejay. Talk about your fans a little bit.

Well as I say, I never really met them. I did that one tour when I was on the air. People come now, and they've got kids of course. They remember going to these shows. I never thought there were that many people in the theater. But they have great memories of me up on the stage. Kids here in New York have a way of greeting you with eggs! And they have a way of throwing them so they won't get caught—from their laps. I walked across

this stage with a big beautiful curtain behind me, and every one of them missed me. At one point, just as I was walking, one went right through my leg, never touched me, you know? "Raaayyy!" Big cheers echoed ... except for the guys who had to clean up the mess. But I meet more people now than I did then. It's too bad we didn't have conventions then to meet the kids when they were kids. They have such memories. They remember things they say I did. I shake my head. I say, I can't remember doing that. Did I really do that? Do I say that? Whoaaa!

You were one of a handful of horror hosts who gained national recognition. Why were you so loved, did it have anything to do with Famous Monsters of Filmland?

That was a big thing, yeah. That started back in Philadelphia, too. (*Famous Monsters* publisher) James Warren lived in Philadelphia and he was watching the show. I was only there a year. But I was in one of the first issues of the magazine. It was one of the reasons I left and came to New York. Another reason was, we made this song called "Dinner with Drac," which was based on limericks people were sending in. I thought these were funny lyrics. Not dirty, just funny ... and semi-scary, maybe. But I incorporated it into the show. The guy who ran the Cameo Parkway record company used to watch the show with his daughter and he got a brainstorm. He calls me up and said, "We'll make a record." And I said, geez, okay. I didn't know any different. He says, "You got anymore limericks?" I said, yeah, I got some. He said, "We'll put some funky music behind it." I didn't know what funky meant. But it turned out it was a pretty good little band he had there. Dave Apple and the Applejacks I think they were called.

I didn't meet James Warren before the magazine came out. But I was on two of the early covers, with big stories. Then I met him in New York. He moved up here, as I had, when I was still doing the show. I don't remember

31

the story of *Famous Monsters*, if it was instantly a big hit. That magazine must have had a great deal to do with my success.

I appeared on other people's shows occasionally, Like Dave Garroway, who was the earliest of the *Today Show* hosts. He was a big fan, and I was on his show, maybe three times with him, and with Jack Lescoulie, who followed him for a while. He was just great. Garroway had his own way. I walked in one time and he'd built a great big set, I couldn't believe it. It was this high off the ground, so it would look like a street, a spooky street. We climbed underneath and came up through a manhole. I thought, geez, all of this for just three or four minutes on TV? It's amazing. And he was great. He said, "I want to call my wife. I go around the house imitating you, and I want to call my wife. We'll get her on the phone. She won't know whether it's you or me." We did and she started laughing.

And you were on American Bandstand.

Bandstand! Oh my god, now we're getting to it. We had a big hit with that "Dinner with Drac." Now Dick Clark, he knew something that I didn't know. Bernie Lowe, who ran Parkway Cameo, was aware of this great thing that was going on with *Bandstand* and Philadelphia was putting out a lot of hits. His company had Chubby Checker, The Orlons, The Dovells and Bobby Rydell. They were, boy, pumping out hits all the time. They were a factory and were amazing. The combination of having a network dance show within a 10-minute taxi ride was great. Dick Clark got all these people on the air and got them interviewed; he loved that too. He was very, very connected.

I got over there Halloween or whenever it was. Probably the first time may have been "Dinner with Drac." How it got across the country as a big hit, I don't understand. I don't think that he played it that often on his show, like a normal hit. It was a novelty song. He thought the lyrics were a little too gory or something and I had to do a separate version for his show. And yet as I've listened

> EVEN DICK CLARK, idol of the teen-agers, invited Zacherley to to share his TV cameras after the latter's recording, "Dinner With Drac," found its way to the juke boxes.
>
> "Clark asked me to go on his show because he said the kids were 'bugging' him to put me on. I had to change the 'Dinner With Drac' lyrics for the appearance though. Clark thought they were a little too ghoulish for network exposure. The lines about mummy's veins were changed to straws from a witch's broom."
>
> Besides introducing the films in "Shock Theater," Zacherle's specialty is to intrude on the movies occasionally to heighten the fright. During a supper scene in Dracula's tomb, for instance, Zacherele is cut in to give the effect he's actually at the supper—a situation which, needless to say, offers unlimited opportunity for ghostly conversation.

Stubenville Herald-Star, October 2, 1956

to his version, and what the original was, it doesn't seem all that exciting a change. The record was banned in England, I was very excited about that.

And he also dubbed you the "Cool Ghoul," didn't he?

Yes, he did. Indeed he did, he did. Anyways, he was great. He and I were going through female trouble at the time and we sat there one night talking. He was breaking up with his wife and I was losing a girlfriend. We had a nice relationship. I never saw him socially at all. But I guess I came back there after the show was on in New York. It was always a lot of fun. The kids were great. But he realized that his audience was, in Philadelphia certainly, the same as mine, the same high school kids— though I used to get a lot of letters from college kids who looked at the shows in a very different way. The fact that I was kidding the films and the commercials, they loved that, you know?

Dick Clark, that's a great memory. People used to make fun of him, the way he used to do the show, but he's been very consistent, you know. And he loves to work; he's got a wife who loves to work. They never stop.

How important has New York been to you? What could you do in New York that you couldn't do anywhere else?

It's been amazing. When I first came here, all three networks, they each had a house orchestra. NBC had a symphony orchestra with Toscanini. ABC had a house orchestra with maybe 30 guys on the payroll. And it was a union thing; they had to have it. So I'm there at ABC. There's a long corridor and all these dressing rooms. All these shows, *The Patty Page Show*, *Pat Boone Show*, *The Voice of Firestone*, were on. All this stuff went on every night. So I'm getting all these people. Pat Boone is a big fan. I would have joined in the fun if I knew how much fun Boone was having. I didn't know he was riding around in a fancy car having a great time up at Columbia University. Anyway, he was a big fan. He had me on his show a couple times.

I met opera stars. Even they were excited. They'd walk past my little room and I'd be in there working. They'd see all this stuff in there. "Ah, Zacherley! Wonderful!" There was this one guy, Italian opera singer Chesere Ciappi. I told him I'd talked about him to this girl down in Philadelphia, and she said, "Chesere Ciappi, oh my god!" She went crazy. So I said to him, would you mind talking on the phone to my girlfriend down in Philadelphia? She's working in a record store. So I dialed her up. I said, Maria, here's Chesere Ciappi. He says, "Hello, Miss Maria? I understand you sell my records like crazy." (*Laughs*) She couldn't answer. But this guy was a big fan; he was lovely. He used to stop by every time he was on. It was terrific experience for me here in show business.

The other guy is Barney Martin. Does anybody here know Barney Martin, who recently played Seinfeld's father? (*Laughs*) He was warming up the audience for the *Pat Boone Show*, doing gags with another guy. Barney was a cop; I didn't really know that. I remembered after I met him again. He came to the convention, I think, about two years ago. He greeted me like an old lost brother. We never hung out, but we used to kid around. I'd go in and watch these shows and they overwhelmed me. I was used to having a cameraman and a sound effect man, you know, and that's it. But you go into a network show, and there's too many people around, supposedly being paid to do something. It was a big experience, a big learning experience.

So that was the best thing about New York, just the density of opportunity?

Yep. It was the closest to a network show. Do you remember the half-hour Boris Karloff series, *The Veil*? He introduced these things. The network decided I should do that. One day I was called down there to another studio, a bigger one than I normally use. There's people running around, and they had it set up. It was just a half hour show. I was going to do these intermissions, but I don't know how they were going to squeeze 'em in. All I remember is once they had a table, a big table. And they had these big silver trays with big domes. You lift them up and there's a roast beef under there. Of course when you lift it up my head's under there looking at the camera. It was a very elaborate set they had built, but it didn't make it. But that was my first taste of what it would be like.

And even with the *Pat Boone Show*, it was a little unnerving to step in front of an audience. He never had an audience, actually. But just the fact that there's so many people around there. Or the few commercials I did, they would also have a whole lot of people around. I always thought it would be really great if you were nearsighted and couldn't see all those people. The few times that I ever did a play, I thought, God, how can you ever get used to this, all those faces looking at you? It would be better if it were blurry. But actors don't mind that at all, the ones who are used to it. They love it, I guess. But it's very hard to get used to. You're supposed, occasionally, to look in that direction. But when you look in that direction, there are three hundred pairs of eyes looking at you. It's kind of weird.

With TV, when you get into the big time networks, it's a lot different than doing a little local show. Local shows are really more fun, because they're usually just a couple people there. They're people you know, and they can enjoy it and laugh and make a little fun. The only thing that was tough about the kid shows was all the advertising. It was always on tape or film, but you were aware of the fact this was an advertising machine that was going on here. And that's what they were after. They were after ratings.

1960 was a banner year for Zacherley!

But you skewered your advertisers pretty good. You had a lot of fun with your ads.

Oh yeah. "An uplifting commercial" and it would go to the Wonder Bra. (*Laughs*) We got away with that. The only one I had trouble with ... I had a spark machine, one of those Tesla coil things, you know? And the spark goes ZZZZZIIIITTTT! I decided to put two rubber Spaulding balls on the top, and it would look more realistic going across there. I was going to hold these balls and the spark was going to go through them. It didn't work right. I either got shocked when we rehearsed it or something. So instead I was just twisting the Spaulding balls and they faded into the Wonder Bra commercial. We heard about that, we really did. I don't know if the guy in charge said, "Roll the commercial" or "Fade into commercial," but it really happened. And that's the end of that story! (*Laughs*) It was no big deal, but they mentioned it the next day.

That's wonderful. There are a lot of memories here that we're trying to get before they're gone and nobody remembers anymore. Because there's no tape, nobody's done systematic histories, and there are these guys who did horror hosts and children's shows ... that did Bozo.

Bozo, yep, Bozo! We had a guy with a parrot and Chuck McCann was so annoyed because the guy left the parrot in his office over the weekend. Chuck said it was disgusting when he came back on Monday and the parrot had messed all over. He says he taught the parrot... (*Laughs*) He may have exaggerated, but he says he taught the parrot to say, "Fuck you! Fuck you!" He claims that during one of the shows, when the parrot was on Beachcomber Bill's shoulder ... it yelled, "Fuck you!"

We've talked with a number of people who are fans of yours, including Leonard Maltin, who said he got his sense of what is funny and what is not, and his sense of humor, from watching Zacherley.

Well, it was fun, because we sketched out what we had to do. In an hour and a half film there were maybe eight intermissions. So if you're going to do an experiment, you have to not finish it too soon. You've got to stretch it out. So you'd write out a kind of a sketchy script that would also give the director a clue when to go to the film, when go to the commercial or when to go back to the movie, so you wouldn't make a mess of the evening. Then you had to just kid around and say whatever came into your head. The guy who helped me the first year when I came to town created little operas. We had a guy playing piano; his day job was playing piano for the ABC orchestra. But his real job was classical pianist. His name was Earl Wild. He's a classical pianist—comes to town, plays Carnegie Hall all the time. He's still doing it, an old man. He was in this thing we did called "Il Draculari." It was just made up of a lot of tunes that Ellis Sard remembered. He just changed the words to them. There were old vaudeville type songs. It was very funny. We did a whole bunch of them.

I want to ask about a specific bit, "the amoeba." How did the amoeba come about?

Well, we must give credit where credit is due. The Chestnut Hills Diner in Philadelphia is where it struck me. We were trying to pretend we were making heart transplants and things like that. There would be a piece of liver sitting on a table with a hole underneath, and I would have a dowel stick under there on my foot and I could make the liver jump up and down, you know? Sometimes I'd poke it too hard and the stick would come up too far, that kind of thing. "Whoa! Get down there!" We used cauliflower for brains...

So I was having dinner at the diner, nothing could be finer! And I noticed somebody along the counter had ordered Jell-O. So they brought out this great big tray full of Jell-O and started slicing it. I thought, wow. I went home and made a big Tupperware basin full of Jell-O and took it in. And just before we were going to use it, I said, let's dump it upside down, tell 'em it's a big amoeba. And they had a real close-up of this thing. We dumped it — which we didn't show — it was just there when the camera went on. It's there shivering, you know, and I poked it. And then it split open. God, it looked to be the ugliest thing you ever saw. It split of its own weight and went bleeeeeech! Like a big, ugly mouth. We thought that was hilarious.

Then we decided it should have a skin. So we took a big piece of cheesecloth and put it in the middle, then tied the four ends up and turned it over. And we had a string on it, so we could pull it and jerk it. You could cut it open and that would look even funnier as it oozed out. You could lean over and squeeze it. Oh my, look at that, and so on. And stuff would be in there besides the Jell-O. That was a great thing to play with. We had an amoeba that became invisible, too, one time.

The best thing we ever did with the amoeba was up here in New York. We decided to mate two of them, have them mating on camera. Then it turned out they didn't like each other. I had to force mate them. That got really messy, forcing these things together and slapping them. And of course, that's an effect you didn't expect. When you slap it, it's funnier when the Jell-O is kind of juicy, rather than too solid. During the intermission we had six or eight smaller amoebas on strings. So we went to commercial, and when the camera came back, whoa, we've got a real marriage here or something!

And the guys, they were having a great time. The stagehands were pulling these things and they (the amoebas) were going up and flying around and getting tangled and hitting each other. And when they hit each other — wow! You get this big splat. They were so tangled, and they couldn't move them any more. But that was terrific. We never got that on tape, unfortunately. But that was the height of our amoeba situation. It was a great thing to play with, it really was.

What other routines have people come to you at conventions and said, "I remember that"?

Well, the amoebas and the brain transplant. They still haven't transplanted a brain yet. They're getting pretty close with these little infants who were stuck together at the head. Whoa! My god, that's frightening. But the real medical people haven't figured out how to transplant a brain. You know, people ask me what's the funniest thing that ever happened. I don't know. I can't remember anything that happened that was totally unexpected. I'm sure it did happen. But you just had to swing with it. And what you came up with was fun.

How much of this was play? You mentioned play a couple times. When you came into work, did it feel like work doing that show?

No. It was interesting to do. Because when it was being done live, you were kind of tired by the time the show started, from being up all day getting a look at the movie and getting things ready. Then the stagehands were very strict about what you could use on camera. You couldn't move something; they had to move it, that kind of thing. They only eased up after the kids in their neighborhood found out they were working on the show. Then they were relaxed a little bit. But there were times when it was so freaking frustrating to have somebody say, "You can't touch that."

I remember doing the dancing show. Even over in Newark, we'd have a live group on playing. We had high school bands come in and play, but we often had big time people come by. But they didn't attempt to play, because we didn't have the facilities to make them sound right. But I would grab a microphone. Because I would realize this microphone is over here and the singer is way over there. And god, the shop steward up in the Control Room would get furious and slam his earphones down, screaming and hollering that I'm not allowed to do that. It was on camera. I'm not sure why I wasn't able to do it. But I think he was wrong. As long as it was on camera, he shouldn't have fussed around with it.

Was there anything you wanted to do in your career that you weren't able to do?

I was never red hot to get on the stage, though I did enough of it to realize it's not easy. I also had the attitude it might be pretty boring. If you got into a hit show, how could you do that every night, you know? Maybe comedy, but imagine what it would be like to do a dramatic play every night of your life for a long run? God, it's no wonder they get drunk when the play's over. I should have taken singing lessons and things like that, and maybe dancing a little bit, to learn how to do a little tap or something. That would have come in handy. As far as dancing skill, I remember doing dancing once, like a waltz. I could do that.

I see now they're showing all the old tapes of the *Carol Burnett Show*. It's hilarious. You sit for an hour and half just watching what they want you to buy. What these people did, it's just amazing. They knew how to

Which was more important in your career, doing the deejay stuff or doing the hosting?

The radio thing, when I was at WNEW FM, was pretty amazing because the Vietnam War was raging. It had a lot of meaning, what we were doing there. We were playing all the anti-war songs that were coming out. We were advertising all the parades that were going on. I realized, too, there were guys over there in Nam, and people who were not yet going still remembered me when I first came to New York in 1959. These kids grew up and the next thing you know, 10 years later, they're over in Vietnam. So I had a real interesting life of growing up with these kids. And I stayed on the radio 13, 15 years, I forget.

What is it that the audience means to you, having them out there? Here it is 10, 12 years later, and you feel like you've got a mission now to keep helping these kids.

Well, it's just a connection. I don't know if it's a mission. The mission I had was when I was on this great free-form radio station. I had this little yellow Volkswagen, and I was on late at night. Whenever something was going on, I'd jump in the car, when I got off the air at 2 a.m. and whiz on down to The Fillmore to catch whoever was still playing. Maybe by two o'clock most of them had closed. But when The Grateful Dead was in town, they hadn't even started by then. And there, I ran into people all the time. I had forgotten that. I was telling you earlier that I didn't meet the audience. I didn't meet them when I was doing the horror shows. But when I was doing radio, I met them. Especially down there. I got to introduce some of the bands on the outdoor stadiums, before they went to the gigantic football stadiums. In Central Park we used to have concerts and you used to mix around with the crowd. It was great. I'd forgotten that when we were talking here a while ago. You know, it's been a great life. Really, I've been very lucky.

What were some of the major elements of your horror host show, the other characters and such?

As a local show, the one thing we had to hold back on was spending money. Chuck McCann had a puppeteer

do everything, Tim Conway especially. And what was his cohort's name? Harvey Korman. God! These people deserved to be on network time! They were just terrific. I don't know what their background was. But, gosh, they could break out anything.

I saw something the other day that I should have remembered. Frank Sinatra was a guest with Gene Kelly and they were both dressed up in tuxedoes with tails. It was not from a movie. I was surprised to see Frank Sinatra really keep up with Gene Kelly dancing. It was amazing. He was terrific. The two of them did a little duet. Then of course Gene Kelly went off and did a more exciting one. But he was great; he knew how to do that. But those kind of skills I never learned. I should have.

and he was shown occasionally. But you had to pay. You couldn't just have some friend come in and help without any pay. And producers were unlikely to give you any money to do that. And so we had to make believe. The guy in Chicago, whose name I can't remember (*Marvin, played by Terry Bennett*), had a wife on the air, but you never saw her face. The camera's always showing the back of her head. He came to New York and did a lot of producing here, had a very successful life. In fact, he and his wife were on the radio about the same time as I was.

But we decided I should have a wife or something in a big box that you never see, and an off-stage character moaned and groaned like a monster. But you never saw him. In Philadelphia, he ate the mailman all the time. Every time mail was delivered, he'd eat the mailman. I mean, eat him whole. We'd hang the mailman's whistle up on the wall like trophies. But the wife would moan and groan and I'd hammer in the stake on her and tell her to shut up or whatever. Or else I was making cozy talk with her and maybe jump inside the box occasionally. We had a record of monkeys chattering, and we either slowed it down or speeded it up, I can't remember which it was. And she made a noise like "*HUQUAGHK WUHK WHUK!*" And I would answer her back the same way. That would be a funny part of the show. One time I had to give her a bath without her being seen. We gave her the big pillow that was stuffed with everything all the people sent in.

Then we had a character called Gasport who lived in a burlap bag hanging from a meat hook. He would moan and groan. We used a recording of a crying baby, slowed down. And I would operate on him and tell him to shut up and kick him, make him do things. But that's all we could afford, that's how it worked.

Do you remember inserting yourself into some of the films?

Yeah, yeah. We started that in Philadelphia. A guy named Ed White was the brain behind it all. He had seen every one of these movies in a movie house. I hadn't. He was a little younger than I was, but he wasn't as young as the high school kids. We used to sit and watch the movies, only to find out what the words were being said by the actors when the commercial breaks came up. We were showing these things for the first time on TV, so he had to pick a spot, like eight minutes in, to break. So we'd pick a spot, by minutes and seconds, so the director would know. For our benefit, we wanted to know the words that were being said, so we could say something right back to the character or whatever. And we'd lead back into the film the same way.

When we started doing that, about one-third of the season was gone already. We were watching *The Black Cat* (1934). They were having a ceremony of some kind and Boris Karloff was standing up there in this big black robe, intoning to the people down here. I don't what he's saying. Then they were showing the faces of the people looking up at him, half whacked out, as if they were really mesmerized by him. So he says, "Why don't we pop you in there?" Okay, seemed like a good idea. So we set it up. We're all nervous; the camera's high up and aiming down. It was very easy to do, because the camera just went on and on. And they popped me in there, just for that second. Just pop, like that.

Well, god, we thought that was just the funniest thing that ever happened. I don't know if we did any other one in that movie. But from then on, we just never stopped. The only tough thing was when the movies were really terrific movies, like *Frankenstein* (1931) or something. We normally would do it in a real double-B movie, when you're having fun. Or if it was a Frankenstein film, just a crowd scene, not answering back, you know.

I'm sure everybody did that. Ghoulardi did that, right? Now you could do it perfectly. But live, you couldn't always do it perfectly. We picked half a dozen places to jump into the film, because the film was always rolling. You couldn't stop it. We might not get in just in time, we might not get off in time, depending on when they switched. In Philadelphia, the director switched himself. I came to New York, and there's another guy who had to do this while the director says, "Take two, take one…" But it was much tighter when the director just did it himself. We would try to time what I was going to say to the scene that was being covered.

What about other horror hosts? Did you know any or know of any?

You know, it's a shame Ed Sullivan, Dick Clark or somebody didn't gather us all together. We never met, but that would have been kind of neat if somebody had done that. Dick Clark would be the obvious one, because eventually he was on the network while we were still doing this stuff. I stopped doing it about 1963 or '64, but I think other people kept going for a while. I understand in Cleveland they're still doing it. But that would have been kind of fun.

Terry Bennett, that was the horror host guy from Chicago, I met him in New York when I was working for Channel 11, or maybe when I was on the radio. But he's the only one I met and we weren't really doing our act at that point. He and his wife did a great radio show, and

Dr. Shock, the Shocky Doc. With John Zacherle's permission, Philadelphia magician Joe Zawislak resurrected the Roland image for a decade-long run, beginning in 1969.

they were trying to keep free-form going. I think it had died. I had moved to another station, after the first one, which was totally freeform. And they were even more open, even playing jazz. And Alex Bennett, remember that name from San Francisco? He was there with a late-night talk show.

What about Dr. Shock?

Dr. Shock, yeah. The station called me and asked if I wanted to come back and do the show. But I said, no, I'm working in New York. I can't come back. And they said, "Well, do you mind if Joe Zawislak dressed up like you?" And I said, good heavens, no. Just go ahead and do it. He was a magician. My neighbor was so excited, because she knew him as a magician. She heard that he was going to do it and she was all excited. I would come back from New York to Philadelphia when he was doing his show. But I don't think he was on weekends. There was some reason I wasn't able to see him. And it was only recently that somebody gave me a kinescope of his show. He was having a lot of fun, like we were all doing.

Joe Bob Briggs once got you together with a couple other hosts, Elvira and Ernie Anderson, for his show. Did you know Ernie Anderson?

No, I had never met them before. Yes, there was a Hollywood trip, it was kind of fun. It was a special thing for the month of October, leading up to Halloween. They had a guy come up. Stanley, I think, from San Francisco. And then Ernie Anderson and Joe Bob were there. I never saw the show. In fact, I never saw any of Elvira's syndicated shows. She was not syndicated in New York. She was shown in Connecticut and other places. But she's a really nice lady, I knew her husband. He was a nice guy also. But it was a really good time. Apparently everything she's got is absolutely real, I can tell you that.

But that was your first experience with Ernie Anderson?

Yes, yes. We had a good time; we talked. He was so happy out there with his children, telling me how his daughters were winning prizes with their horses and all that. I don't know how he landed that great job of being the voice of ABC. God!

Is there anything we should have asked but didn't ask? Is there anything you'd like to say about Zacherley and horror hosting?

I just want to say I feel real lucky with what happened. I had no big desire to be on a stage or be an entertainer or whatever you call it. I didn't know what I wanted to do. I wanted to get out of the Army. I was just bumming around. I somehow knew this little theater group and this one lady who worked for the board of education. She was doing these little educational radio shows to be played in classrooms, historical stuff and all. They always had a hard time getting people to be in the plays, you know? They'd say, "Who are we going to find to play this part?" So I just started to do that at this little theater. I had started off making scenery, and I enjoyed doing that. She eventually told me, "Hey, they got a cowboy show. Didn't you know anything about that?" I didn't know anything about it. I had no idea and would never have gone anyway. So I went up to the studio. I don't know how I introduced myself. But the open call had been done weeks before. And they must have had so many people show up that they just threw out all the pictures after they left. So the minute I walked in they said, "Oh yeah, we need somebody to hold the horses or whatever, and be an extra." Then the lady in charge of costumes, Lois Pennybecker, I should never forget her name, she ended up in the studio one day in the control room, watching the show and watching her costumes. She says, "Why don't you give that guy something to say? He looks so forlorn over there holding the horses." So that's how it started.

And the New York people who came down to be leads each time were very confused about the excitement of rehearsing, rehearsing, rehearsing, and then doing a dress rehearsal for the director—and he didn't like it, he'd change it all. And the next thing you know, you're doing it live. And they got so confused, running from this tree stump to another, looking for the microphone. There's one kinescope that I've seen where the sheriff is talking to this nasty guy in front of the barroom. The nasty guy says, "To heck with you. I'm going in to have a drink." And he goes in to have a drink. The deputy starts walking along the storefronts and he gets over here. And suddenly, you see this guy running—he wasn't supposed to do that—behind him to get in the studio. And that confusion was so much that they started getting local people for the feature role each week. I played an old prospector once. I played the husband in some farm family who was having a tough time. Then I played that undertaker thing. It was fun to do. But I still had no great desire. I didn't know what was going to happen next.

And then I made that record and that made management mad. They took me off the air for a week or something. Then they realized that I didn't have a contract and I didn't use their name (*Roland*) on the record, I used my own name. So they really had to back down, because they got so many complaints, and I got back on the air again.

My friend, Dick Strome, who did the *Zacherley for President* book, was one of the writers on the cowboy show. He was in New York and commuting all the time. He had a big job up here in an ad agency. He says, "You should come to New York." So after the big excitement of how many people came to the studio that day, and the fact that the record was in the top-10 for I don't know how many weeks, all that stuff, next thing I know, I'm up here talking to the big William Morris Agency. I did wind up at a lesser agency, but it was fun.

So what do think a horror host is? How would you define that?

As I said earlier, I don't think any horror host was trying to be more horrible or totally frightening. I guess

John Zacherle sits down with Sandy Clark, in 2004, to discuss his career.

you could have been, these days, especially. You could be really disgusting, unless Congress changes the rules again. But being interested in getting and keeping a show on the air, you're faced with some great movies and some terrible movies. I mean really early quickies and stuff like that. All those movies seem to have disappeared. You don't see them on the air, not even on the Sci-Fi/Sy-Fy Channel. They got so many, many more modern ones in color. Black and white isn't seen much anymore. But we had these old black and white movies, some of which were not very exciting, or interesting or fun. You're there to add a lot of fun to it all and take the curse out of the commercials somewhat. The commercials are just overwhelming now, the number you see. It's just appalling. The same is true with radio.

To make the show work, we used to make fun of a lot of the commercials, especially when we knew what they would be. Unfortunately on Channel 9, they would repeat the show three times over the weekend. And people would say, "Oh it was great!" What do you mean? He said, "We'd watch it Friday night and we'd get together Saturday and watch it again. And then we'd watch it Sunday morning all over again. We didn't care it was the same show. We'd never miss it." But when you knew what the commercials were, what the words were and when they were on, you could make a lot of good fun. You could pick out a phrase from deep inside the commercial, or maybe even the *second* commercial. And if you knew how the commercial ended, you could make some caustic comment.

Why do you think you've remained so popular?

I don't know. But you know, it's been a great trip. We did all these wonderful things. And aren't you glad we did? (*Laughs*)

Fiend Without A Face
Dr. E. Nick Witty (Alan Milair)
Interviewed by Michael Monahan (2004)

For two decades, monster movie fans in Syracuse, New York talked to the hand. Or rather, the hand talked to them. The extremity in question belonged to Dr. E. Nick Witty, an evil scientist whose unholy experiments had left him with a face too horrible for human eyes to behold. Beginning in 1964 with *Monster Movie Matinee* on WSYR-TV 3, and continuing on cable Channel 13 with *Chamber 13* in 1980, the doctor's diabolical presence was represented by shadowy outline, a cadaverous, bejeweled hand and the darkly mellifluous voice of Alan Milair.

While some other hosted horror programs may have featured a semi-regular cast of characters, *Monster Movie Matinee* offered a fully developed macabre soap opera, pre-dating *Dark Shadows* by two years. Story arcs could carry over for weeks, often centering on some new and terrible experiment performed upon the bad doctor's faithful assistant, Epal, played by Willard Lape, Jr. (aka Bill Everett), who died September 19, 2004.

Like many other television hosts, Alan Milair had enjoyed a career in radio, and his love of vintage radio shows, particularly of the horror variety, clearly influenced the serial format of the show, as well as its serious and sinister tone.

Can you tell us a little about the genesis of the program? What you were doing at the time, how you got into it, how the show was developed?

We, my faithful companion Bill Lape and I, were both film buffs from a long time ago. One of the other television stations in town ran a summary of who liked what kind of movies. Out of their survey came [the information that] 37.5% liked horror movies and horror movies were not being shown to any great extent. That stirred something, and I talked with Bill, and then with one of the directors, Gene Flaven, and Joe Torrisi, who was the studio crewman. We said, there's got to be something we can do. Bill's already doing a children's show as Salty Sam. We said with that many people out there, there's got to be an audience for horror movies and we've got some in some of the packages available. We proposed it, expecting a no. But we got an enthusiastic, sure, why not? The only thing is, the money never came up. (*Laughs*)

So we went ahead and put together the idea of a mansion someplace, a spooky mansion, and a doctor—myself. It sounded better than mister or sir. Doctor made it sound very official. So I became Dr. E. Nick Witty, as in "the den of inequity." Bill couldn't figure out what to do with Bill. We wanted something that was similar to Igor, but we didn't want to do any of the usual repetitions. We were pushing that one around and he said, "How does Epal sound?" Great! That was it! That's what we needed. Nice and short and punchy, and similar enough to Igor that there was a connection in your mind.

I said that sounds great. He said, "That's my last name spelled backwards." His name was William Everett Lape. But for his air name, he stopped with the Everett. So he was Bill Everett on the air and his last name had never come up. (*Laughs*) And I had only known him for four years at that point! So that was how he got his name and that's how I got mine. And we were the entire program, until later when we brought in a few dear guests to assist us whenever we needed them.

The studio, the mansion, it looked beautiful: absolutely beautiful, absolutely real. They created a landscape that included a memorial garden that was down the hill to the viewer's right. And then there was a path that went up to the porch on the mansion. That is where we dissolved into the mansion, into one of the windows, or into an obvious entry to the building, wherever we had the set-up inside. We expanded it later to include a swamp. Dry ice was our stock in trade. So that was the genesis of everything in that respect. There was a wing chair and I thought great, we'll make it spooky, because you never see the character. It also gave me a chance to hold my script in the other hand off camera.

Originally the promotion depart was thrilled. They thought it was great. "Good! We can have a contest. What does he look like? What does he really look like?" And so on, so forth. We got about six weeks into the show and it suddenly dawned on us that if we did that, we would blow the whole thing, because people would say ... "Yaaawn." Or they would laugh, or they would be upset. Everybody has his or her own idea of horror, and the worst horror is in the human mind. Each of us—there's one thing in our mind that is the most horrible thing imaginable. Everybody's got his or her own. So we decided we'd never show him. And we never did. All they ever saw was my hand (*gestures with right hand*).

Bill they saw. He was the subject of most of the experiments that we did and he suffered all of the slings and arrows. He started out with a hump and he had an enormous nose and age lines all over. That was the beginning of the character. Well, at some point along the line, as we got into it, he decided he did not like his nose. It just was blowing his mind. So I said, well, we can re-construct the nose. So we re-constructed the nose. But there was one little error during the operation, and he lost the sight of his right eye. So after the operation he came in with his brand new nose, which was classic, and a patch over the eye.

The one point we carried over in all of the scripts we wrote for the show: Dr. Witty *never* succeeded. Everything he tried turned wrong somewhere. Something went wrong. Even if he was successful with the nose ... a little slip of the scalpel and he lost an eye. This established the pity that is felt by almost everyone who watches any of the horror movies. There is a point at which you feel sorry for the monster. I mean the monster, Frankenstein's monster, is blown away completely when the little girl is in the water and doesn't come up. He didn't intend it. It happened and he didn't understand it. And we feel a touch of pity for him, because he doesn't understand what's happening. The same is true with the Mummy. He didn't design evildoing. Somebody else did, and they brought forth a creation of the gods. So that was the other thing, under the little pity was the fact that I never succeeded. (*Laughs*) So that's how we got started.

Dr. E. Nick Witty (Alan Milair), his face too horrible to behold, nevertheless poses for a portrait with his faithful assistant Epal (Willard Lape, Jr.).

How recognizable is that laugh? How often do you do the laugh and people recognize it?

I enjoy the laugh enormously. People, who recognize me and know I did the show, always want to hear it. It was the most identifiable thing. When we first started, I had three very young children. And if we went grocery shopping, I had to be very careful not to laugh at all, because people would turn around, just with my normal laugh. I had to be very, very stern with the children. We had to explain that to them. "Don't worry if daddy doesn't laugh." Somebody would stop me and say, "You must be…!" So it was a trademark with the show.

Marvelous! Back to the mechanics of the show, gathering the props and then the launch date in '64.

When we finally had the crew and the okay, and Bill and I had established our characters and so on, we were at a loss at what to do in terms of a setting. We felt that we needed something we could vary. We didn't always want to be in the same place. But at the same time we wanted something identifiable to use as a base. This was handled during group discussions. This is not Bill or I or somebody coming up with this whole thing out of one piece of cloth. We decided that a house would be the best thing, because it has lots of rooms. A haunted house, obviously. So then we said, well, how do we get it? What do we use for a house? What do we use for a living room or whatever?

Building the sets was a little complicated, but nothing spectacular. Being a frequenter of model stores, I had seen a Victorian mansion for toy trains. One of the members of the crew was a man who was bigger and heavier than I was. He was an ex-Marine and had hands like hams. You were sure he would not even be able to write his own name carefully. But he was absolutely unbelievable in working

41

The title card used on the TV program during the early 1960s; courtesy of Joseph Capuana

with these miniatures. He created the miniature-haunted house that we lived in. He took the basic Victorian mansion and made it look decrepit, haunted and so on. His work with it was absolutely phenomenal. And then he also designed the hill on which the house sat. The stairway and the path running up to it became sort of a joint effort with everybody on the crew.

With other additions to the set over the years, it was the same kind of thing. It was the crew. We would come up with an idea, or they would come up with an idea, and they would go ahead and do it. There were about 13 people put the show together every week, and every single one of them was part of the show. We used to make a joke to a certain extent that once we got a hook into somebody and we saw their interest in it, they were ours for life. They would work anything, do anything, come up with any idea that they could.

One of the basic things we first did was establish that the cameras were the viewer. That one we stole from Robert Montgomery (*Montgomery used first-person camera techniques in the film* Lady in the Lake, *1947*). When people came into a room they were supposed to look around, the way that you would if you were walking into a strange room. And the sets were large enough so that they could do that. We did it with the library. The viewer went over and looked at all the shelves as you would, just sort of scanning them up and down and so on. There were little horror gadgets on the shelves and so on. But that was, I think, one of the things that made the show so successful, the fact that the camera was interested in just what other people walking into the room would be interested in.

And the introductory line "Dear guest" served two purposes. It involved the viewers individually. We weren't talking to them; we were talking to *you*. And we always had your best interests at heart. That sort of thing took it out of the ordinary—and the fact that we scripted it into every show. Those things were different.

What was the production schedule like, from writing to filming to air?

We had two hours a week in the studio by ourselves (*Laughs*). The studio crew put things together for the filming, for the video work. The sets were built. But the big things were on rollers, so that everything could be rolled off, or carried off, easily. Setting up and breaking down the set was not an onerous task. Sometimes it took a lot of work to get the light right. And whenever we did something that was new, there was a lot of experimentation. But we used the time to set it up. Then it was torn down for the next week. We saved everything. Fortunately we had an enormous warehouse near the studios where they could put things. So we saved everything.

We had a gorgeous fireplace. When we did the library, we had four by eights, ceiling to floor bookshelves. The artisan at the studio, Bill Brown, did all of the books. So that with each book there was something in each title that you could catch as a word. Some of them, if they were short, would simply be the name of somebody: "Frankenstein" or "Monsters" or something like that, so that each of the bindings could be seen. You got an impression even if you didn't get a chance to read them as they panned over them. And we found some wonderful things to work with, such as little knights and little models of various kinds ... a guillotine.

Was the show done on tape, or was it done live?

It was done on tape. But we very seldom went back; we didn't have the time to go back. We corrected errors, no question. Or if somebody blew up in the middle, we would go back. But we were under time constraint. And we were under the constraint of using some of the effects. Dry ice only lasts so long, and then it just sort of peters out. And there's not much that you can do, because the water's so cold. You could drop another piece in; it doesn't do anything. You have to have hot water. So this is another minor thing where we would do retakes. The tape was erased every week, ready for the next day after it played. We did just the opens and closes originally. Then later we added some bridges to accommodate the breaks in the film, very quick stuff.

Could you talk about the gathering of the props, like the casket, the organ?

Well, the organ! I had seen it on a second floor porch of a house on James Street and had been tracking it for a year. I noticed it one day and I just kept looking to see if it was there every time I went up and down James Street, which I traveled with great regularity. Obviously nobody was doing anything with it, except the pigeons that were living on it. I thought, what the heck, it doesn't hurt to ask. So I checked that I had some financing from the station, not having any idea what the owner was going to ask for the organ. I went in and said, I've been admiring the organ that's on the front porch. Does it belong to you? She said, "No, it's my brother's." I said, would you consider selling it, and her "yes" was too quick to pass up. I said, well, how much would you want for it? And she said, "I don't know. I'm just glad to get rid of it." I said, $25 dollars? She said, "Fine. You got to take it out, though." So I cheerfully handed over the $25 dollars.

It took us about the best part of a week to get the pigeon droppings off it. It was literally covered. And it had no cover at all. So it had been exposed, at least a year, to the elements. But we got it cleaned off and polished up to some extent. We didn't want to polish it too much. It had to fit in with the rest of the décor. That became a specific piece of the main set, which was the living room, where Bill and I each had our chair. My chair was at the organ. Prior to that we had used the keyboard of a regular organ, but suddenly we had this gorgeous thing that came within the scope. We could take different pictures, different angles, with that working organ. And it got us in and out, with my hand running over the keys. Not playing, just pretending.

Bill had a chair that was directly opposite me. We had a table in the center and on the table was usually a foaming silver chalice. That was dry ice in warm water. Occasionally, if the script called for it, I would pause while Bill was doing a story and the chalice would come up (*gestures with hand, as if to drink*) and go back. Bill would sometimes have a similar container if we were about to toast something or share a thought or relax for moment or two before our "dear guest" came. The table was the center for anything that came into the mansion. If we were gifted with something, we would use it as a centerpiece on that table. So then everything worked in this general area. Then we had other sets, other circumstances.

There was nobody on the crew that we could have done without. We would not have been able to do the same excellent show if we were missing anybody. But people on the crew would go on vacation. One of them, Bernie Wyman, brought back from her Florida vacation a movie prop hand. It pulled itself across a table with a bloody bandage trailing off the end of it. That got a lot of use over the years. I cannot remember all the times we used it. It escaped into an atomic energy furnace-type thing, where the door went up, the fog rolled out and the hand crawled into the fog and disappeared inside. We used it as a prop when we worked on Bill's hand. Originally he had a hand, just like everybody else. And then something happened. I do not remember. Something happened and he lost his hand. So for a while he just had a bloody stump that had a bandage on the end of it. And then we worked on it. He needed something to work with to do things around the mansion.

And so we went through a whole series of hands. They always involved telekinesis; something in a box communicating to something in another box. But in the other box was his stump. We worked it out so the audience could see us put on the tentacle, the hook. He ended up with a barbed wirepuller glove, which is an iron mesh that they used in the Army to pull barbed wire, so you don't get stuck with it. But it looks gorgeous on the hand. It sort of does things. It jangles a little bit. But it flops down if you turn your hand; it flops the other way. It's just disgusting enough to use. That's what he ended up with. It took us, I don't know how many months, to get to that. We went through a whole series of things. We transmuted this—whatever we were using—to his hand. And his hand was simply where his hand was. It was grafted onto his arm—believable (*laughs*), if you're inclined that way. We made it sound as believable as possible.

Were there any other continuing story lines? Because it sounds like you created serial stories.

Yes. We already had the living room; we had the memorial grounds. We had the tower room. And we put the tower room to a new use, which was simply that little gazebo on the top of the house. We put that to use, not as it was originally designed, but as a place to put the casket.

43

We wanted to do a theme about a casket. But we needed a casket to put me in. We didn't want anything special; we didn't want anything elaborate.

We were looking for the Western kind they used to display the outlaw's body in and so on. Nobody could come up with one. Nobody had the vaguest idea, even though they were fantastic carpenters. It just wasn't worth the effort to build. My wife at the time suggested, "Why don't you call Norm Jacobs?" He was the man who ran National Casket Company, and she formerly baby-sat his children. We knew them very well. She said to call him. I said, are you serious, call a place like that and ask if we can have one of the coffins? She said, "Oh, he'll be delighted!"

She called him and we set up a meeting. I went down and we talked. I told him what I needed and assured him we would treat it gently and so on. The first thing he showed me was a gorgeous sterling bronze casket ... magnificent! It was only $37,000, and I said, noooo, I don't think I want something I need to be that careful of. So he showed me everything. Finally I said, don't you have something that is really cheap? He said, "Well ... um ... uh ... there's the ... welfare casket." He was a little taken aback by having to mention that they did them. And I said, well, let me take a look. At least let me see it.

Well, it was gorgeous. It was a flocked, gray standard casket: viewing lid, satin on the inside, ruffles across it. So it was a very attractive piece. It had the bars you carried it with along the side, and they were aluminum color. But it looked great on camera. It was fuzzy from the flocking, which was in a pattern. It looked great. But it didn't reflect anything, and you couldn't scratch it. So he said, "I hate to let you. But if you can use it, go ahead." And so we did. Twelve years later he wrote me a letter and said, "And by the way, we've finally taken the coffin off the memo list. So it's now yours." And we had used it in every conceivable way, with the viewing lid open or closed—but closed so my hand could stick out. It was never closed totally. My hand sticking out, holding it, ready to open, or it was already open. We worked those bits to death.

We did the old routine, about coming up out of the cellar on a level floor. Epal came up into the tower room where the casket was. That was one of the bits that we loved especially, because it illustrated a lot of things. The first thing the viewer, "dear guest," saw was the coffin, viewing lid open, with a great big chunk of wood sticking out of it. And then we hear Bill, mumbling to himself and so on, coming up the stairs and coming over. And he put the candelabra on the end of the coffin and said, "Well, really, I'm not late. It's almost time for him to be awakened." He takes hold of the stake, and with great effort pulls it out. Just as it came out, from the coffin came, "Ahhhhh ... thank you, Epal." (*Laughs*) That was it. But then we continued our conversation.

It was one of the continuing themes that we were not out to scare kids. It was not a kids' show in that sense. We never talked down to them. We used lots of words that they never heard of before. But if they didn't know about vampires and wooden stakes, it wouldn't mean a thing. But they would still laugh like the devil. We presumed that there was some prior knowledge with most of the bits we did. So we never had to describe what they were. Dr. E. Nick Witty had black fingernails, and nobody ever realized that ghouls had black fingernails. So we never had to say anything about my being a ghoul. It was, if you knew about black fingernails, fine. If you didn't, it made a great picture. So that was it with the coffin and the tower room.

What was the audience reaction like? Did you get a lot of fan mail? Fan art?

We got a lot of fan art. It was one of the most interesting things. One of them wound up on the show. We had the Fickle Fingers, which is a marking pen drawing—quite large—that one of our viewers sent in. We ended up using it as a regular piece in the living room. We had a wide variety of pictures of us, not having any idea what I looked like. The reaction was great. And the reaction since then has been great. There are still a few dyed-in-the-wool fans out there that I run in to from time to time.

When the original Monster Movie Matinee *program was cancelled, that wasn't quite the end. Can you talk a bit about the show's revival on cable as* Chamber 13*?*

We had done this for 15 years with WSYR, Channel 3. When the station was sold, it separated television and radio. Various people stayed with the television and various people stayed with the radio department. I stayed with radio, by the boss's instructions. But my partner Epal (Bill Everett) stayed with television. And the new owners, *Times-Mirror* out of Los Angeles, had a standard policy: If you don't work for us, you don't get on the air. So that meant that the show was kaput at that point. That was in 1979.

The same people that had owned WSYR-TV also owned the cable system, and they wanted some fill for some of their airtime. Somebody remembered *Monster Movie Matinee*. So we went over there and did 38 shows, with everything the same except the setting. We had a different setting. We were no longer in a house; we were in a castle. And it was called *Chamber 13* instead of *Monster Movie Matinee*. We did 38 shows and that was the last of it.

Why the continuing appeal?

As far as kids are concerned, I think they enjoyed it because it wasn't talking down to them. We did not play as though we had children for an audience. That's what Bill did with his morning show as Salty Sam. He played to the kids. He had an uncanny and unreal empathy with children. That was a joy to see anytime that he worked. And that's still true. He does storytelling now. But people could sit and watch it. They didn't have to worry about whether or not they saw the ending.

Sometimes it was a climax and sometimes it wasn't. Very often we just trailed off into nothingness. Like, if the storyline involved the necessity of having blood, for whatever reason, we'd save the last line for the close. Epal would say something to the effect of, "Well, I've got to be off, kind host." And I'd say, "Ah yes. Remember Epal, it must be fresh." And we never said blood. We talked about body fluids; we talked about fluids. We never said blood, so that nobody could get upset. At the same time they could build their own bit for whatever we were talking about.

The biggest effect that we had was the bodiless head. One of the guys on the crew was an amateur magician and he said, "What you should have is a head that just talks to you." I told him I'd love to do that. The more I thought about it, and Bill thought about it, the better we liked the idea. We asked what do you know about the bodiless head gag? I mean, heads on tables and stuff. He had a magician's catalog. In the catalog they had a whole set you could buy for, I think it was, $499. That ruled it out instantly.

But you could buy the plans for $15. So we bought the plans and built it. We had to have a mirror. We had a huge woman's dressing mirror from a store that I had saved over the years, and that was cut into two pieces. The table was diagonal and you would be looking at the corner of it. There was a leg in this mirror (*indicates left hand*) and a leg in this mirror (*indicates right hand*) offstage. And when they were reflected, it created the fourth leg of the table. So that you saw the two on the ends, the one here (*gestures forward*) and obviously assumed there was one

The house that HO built! A model train Victorian mansion was transformed into the diabolical dwelling of Dr. E. Nick Witty. Courtesy of Joseph Capuana

at the back. Then we cut a hole in the table and various people put their heads through it. They were mounted, like, here (*brings hands under chin*) and there was about this much (*holds fingers four inches apart*) of a collar that we fitted out with all kinds of things. Sometimes colored lights, sometimes just plain lights, depending on what was going on. The bits included things like keeping the head alive for a particular body.

How did the film package change over time? Did you have the Universal classics and later Hammer films?

We had the cheaper product in the beginning, the ones that were almost public domain. And it wasn't until later that we got into the *Shock* packages and so on. We never got *The Mummy* (1932), but we had all of the other various titles: the Boris Karloff, the Bela Lugosi, that type of thing. We had most of the Japanese monsters, like Godzilla and that type of thing. This would go into the last years we were on. We had all of that.

The only problem we had was this. We started out originally building our opening on whatever film we were showing. In other words, if the film was about a werewolf, we were doing a bit about a werewolf. We found out after about two months that you couldn't depend on that, because films were bicycled. Which means that station A used it, and when then they finished with it, they sent it to station B. When they were finished with it, they sent it to station C. But you couldn't be sure the station ahead of you would get it out on time. So the show would go

45

The shadowy figure of Dr. E. Nick Witty greets his manservant/guinea pig Epal in an early 1960s episode. Courtesy of Joseph Canuana

on and the film would arrive the next day. But we always had a standby. So we had to stop keying the two together. That was one of the challenging things.

Were you involved in any radio drama? Were you a fan of old radio mystery and drama, like Lights Out*?*

All of it, from the time I was a child. I was about seven. My family, at that point, was living in an upstairs apartment. I once woke up in the middle of the night. It was dark and I was looking for Dad and Mom. I got up and I wandered in and I could hear something that was going on, but I couldn't see anything. Well, they took *Lights Out* very seriously. They turned the lights out. And I could hear this forest fire raging. They were talking to themselves, but not a great deal. This whole drama was unfolding and I was in the hall. I came rushing into the room, because they were talking about fire. (*Laughs*) So they let me stay till the end of the program just to make sure that I knew it was a radio program, then put me back to bed. And I listened to all of them. My family, as I said, loved those things.

My father was an amateur actor. Everybody enjoyed it. So I was exposed to radio and its tricks very early on. Then when I started working in radio when I was 16, I learned a lot of other things. These were the days when the only recordings were the gigantic 16-inch enamel discs, and every station cut their own. When these discs came to Syracuse, they were network ones. They cut things by themselves or picked things up from the network and played them back at a different time.

There are shows that I know, that I'm sure in my own mind, were too good for television. There was the one story that remains in my psyche. I think it was called *The House*. It was about two young people who bought a house and moved into it. Everything in it was modern and it was just spectacular. Except that the house had a soul, and it did things to them. And it didn't like some of the things that they did. That was the basic theme of what went on—two people and a house. And it was a great show. I mean, it was a great, scary show. I don't even remember the end of it. I just remember the impact of the whole thing, because they had this mansion and everything was working, and then suddenly the house decided it was going to do what it wanted to do. And if you didn't go along, there was a penalty to pay. So that carries through from everything that I had in radio, everything we did in radio.

Were there any particular elements from radio that you pulled out for your program?

Yes. The laugh is a combination of Raymond and The Shadow; those are the two identifiable ones. They're part of the laugh. I just do it my way. And my way was different from Orson Welles when he was The Shadow, or the four or five Shadows that were on the radio. And they all had a different laugh, slightly different, but much the same. So I just pulled a little piece from everybody.

I did a show late at night, from 11:15 to midnight, on radio. And I dearly loved it, because it was fun and because people remembered it. It was 45 minutes and it was mood music. I made the selections and I played two records at a time, which was not the way you were supposed to do it. But at that hour, nobody else on the staff was listening. The whole thing was done in a very soft voice. The whole bit was "Music just for you …" and then, bang, into the music. At another point we would be

Syracuse TV horror hosts Dr. E. Nick Witty (Alan Milair) and Baron Daemon (Mike Price) get together for the shoot in 2004.

slightly past 11:45 p.m. and I'd give a time check and a temperature. "The temperature is 32 degrees in Syracuse, and its 4 minutes to a brand new day." I got calls from students on the hill. It was the only thing they could listen to, because it didn't interfere with anything they were doing. They could get their homework done and so on.

For as long as you did the Monster Matinee *TV show, it's amazing to think you were so well known solely by your voice. In a strange way, that's almost like an extension of radio.*

Yes, it is. It is, exactly. We used a lot of tricks from the old radio days. As I said, we did it with only two men. Whenever we were talking to each other, we always identified ourselves. If Epal was talking to me, he'd say, "Ah, but kind host …" or something else. "Dr. Witty …" We always identified who he was talking to. I did the same thing. "Epal …" and I'd go on from there. Or "When you have made the arrangements, Epal …" And that's an old trick from radio, because you couldn't see the characters. You'd better identify them some way or people will lose track, especially if there's more than two.

One thing that strikes me about horror hosts in particular is that they are a flashpoint for eccentricity.

Yeah.

That they're waiting for an audience to feed their own personality.

Yes, yes. I think that's very true. It's one of the reasons we're always very careful in our scripts about how much we told them. In all the years we were on the air, we were only criticized once. (*Laughs*) And that was because of a gigantic snowstorm that central New York suffered. It was in the early years, when we were on. It was sometime in the 1960s, I think, or early 1970s. There was a huge snowstorm and everything stopped. We got three complaints. One was from a college professor who objected to the content of this film. The movie involved a tree that bled. That was the bit. And they showed copious blood. He said, "This is a terrible thing. You shouldn't show this to children. This is just an awful thing." It was probably the one and only time in his life that he saw the show, because he was stuck in the house and there wasn't anything else he wanted to watch.

We got a beautiful letter from a sister [nun] in Buffalo, from a convent, basically saying the same thing. She was concerned about the effect on children, young children, of seeing so much blood. It wasn't really a criticism, but she didn't think it was the best thing. Well, we decided

Dr. E. Nick Witty's Monster Movie mansion, scene of many strange experiments in his 20-year run on Syracuse television.

immediately she caught us only because she was turning the dial to get something on and there weren't that many stations around. She could pick us up off the relay. And we got another one from somebody in Utica. There had been a recent news story about a young lady who had been tied to a tree and died. This letter proceeded to say that we were the reason that horrible things like this happened.

Frankly, our opinion was none of these were genuinely valuable criticisms. We didn't find anything wrong with the film. Anything that was wrong was edited out. Bill was magnificent at editing film. You never knew. There are people who swear today that what they saw was the original film in its entirety—in an hour and a half. (*Laughs*) I'm sorry, but we used up five minutes at the beginning and the end, and then there were the commercial breaks in the middle. So it was like, sometimes the film ran for an hour and 10 minutes. (*Laughs*)

What does it take to be a good horror host?

It's difficult. I think that to be one you have to like the venue, like the old horror shows and all of the things that have been generated over the years. You have to enjoy all those things and then you transfer that enjoyment to the audience. You have to identify with the audience. Much more so, I think, than in any other media format. It's similar to a newscast in the sense that it's one-on-one. But the empathy with the audience is, I think, the most important thing for anything like that. And obviously you have to like the product. I mean, you have to be a little crazy.

Bloody Buddies
Baron Daemon (Mike Price)
Interviewed by Sandy Clark and Michael Monahan (2004)

Mike Price enjoyed the classic local TV career: He started as a staffer when WNYS 9 (*later WSYR*) went on the air in September 1962. He entertained kids as Cousin Orky, a lovable hayseed who introduced cartoons. When the station acquired a package of horror movies, Price offered his hosting services in a goofy Bela Lugosi accent and became a local legend as Baron Daemon.

The Baron was broad burlesque of the Lugosi-style vampire that drew heavily on Price's kid show roots. His sidekicks, Verry (sic) Hairy (Dennis Calkins in a rubber caveman mask) supported him and Boris, the world's smallest monster (a diminutive Bill Eadie in a Frankenstein mask).

The Baron's late-night monster movies were so popular with kids that the station gave him an afternoon show, *The Baron and His Buddies*, which, like Cousin Orky, featured cartoons and a live audience. The Baron followed the familiar trajectory of local horror hosts, making frequent public appearances, cutting a novelty record, "The Transylvania Twist," and maintaining a multi-generational local fan base decades after he went off the air.

In the Baron's case, his exit was premature, precipitated by a fire at WNYS in 1967, which destroyed his props and set. But Mike Price remained at the station, becoming a respected and beloved newscaster. In later years, Price developed a popular editorial segment on the nightly news called "The Good News."

Mike Price revived the Baron post-Millennium for a couple of one-off Halloween specials, and retired from the station in June 2008, after 6 years.

Michael Monahan: Can you please tell us about the creation of the Baron, the circumstances that led you to hosting a show and how you came up with the program.

Back in September of '62, just in passing, in the hallway, I heard our general manager and program director talking about a package of old horror films that they had leased. They were the old *Frankenstein* (1931) and *Dracula* (1931) and *The Wolf Man* (1941) and *The Mummy* (1932), and all of those. They were discussing where and when they would use them. And the general manager said to the program director, "You know, Jeff, where are we going to put these? Where are we going to use these?" And I overheard them and I said, I've got an idea. I've heard of these late-night horror hosts in other parts of the country. And I can do a fairly decent imitation of Bela Lugosi as Dracula. If I could do that accent, perhaps I can host these movies late at night and we can have funny little skits in the breaks, in between and during the movies! And they went, "Yeah, that might work. Let's give it a try." So we did.

I ran next door to a department store. We were in the Shopping Town Plaza, and right next door to our studios was a W.T. Grant's, a department hardware store. I got about three yards of black cotton cloth and tucked it into my shirt collar; I threw some baby powder into my face, and I eye-browed in some darker eyebrows. And I started talking like that *(Bela Lugosi accent)*. It was really horrible! *(Laughs)* I was a horrible horror host for a horrible horror show! So it worked out. And as it progressed, and we did it two or three weeks, or a couple of months, gee, we started getting phone calls and letters from people. They seemed to enjoy it. So that's when they decided to go full-blown and get a set and a couple tailor-made capes with the red lining and everything. Then get the paste-on bushy eyebrow, the mono-brow that goes all the way across, one big eyebrow. That's how it all got started.

MM: What was the process for putting together a show?

Well, when we first started on Saturday nights, we did these double-feature movies, and we did live skits within the moves and between the movies. We had a guy who was the creator of a lot of it. His name was Bill Eadie, who was our studio floor manager at the time. And he would write it out, but not line for line. He would come up with an idea, with a concept, and from that we would pretty much ad lib from there. It was all made up on the spur of the moment. It was a lot of fun, and some crazy moments, too.

MM: Were the skits that you did for that week's show linked to the movie at all? Or were they completely separate stand-alones?

Both. Sometimes we would get a chance to look at the movie. Or we knew something about the movie. It was an old movie; we all had seen it at some time. And we would try to match things with the movie. And then other times we would do things that had nothing to do with the movie, but these bits related to current topics. We created skits involving news, sports, or something happening in the community. We created something timely, but bits that had nothing to do with the movie. I know there were some late-night horror hosts who would put themselves, somehow, into the movie. We never did that. But we did take-offs on a lot of different things.

MM: Who else was involved with the production end, building sets and props? Did they do this on their own time, or on weekends?

They would mostly do this on their regular time, on the clock. Dennis Caulkins was a commercial artist, who drew up most of the sets and the background for what we did. But he was also a character. He was a sidekick for me. His name was Verry Hairy, and he wore a big pullover mask, sort of like a Neanderthal; a cross between a Neanderthal and an ape of some type. And he didn't talk. He just used a lot of hand gestures and nodding and so on. He was one of those guys.

We went to a kid show eventually, and the kids would scream, "Look over here! Look over here!" And I'd say, "What? What's over here, boys and girls?" And of course he'd be on the other side of me, tugging my cape or something. And the other guy I mentioned, Bill Eadie, he came up with most of the concepts and ideas for the skits that we would do. But he would also put on a mask. It was a Frankenstein monster mask. But he was smaller than I was and would bill himself as the world's smallest Frankenstein Monster. "I'm a monster, but a little one."

MM: What was fan reaction like, and how did it manifest itself in art and letters?

The fan reaction was outstanding. We did it live, and then we started to tape things. But after six or eight months, a lot of fan mail was coming in. A lot was from kids, or parents of kids, that said, "Gee, we like the Baron and what he does. But we think the movies are too scary. They scare the kids and we don't like them watching them," or "It's too late for them to stay up. Too bad he isn't on earlier in the day." So our bosses here, our general manager, thought what a good idea it would be to have a kids' show for the Baron. So the Baron, in the same vampire outfit, with the same dungeon set as a background,

The Scarin' and Carin' Baron Daemon (Mike Price), Syracuse, New York's popular horror and kiddie show host; photo courtesy WSYR-TV 9 and Joseph Capuana

had a peanut gallery. We brought kids in and set them on cut up logs. We maybe had 10 to 15 kids every day.

And the movies that we ran ... forget about *Frankenstein* and *Dracula* and *The Wolf Man*, we ran *Buck Rogers* and *Flash Gordon* serials with Buster Crabbe. Had no tie-in to Transylvania or late-night horror or anything. The kids loved it. But I was still Baron Daemon, saying, "Hello boys and girls! How are you today?" And we'd put them on this makeshift rocket ship that we had, as if we were going to take them to meet Buck Rogers on Mars, or some place. And we would flash the lights off and on and move the cameras around, and throw a little fog in there. And what was too bad is that the kids at home really thought we were going someplace. (*Laughs*) And then they'd come in one of these potato chip plastic chairs and think, "We didn't go anyplace. We're still sitting right here." You know? The lights would come back up and it's like, what a let down, what a disappointment for the kids. They didn't really go anywhere.

MM: Did the Baron make any personal appearances?

Oh, nearly every weekend, sometimes twice a week on Saturdays and Sundays. And it was all different places. I was at hardware stores, openings of automobile dealerships and supermarkets and all kinds of special places. We had some interesting moments, too. I remember one where I was at an automobile parts place called Meltzer's Auto Supply. And that was one of the first appearances I did. They made up Dennis, who was our commercial artist. But he did a lot of building of sets, too. And he built a crypt, a portable crypt that we could take along with us. We set that up, and I was in the crypt. Kids would come up and I would pose for pictures and shake hands and sign Baron Daemon autographs, in blood of course. I always had a red bloody pen with me.

One boy came up one day, and I shook hands with him. I would wear these white parade gloves. And he said, "And now, Baron. It's time for me to bite you!" And the kid grabbed on to my hand like a bulldog. There were two security guys there and they were trying to pull him off. I'm going, "Whoa! Wait a minute!" And he didn't want to let go. I'm probably exaggerating this to some degree, but it almost seemed as if they lifted him, his legs and his feet, parallel to the floor, trying to pull him off my hand. Finally I gave him just like a little chop, a little karate, and the kid did let go. Luckily they caught him, so his head didn't hit the floor or anything. I remember I took the glove off, and there were teeth marks on my hand for about three days. Didn't break the skin, but just the teeth marks were there.

MM: Can you tell us about the Baron's 45 rpm single?

Our manager here thought, gee, this thing is going so well. What are different ways that we can promote it? We had Baron Daemon t-shirts and sweatshirts, Baron Daemon fan clubs. And the last thing that he thought of was, "Hey, how about a 45 record?" You remember those. They were a small record with a big hole in the center. They were flat, on this thing called vinyl. (*Laughs*) We had a 45 record called "The Transylvania Twist with Baron Daemon." It went like (*singing*): "Grab a hold of your baby/And hold her tight/'Cause Baron Daemon is flying tonight!" Well, that's enough of that (*Laughs*). We had a vocal group in town, a trio, The Vitree Sisters. On the record, they were labeled as 'The Vampires," and they backed me up. And we had a combo, a four-person combo. Sam and the Twisters was the group that backed me up.

Capitol actually did the pressing. But the label, it was a red label, was the WNYS label, which was our call letters at the time. It was just a promotional gimmick. So there was no distribution outside our viewing area. Once you got 50 or 60 miles outside of town, you couldn't buy it anywhere, but it did very well locally. And supposedly it's still the best selling locally produced record ever produced in Syracuse. We sold about 12 thousand, maybe more than that. But it's done well.

MM: How do think that television has changed since you started to do the Baron? And how much fun was it then?

It's a lot different today. Technology, what they can do now, is so far advanced than what we could do in those days. But for what I did, it was more fun in those days because we used to think of ourselves, back in the 1960s, as a part of show business. So we did a lot of locally produced programs. In addition to the Baron, I did another character called Cousin Orky, which was like a hayseed farmer character that introduced cartoons. And we had a variety show on the air; we had quiz shows on the air. We had other kid shows, like *Romper Room*, on the air. We had a Bozo the Clown. So there was a lot of local origination, right here from our studios. We don't have any of that anymore. Everything is news or public affairs.

A vampire piloting a rocketship? Sure, why not? It's the Sixties. Photo courtesy of WSYR-TV 9 and Joseph Capuana

MM: What do you think we've lost with the absence of that direct audience contact?

I think what we've lost is the identification with the community. I think we've retained that here at Channel 9. We've been lucky over the years, because a lot of our news people—our meteorologists, our anchor people, our reporters—are local people who have stayed here over a period of years. Or if they're not local, they've come in and made this their home and stayed over a period of years. There's still a connection with community, and the feeling that you're part of the family here. And I think that's the way people look at us.

I'm lucky in that, for the last 20 years, I've been doing a feature report that's part of the news called "The Good News." And for me, that's very enjoyable. I love it. I could have retired a couple of years ago. But I don't want to, because I'm having too much fun. I'm having too good a time. While the other people are out covering the hard news of the day, the disasters and the tragedies, I'm doing things that are fun and enjoyable to do. And I really feel I connect with the community when I'm doing that.

Sandy Clark: Continuing on that thread, reflect upon the idea of a local celebrity as someone you could touch, as opposed to being off in some distant land. Talk about that sort of celebrity. Do people still recognize you as the Baron? And what do you think the benefit is to having local celebrities over the national ones?

In those days, local people who appeared on the air were celebrities in their home community. I can remember when I was doing the Baron, and I would go out someplace, either in costume or afterward, I would have to hang around and sign autographs for a couple of hours. I always enjoyed doing that, and never brushed anybody off in that regard. I always thought, I'm fortunate to be doing this instead of having to work for a living. I can

The Baron holding court on his afternoon *The Baron and His Buddies* show. Note sidekick Verry Hairy (Dennis Calkins) exiting stage right. Photo courtesy of WSYR-TV 9 and Joseph Capuana

do this and have a good time. So any kid, or anybody, that wants to talk for a couple of minutes, or wants me to sign something, I'm more than happy to do it.

The guy who was one of the producers on the record that we did, "The Transylvania Twist"—he's deceased, he's left us, his name was Huvey Larrison. He said to me one day, after booking me for a personal appearance, "You know what? Here in Syracuse, you're as popular as Elvis Presley." And I said, well, that's pretty nice; it's very complimentary. I like that. Now, of course, if I drove to Rochester, nobody would know who I was. But here locally, within our viewing area, for me and for other people, we were like celebrities out on the street. And today, even now, 40 years later, I'll see people across the street that are contemporaries of mine, who will look over and say, "Hey, Baron! How's it going?" (*Laughs*) And then they'll say to me sometimes, apologetically, "I'm sorry. You probably wish that was over." I say, nah, it comes with the territory. That's part of it. I don't mind that. I'm very flattered that you still remember. They say, "Yeah, that was part of my childhood. I remember that growing up." It's a nice feeling, that people do remember that.

MM: Continuing along the lines of the community aspect. You did a "Drop and Roll" tape with the local fire department.

One of our news producers here at the time, Dexter Blake, was also working like a PR guy and producer to help the fire department. So he said, "You know what?

Can I get you to come down?" It was maybe 20 years after I was off the air with Baron Daemon. "Could you suit up again, rent a costume or something, and come on down with the fire department and the kids and do a stop, drop and roll as Baron Daemon?" And I did. (*Laughs*) The kids then didn't know and didn't identify with who Baron Daemon was. So I don't know how effective it was, you know? I came out and they all sort of went, "Whoa! Who's the weirdo in this outfit?" But I nevertheless went (*Bela Lugosi accent*) "Alright, boys and girls, remember. If your clothing, like my cape, was burning, remember to stop, drop and roll to put out the fire! Mwa-ha-ha-ha-ha!" Then the kids just sort of scratched their heads. "Where did they get this guy from?"

SC: As part of Syracuse horror host history, I'm wondering what your thoughts are on the other Syracuse host (Dr E. Nick Witty). *What do you remember about his show?*

What I remember about Dr E. Nick Witty and his pal, Epal, was that they did a lot of things I wished I had done. They came on the air, actually, right after we finished. So we had run our course for about five years.. I looked at the things that they did and I was somewhat jealous. Darn, why didn't we think of that? Or why didn't we do that? But I always held them in admiration, and thought they did a fine job. They had this thing where they did a little Monster Mansion. They had the Monster Mansion there, and they'd have the fog around it, and a little pond and cricket sounds and so on, and howls and dragging chains. And then they'd zoom into that. Later I talked to adults who said, "We thought it was a real house. (*Laughs*). It was a real mansion." And then they'd dissolve into something that was an inside set. And the kids thought, "We thought that was a room inside their house." That was pretty clever, that was pretty unique. Too bad we didn't come up with that idea first. I hold them in high regard, yeah.

SC: Did people ever confuse the two of you?

Oh, yes, all the time, especially now. I'll run into middle-aged and older people who remember the two programs, and they'll go, "Baron, I remember you on that *Saturday Movie Matinee*, with the Monster Mansion! It was great!" And you know what? I don't want to make people feel bad or tell them that they're mistaken. I just say, oh, thanks very much. It's very nice for you to remember that. And if they think that's the way it was, that's fine. It's okay with me. They remember I was the Baron, they just thought I was in the Monster Mansion, which I wasn't. "We loved when you were there with *The Baron and his Buddies*!"

SC: Can you give some of the details of Baron Daemon? Did you have any catchphrases? Can you remember anything about how the Baron opened or closed his show?

I can remember we had a segment called (*Bela Lugosi accent*) "Readings from the Transylvania Tome." And I would open up this book, and we had poems in there, like: "Jack Sprat could eat no fat/His wife could eat no lean/So betwixt them both they starved to death/ And turned a sickly green." Mwa-ha-ha-ha-ha-ha! Wonderful, wonderful, wonderful! "Little Miss Muffet sat on a tuffet/Eating her curds and whey/when along came a spider/And the spider bited (*sic*) her and died!" Mwa-ha-ha-ha-ha-ha! Wonderful, wonderful! And let's see, "Little Jack Horner sat in a corner/Eating his piranha fish pie/ He stuck in his thumb and pulled out a stump/And they called him Lefty." Mwa-ha-ha-ha-ha! Wonderful! These readings from the Transylvania Tome!

Some of the things we used to use were just catchphrases, like (*Bela Lugosi accent*), "Well, why don't you join me in Transylvania for a little Blood-weiser? Mwa-ha-ha-ha-ha! Or a little clots on the rocks is delicious, too! I have to go make a deposit—no, a withdrawal—from the blood bank. It's much better to receive than give when you're at the blood bank!"

SC: How has horror changed, making it less of a family thing?

The Baron makes some identifiable moves on an unidentified woman. Photo courtesy of WSYR-TV 9 and Joseph Capuana

I think what I did was to become a clown in a vampire suit. It was slapstick comedy, and we all had a great time and lots of laughs. Now I think they're very serious about it, the people who do it, and they really think they're going to frighten people. And a lot of it is blood and guts and gore. We weren't involved in any of that. We just had a good time and a lot of fun. You know, simple things, like roasting skulls over a campfire. (*laughs*) No gore involved in that, of course. It was a good time. It was all silly stuff. Who was that guy ... there was a show a few years ago. A guy used to suit up in a vampire outfit and say, "Whoa, we have a real scary movie ..."

MM: Joe Flaherty as Count Floyd on SCTV?

I've run into people after that—because I was on the air a few years before that—who said to me, "I think he probably saw, or somebody sent him a clip of you. That's a direct imitation of what you used to be." It might have been me, I don't know. I never met the man.

SC: If it turns out is was you, how would it feel to have influenced this character?

It would be very flattering, yes. I'd be very proud of that. You guys know of the comedian Jeff Altman? He's from Syracuse, used to do a lot of Vegas shows and move around a lot. He comes back to town once in a while. We go to talk to him about his career and so on. And he says one of the things he remembers as a kid is Baron Daemon. And it's funny how certain things will strike different people. He said, "The thing that I thought was always great was when you called your sidekick Verry Hairy. You'd say 'Verry! Come over here, Verry!'" And I was always doing this with my hands (*rubbing them*). Jeff continued, "You would do that and say, 'Verry, come over here. He's very hairy! Mwa-ha-ha-ha-ha-ha!'"

The Baron Daemon with his munchkin minions, along with Verry Hairy. Photo Courtesy of WSYR-TV 9 and Joseph Capuana

Can I tell you something that's one of my little anecdotes? One of the more interesting things was years ago when I would go up to The Enchanted Forest. That's, like a kid's village in the lower Adirondacks, in an area called Old Forge, New York, about 100 miles from here. And they would call me up there in the summer time, usually in June, to do a weekend thing with some of the kids. This is my favorite story. And they set my crypt up. They thought the best place to set up this crypt was in our old Western setting here, our village and Boot Hill, with the rest of the phony tombstones here. So I was up on the top of Boot Hill.

Well, the night before, my partner and I went out, and we maybe over-indulged ... over-imbibed, you know. We went to this place and that place and another place. We had to get up early in the morning, and I had—phew—an awful headache! And a lot of belching and other things was going on. A lot of gas, let's put it that way. I had this cape on, and we get up there in the crypt. They opened the gates at nine in the morning. And wouldn't you know it; I'm in this enclosed area here in the crypt.

And this woman comes in with her young son and she says, "Well, there he is, up there in Boot Hill! Go up and see him. You've been talking about it for a month now. You can't wait to get in to see him!" So he ran up the hill to see me and I said (*Bela Lugosi accent*), "Bluh! Hello, Bloody Buddy! So good to see you this morning!" And I had to breathe on the poor kid ... plus other scents that might have been coming from the crypt. The kid kind of blinked his eyes and shook my hand. He turned around and ran back down the hill, and he said, "Mom! He really is dead! You oughta smell him!" (*Laughs*) That's a true story, too. Embarrassing, isn't it? (*Laughs*) They used to pay me to do this! (*Laughs*)

I told you about this other character I used to do, Cousin Orky. Cousin Orky was a Mortimer Snerd kind of guy. (*Mortimer Snerd-type voice*) "H'yut, yut. Hiya, kids!" And I'd have this old soft hat pulled down, and an old coat, big Boondocker's shoes and a corncob pipe. "Yeah, boys and girls, I'm glad you could join us for our cartoons this morning." That was that voice. I talked like that. Well, one day I came out to host the kid show in the afternoon, and I was Baron Daemon. I had the whole outfit on, with a big cape and everything. I had the big eyebrow!

And I came out and I went (*Cousin Orky voice*), "Well, hello there, boys and girls. How are you today?"

Ummmm ... that's the wrong voice, isn't it? That's what I'm thinking, you know. Luckily, I was able to squat down next to one of the kids, and within three or four seconds I went, (*Bela Lugosi accent*): "And what brings you in today?" And I went whew, what a relief! Until I got locked into that right voice I spent an awful few seconds. The kids all sort of went, "What the hell happened to the Baron?" I mean what the *heck* happened to the Baron? (*Laughs*)

I remember the time I came out in full costume as the Baron, and the floor man, Bill Eadie, held up a cue card in front of me that said, "You forgot your pants." (*Laughs*) So ... you know ... casually ... (*glances down*) I say: "Well, boys and girls. Everything is fine today!" But I had to look. I had to cheat and look *down*, because I thought, "Did I forget my pants? Have I got the cape on and under shorts?" No, I did have my pants on. I did, I did have my pants on. Let's be clear about that.

The Baron at the controls of his rocket, a surreal splicing of Gothic horror and space age s.f. reminiscent of *Plan 9 from Outer Space*. Photo courtesy of WSYR-TV 9 and Joseph Capuana

MM: You've heard of some other horror hosts, like Zacherley. What do you think are the elements of a good horror host?

I think from my viewpoint, and the way I did it part of it was to be able to get into that character and do that character, and present it properly. And I liked doing that poor man's imitation of Bela Lugosi, which I think I did fairly well. Plus I think you have to have a good sense of humor and just not take yourself too serious when you're doing it. I mean, remember that it's fun, and have a good time. Enjoy the comedy and the comedic part of it. Otherwise it wouldn't have been fun for me and it wouldn't have been fun for the audience. I guess there's a lot of people who want to be serious about it. But I think it has to be tongue in cheek.

MM: What do you think is the lasting appeal for the generation that's grown up with this? What's the lasting appeal of a horror host?

Well I think lasting appeal for the era in which I appeared, the mid-'60s, was that it was live television. And we would make mistakes as we were doing it. And the audience at home wasn't sure, with the way we did it, it wasn't sure, did they just mess that up? Was that a mistake or was that intended? We always seemed to be able to carry it off so they never were sure whether it was intended, but most of the time it wasn't. It was a legitimate mistake. Is there such a thing? And they were. We did make mistakes and enjoyed it and worked around that. And the fact that it was live really made it interesting. But even when we decided to roll tape, years ago, we would never go back and re-do it. We'd say, "Can we do that again?" And the director, from the other room, would say, "I'm sorry. Wrap it up. Let's get on to the next one. That's it. No. That was funny the way you did it." So even on tape we would never go back and do it again.

MM: Did you ever go back and use the same tape again?

That's the sad part of it. You know, our shows were on these hour-long, two-inch wide reels of tape. And even before we had a fire that destroyed some of the material, a lot of the tapes were lost, in that we would tape and the production crew would just rewind and record over what we had done the week before. So we had nothing to show, because the old show was wiped out with the new taping that we did. So that was a shame.

"Here We Go Again ..."
Big Chuck (Chuck Schodowski)
Interviewed by Michael Monahan and Sandy Clark (2004)

Cleveland native "Big Chuck" Schodowski is a genuine television pioneer, with an on-air career that spanned 47 years. He was a life-long friend of Ernie Anderson and worked closely with him developing Anderson's landmark Ghoulardi show on WJW-TV 8 in 1962. It was Chuck's love for blues and polka music that provided Ghoulardi with his distinctive musical language, an appreciation for the surreal sight gags of Ernie Kovacs that inspired his own visual experimentation, and his deep affection for Anderson that gave the show its heart.

Schodowski immortalized The Rivingtons' classic nonsense tune "Papa-Oo-Mow-Mow" by marrying it to the image of an old man "gurning" (*essentially swallowing his own nose*). He introduced the idea of adding comic audio drop-ins to enliven the awful movies common to *Shock Theater* and placed Ghoulardi into the movies themselves, allowing the host to kibitz with the B-actors and rampaging monsters.

When Ernie Anderson left to pursue a career in California, the notoriously shy Schodowski found himself thrust in front of the camera as the new co-host of the Friday late-night movies, along side Bob "Hoolihan" Wells, the station's weatherman. *The Hoolihan and Big Chuck Show* ran from 1966 to 1979. When Wells left for Florida, he handed off his spot to semi-regular cast member Lil' John Rinaldi. *The Big Chuck and Lil' John Show* remained a popular fixture on Cleveland television for decades, until their final show on June 22, 2007.

Michael Monahan: Let's start with the early days in Cleveland and Ghoulardi. Can you talk about how you met Ernie Anderson, how the show started, and finally, how Ernie started to pull you in front of the camera?

I started in television as a summer replacement in 1960 at Channel 3, KYW-TV. And when I went there, Ernie Anderson was the announcer. He had a fantastic voice, as you know. I was only there for the summer, and then I came here to WJW-TV 8 in the fall of 1960. While Ernie was at Channel 3, a young writer came there by the name of Tom Conway. He later changed his name to Tim Conway. And Ernie and he became very good friends. Ernie was going to come to Channel 8 to host an afternoon movie called *Ernie's Place*, and he talked the station into letting him bring Tim Conway with him, telling the station that Tim was a director, which he wasn't. We needed a director, so they brought Tim along. Then Ernie and I joined up again. I was usually working tape or switching.

This early show, *Ernie's Place*, was a movie show in the afternoon. Tim was supposed to be directing it, but he didn't know how to direct. But the station didn't know that. Ernie would tell me as the switcher, "Do what's right, don't do what Tim says." Ernie was the host, and they would try to get guests. Well, someone wouldn't show up, and Tim would become the guest, no matter what it was. And it was hilarious, because it was so impromptu and Tim was so good at that. It caught on like wildfire, because everybody knew the show had stopped getting guests and would just create these things for Tim. They did a bunch of commercials called Bon Jour Coffee that Tim and Ernie wrote.

Back in those days, CBS used to send people who were in their TV series around to do promos at the stations. Now everybody goes to Hollywood and does it in a hotel room. But back then, they sent various CBS celebrities, one of whom was Rose Marie from *The Dick Van Dyke Show*. They took her out and got her half-loaded, then came back to the station. I was working the tape room, and they said, "Put these tapes up for her." And she was laughing, watching these Bon Jour Coffee ads. She asked me if I'd make a dub. So I made a dub, she took it to Steve Allen. Steve Allen saw Ernie and Tim, and he said, "I want the little fat guy. I can do the other guy's job." So they took Tim, and left Ernie.

When Tim left, the station wanted a horror host. So Ernie naturally would be the guy, because he was the afternoon host. They had a contest to name the thing, and it turned out to be Ghoulardi ... actually Ghoulardo. But he didn't like that name and changed it to Ghoulardi. First he figured the station just wanted him to talk about the movie and do the typical thing. He did that for, like, two weeks. Then he started throwing in his own stuff, which was way, way ahead of its time. And it caught on like wildfire. I was doing a lot for him. I was picking film clips; we were dropping funny things into the film. All the music we had was my music, because he only liked big band stuff.

I came out of high school and went directly into the foundry, like every other Polish kid in my neighborhood.

And I worked there for eight years on the night shift. I was the only white guy on the night shift. All of the black guys would listen to Alan Freed, the *Moondog* show. And I started to like that music a lot. So I brought that taste of music with me to Ghoulardi's show. And that's where some of the background music, like "Desert Rat," came from.

Ernie and I became very good friends, and he wanted me to do some things on the air, which I had wanted no part of, absolutely not. So one time, I was in the switcher. The announce booth was right next to it. He was in there, and he flicks on the talkback and says, "What size pants to do you wear?" I tell him. He's says, "What size shirt do you wear?" I say why? He says, "Never mind."

So I tell him I'm not doing anything on the air. He said, "Don't worry about it." Meanwhile, he wanted me to be in this skit. He wanted me to interview a Cleveland Indians batting coach. And that's what they were getting for me, a Cleveland Indians uniform. I told him I'm not going to do it. So he got, like, the three biggest guys on the crew and they threatened to pants me. I figured it would be easier to do it than to fight these guys.

He liked the subtle, wry sense of humor I had, and he thought it would be hilarious. I was scared to death. But he was right. It was really funny; because people believed it was real. First of all, I wasn't acting; I was scared. And people saw this and they felt so sorry for this poor batting coach that Ernie was embarrassing. That was great, because that's what he wanted. They were writing and calling—and always watching, of course. So I was the batting coach, then I was the pitching coach, then I was a karate expert. And each time I did this, it got easier and easier to do. As long as I was off-camera most of the time and only did an occasional skit, which was all the TV I wanted. And I sort of started to like it.

We did this one skit, which was a take-off of *Peyton Place*, called *Parma Place*. It became so big here in town, that some people in Parma got together and sent the mayor down here with a committee and made us take it off the air. But it was outrageously funny. I loved doing this as long as Ernie was heading it up.

When Ernie went to Hollywood, they were taking auditions for people to take his place. I think every deejay in Cleveland auditioned for the job. Bob Wells, who was Hoolihan the Weatherman, knew that I wrote stuff for Ernie and asked if I would help him with the audition. So I wrote a couple skits for us to do. Hoolie came out much like Ernie, sitting on a stool, and he would lead into these skits. I thought this is great. If Hoolie gets the job, I'll continue being a bit player. That's all I wanted to do.

So they called us one day and said, "You guys won the audition. We want you to be co-hosts." I went, wait a minute! Are you kidding me? There is no way I can go out there. And it was live then. I said I couldn't do it. They talked me into it. I was so scared. I figured I was going to embarrass my family and my friends. But then I thought, it's only going to last 13 weeks, it's not going to make it. Here we are 42 later. To make a long story short, it got easier and easier. I got more into the creative end and I started writing the skits. And it's so much a part of me now; it seems I can't remember when I wasn't doing the show. It's just great. It's like John (*Lil' John Rinaldi*) always says, "It beats working for a living. We tried that and hated it."

MM: Who were some of your influences? I've heard you talk in the past about Ernie Kovacs.

Well, I soon realized I was going to be doing all the writing for *The Hoolihan and Big Chuck Show*, and I had to draw on things that I liked. And Ernie Kovacs seemed to me to be way ahead of his time. I was an engineer at the time, and he did very creative things with the limited technology. And I liked doing that. When Ernie was on, I put a modulated circle around him. Nobody ever did that. I modulated the circle with 60-cycle tones. And I figured if I could do that, I could modulate it with music. Then I put Ernie's mic in there, and when he would shout, you know, it would affect the circle.

Anyway, I did that sort of horsing around with technical stuff. And so did Ernie Kovacs. He did gimmicky things in his skits. So that sort of challenged me

Big Chuck Schodowski (right) and Lil' John Rinaldi (left) on the set at WJW-TV 8 studios in Cleveland, Ohio (2004) —Chuck is admiring a pink flamingo oven mitt.

the Entertainment category was the first category that night, and it won. So it won the very first Emmy ever presented in Cleveland. We've won dozens of Emmys since, but that's always my favorite. It was a great skit.

To get back to Ernie Kovacs—he also did a character called Percy Dovetonsils. And Bob Wells, Hoolihan, could do this lisping voice so well. His name was Robert, so I changed Percy Dovetonsils to "Readings by Robert." People would send in stories—you know, shaggy dog stories—and he would read them. I appeared as a jazz ukulele player with a long wig. At that time it was the 1960s and '70s with that hippie look. My name was Carlos and I would accompany him. Anyway, a lot of stuff came from Ernie Kovacs. It still does. I like that sort of slapstick humor and off the wall ethnic stuff.

to try and think of something, and create something, and make some new effect. But Ernie Kovacs also had a few things that were really ethnic, and you didn't see that on network television. He had a thing called *The Kapusta Kid in Outer Space*. He was Hungarian, I believe. And kapusta is a Polish word for cabbage. And I thought that hilarious. Here was a guy on network television using an ethnic word, you know?

So I created a character called The Kielbasa Kid. Kielbasa is a sausage and I had a sausage in my holster instead of a gun. We had a big run of those skits. Even today, people call me The Kielbasa Kid, the old-timers. We did a skit, called "King the Wonder Dog" for the Kielbasa Kid. And there again, I took that from *Yukon King*. There was an old series called *Yukon King*, and they called him "King the Wonder Dog." We did a skit where a tree had fallen and it was wintertime and I was trapped under the tree on a mountain, and a dog comes running to save me. He runs and runs and runs, and the music swells, and he's running and running and running. He's running up toward me and … he jumps over me and keeps on running.

In 1969, Cleveland, for the very first time, had a local Emmy awards. I entered that skit into the Emmy awards, in the Entertainment category. As it happened,

MM: *Actually placing Ghoulardi into the movies, was that another Ernie Kovacs–inspired bit?*

I never saw Ernie Kovacs put anyone into something. You see, I used to "switch" the news. Now we have Vita fonts. You type it in and it'll appear on the screen. Back then when you had a news story, and you had someone's name in it, you would have to go to the graphics department. They'd take a black piece of paper and actually put on white letters, like "Mr. Jones." Then we would put all these big pieces of paper on easels, and one camera would do nothing but shoot names. And I would superimpose the names. And it would superimpose real easy without getting anything else in.

So when you had a news story and someone was talking, you would superimpose it—boom—lose it, then the camera would go to another name. It took forever, a lot of camera work and so on. One day I was thinking, "If I can superimpose this white, if Ernie wore light clothes, I might be able to put him in the movie." We both worked the sign-off shift. After the news, we had three hours to kill, because they had late-night movies on next. So I would horse around, trying to superimpose him into the movie, but only on the studio monitor.

We could get it down if he wore white pants and something light, but we always had trouble with his hair. We would lose the top. So I said, why don't you wear a fright wig? And that's where the fright wig came from.

So we had a wig, he wore that. He had a lab coat, which was white, and that became his uniform. So we started putting him into the films. And as it happened, Ernie was absolutely perfect. I don't know if you ever looked at yourself in a monitor. But it's really hard to look at yourself in a monitor and move the right way if you're trying to fit yourself into the background of the film. But he never had any problem; he was excellent with that.

We had *Attack of the 50 Ft. Woman* (1958) on. We would look for cheap films with long scenes with no edits, because then you could put him in easily. Everything was live. He would have several minutes, sometimes, without an edit, if you can believe that. And those were the best scenes because he could work his way into the characters, move around in the background and so forth. So they were in this cave, and guys were running back and forth. They wanted to go this way and that way. And Ernie would say, "Hey, come this way!"

Everyone in the control room was dying laughing and I was out in the studio looking at the clock. I knew we were going to have to get out, because the scene's going to change. So I gave him a wrap. But he just kept going on, because he was sensational, and he knew it. And he was throwing out these one-liners, but he wasn't getting out of the scene. So he puts his hand up and leans against the wall of the cave, and the scene changes and he's got his hand right on the giant woman's boob! He looks in the monitor and goes (*whipping his hand away*) "Whoa!" and runs out of the scene. You couldn't have planned it any better. It was hilarious. And of course we got letters and calls saying we did that purposely. But we didn't.

MM: Ghoulardi's popularity produced some pretty amazing statistics. The crime rate went down, right?

Ernie holds the local ratings record. I don't have the exact numbers. But the year after he started, he was so big. Nobody could touch us. I mean, it didn't matter what they ran against us. It was incredible. The share number was just outrageous. Nobody's done that here, locally, since. Almost everyone watched it. We were doing a thing one time, a charity game against the police department, and they actually told us that the crime rates on Friday nights was so low that they wanted Ernie to be on every night. It was ridiculous. They said everybody watched Ernie, even the criminals. Nobody did any crime on Friday night. Everybody watched him.

MM: What were public appearances like?

Ernie wouldn't have much of a show. If they had a band or something like that, he'd just poke fun at them. "You are all playing the same song?" Or he'd say, "This is it. I don't do shows, I just show up." The audience would ask him questions and he would just insult everybody. People loved it and they'd cheer him. And he'd say, "Don't you have anything better to do than come to this stupid shopping center?"

MM: What kind of crowds were you pulling for the Ghoulardi All-Stars games?

When we played, they were sell-outs. We would announce we were going to play basketball. It would sell out, like, the next day. There would be people trying to get in as we pulled up, and the place would be standing room only in gyms. It was incredible. It was like the poor man's Beatles—people running to the cars and running along the side of the bus. It was phenomenal.

MM: The Ghoulardi All-Star games—basketball, baseball—these were charity events. How much of this did you do?

We carried the tradition on, but it started with Ernie. Ernie thought he was a great jock. He was okay, but he was nowhere near what he thought. At that time, he was 40. And he was going to prove that he was macho. So he would go from one game to another. He would book hockey games, and half our guys never had skates on in their life. We actually accumulated some pretty good athletes who didn't work at the station. We were really good. We had a few ringers, you know? Ernie really enjoyed just beating up these teams, because they'd say, "We're gonna kill Ghoulardi." Then we'd pull the ringers out.

One summer, he booked 65 softball games. Now you figure you spread that over three months, and we're playing a game every other day. We're taking bus trips. We worked all day, and after work we would get on a bus to go to Canton, somewhere else the next day, 65 in one summer. Anyone could challenge Ernie for charity and he would agree. I don't how much money we earned, but we went right from baseball to flag football. Sometimes they'd overlap, we'd play football one night, baseball the next night, then hockey. Our wives were threatening divorce. It was incredible.

MM: Could that have happened in any other town? What is it about Cleveland that would embrace something to that extent?

Cleveland loves people if they think you like Cleveland. Cleveland is a unique city. People there can laugh at themselves, they always have. I don't know why this is. Maybe it's because Cleveland is a big city, but it's made

Ernie "Ghoulardi" Anderson, still the single most important cultural influencer in Cleveland television.

up of small neighborhoods. And each small neighborhood has stayed the same, with their own little theater, their own little shops. And it's pretty much like that now. You got Little Italy, and you got the Polish section, Slavic Village. It's just like that. And Clevelanders like it if you come in and say, "I want to play for Cleveland," like Bernie Cosar, that's it. You can stink, but they love you. I mean, because you wanted to play for Cleveland. And they'll support athletes like that.

Cleveland, interestingly enough, is a pretty hip city. When I first started in television, they used to have test marketing. We never knew it, but a network show would run a commercial at a certain time. They'd send us the exact time, and we'd have a 60-second film they'd sent us that we would have to put in. And we were blocking some other commercial. We found out years later that Cleveland was a test market. Because if something made it in Cleveland, it would make it anywhere, that's what they said. We had the Princess phone here for two or three years before anyone else in the country even heard of it. But Cleveland is very unique. Like I said, residents can laugh at themselves, I think, easier. We got very little flak. Because like Lil' John says, "We really like people, and they like us."

MM: We would be remiss if we left the subject of Ghoulardi without talking about the "Boom-Booms." How did the idea of using fireworks come up in the first place?

Ernie never thought he was going to last as Ghoulardi, so he really didn't put any work into it. He would come out—and I mean literally—I would be in the control room and we would be into the opening theme. There would be nothing out there, and I would still come up on the shot. I would hear him running down the hallway. He would be running past the control room and I would see him putting on his moustache. See, he was in a bar next door, and he would be watching the monitor. This one time, he was saying, he was watching the news and this and that, and they were telling him, "You better go, Ernie." He's just sitting there having a great time, and he looks at the monitor and sees a picture of the chair. That's where he was.

He was so blasé, since he didn't think it was going to work. Actually, it worked to his advantage, because it was like, "Oh, I'm not here? So what?" He'd tell the people, "Don't you have anything better to do? It's a terrible movie." And every time he'd do something, they loved it more and more.

So anyway, he started using mail, because he didn't have to create anything. The kids would send in pictures and some of the things were pretty good. They were sending in gimmicks and things. So one time, someone sent in a model car that they made. And they put a firecracker in it since they didn't like it. And he thought that was great. He lit it and it blew the car apart. That was it. Every week, we would get dozens and hundreds of things. And the firecrackers weren't just the small ones; they were getting pretty good, big whopping firecrackers. And they got to be quite the thing to do.

So I used to help Ernie with the mail. We got this big box, and we're pulling out stuff, and Ernie goes, "Wow, look at this." And it had a cylinder about that round and about that big. It looked just like part of a stick of dynamite. I said, I don't know anything about explosives, Ern. But, I said, this is just too heavy, you know? This is heavy. I mean, I don't know what this is. I wouldn't light it. And I immediately knew I'd said the wrong thing. "I wouldn't …" Oh, man. And he says, "Don't worry about it." He always said that.

That night on the show, he goes out there, and he's got this little coffee table out there. And he's always smoking. So he takes this thing and puts it on the coffee table. I'm looking at the monitors and I tell the guys in the control room, I said, if he lights that thing, get away from the window. I said, this thing is so heavy, and I don't know what it is. It might be a plastic explosive. God, I hope he doesn't light that. So, Ernie's talking and he's going, "You know, Big Chuck's back there. He's from Parma, and he told me not to light this." He reaches down and puts his helmet on … and a pair of goggles. So I said, he's going to light it. He's sitting there and he lights a cigar. He's talking about me and he touches the cigar to the fuse. And he sort of eases out of the picture, you know? And we're all looking, looking … and *BOOM!*

All I could see was white. And then it was smoke. We had a window in the control room that was about six inches thick. When this thing went off, it pushed the window in about a foot, but it didn't break. When the smoke cleared, it was nothing but flames. The drapes were on fire. It must have been a plastic explosive. I went to commercial. We went and ran and got every fire extinguisher in the building. And it was blazing! We were putting this stuff out, since we did not want to call the fire department. Ernie would get in trouble every week. We used every fire extinguisher there was, and we put it out. Of course we got called on the carpet, because the next Monday there were all these empty fire extinguishers to be refilled. I don't know what it was, but Ernie would never hesitate to do things like that. He was one of a kind.

MM: That sort of thing must have strained the relationship with management. I've heard stories about Ernie's conflict with Ted Baze, the general manager.

Oh yeah, like I said, Ernie was 40 years old, and he had that macho thing where he wanted to be the great athlete. And he never rode a motorcycle. So he buys this motorcycle. And during a break, he said, "Come on, I'll show you my motorcycle." I thought if he bought a motorcycle, he knew how to ride it. So he says, "Get on." I get on the back. We're in the alley behind the station, and he guns it. And we did a wheelie! He didn't mean to do it! We were doing a wheelie down the alley, and I'm holding on to Ernie. We're going, *RRRRRRRRRRRRRRRRRRRRRRRR!* And all the while I thought, wow, he's pretty good! But he didn't know what he was doing. He could have killed us. We went right out onto Euclid Ave, he couldn't see, and the cars were screeching by and all.

So anyway, he gets this motorcycle and he's determined to ride this thing to work. I don't know how he wasn't killed. He wasn't very good. So one day, it was raining, and he didn't want to leave his motorcycle outside. It's raining real hard. He opens the front door while he's on his motorcycle. It's all muddy, and he drives it through the lobby, which was carpeted. And he figures, "I'm going to drive through the newsroom and scare the hell out of everybody," which he did. He goes through the newsroom, and you know how loud a motorcycle can be in a room? *RRRRRRRRRRR!!! RRRRRRRRRRRR!!!* And he goes right through and up into Norm Wiggy's office.

To make a long story short, they didn't know what to do with Ernie. They had to do something. So they typed this official memo: "You will not ride your motorcycle through Norm Wiggy's office anymore." It was so ridiculous, taken out of context. That's all it said. He had it framed in his house; I've got it on video. So that started the battle with the management. Ted Baze actually loved Hoolihan and me, but he didn't like Ernie. And they would battle every single week. Ted Baze would think of something that would tick Ernie off and Ernie would think of something that would rile Ted Baze. Every week, something, they were getting pretty vicious.

Because Ernie didn't like to do a lot of production, he would broadcast footage from these Ghoulardi All-Stars games. He would have a station photographer shoot them on overtime. And he'd show way more than you wanted to see, but he made it funny by his narration. And he would show a lot of audience shots; they were all sold out, like I said. And of course they'd go home and tell their families, and you'd have a pretty good audience just from the people at this event. So Ted Baze, to get at Ernie, figured he'd say, "No more photographers, no more overtime."

Ernie was real mad at the next game, since there were no photographers. I knew he was going to do something. We played on a Thursday, and Friday night he was on live. And he said, "I'll tell you what the station really thinks of you folks. You know, there were 10 thousand people at our event last night, and I know you're all waiting for the film, because your family is waiting to see it. And I know you told everyone, all your relatives, and everyone is gathered around to see it. Well, Channel 8 … they don't really care about you. Ted Baze, the production manager, cut out all the film. He doesn't care about you folks. He doesn't care that maybe 30 thousand people are out there waiting for this film. Now, I don't want to get into anything. But if you want to complain …" He reaches down—nobody knows he had done this—and pulls up a card. "Here's his home phone number." Baze had to get his phone number changed, since it rang off the hook for two days.

But he would do things like that. And they would do things back and forth. It was constant, but they were afraid to get rid of him, or try to get rid of him. It was like holding the tiger by the tail. They were not going to let go. Man, he was something. Three and a half years of this and every week it was something. I don't think there was a dull week.

Every time he showed something on the air, we'd get tons of it next week. Well, someone sent him a squirt gun. Next week, we must have 150 squirt guns. So everyone in the station had squirt guns loaded with water, and it was like the old West. Ernie would do things all through the night to keep things moving. He couldn't just sit in the announce booth to do his half hour I.D. He would either have gambling games going on, or he would always create something.

So now everyone hides and you creep around the building. And everyone was sopping wet, since we're shooting squirt guns. Until we're squirting too much and it gets in the switcher and blows the switcher up. We're off the air about an hour. It's just one thing after another. So the squirt guns … we're squirting, squirting. This went on for days with the squirting, before we blew the switcher up. But then the squirt gun wasn't enough, we had buckets of water hidden every which place. We'd be sopping wet when we came home. And it was just a normal thing. The next week, Ernie would do something else.

Like, during the day or the late afternoon, we'd have these game shows. He used to be in the announce booth and everyone had to put a dime down and play along. But he could not just sit there and do the announcing. During the late-night movie, after the news, there would be nobody there except the skeleton crew. He'd sit in the announce booth and say, "Welcome to the late-night movie." Then he'd go on and say, "Tonight's movie…" and then the title would come up and he'd read it. Then he'd look for whoever was in the control room. "Starring Chuck Schodowski and Dominic Lollie." We never, ever, once got a call. He'd just mention whoever was there. In fact, if I couldn't be there, I knew who the crew was, because I'd listen to Ernie open the movie.

Then we got transferred to early morning and that was another thing. He had to go there early morning and prepare a six-minute newscast that he would read over a news slide from the announce booth. Well, he wasn't about to go to the newsroom and edit. He'd buy a copy of *The Plain Dealer* and read the front page. He would just read the paper, you know? Just read it in that beautiful voice.

Occasionally, they wanted him to do a short news show in the afternoon. Here again, he couldn't just do a short news show. When the news was over, the people would generally sit there and fix their papers, you know? They were playing the theme. Ernie would say, "And that's the news," and get up and walk off. And we still had to go through the closing. We'd tell him, "Don't do that!" So he would go, "What I am gonna do? I got nothing more to say." So they'd finish the news and play the theme, and he'd put his feet up. The management would write a letter, but they were afraid to get rid of him.

MM: Besides his work at the station, Ernie also did freelance work on commercials.

Probably the best announcing voice in the history of television and he was in our market. He had it sewed up. He did all the commercials here. And when he went to Los Angeles, he did all the commercials there.

MM: What was the actual production history of Ghoulardi? He began on Friday nights, but that soon expanded.

The news was only 25 minutes then, so he was only on 11:25 on Friday nights, *Shock Theater*. Then they gave him *Laurel, Ghoulardi and Hardy*, Monday through Friday afternoon. Then Saturday afternoon: *Masterpiece Theater*. He did a daily thing for a while because we were supposed to have a syndicated show that didn't happen. Hoolie and I did the same thing too for a while. I forgot what the format was.

Basically the Friday night show is the thing everybody remembers. Saturday afternoon he had the other movie. It was usually a horror show, like the Friday night. It was totally different from the Friday night. There were lights on the set and he would show things that were sent in. But the Friday night show always had the circle effect. But he was always the character. On Saturday's you would see the full thing. He'd wear the lab coat and that stuff. He bounced around more, and did more. Friday night was with the bluesy music, and he never got out of that circle.

MM: Did you and Hoolie have any trepidation taking over the Ghoulardi time slot?

Yeah, I thought Hoolie was crazy. Ernie just earned the world's record for what he did and we're going to try to do that? That's another thing I talked Hoolie out of. In the audition, Hoolie sat on a stool with the same lighting we used for Ghoulardi, with the light we put on the floor. And I was thinking that would be a direct comparison. People would look and say, "He's trying to imitate Ernie." I said, what we should do is just be two guys. At the time, I didn't know what kind of set we'd use, how we would package this thing. I thought for the first one or two weeks, we'd be roommates. But then I thought, naw. We did it, but people started calling us gay. So, forget that.

As it turned out, we did it pretty much like the Steve Allen show, which was on at the time. We had a desk and talked about the movie. One time we had a casket, because we had a lot of horror movies. Actually then we just started to use things people sent in for the background—drawings of monsters, stuff like that. And because we didn't have sets, we started doing our skits in and around the city. People would love that because they'd recognize places. That's how it started, doing skits on location. We still do skits on location more than anywhere else, more than the studio.

MM: Was that a conscious effort to change the identity, separate it from the Ghoulardi show?

It was for me. Hoolie, when he did the audition, wanted to do it the old Ghoulardi way. And they bought it that way. But I knew it wasn't going to work for both of us. We couldn't both be out there with the lights on us, so we had to do something else. And as it turned out, Hoolie was probably one of the most incredible talents. He could do any accent; he could do anything. I wouldn't even ask if he could do it, I just knew he could do it. I would write stuff, and it became apparent very early Hoolie was the talent and I was the writer. So I would only write things for myself that I knew I could handle, which was, compared to him, very little. So I would always be the shy guy, or something like that, or the hero who never talks much. But Hoolie could do anything. It sort of evolved that Hoolie was the multi-talented person, and I would be just the writer and all that.

We'd sit out here live. And I'd be scared to death, because I'd get all tongue-tied. I would get real nervous, till I learned to just shut up. Hoolie could talk for 10 minutes and say nothing. And you would be entertained. You would be looking at him and listening and he would say absolutely nothing. And he would not be nervous. That amazed me. If you could tell him we were going to be live by satellite around the world right now, he would finish what he was saying and just come on and just do it. I would be stammering and stuttering and he would sound like he was saying something. But he wasn't.

MM: At one point, you started doing what were essentially music videos: Snoopy vs. the Red Baron, Guitarzan, *things like that.*

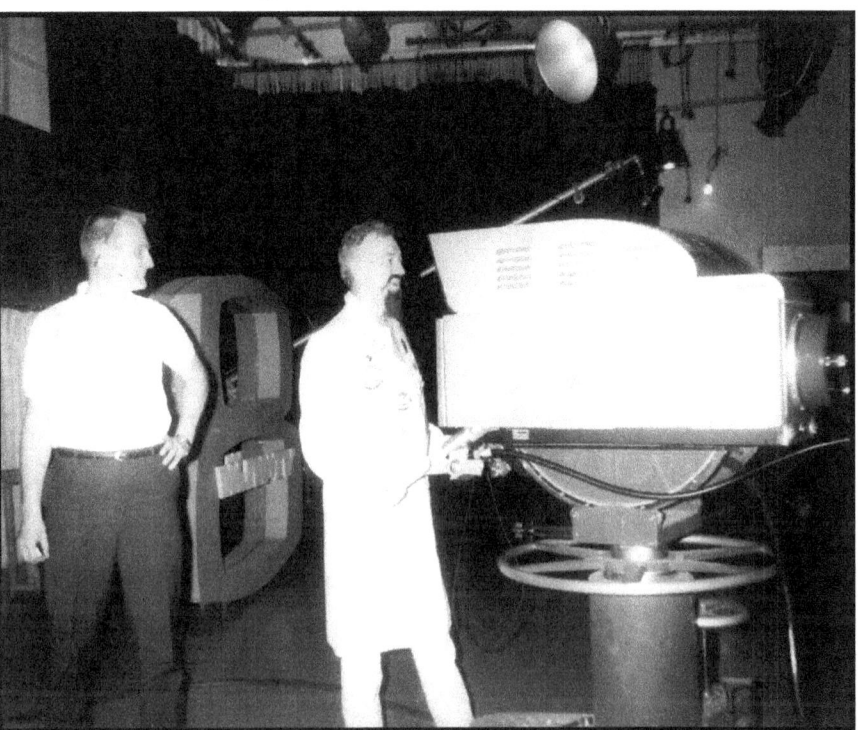

Ghoulardi mans the camera, circa 1965. Photo courtesy John Hlucky

To my knowledge, I hadn't even heard the words "music video." To me, I just had an idea to take this popular piece of music and put video to it. I just thought, well, that's not unique. But as it turned out, it was. I did so many Ray Stevens songs and one Christmas he came to town. He was appearing here singing. And he was selling music videos of the songs he did. And I was looking at them and saying, I did every one of those ... and better. I didn't see him, but I had a friend who was going down to the show. I told him, tell Ray I've been doing his music videos long before he ever thought of it. We sent him some tapes and apparently he loved it.

MM: And then you did Bridget the Midget, *and that's how Lil' John came to the show.*

63

Yeah. I liked doing these music videos, since they were easy to do. You didn't have to create anything; you just had to follow the music. You know, create a little bit of a side thing. We did several of them. Then I heard this *Bridget the Midget*. It was a good nice song, and it was sort of popular. So I said, we've got to get this little girl, and I was thinking of a place we could do it. So I called a guy, he was a dance instructor in Cleveland, well known. And I said, do you have any little girls who can dance? He said, "Nope ... but I have a little guy." I said that'd be even funnier. What's his name?" "John Rinaldi."

Now, John's uncle was a very famous doctor in Cleveland. His name was Rinaldi. He was my doctor. I had rheumatic fever when I was five years old. He took care of me for my entire life. He delivered my first two children. So I'm thinking, it can't be," since his son's name wasn't John. So I dismissed it. Then after we got started I

water, fishing around, pulled him out. He never told me he couldn't swim.

So after that, I was tentative about asking him to do things. But he would do anything. As long as he thought it was safe, he'd do it. If I couldn't swim, I wouldn't go close to water. John still, to this day, will do things under water. We attached him to a log floating on Lake Erie one time.

MM: There was one great, animated skit you did where you were a state cop...

Oh yeah! Ray Harryhausen, he was in town one time. Bill Strauss, the skit animator, took the film to show him, and he called it the best amateur animation in the world. That was great, coming from him.

MM: Is Bill Strauss the guy who does the various gorilla openings for your show?

Ghoulardi's late-night popularity led to a less-successful children's program, *Laurel, Ghoulardi and Hardy*. With movie shows on Friday night and Saturday evening, Ghoulardi was on the air six times a week.

said, is Dr. Rinaldi related to you? He said, "Yeah, that's my uncle." This doctor was very famous. Everywhere we go—even today—someone always brings up that Dr. Rinaldi was John's uncle.

Anyway, so John became "Bridget the Midget." That was his very first thing. And he was so good at it that I figured I didn't want to let this guy go. He's just too good; he was a natural. And no matter what you asked him to do, he'd do it. He never told me he couldn't swim. He damn near drowned. In fact, my son saved his life. My son was going to Cleveland State at the time, and he was a lifeguard. I had walked out into the water pretty far, and I said, it's okay. Just walk straight out. So John goes beyond where I walked, and there was evidently a ledge. I was watching and he's laughing and laughing as we were shooting and—vwoop—John disappears. And I went, oh my God...I'm looking and looking and he's not coming up. Before I could even look around, my son was in the

Right, yeah. We've got some things pending that we're going to do. He's already made the animation for it. Now I just have to do the studio work. He's fantastic. But that skit he did was called *The Chase*. And it was really the last bit of stop motion ever done, because now a computer does everything. Nobody does the stop action anymore, unless you want to win some art award or something. But that was all stop action. That was done a few years ago, not that long ago. We would do one frame at a time. I figured maybe we'd do two. But no, he did one frame at a time. Then he'd have to move the camera, get a little thing and measure it. Click! We slide on our butt up to here, and he moves the camera.

We would work, like, two hours every morning. "How much did we get today?" "Oh, six and a half seconds." "Oh, man ..." It took two years to do, sliding on our butts. John and I both wore out about two pairs of pants; we really did, just scooting on the ground. And if you ever sat for a really long time with your legs out flat, you won't believe how they ache after a couple of hours. It was torture. But as we were doing it, and I saw bits and pieces of it, I said, this is going to be a gem! And it was. But man, two and a half years. That's a long time to work on something.

MM: Lil' John was a featured player on the show at the time Bob "Hoolihan" Wells was still co-hosting. What were the circumstances behind Bob leaving the show?

Bob and I were co-hosts for almost 13 years. Near the end of the run, Hoolie was doing a lot of freelance. He was a very good announcer, just like Ghoulardi. And he was flying to Chicago, doing things like this, and he was getting away from the show. He had an offer to go to Florida and be the general manager of a religious TV station. So he decided to end it. Like I said, he was branching out and not staying here all that much.

I didn't want to do the show alone. At that time, Bill Flynn said I could get any co-host I wanted to, so I thought about who would be good. John—Lil' John—had more skits than anybody on tape. So I figured if we became co-hosts, John and I, I would have enough of John's skits to show while we were doing new ones. That would be the easiest transition.

So Hoolie left for Florida and John and I took over. We actually ran reruns of Hoolie's skits for several years, until we built a backlog of our own. But some of the things that Hoolihan did were absolute classics that people still want to see, and we still run them on oldies nights. Of course some of the better stuff we did, we re-did, because we had better production values and better everything. So I re-did it. But there are some things that I just wouldn't even consider doing because they were just so beautiful at the time. Hoolie was so good at some of this stuff that we still run them. Can you imagine anything on television where they would run things that are 40 years old?

MM: What was the first show like with John in the co-host position?

When Hoolie was here, like I said, I was so nervous. But then I learned if I get tongue-tied, I just shut up. Hoolie would just talk and I would just sit there and smile. Hoolie was the ultimate pro. He was the announcer, he was quick-witted, and I was just the average guy, who was writing behind the scenes, and I was shy and scared to death. He was the professional and I was the amateur.

But I was the blue-collar guy that everyone related to in Cleveland. I was Polish, they knew I was from Cleveland; I would talk about working in the foundry and stuff like that. So I had that going for me. But when Hoolie left, I said, the only professional part of our show is leaving. Now I got John, and John was so hyper and nervous. Now we've got two amateurs out here. So I figured I've got to take Hoolie's role and calm John down. John was just the opposite of me. You had to give him a tranquilizer. Those early shows, he couldn't even sit in his chair.

We got a good chemistry going, mostly from doing the skits. It worked out. At first though, it was really rough. Dick Goddard, a good friend of ours, saw that we were struggling. So he would come in—and I didn't realize what he was doing until maybe a year later—he was sort of smoothing out the transition with us. He would come in and be in skits, and he would just come on the set while we were live. He's a very beloved guy here, and he helped us out a lot. The transition wasn't easy though; it was scary. But now John and I are like two Clevelanders and everyone relates. John's Italian, I'm Polish. He's from the East side; I was from the South East side. We're local guys who made good.

MM: Talk a little about that ethnic blend in Cleveland. What is it that allows you to mix polka music and blues? You were doing that from the earliest days, and when you see it laid out, it really paints a picture.

You would never hear polkas on a radio station, but it would be on TV (*notably the Cleveland television program,* Polka Varieties). Cleveland has a huge Slovenian population, and it would be, like, wow, they're watching TV and these guys are playing polkas. We were joking about it, and the joke turns into this Polish character. I didn't know if it was going to work. But man, it sure did. And then I figured if that works with the Polish Slovenian people, then maybe getting a character like Soulman, have him eat soul food, maybe that's going to work with the black community. And it did.

And we got Lil' John doing Godfather skits with the Mafia. Then we had a Jewish character. And every time we did it, it was working. So I figured this is great; this is easy. Then we went to Detroit. Everything we did, they were complaining, complaining. We had people coming down to the station. We had a week before we taped our shows where we would have to talk to these people. Anyway, Cleveland was great. We could get away with anything, and we still can. Because we've been doing it for 40 years, and people say, "Aw, they don't mean that."

MM: What do you think has changed over time, in terms of the local market, the city itself, but mostly with television? What's changed?

Well, he's right most of the time—Hoolihan the Weatherman reports weather for City Camera, weekdays at 12 noon on WJW-TV.

sunshine to ya

The Rain Man Bob "Hoolihan" Wells was the station weatherman at WJW-TV 8, when he auditioned to take over the movie hosting spot vacated by Ernie Anderson. He would co-host *The Hoolihan and Big Chuck Show* **from 1966 to 1979.**

I don't think people have the sense of humor they used to have. Everybody is so uptight now, the politically correct thing rules. I don't know. They seem to be too restricted in the way they feel. So you want to do a Polish joke, so what? Cleveland's got a lot of Polish people. They used to laugh at it, but not today. They wouldn't even think of it. Too politically correct for one thing. And there aren't really any more local productions. Everything is syndicated. It's really sterile, television, period.

We're on FOX. They've got the *American Idol*, and it's as popular as can be. These people are getting million dollar music contracts, and they can't sing! I don't get it, I really don't. But people watch it. My wife watches it. But they really can't sing. Survival shows and reality shows. They're not reality. Someone's on this island shooting this film, you know? It's like the old joke about the mountain climber. He crawls up to the top, but who's shooting it? I wanted to do a skit like that.

MM: Do you think reality shows are an attempt to take the place of locally produced shows, in that people tune in to see "real" people like themselves, what they used to see on local TV?

I guess. I think you're right. I don't like any of that stuff, mostly because I'm still doing what I've been doing since 1960. Occasionally you'll see a show like ours with good skits in it. Like Tim Conway, he's a good friend of mine. You know, you're looking back at some of that old Carol Burnett stuff. And you see the audience, and they love it. They still love it. So being a producer, I'd say, look, they still like it. Why isn't this on television, you know?

MM: What do you think we lost with the death of local television?

I think we lost some soul. I think people don't have soul anymore. They don't get passionate, they don't get angry, they don't get laugh-out-loud happy. It's like everything is "don't show your emotions." I don't know. I'm not a psychiatrist, but people are just too afraid to let loose. Even if we get a young audience in here! If you see something that's funny, it's ageless. It doesn't matter when it was made, funny is funny. But they don't laugh. And I ask them, was that funny? "Yeah, it was funny."

But they don't laugh; they don't get angry. I don't know, it's just like a bunch of clones. People are different. And because of it, TV is different. I hate to get that deep into it. But you know, I'd worry about our country. We used to be a very passionate country and every city had its local people. People loved them, because they were from Cleveland, they were from Detroit. All that's gone. I mean, you get a show now that's made in New York or LA, and it'll be gone in six months, and there'll something else. Nothing lasts 40 years, like we have.

SC: Do you think TV did it to itself? Forty years, 50 years ago there were still a lot of community events. People would go to the movies, go to plays. You started getting isolated because you would sit home and watch TV.

I never thought of that. That could be a very good reason. People used to go out and do all these things, you're right. Then they'd watch TV and sort of isolated themselves, even more so now with computers. We have a real close family, and my grandkids are glued to these computers. They listen to music on computers; they watch movies. It scares me, you know? It really does. I tell them, "Get out. You like watching this? It happens in real life, go see it."

SC: What worked in the early days that created that spontaneity, that energy, that willingness to try anything?

I think people in general were different then. They all had the attitude of trying something new. People would be less apt to hold back what they feel, or to do something silly. People were less afraid of losing or failing. It didn't matter, you'd laugh at it. You'd have a beer and say, "Boy, that was stupid." But then do it. And do practical jokes. Practical jokes were big. Like I said, when I worked in the foundry, somebody would pull something every day. Now you wouldn't dare, you'd get sued. It scares me.

SC: What kind of stuff would you get away with in a foundry?

We did a lot of things. I worked on the night shift, where I was the only white guy. I worked in the lab and I worked in receiving. And I used to think of things to scare all these guys. We used to do things such as I'd bring a rubber snake in. We had these furnace logs and I'd put the snake in there, stuff like that. The funniest thing I ever did one time ... we had a hallway and the walls weren't very far apart. I was sort of strong, and I could push my hands and my feet against the sides and I could work myself up the wall. And I'd go up there, and it would be pretty high. Guys would try it and they'd fall eight feet, flat on the concrete. We'd do this in between shifts.

So one time, the owner of the foundry was there and I didn't know it. I walked up the wall and everyone took off. I thought they were going to leave me, big deal. I'm up there, and here comes this guy with an entourage of people. And they're right under me when they decide to stop and talk a little bit. And I'm shaking like a leaf. I'm going to fall right on them. As luck would have it, they never looked up. But these guys in the background were just ... they had tears in their eyes. They had their clothes in their mouth so they wouldn't make noise, and I was up there shaking.

Anyway, we would do things like that. And it was not just me; it was people in general. People in general would do silly things. But you don't see that anymore. You do a little thing like that and people go, "Oooooo, you're gonna get sued!" And they will.

MM: As I began looking more deeply into the whole history of the TV horror host, it struck me that there was this distinctive element to the East Coast and Midwest, especially in the earliest days, when there were a limited number of stations. You have hard winters that create something of a captive audience on those cold nights.

That's exactly right. You hit it right on the head. If you lived on the West Coast, there'd be more things to do. If you lived in Cleveland in the wintertime, and you had television, man that's perfect. You stayed home and popped some popcorn and sort of watched a good movie or a bad movie or whatever. I think that's probably why the East Coast probably drew closer to their local horror hosts. It was just a natural fit, to sit with a howling storm outside and watching a chiller movie.

And it was a comfortable thing you grew up with, because probably your father or your uncles were watching that earlier, and it was just a natural thing to do. I know to this day we get people sitting in the audience and a guy will whisper to his little kid, "Daddy was here when he was a little boy just like you." I hear that almost every week. I think the whole movie thing was passed down like that. People would sit together, maybe brothers, family, and watch it. And then when they get together later, they'd do the same thing, since we're still on. But you had a good point about the wintertime. Anytime I think of that, it was the wintertime, when you're cuddling around, sending out for a pizza.

SC: What was it like for you personally to work with Ernie Anderson? What did that make you feel like?

Ernie, I used to call him the original hippie. He was a hippie long before anybody knew what hippies were. He was painfully honest. You asked him something, you better be sure you want to know the answer. He would tell you if he didn't like you. He'd tell you. He'd announce if you were ugly, whatever. He'd just tell you. So people learned not to ask him things, because he would tell the truth. He was one of a kind; he was a fantastic man. Every day would be an adventure, being with him.

He would never stop joking. He would never stop doing goofy things, and he was just an adventurer. There's nothing he wouldn't try. He'd do anything. He'd do it twice if it hurt, you know? He was something. He could not just come to the station and do booth announcing. In between the half-hour shows, he would invent something to do. Like we'd take a football and go in the alley and throw it around...until we'd break a window, which we did. And then we'd get a memo: We can't do this anymore. Then we'd do something else.

He was one of a kind, plus the fact that he had so much talent. He was the biggest, the hottest voiceover here in town. Everybody wanted him. Money meant nothing to him. When he moved to Hollywood and he was making a couple million a year—he was the highest paid announcer at the time—he was actually the same person he was in Cleveland. And when he was in Cleveland, he never paid his bills. There were checks in his desk that were six months old, big checks. He just didn't think about it. When he needed money, he'd just take it. He'd take you out and pay for your stuff at the bar. But he wouldn't bother with the little things.

So finally, Ernie got a manager. He gave him all his checks, and all he would do is pay his light bill, pay his milk bill, stuff like that. But then when I went to see him years later, with all this money, he was the same way. He wouldn't pay this, then his wife would be yelling at him. He had a manager out there. Money meant nothing to him. He's just that kind of guy.

MM: I always loved the story of people offering to buy him drinks.

Ernie drank a lot. We'd be in and out of bars a lot. Everybody recognized him; he was the hottest celebrity ever. And it would be, "Hey, man! Hey, Ghoulardi! C'mon, sit down. Lemme buy you a drink!" Guys having a drink would leave their change on the bar, you know? So it would be, "Come on, lemme buy you a drink!" And Ernie would say, "Naw man, I gotta get going. Here," he'd take some money, "lemme just take 75 cents." He'd take the change and the guy would look at him like, "What the heck?" And he did that every time. I used to think, man, he has lots of guts because some of these guys were pretty big. Truckers would go, "Hey Ernie, lemme buy you a drink." "No, just give me a dollar." And he'd take it. And *keep* it! And the guys would sit there not knowing if they should laugh or not. They just look at him, you know?

SC: You've talked about how nervous you were getting dragged up in front of the camera. Did Ernie's fearlessness empower you at all?

If Ernie wanted me to do something—after I got used to it—I had no fear, because he was like Superman. Nothing fazed him. He'd get out of any jam and everyone was afraid of him. You couldn't lose if you were his buddy. If you were his buddy, you had it made. Ernie didn't like that many people. But he would do anything for someone he liked. He was quite a guy.

Just to give you another example: We were walking out the front of the building, and there were two nuns sitting on a bench, waiting to be guests on a show. They had their habits on. He walks out and he stops, and they're looking at him because they recognize him. He stops, lights a cigar, and he says, "You know, you two look enough alike to be sisters." He would just throw this stuff away. We'd go to a bar and he'd pull that bar thing. It was never-ending stuff! He'd go around the corner and make a joke about the guy in the parking lot, and they'd be hilarious and brilliant. But he was just Superman.

MM: You just reminded me of the story you've told before about WJW's first color broadcast.

Ernie was really popular, and this was before color TV came on. So we got this big—I can't remember what it was—a TK-47 or something color camera. It was as big as a Volkswagen. It was huge, a great big color camera. And everyone's making this big fuss about it. Then the station realized that we only had one color camera. Therefore you could only do a show that would require one camera, because you couldn't cut back and forth between black and white. You couldn't do the news; you couldn't do the interview shows. So they're sitting there wondering, what can you do? Well they wanted to try out the camera, but they didn't want to do Ernie's show and they didn't want to do a big production. So they decided to do *Mass for Shut-Ins*. I don't know if it was Lent or what.

As it happened, the priest comes out and he's all in black and white. And the audience was entirely made up of nuns. When we took a shot, I'm thinking, there's nothing there that has any color. Everything is black and white. It was like you planned it. We were even looking for something in the background to shoot that was in color. There was nothing. The drapes were black and the floor was creamy white, and the nuns were black and white, and the priest was, like, nothing! The priest had a table with a white cloth. I just couldn't get over it. We couldn't find anything in the picture that had any color.

SC: Skin tones?

Skin tones were whitish anyway. It was hilarious. I think we even got a mention in the paper.

SC: Did Ghoulardi sneak himself on in color?

Somebody had a logo with a joker or a jester on it. So on his first color show, he rented a jester costume and he came dancing around. It was real colorful. But the color camera on Ghoulardi meant nothing, because he sat and all you saw was his face and a black background. There was no color there. But they had to get their use out of that color camera. He would make fun, constantly, of the color. And he would purposely show things that had no color.

Bob "Hoolihan" Wells (left) and Big Chuck Schodowski (right). A big hand for a couple of cards.

MM: There were a number of musical items that related specifically to Ghoulardi: "Ghoulardi Surf" and "Turn Blue."

Yeah, "Turn Blue." Jimmy McGriff was a local guy who played an organ. I don't know if he was local. But he was from Cleveland, and he was a big fan of the show. He wrote this song called "Turn Blue," because Ernie would always say, "Turn blue," and that more or less became the theme song. Jimmy McGriff had done "I Got a Woman," which we used, and so he wrote "Turn Blue." Another guy, because we used so many polkas, wrote "The Ghoulardi Polka." We played that a lot. But "Turn Blue" was the big theme song for Ernie, and that was Jimmy McGriff.

And people to this day, in Cleveland, if they hear that or something like it, they'll say, "Hey, that's Ghoulardi music!" All this music we used to play was labeled "Ghoulardi music." In fact, several people have put together CDs you can buy. And they're pretty accurate, all the music's on there.

MM: He'd pull pranks on people, offering them a ride in his sports car.

Oh, several things. He got me on the motorcycle, which I didn't want to do. Every time I would get in trouble. We had a station manager who actually liked me. His name was Dagwell. He was really good, a sharp station manager. He liked Ernie, too. But he'd always talk to me, "You're a nice young man. But you've got to sort of watch it with Ernie, because he's going to get you in trouble." I'd do things like playing football in the alley when I was supposed to be at the switcher. Then I'd get a warning with the union: "This is a written warning …" But if I do it again, I could be reprimanded, I could be fired. I used to worry like crazy. I'd say, Ernie, I don't want to do it anymore. "Naw, naw, come here. I want you to take a ride on my bike," he said. "I just want to show you something." I said, nope." He says, "Come on, we've got half an hour before we have to do the station break." So he talks me into it. I go on the back of his motorcycle. He said, "We're just going around the block."

So, okay. *VOOM*, he goes down the street. *VOOM*, on the Shore Way … and we're just barreling, man. I'm thinking, we're going to each a point of no return, where we're not going to get back for the break. So he goes all the way out to his house. He pulls in and I think, that's it, I'm fired. I felt bad, but I wasn't mad. I felt, you know, it's over. I'm through. I got all these warnings. He pulls in, gets us a couple beers. "Try this cheese; I got it from

They called them Big Chuck and Lil' John for a reason! John Rinaldi took over co-hosting duties in 1979 and continued through the final episode special, June 22, 2007.

New England." I'm thinking, what am I going to say to my wife? I'm going to have to go back to the foundry.

We're driving back, and we got in. A good friend of ours, Don Loley, meets us at the door. He's in on it too, but I didn't know. He's going, "Where were you guys?!" He says, "They threw the station break and it was two minutes of black. The station manager is calling; the phone is ringing off the hook." I'm saying, oh, God …" He's saying, "Yeah, no one was here, the station was black. The commercials didn't run. The clients are calling, they want their money back." I'm saying, oh God, there's no hope for me. Then it turns out, the guys who had said they were going to lunch, they didn't go to lunch. They just left the building, but they didn't go. Ernie taped his part. So everything was covered. But I didn't know that. He let me go on for over two hours. That was just one thing.

Like I said, that would be one week and the next week would be something else. I used to park far away from the station, since I couldn't afford the expensive lot where Ernie parked. So I used to walk a block. Ernie had this sports car, a little AC Ace, just a two-seater. Bob Soinski was with us and Ernie said to Bob, "Jump in." This is right after we closed the bar. So Bob gets in and I said, there's no room for me. And Ernie said, "Just jump on the front. Jump on the hood; I'll drive you to your car." So I get on the car and I'm sort of leaning back against the windshield. And he goes WHOOOOOOM.

As soon as he started I thought, how stupid can I be? He goes right on the Shore Way, man, and he's flying down there. The wind is killing me. So I reach over, and I'm trying to stick my hands down in that little place in the windshield, you know? I'm hanging on and he's laughing. Then I figure, if I block his face, he can't see. So I do that, and he purposely starts swerving the car and I'm trying like heck to hang on. You know, I think anybody else would say, he almost killed me, but then I started laughing and he started laughing and then he finally stopped.

About two months later, the same thing happened, coming out of a bar with Ernie and Soinski. This time, I get in the car and say, come on, Bob. I'll drive you to your car. The minute he said that, I looked at Soinski, figuring, nope. But he was just a little slow. He gets on the back, on the luggage rack and *PHOOOM!* Ernie takes off and Bob's hanging on the luggage rack. Most people would kill him, but you were like his chosen few that he would do this to. We just did things like that.

He'd park his car on the street at night and go into the station. This was at a time when people were stealing cars for some reason. I said, Ernie, someone's going to steal that car, because it's a convertible. He had the top down. He'd leave the keys in it. I said, at least take the keys out. He said, "Come on, who's going to take it?" So I'm coming into work and I see his car parked. I walk over and sure as heck the keys are in it. So I get in the car, and drive it around in back of the building. He had a life-sized stuffed Frankenstein on his set, with coveralls and all that. So I put that in the driver's seat and come in through the front.

I asked Ern how he was doing. "Good," he responded. I'm talking about this, saying something about that. I don't know how I brought it up, but I said, I see you took my advice and didn't keep your car out there. And he goes, "What do you mean?" I say, your car; it's not in front of the building. And he smiles, like, sure, and he goes out to the front of the building. He comes back. "Oh yeah, that's a real Parma joke, that's real funny." He wouldn't admit it got him.

So about a week later, same thing, car's out there with the keys in it. I'm thinking, what can I do? So I drive the car around in the back. This time I take all the clothes off Frankenstein and put them on me. I'm sitting in the car like this (*slightly flopped over*) and we put a camera across the street in the parking lot. So I'm sitting here like the dummy. I could hear him swearing, "That damn Shodowski … Parma." He's walking towards the car, and he grabs me to pull the dummy out, and I go "*RRRAARR!!!*" and grab him. He jumped, and the first thing he said was, "You didn't get me!" (*Laughs*) Just like that, I grabbed him, "Ahh! You didn't get me!" We had it on film.

SC: The footage still exist?

I had it for so long. I think he took it, because he knows I was going to show that forever.

SC: You mentioned something about him always being like this. Tim Conway is the same way. Is this something they got from each other?

Tim Conway and Ernie had pretty much the same personality. In fact, I only saw Tim serious one time in my life. That's a whole other story. Anyway, one time when Ernie and Conway did this comedy record—*Are We On?*—they came back to Cleveland to promote it. And for some reason, they wanted me to go with them. So we were going around to shopping centers all over the viewing area to pump this comedy record. It was sort of dull.

And as we were driving, Conway would be making remarks about whatever we were passing. One that sticks in my mind was a crappy used car lot. We're driving by, and it's really raggedy. There was a trailer for the office and it had cement steps. Conway's sitting there and he reads the sign, and he says, "And you know we're in business to stay, because we have cement steps!" (*Laughs*) I just thought that was brilliant. He would see something and make the most brilliant joke about it, just common stuff.

One time we were playing golf. Ernie is the worst golfer I've ever seen in my life. We were at Manakiki, and we were on a hole, and to the left was Route 90. It was a street, but the hole was along side of it, you know? So we tee off. Ernie comes up and he hooks it. It goes way over the road. We're watching it; there's a guy cutting grass and the ball's coming down. I don't know if the ball hit him or came close to hitting him, but this guy goes nuts. He had a rake or something, and he comes screaming towards us. Now, I'm pretty macho. I'm a young guy. I think, I'm going to stand here and I'm going to cool him off. This guy's running and he's swearing and he's got this thing, and he's not slowing up. I'm thinking, oh, man… So I turn around to maybe get some advice. Ernie and Tim are running into the woods, and they're laughing hysterically.

I'm figuring I'm not going to talk him out of it. So the minute I turn to run, I start laughing. And we were running and laughing. This guy, as it turned out, is an older guy. He's puffing and he's gagging. He's retching and he's almost out of breath. He's not stopping though. We run into the woods, and we're laughing so heard we're out of breath. This guy comes into the woods, and he's huffing and he's swearing and he just out of it. So we all run, but we couldn't get rid of this guy. Every time we'd think he'd stop, he'd keep coming and swearing at us. I don't know how you can hold anger that long, but he did.

So we all run into a thicket, and we're sort of crouched down. Ernie pulls his shirt off and sticks it in his mouth, because he didn't want to laugh. And I'm biting my lip. We're sitting there, and this guy is right in front of us swearing and walking around. He can't see us. So he's puffing, just about dying, and he starts to walk out of the woods. We're real quiet and I'm figuring at last it's over. I turn around, Conway's not with us. Turns out Conway's out behind the guy. He goes, "Hey!" (*Laughs*) It starts all over again. The guys chasing us, and I'm saying, "That's brilliant." I'm sort of relaxed, it's all over and Conway starts it again.

When we were going back, we realize we can't walk back to where our bags are, because the guy's going to know and be laying for us somewhere. So we walk back to the clubhouse where our car was. It took about a half hour. It just so happened I was driving. So as we're driving, Ernie and Tim get in the back and lay down so they wouldn't be seen. I'm kind of slouched down, since I don't want the guy to see me either. I just want to see if our bags are there. So we go past the hole and I say, yep, they're there. "Is the guy around?" I say, no. But he could be hiding anywhere. It was like a bunch of little kids, man. We come around—BOOM—open the door,

71

grab the bags, all of us laughing hysterically, and took off. But with them it was just a daily routine. There was no such thing as a normal day with them.

MM: You have had such a long career in Cleveland, 40 plus years. What have you gotten from your time here?

It's such a rewarding life that I've had on television. I met so many good people, people who are very loyal to the show and movie buffs. I like old movies, and I like horror movies. At some of these conventions, you meet their children. And I think that's great, because I love tradition. I think Cleveland loves tradition in general, and I think that's why we are still here. Cleveland doesn't like anything to change. If they grew up, and you were the movie host, then they want you to always be the movie host for their kids and their grandkids. I can't explain it. They don't want anything to change. I play the same music all the time. The minute I change it, I'll be darned if I don't get letters. "Why did you change this?"

But Cleveland is like that. It's very rewarding to be in this market. Clevelanders have something very special about them. They can laugh at themselves and they're very ethnic. They have a lot of ethnic pride. Not that they bicker among themselves. But they respect the fact that you're Polish and you like Polish tradition, or you're Irish, or you're Italian, or Slovenian or whatever. They like the fact that you stick with those roots. Cleveland is made up of pockets of ethnics. It's a big city, but a bunch of little neighborhoods. I've never seen any other city quite like that, where to this day you've got the Italian neighborhoods, the Polish neighborhoods, and they've stayed pretty much the same.

SC: Can you give us a few words on Ron Sweed and the time he worked on the Ghoulardi show? He was pretty young; he was a kid.

Yeah, we brought him along with us. When Ernie started his show, he did a personal appearance at Euclid Beach. This kid comes up in this ape costume and started jumping around. It was real hot and he almost passed out. And Ernie said, "Hey, you come on down to the show when we tape." The kid was Ron Sweed. Ron later said he found the gorilla costume in the garbage, and it was all mothy and maggoty. He cleaned it up. We still had that gorilla suit for I don't know how long. He gave it to us.

MM: That was the same gorilla suit you guys used in the "Stronger Than Dirt" and "Guitarzan" skits, wasn't it?

Yeah. Ron was only 14 years old. But he was very sharp and quick-witted. He wasn't like a 14 year old; he was more like a young man. He started hanging around Ernie and he had some good production ideas. So Ernie sort of kept him around as a mail boy. Ron was very, very devoted. He would do everything for Ernie. He would lay out his beard and costume before the show, stuff that no one ever did. He took care of the mail.

He became very good friends with Ernie's oldest son. They became really good friends because they were both in the same neighborhood. So Ron was a fixture on Ernie's show. Ron and I were good friends by the time Ernie left. I'm older than he is, but I recognized that he had talent. He had talent for knowing what would be good music for the show.

He had an idea for a birthday segment that was real big on the *Hoolihan and Big Chuck Show*. People would send in their birthdays. We were both good singers and we'd sing "Happy Birthday." It was his idea to have the PJs at the end of the show. He even went out and bought the nightgowns. He had a lot of good ideas. I always told him, "You're going to do something on TV," because he had this talent. He sure did, he became The Ghoul.

When Ernie left, he sort of grabbed all of Ernie's stuff, because he idolized Ernie. He wrote Ernie when he was in Hollywood and asked if he could take his character and audition. Ernie said, go ahead. And that became The Ghoul. He would even listen to old tapes and get that, "Cool it ove'day!" He would get that all down. He got it down pretty good. It was, at first, a direct copy of Ernie. But he went on to do his own creative stuff. But Ernie gave him his blessing, and that's how The Ghoul started. And of course The Son of Ghoul worked for The Ghoul. Then he branched off. It's like Cleveland keeps spawning these things. So we're going to get The Grandson of Ghoul, probably.

But Ron had the talent to think of these crazy things. It's fun, kind of like a friendly competition. Nobody knows The Ghoul and I are real close friends. They would think we were bitter enemies and they just love this bickering and stuff like that. But that's fun. Cities that don't have horror movie hosts are missing something. I can't imagine not growing up with that. Of course I was around before TV started. But when it started, you would latch onto a personality. Heck, I used to watch Ghoulardi. I never missed it, even though I was a part of it. If I was home, there was not a time I wouldn't watch it. It was good.

SC: What were some of the other differences between television then and now?

TV in the 1960s—I started in 1960—everything was live. We had a tape machine, but it wasn't on line.

Everything was live; every single show was live. You can imagine. Nothing was syndicated. You had to fill hours and hours, from show to show. While you were doing one show, they were setting up another show in the next studio. And during the station break, man, you would switch over those cameras. You really earned your money back then.

And talk about mistakes! A lot of these shows you couldn't rehearse. There would be mics in the shot and boom mics and things falling and people in the background who would scurry out. Every day was filled with that, and it was fun. It was exciting, because at any moment you'd be making these horrendous mistakes. With tape, you could stop and do it over. But live … it was being broadcast.

MM: Do you think that live brand of television, particularly the mistakes, made a direct connection to the audience?

Absolutely! You were really linked to what was happening, because it was live. And you didn't know any different, 'cause there wasn't any tape. TV at the time, everything was live, even *The Milton Berle Show*. These big network productions, they were live. Live things, funny things, happened, you know? And you're right, people got used to the idea that this thing was happening now. It wasn't edited; it was done and critiqued. It's happening and it was live. It was bound to happen that the technology would get toward where we are today.

But it's taken away the spontaneity and the chance for something to happen … except for the Super Bowl and Janet Jackson. That was live; you know what I mean? Something stupid like this could happen. I remember when someone had to do this blender commercial and they kept jamming too much in the blender. The thing started smoking. They were trying to tell you what a good blender this was and this thing was just blowing up, man. A little flame on the bottom, a spark, and then the woman's trying to put a carrot in there. But that was a daily occurrence back then.

When I first started at Channel 3, I had never run camera, and the cameraman got sick. So they said, "You're gonna have to run camera." I said, not only have I never run a camera, I've never seen a real camera. I worked in the projection room. They sent me into the studio and give me about a 15-minute course on running the camera. It was a news show. They said, "We made it easy. All you have to do is get this shot here of the guy, and then you have to truck over…" and they had a display, a pyramid

The winning formula for *The Big Chuck and Lil' John Show* remained virtually unchanged throughout its run. Only a new set, designed by local artist John Hlucky in 1991, altered the formula.

made out of beer cans. I'd get a shot of that and the booth announcer would read the copy. So I said, how much time do I have to get from this shot to that? They said, "A lot of time." Now, a lot of time to a director back then was, like, 10 seconds. To me, a lot of time is, like, five minutes.

So I practiced before the news. I practiced bringing it over here and turning the ring on the camera. Pull it, turn it this way! Pull it, focus … real smooth. I must have done it 15 times. So we're on the air and man, my heart's pounding. I know I only had two shots—that and the beer shot. So I got this shot, man. And they say, "Okay,

go Camera Four, go!" And I'm casually setting up. "Get it! Get it! Get it! Get it!" You know, he said I had a lot of time. "Get it! Get it! Get it! Get it!" So I'm going faster, man, and he's *screaming* at me. I start pushing the camera and—you get a camera going, they're heavy! I'm pushing that camera, man, and I hear the announcer reading the copy and the director says, "Take it!"

I'm out of focus and the camera's bouncing like hell. I'm coming in on this thing and the announcer's going, "Iron City Beer…"; he's going on and doing his thing. I'm coming in, man. And I'm trying to focus at the same time. The table with the display is here and I hit the table with the camera. All these cans fall down. I hear the announcer laughing at the top of his voice. I heard the director dying in the headset. I figured I was canned because I was just a summer replacement.

But anyway, things like that would happen daily. There was another time, almost the same week. I never ran a boom microphone; again someone was sick. This guy wanted to open the back door and walk into the studio. He wanted to open the show like that. So I'm top of this thing, and I'd never worked it. So again I'm practicing.

He's coming in like this and he's coming into the studio with all these klieg lights. And he's walking and I'm doing pretty good. But as he's walking, I start hitting the lights above his head. *PWOM! PWOM!* He's trying to talk and he's ducking, because these pieces of glass are falling down. And they're hot. This stuff is flying and I'm hitting all the kliegs. But things like were commonplace and it was so much fun back then. Now, if anything like that happened, you'd stop and you edit it, you do it again. But back then it was exciting. We did it live for years. We would be up here at two o'clock in the morning and it was fun. Because when you got end-of-your-rope tired like that, you'd get really silly. And it would add to it. People knew that you were really there, you know?

We were right next to a bar when the station was on Euclid. Hoolie and I would have our PJs on and I'd run across for a quick beer—in the summertime of course. And the people in the street would see me. They would know what's going on, because they'd know we were on the air. It was great. We used to run next door to have a beer when the movie's on, real quick. It was a whole different life. But it was so much fun. You had a camaraderie that you don't have now. It was, "Did you hear what happened yesterday?" It was always one story after another.

SC: What do you think a horror host is, how would you define it?

In one way, they're pretty much alike. But they're all different. If you're seeing a monster movie, he's really not you and he's not really a monster. He's like somewhere in between. He's part monster and he's part viewer. I think he sort of brings the horror movie into your living room, because you can trust him. He's not really a monster, but you wouldn't want him to come over, you know? He was just a character who was in between. He understood your life and the monster's life. He was just a go-between. That's what I always got out of a horror host. They seemed like they knew the characters in the movie and they seemed like they knew you. It was like we had a mutual friend, the monsters and the audience.

SC: What does it take to be a really good horror host? What does it take to make that connection?

I think you really have to be into the movies. I don't think you can fake it. And that's why Ernie never said he liked the movies. Some movies he liked, he loved *Little Shop of Horrors* (1960) and *House on Haunted Hill* (1959), which I finally got for our show. He loved those, and he'd say that. If he said he liked it, you could bet on it. He didn't say it much. But if he said he liked it, he liked it. Most of the time he didn't like it, and he'd tell you to watch out for the papier-mâché this and that coming up. He was just a different breed.

What appealed to everybody is that the horror host really liked the movie. They like that kind of movie and their enthusiasm flowed into you. Most of them know a lot about the movies, and they'll tell you little background things about the people in the movies. You know, no one really talked about movies back then. Some of the movie hosts now tell you a little story. That probably sprang out of the horror host. I don't know the ones you saw, but the ones I saw always knew a little bit. It's a shame. I can see we're a dying breed. I don't think there's anyone going to take our place. I don't think there's anyone young up and coming.

WJW 'stars visit Lorain

LORAIN — WJW-TV8's Big Chuck and Lil' John will bring their unpredictable team of softball all-stars to Oakwood Park Thursday at 7:30 p.m.

"Big Chuck" Schodowski and "Lil' John" Rinaldi will be playing against the managers and coaches of the Lorain Buckeye Youth Baseball Program.

The game, to be played at Oakwood Park field No. 1, will feature special celebrity guest appearances, prize give-aways, autographed pictures, and Big Chuck and Lil' John's renowned "certain ethnic" humor.

A minimal admission fee will be charged at the gate to benefit the Lorain Buckeye Youth Baseball Program.

MM: Some of your local fans have actually become part of the show. Art Lafrado sent in some skits, and has been a regular for years. John Hlucky designed your set and does some of your artwork...

Some of the charm of our show is that we don't really go out and get professionals. Any day, I would trade desire for talent. And there are a lot of people who just want to do it. They'll do a darn good job, and they'll be dedicated to it. As opposed to someone who's good at it, but not in the mood, you know? Because of that, we developed quite a few blue-collar characters. I mean guys who are very good, just finding out what they do well. Just like myself.

SC: Do you see yourself as a horror host, or as a general movie host?

Hoolie and I started out primarily as horror hosts, because those movies were the cheapest to get, those packages. Everybody had the classics. And as it turns out today, everybody wants to see *Frankenstein* (1931) and *Dracula* (1931) and you can't get 'em. If you do, they cost a fortune. But back then, they were by far the cheapest things you could have. That's why everybody had them. And then the '50s and the '60s sci-fi stuff, that was great. For the kind of show that Ernie had and that we had, they were perfect, because you could make fun of them and no one would be offended. They were so bad they were good.

SC: How do you feel being part of that tradition?

I love it, although I'm not the traditional horror host. I'm not the traditional anything. I didn't want to do this. It was thrust upon me. I used to crack Ernie up. After he went to Hollywood, he would razz me about the job I was doing, and I'd say, I didn't want to do it. It was thrust upon me. He'd die when I said that. Anyway, I'm not the typical host. But I can see where it's going. I'd hate to see horror hosts go out, it's their own little niche. They actually brought horror movies to television and made them more television entertainment than movies, because you can only see this on TV with the horror host. It's really a TV show.

Regarding Ghoulardi
Tim Conway
Interviewed by Sandy Clark (2004)

Tim Conway began his career in Cleveland, Ohio in the early 1960s, where he was writing material for the popular radio and TV personality, "Big" Wilson. A chance meeting with Ernie "Ghoulardi" Anderson led to a fruitful comic association and lifelong friendship. Conway worked with Anderson on a weekday movie program in Cleveland called *Ernie's Place*, and later collaborated on a pair of comedy albums, *Are We On?* and *Bull*.

Conway had gotten Anderson work on his post-*McHale's Navy* series *Rango*, and later introduced him into the *Carol Burnett Show* family, a footing that helped sustain Anderson in California until he eventually found fame as the voice of the ABC network.

How did you meet Ernie Anderson, and how did you come to know him?

Ernie and I met about 40 or some years ago. I was working at Channel 3 in Cleveland. I was actually driving down Euclid Avenue after work in a Volkswagen. And I had blown the last three gears of my car—second, third and fourth. So I was driving in first. I was driving home to Chagrin Falls, and I was going *HHHNNNNNNNNNNN!* A car pulled up along side, a window rolled down, and Ernie said, "Hey, schmuck. Are you charging your battery?" And that's how we met. Then we went to a bar after that and sat around for a couple of years. He eventually got into promotion work in Cleveland. I was working in promotion; I had just come out of the Army. I was defending Seattle. I had been there two years, and as you know they were not attacked, 1956 through 1958. I came back to Cleveland and ended up taking Jack Riley's place. He eventually ended up on *The Newhart Show*—writing for a disc jockey here, "Big" Wilson. Ernie became part of the promotional program of Channel 3, so we did a lot of stuff, just horsing around, promoting shows. So, that's how it kind of started between he and I.

What made you want to work with him?

(*Laughs*) Ernie was a very unusual personality. I mean, he just was a very, very loveable guy. He just was fun-filled. We had go-carts; we did silly things together. So it was fun to work with him. He was fun to be with. He had no respect for the business or people ... as I didn't at the time. I have great respect for the people in the business now, as you might expect. But neither of us really cared about being in the business. So it worked out very nicely, because we just had a very nice relaxed attitude about it. We were fired from most of the stations here in Cleveland. But you kept moving, you know. You try to get a job at the next place. If they call you in on Friday at 4:30 p.m. you know it's pretty much over. They don't like to fire you on Wednesday, because you can steal things between Wednesday and Friday. So on Friday, they know they got you locked up. You can leave and go home. So we did most of the stations in town, radio and TV.

*Tell me a little about the Ernie show (*Ernie's Place*) that you ended up directing.*

The morning show started on Channel 8. We talked the manager into a show. Ernie was going to be the talent; I was going to be the director. I had never directed and Ernie had minimal talent. But we talked the manager into it. It was a movie in the morning and little bits with guests. The show was so bad we couldn't attract guests, so I was always the guest. I just locked the camera to "on" and come out, and I was the guest *every* day. I couldn't back time the movies, so we never showed the endings of the movie for the first week. People were annoyed. You know, *Citizen Kane* (1941), people wanted to see the sled burning up and all that. Get a book, read it. And so we showed endings on Fridays. We'd show the movies during the week, no endings. And then on Friday, if you want to catch the ending, you could catch up on things. That became amusing to people, I don't know why. We were inadequate, really.

And from that Ernie became very, very, very popular in Cleveland. I mean, he just exploded in Cleveland, when this package of "ghoul" movies came out. There were about a 140 in there. None of them were worth viewing, except maybe one. But nobody you knew was in the movies. They were just these horrible, horrible, horror movies. So Ernie was perfect for that, because (*laughs*) you really didn't have to say anything nice about them. He said, "This thing really stinks and I hope you stay tuned." And people did.

I think Ernie, on one of his initial shows, blew up a frog. Which got a great deal of comment from the people in Cleveland. And he just had fun with them. He put on this stupid beard and a doctor's coat, and he was Ghoulardi. He just made fun of Cleveland. Cleveland's a very hard city to make fun of, as you know. It's not a city that you can make fun of. Although the river did catch on fire here in Cleveland and burned for three days, which is kind of unusual. They were putting water on it for the first couple of days. Someone says, "Hey, it's not working." So they finally put foam on it and put it out. It burned a lot of the docks down and everything.

We had a promotion at the station one time, throwing baseballs off the Terminal Tower here in Cleveland, a very high building. And if you caught the ball, you got a season's pass to the Cleveland Indians. We tossed the first ball off of the building and it went through a car roof. So we decided, maybe that wouldn't work. Maybe we shouldn't be doing this. We're going to kill somebody down there with this.

Ernie and I were also in on a promotion at Channel 3 where we sent out invitations to come to a special meeting for all the sponsors on Monday, and we sent it out with carrier pigeons in a little box. We sent it to all the advertising people. And when they opened the box, there's a pigeon in there with the note. It's a homing pigeon. If you wanted to come, you'd write, "I'll be there," and let the pigeon go. Of course, on Friday everybody went home. The pigeons were delivered on Friday, and of course they died over the weekend. I think two came back, actually walked back. So that wasn't successful. We were known for quite a few unsuccessful things here in Cleveland.

That leads into the story of how you guys tried to sell a puppet show without puppets.

Yes. We were going to do "The Best of Carson." That's when we were trying to work for another channel, because we were pretty close to getting fired from this one. So we worked up a thing where two puppets—actually, four puppets—would come up and, "Oh, Johnny was great tonight. Remember that thing where he...?" So we practiced at home. We had a script and everything. Now we had never done this by really holding our hands with puppets on them. We had just planned "Well, you say ... and I'll say ...," that sort of thing.

So they were taping this. We had a lot of sponsors from Ohio, big, huge guests coming. And this show was being broadcast live. Well, the stage was here, and Ernie and I were down below. (*Raises arms to indicate a puppet on each hand.*) And we are going, (*puppet voice*) "Yeah, well what do you think about that?" "Yeah, that would be good." "I think so, too." Now, we came to the end of the first page, and realized both of us have our hands up here and couldn't turn the page. So I just went (*mimes sucking up page with his mouth and spitting it away*) ... sucked it up and blew the next one over. Now if you've ever tried to hold your hands over your head for more than a minute, it becomes *extremely* painful. So we're going ... *ack!* We couldn't afford puppets, so we had hair on

Tim Conway began his career in Cleveland by writing jokes for popular TV host Malcolm "Big" Wilson, a former disc jockey and late night movie host.

In order to con WJW-TV 8 into hiring Tim Conway, Ernie Anderson had him brought on as the director of *Ernie's Place*, a morning movie program.

our hands and just two eyes drawn on them. "Yeah, what do you think?" I don't know" And we're going (*pained*) *ack! suck! spit!* And it got to the point we couldn't talk; it was so painful. And I went (*pained*), "Braddis, kay now, food is ep!"

And finally it just came to the point where we were hanging onto the stage with our hands, these hairy hands. We kind of stopped, and we looked up in the booth. And naturally, everybody had left. So we went to a bar. We were sitting there having a beer, with this hair still all over our hands, going, "Huh, I don't know why that didn't work. It seemed like a good idea at the time." That's another successful moment in our careers, yes.

It wasn't long before you went out to Hollywood, and you heard about this Ghoulardi thing. What were your first impressions? Did he send you tapes?

No. I was actually here for, kind of, the beginning of it. The thing was just coming in and Ernie was go-ing to do this ghoul guy. I had just left as he was doing Ghoulardi, and I'd heard it was extremely successful. It just exploded, you know. He became Mr. Cleveland. I mean, he could fill practically the Cleveland Stadium for a benefit softball game or whatever. So he did a lot of good for Cleveland, did a lot of benefits, a lot of stuff in this area. Made a lot of fun of the people, but of course, as I say, that's kind of easy to do.

What about Ernie Anderson worked in that role? What was it about him that made that character work?

The thing that worked best about Ernie is, he didn't care. (*Laughs*) He never prepared, which is important, I think, in this business, if you want to do something like that. He had no respect for Cleveland. (*Laughs*) He did, of course. He was just carefree. Whatever came to his mind, he did. He was the host of these ghoul movies and everybody just fell in love with it. You could see that he was not trying to do anything more than occupy this time and show films to these folks.

Did you ever make it back for any of these shows? Did you ever see him in make-up? Did you ever see any of his appearances or see his adulation first-hand?

Yeah, I came back and did a couple specials with Ernie, a couple of hour shows. And I saw this character. I used to come back to Chagrin Falls a couple times a year. I'd go to Chagrin and he'd be on television here. So I saw quite a few of them, yeah.

What were your impressions of the shows themselves? Did you watch the movies?

Ernie didn't even watch the movies. The movies stunk. They were these cheap, cheap films. He would put himself into the movies from time to time. That was in the early days, when supers never did work. But he'd take a picture of himself and he'd be in the movie. It never matched or made sense or anything. That also became part of the intrigue of what this whole thing was about, you know. It was just a bad show, with a great guy doing it, and some really bad films. And people loved him.

You did a character with Ernie called Dag Herford.

Well, Dag Herford was the character that we used on the early talk show. We couldn't get anybody to guest, because it just didn't appeal to anybody. We'd say things like, "Bob Feller's going to be on the show today." Then the next break we'd say, "Bob's on his way, he's a little tied up in traffic." And Bob would call and say, "What are you talking about? We're not doing this. Are you nuts?"

So we never had a guest. And the guests we did have weren't all that thrilling.

Rose Marie, from *The Dick Van Dyke Show*, came by one time. She saw this whole mess and said she thought it was amusing. She showed this to Steve Allen. That's how I got hired on Steve Allen. Later in the years, I had Ernie come out and he just exploded in voiceover announcing in Los Angeles. He was the voice of ABC, the guy who did, "On *The Loooove Boat!*" So he became very, very well known in the industry in Los Angeles, too.

Tell me a little bit about that. I understand when he first got there, Carol Burnett used to introduce him from the audience at the beginning of the show, just to give him some free publicity.

Carol opened the show for about six months saying, "Oh, Ernie Anderson's in the audience!" And he'd stand up. Nobody had any idea who he was. Everybody would applaud and go, "Who is he?" (*Laughs*) So that just became our sort of mascot on the show.

When you were working with him, especially in the early days, what do you think you learned from him? What impact did he have on your life and how you approached your career?

I learned from Ernie where most of the bars are in Cleveland. There was a place, used to be called Iggy McIntyre's. He had the key to the front door. Iggy would go home. He'd say, "It's 2:30, I got to go home." He'd give us the key. We'd lock up, then we'd actually open up the next day. I learned nothing from Ernie. He learned absolutely nothing from me. We just kind of palled around together. We didn't do a lot of preparing for the show; we didn't think that was important. And as it turned out, it wasn't.

Can you tell us about the famous incident on the golf course? The one where you were with him and got chased by a guy?

Some guy hit a ball and Ernie hit it back to him. I mean, actually, he was in the wrong. We were at Bel-Air. We were on one hole and Ernie had a 27 on this hole—which is a lot in golf, considering he was on the green in 3. But he over-putted; it went in the sand, so there's this continuation of explosions and sand. It went from one trap into another. He had 27. He's trying to line up this putt, and some guy hits a ball from in back of us. And it's on the green, too. So Ernie hits it back. The guy wasn't pleased; I don't know why. But he did come after us a bit. We went into the woods. Then we indicated where we were by going, "Yoo-hoo!" and then running. We weren't allowed to come back to that course. That was Bel-Air, too. It was a big course. It's a beautiful course. We only played nine holes, then we were asked to get our own clubs and go, obviously, to a public course.

What other stunts do you remember?

Joe Hamilton—Carol Burnett's husband—Harvey Korman, Ernie and me used to play golf every Monday. We had a revolving trophy. Most of the scores were well into the 100s, 140 or 150. But Ernie, he was one of those kinds of guys. If he hit a ball into the woods, he wouldn't come out till he had a dozen of them. He just looked around in there. And we lived in snake country in California. So one day he bent over to get a ball and a thorn went in his eye. He hit a bush and the thorn went in his eye. So he comes out crying, "Ahhh! Ahhh! I got to get to the hospital!" So we said, okay. He's says, "You got to take me." The group responds, "Ernie, we're on the third hole. You gonna break up this game at the third hole? It doesn't make any sense." He says, "How am I going to drive?" We say, "It's not our problem." So we actually flipped to see whose cart we were going to let him take back to his car, and he drove himself to the hospital. He was okay ... eventually. It wasn't that big a deal.

Why do you think Cleveland is conducive to these sort of hosted shows? What is it about Cleveland that draws this sort of humor, that sort of program?

I don't know, not many ghouls live here. There used to be a lot of ghouls, every other house had a ghoul. But a lot of them moved out when the steel industry moved out. They figured, "There's nothing here for us anymore." I don't know. But Big Chuck and Lil' John have been here 40-some years. Everybody in Cleveland knows them. And it's the only live local show now on television in the country. There's just something about the fact that if you have likable people and a premise, you can hang around for a long time if you want to.

Back when it was The Hoolihan and Big Chuck Show, *you went on with Ernie to promote* Are We On? *and you couldn't get a word in edgewise.*

(*Laughs*) Yes. We made an album, Ernie and me, for Liberty Records. They went out of existence right after the album came out, I think. To show you how popular it was, several of the album jackets—this is the truth—somehow mistakenly were shipped with a record of Elmo Tanner whistling. So it said, Ernie Anderson and Tim Conway, *Are We On?*, and it's just Elmo Tanner whistling. And nobody returned them. So that'll give you some idea how

Conway and Anderson worked on a nunber of projects over the years, notably the comedy albums *Are We On?* and *Bull*.

popular the album was. I think they sold four or five of them, in the entire run. So they asked us to do another one. Of course, we had to.

But I heard about this one show where you guys couldn't talk.

Oh, yes. Yep. Chuck and Hoolihan interviewed us, and they wouldn't let us talk. I had traveled 3,000 miles ... hmm ... I'd forgotten about that.

I was going to ask you how you guys shot "The Indian Guide" segments back then, because you were out and about. Were you shooting 16-millimeter? How difficult was it to pull these things off?

The production in that was just awful. It was about as bad as you could get. But that was just part of the thing. It was terrible. The material was terrible; the film was terrible. It was just what the show needed, just that touch of terrible. (*Laughs*) But yeah, I was an Indian guide, and I used to do stuff with Ernie out in the woods. Yeah. We just did nonsensical stuff. It made no sense whatsoever.

Did you notice a change in Ernie after the Ghoulardi experience? I mean, before that he was well known and he had a show locally. But Ghoulardi was very different. Did he change at all? Did you notice a change in his character, his desires, what he wanted to do? He left Cleveland not long after that.

No. Ernie *never* changed in the business. He was nasty when he came in and he was nasty when he went out. (*Laughs*) He never had any respect for management. That was the one nice thing about Ernie. He was supposed to come out to Cleveland and do a radio stint on WHK. He was going to be the morning man. He came from Connecticut. And there was a lot of publicity in town. "He's coming! Bleh, bleh, bleh!" He went to a party a little bit before he was supposed to come on WHK, and one of the people said, "Hey, Ernie. Get up and talk." So he started to talk, and he started telling some jokes. And every time, just before he got to the punch line, someone in the audience would say, "Yeah, well his sister is, too!" Ernie said, "How do you know all these jokes?" He said, "Well, I can anticipate them. I know these jokes."

"Really?" said Ernie. "Well, anticipate this..." And he told the gentleman where to go in no short terms.

It happened to be the manager of the station. So the guy said, "Pfft! You're out." So he never was on the air—a lot of billboards plastered the city, though. And people were going, "Hmm, I wonder what he was really like?" So that was his attitude towards management. But he had a very strong respect for people. And as I say, a lot of benefits that he did in this town helped a lot of people.

What do think was the funniest thing you saw him do? Be it a stunt—riding a motorcycle through someone's office or what have you—or something he did on the air with you. What's the funniest thing you saw?

Well, one time we went to a party. I don't think we were invited; we were never invited. But we just happened to go to this party. And this lady had a *huge* aquarium of fish. It took the whole length of the room. Ernie and I were at the tank, looking at all these fish. He was knocking on it and hit it with his beer bottle and he broke the glass. You never saw so many fish on a rug in your entire life. This lady was going nuts. So we filled up the tub and put in as many we could. They were all floating...but we put them in there anyway. I thought that was amusing. Certainly not for the lady, she was quite upset. I don't know why. I guess she had names for the fish and everything. We left the party.

There was a picket fence, and we were both laughing so hard in the car that Ernie took out the entire picket fence, which must have been a quarter of a mile long. It was just biddila-bing-bing! Bing, bing! Biddila-bing bing! And these white things flew over our car. I thought it amusing, you know, to be a part of that. I said goodbye to him one night and I didn't realize that I had put the window up on his hand. I look over and I see he's running beside the car. And I'm going, okay ... (*waves*) and he's still running along side the car. I'm thinking, what the hell's the matter with him? And he had his hand in the window, going, "Augh! Augh!" (*Laughs*) So we had a few good times, you know?

*Another question about another Clevelander—but did you help get Ron Sweed (*The Ghoul*) into Bowling Green University?*

(*Smiles, nods*) No. No. Not that I know of. No. Who's Ron Sweed?

He does a character called The Ghoul. He worked on Ghoulardi's show as a kid.

No. I didn't know him.

He says you're one of the reasons he was able to get into the school.

Is that right? Well, I did a very good thing for him then, didn't I? That's possible, then, that's possible. I don't remember my home phone number, so it's not like the past is really up front here. What is he doing now?

He does a show called The Ghoul.

Well, there ya go. Look at how I helped him. I'm very happy to have helped him.

Do you miss that type of seat-of-the-pants television, as opposed to television today?

Yeah, I think so. We had much more fun in those days, especially when you were live. You didn't have any control over what was happening or what happened. You couldn't correct it on tape, so you just stayed with what happened. And if you wanted a prop, you went and got it yourself. Or you made it. It was more fun, it really was. You'll never see that again, because stations won't take that chance. You see live shows, supposedly, but they're really not live. I mean afternoon and late-night talk shows; they can edit things out. Even *Saturday Night Live* censors itself. It's *live*, but if anything bad happens, there's a delay. You can pull that out of there, or certainly switch it off. Radio's the same way. You'd call up, and if you swear on the radio, there's a seven-second delay.

So you don't see, really, the live stuff anymore, the great stuff in this town, like Lynn Sheldon, who used to be a kid-show host, Barnaby. Lynn was another *great* personality here in Cleveland. He was explaining to the kids at home—he'd have a little hat, a little jacket and a little tie—"Hi, kids. How ya doing? Well, to teach you how to peel, Barnaby's going to cut a potato and peel it for you." He has a paring knife and he says, "When you're peeling a potato, you have to be very careful. Because ..." and he took the end of his thumb off. And he goes, "Well, Barnaby's going to go to the hospital now." (*Laughs*) This thumb's spurting out. "Barnaby will see you tomorrow ... maybe." So, you don't see that anymore.

What was Cleveland like as a place to start your career?

It doesn't get any better than Cleveland. It really doesn't. You just had fun in those days. Everybody from all the stations in the business knew each other. You got together, had a couple of drinks after the day and everything. It just was wonderful. And it's true, if you got fired from the one station, you went to next one. They picked you up and you just kept moving around. There were guys working for all kinds of places in town. It was fun, it really was. It was a challenge. Nobody was any smarter than the next guy, so you were all on the same terms. But it was just amazing how much fun we could have with this.

If you could do live television again, would you?

If I could do live television, would I? I think probably so, yeah. The problem is sometimes, if you are doing live television, you try too hard to make mistakes, to do things that are amusing. So the secret is just to do it. You know, on the Burnett show, mistakes we made stayed in, because it became part of the show. Harvey Korman, who was a very poor performer, was very easy to break up. We had the George Burns, Jack Benny relationship, and he'd just look at me and fall down. But I was also a writer on the show. I could write one thing, and his lines were okay, but mine were never as written. He never knew what I was going to do or say, and that all became genuinely a part of the show. They wouldn't leave in something that was phony. If it was a true break up at the time, we left it in there.

We didn't have a laugh machine in those days. So if you didn't get a laugh, you heard the air conditioner. So we really tried to be amusing out there. We would stare at each other sometimes when we were doing material and no one was laughing. We knew we were bombing, you know, and one gets a gleam in his eye. "Whew! We really stink, don't we?" And the next thing you know, he's on the ground laughing. So those were fun days. As I say, they'll never come back, because producers or networks won't allow them to come back. They can't take that kind of chance. "Be amusing? Are you crazy? We'll make it funny! Or the guy with the laugh machine will make it funny."

Inside Mister Outside
Lil' John (John Rinaldi)
Interviewed by Sandy Clark (2004)

John Rinaldi stumbled into a successful television career by one of those happy accidents common to the world of pre-corporate television. Rinaldi had graduated from Ohio State University with a degree in marketing. He was working at a local jewelry store when a customer suggested the 4'3" Rinaldi for the starring role in a "Bridget the Midget" skit being prepared for the popular *Hoolihan and Big Chuck Show*.

The amateur Rinaldi was a hit and became a regular part of the cast, appearing in dozens of skits over the course of a decade. In 1979, Bob "Hoolihan" WellS left the show and "Lil' John" Rinaldi graduated to the co-host chair. The rechristened *Big Chuck and Lil' John Show* garnered numerous Emmy awards, and both were inducted into the Broadcaster's Hall of Fame before leaving the air in 2007.

Let's start with your horror host memories. Who did you grow up watching in your youth and childhood?

I happened to grow up in the good times, when there were a lot of horror hosts. So when I was living in Cleveland here, it was Ghoulardi. He was the big, big thing going on while I was going to high school. Then when I went to Columbus, there was a guy called Fritz the Nite Owl that we used to all watch. I used to watch when I was working as a janitor, cleaning all the floors and everything. Then when I used to go Pittsburgh to visit friends, there was Chilly Billy. He was around for a long time.

So I saw a lot of them, horror hosts and all that. Then when I came back (*to Cleveland*) after I graduated from college, there was the Hoolihan and Big Chuck Show. And then it became Big Chuck and Lil' John!

Was there a continuity of horror hosts with kid-show hosts you'd seen in your youth—you know, the people hosting the cartoon shows? Can you compare them?

When I was a youth, they were live TV shows. (*Laughs*) It was Uncle Jake, a local guy here. And I was on his show a couple times as a child and did a couple things. *Kukla, Fran and Ollie*, with Miss Barbara, I was on their show. See, I was on every show. Anything that was free, I'd go down and try to win a prize. (*Laughs*)

Just briefly, with Ghoulardi and Fritz and Chilly Billy, tell me what you can remember about their shows. Just a quick sketch of their look, the kind of skits they did..

Well, Fritz had the big glasses. Chilly Billy, he was just a regular guy. Ghoulardi was the one that was the *best*. Not because I'm from Cleveland and that. But there was actually a lot that went into the show, with the skits and getting into things, the way he would talk to the audience. It was a lot more in-depth.

Specifically, what do you remember about the music of the show?

The music on the show was all things from the 1950s and the 1960s, and that timed-in with what was going on in the movie. The other ones just had eerie sounds. There was nothing planned in there like the music.

Coming forward, how did you end up getting involved in shows in Cleveland?

What it was is that I was working in a jewelry store. There was a gentleman who came into the jewelry store and he was upset because we had cracked his stone. We wanted to replace the stone and he wanted money. So we said, "No. We're a jewelry store, not a bank." This would go on back and forth. So nobody really wanted to wait on the guy. Me, being the young salesman at the time, they'd say, "Go make him laugh. Make him laugh."

So I did this a couple times. And he says to me, "Do you like to be funny?" I say, yeah. So he says, "I know these guys, Hoolihan and Big Chuck." I said here's my card. Tell them to give me a call. I just wanted to get him out of the store. Little do I know that he would call Chuck. And Chuck said, "I need a little girl (for a skit). Do you know anybody?"

This gentleman had a dance studio. He says, "I don't have a little girl. But I know a little *guy*." Chuck says, "Who is it?" He says, "John Rinaldi." My uncle was a doctor and Chuck assumed I was his son. My uncle was short also. So he called me up. And when I answered I said, "John Rinaldi here." And he said, "Hi, this is Big Chuck." And I'm going, "Yeah, sure. Nobody answers the phone like that." Meanwhile I find myself today calling people and saying, "Hello, this is Little John." (*Laughs*)

Anyway, he asked me if I'd do this skit, "Bridget the Midget." So I said, sure, no problem. He said, "We're going to do the skit. It's going to be on Saturday night. It's going to be at Bonnie's Lounge, on the West Side." I'm from the East Side. And if you know anything about Cleveland, we don't cross the river. So I thought, okay, they're just putting me on. It's just some guy trying to get me out there to get even for making fun of him. So I went out there.

I've been doing skits now for 34 years. Never have we done one on Saturday night—except that one. I took a couple buddies. I figured if nothing else happens we'll go out there to the West Side and have a good time. We get there and the door is locked. Knock on the door and lo and behold, Chuck opens the door. He says, "Come on in." It was that anybody who was there could stay and drink beer and everything. But once you left, you couldn't come back and bring your friends. That was before cell phones, so nobody called anybody.

An early promotional postcard announcing Lil' John Rinaldi as Big Chuck Schodowski's new movie-hosting partner. Rinaldi had been a regular on *The Hoolihan and Big Chuck Show*, making the transition an easy one.

I had to dress like this little girl. So, I brought my sister's clothes and my combat boots, and I did "Bridget the Midget." Chuck came up to me and said, "After about 20 minutes you're going to lose the crowd. "I said, "Ah, don't worry about that." Then after about 20 minutes I was flipping my skirt and dancing around. I was having a good time on stage. It worked out well.

Had you seen Chuck's show before this?
Oh, yes! *The Hoolihan and Big Chuck Show*.

Tell me a little about their show, just a brief description of what it was like.
Well, it hasn't changed that much with *The Big Chuck and Lil' John Show*! (*Laughs*) The truth of it is that I didn't see a lot of it, because I was gone for five of those years when I was at Ohio State. When I came back, it was only on a few years when I saw it.

What were your thoughts when you went out for this in terms of a career move?
No, no, no! It had nothing to do with a career move. I was just going out to have a good time on the West Side. And I thought it would be a hoot to be on television. Then from there, Chuck asked me if I'd like to be on the basketball team. And I said, "Sure!" He expected me to say no. (*Laughs*) I showed up and that's it.

How long have you been doing the show now, as The Big Chuck and Lil' John Show?
Twenty-five years.

Any estimate of how many skits you've done, how many shows you've done?
Oh, wow … well, you figure one a week. (*Laughs*) We did at least one a week and two on Saturdays.

Are you on every week? Do you do reruns?
No. The shows are all fresh. Once in a while…like, if we went to a special place and did a Disney(land) show—we might replay that. But anything done in Cleveland, that's it.

What was your first show like, your first show as co-host?
The first time we did the show, obviously, I was taking over for Hoolihan. He had just left. And we're talking about me being an untrained guy without any experience. When we were sitting on the set, Chuck had a cutout picture—a full-body picture—of Hoolihan. He

83

John Rinaldi (center) is flanked by Cleveland TV legends, Big Chuck Schodowski (left) and Bob "Hoolihan" Wells, at the 2009 GhoulardiFest convention in Cleveland, Ohio. Photo by Patrick Keeney

welcomed me to the show by throwing the cutout away, and I'm underneath it. And he says—"Here's to another 13 years!" because they were on for 13 years. And I said something like, "Here's to another 25!" And then he fell off his chair. Meanwhile, we are approaching 25 years.

Just briefly, let's get a rundown of how a show gets put together. I'm guessing you have a lot of skit material that you recycle.

I work very hard on the show. I show up and read. (*Laughs*) It's sort of like Mister Inside and Mister Outside. I'm the outside guy and Chuck is the inside guy. So, Chuck writes the show and he pulls all the tapes and does the skits and everything. My part of the show is come in and read it and then leave. Then anybody who would like us for an appearance, some contractual thing, they can contact me and I take care of that end.

Is this job more like play or work, and why?

I happen to have two great jobs. I mean, they're happy jobs. One is, I have a jewelry store, and it's a happy business. People come in to buy jewelry because they're happy to buy presents or an engagement ring. And this (television) is a happy business, too. Because you make people laugh and everybody's happy to see you. So I'm fortunate. I have two happy jobs.

What do you like most about the show? Doing the skits, hosting the stuff, meeting the people, doing live appearances?

I think it's everything. There's nothing I don't like doing. I like doing the skits. I like live. I like when we're at a personal appearance, and I like doing the show. Both Chuck and I are "people" persons. We like meeting people, seeing people and that.

What kind of live appearances do you do?

You name it; we do it, from car openings to old age homes to parades to charity events. There's a little act that we do and it's very high-tech. We haven't changed a word of it in 30 years.

Why has this hung on in Cleveland? What is it you think it is about Cleveland that they love their horror host, their entertainment, their community?

I can only speak for Chuck and me. We've out-lived everybody. I think that Chuck and I are both "people" people. We're out in the public; we're out and about. We don't hide; we don't sit behind the gold-lined film vaults here at TV-8. We're in the public and we like people. And they generally like us.

What do you think it is about the community that enjoys that kind of entertainment and has stayed with you so long?

I think now it's in the generations. It is, like, my father would watch the show; I watch the show, now my kids watch the show. It's gone through the generation thing. And it's clean. We're in the gray area. We never step out of it. We don't try to offend anybody. We try to offend everybody. I think it works out well. For me, I think this is the perfect show. I mean, I can't see myself doing the news or anything straight. I'm not going to be the leading man in love scenes. For me, this is perfect. This is where I like to be.

Are there any movies that you'd like to host on the show sometime? I know you guys don't have a lot of control over what's in the packages. But are you ever like, "I would love to do Dracula *sometime..."*

No, no. To me, whatever they pick is fine. I'm hoping the movie is secondary, and they want to watch *us* during the breaks.

A number of people have mentioned Ernie Kovacs as an influence. Do you see any Kovacs in what you do?

Well, it's burlesque. I think what we're good at is burlesque. And that's what Ernie Kovacs was good at. When the *Wall Street Journal* wrote us up, they said we were the last vestiges of burlesque. That's true. And again, it's the good, clean humor with a little twist to it.

Do you feel yourself a part of a legacy that began with Ghoulardi? And do you feel the flavor of the show is specifically Cleveland, something that can't really be translated elsewhere?

I think I'm very fortunate to be in the history of television in Cleveland, starting with Ghoulardi, then Hoolihan and Big Chuck, then Big Chuck and myself. It's just evolved, and it's a part of Cleveland. And we're a part of Cleveland; we're the history of Cleveland. When you think it's been 30 years—no, 40 years—the show has been on.

As far as being local, a lot of it is local and wouldn't translate into other markets and such. But a lot of it, I think, could be in other markets, because "certain ethnics" are "certain ethnics" wherever you go. But as far as Cleveland goes, I think we've been very blessed. People have opened their hearts up, and their homes, and have let us in.

What is "the certain ethnic"?

Okay ... (*Laughs*). To me, the "certain ethnic" is anybody. You could be Italian; you could be Polish. I'm 100% Italian; Chuck's 100% Polish. You could be Jewish; you could be black, white, Puerto Rican, anything ... Chinese. You're just a certain ethnic. So, we're making fun of, really, *everybody*. We're not just making fun of one group.

Is this getting harder to do? Do you think there are obstacles you guys have to overcome with the humor in a more politically correct world?

I think if we went to another market, maybe yes. But I think people in Cleveland know we're not out to hurt anybody. We're just poking fun at everybody. If we went to another market, I think we'd have to tone it down a little or do things a little bit different. But Clevelanders understand us.

We've been in other markets besides Cleveland. One summer we did 15 weeks in Detroit as a summer replacement show. And it turned out that everybody hated us, except the blacks. Every nationality hated us. The Italians didn't like me. The Polish didn't like Chuck. The Jewish people from the Anti-Defamation League did not like us ... since we did take-offs on certain Jewish things. Blacks loved Soulman, though. They loved that and wrote in.

I think if the show had lasted longer, they would have known that we don't poke fun at individual groups, we poke fun at everybody. But we went up there every week and did a show and came back.

So you traveled to Detroit to tape the show.

Yeah. We'd leave, like, a Tuesday afternoon, go up there, tape it, and come back Tuesday night.

Can you talk a bit about Soulman?

Soulman is a Superman super-crime-fighter that takes soul pills. He's a white guy when he starts off. He goes into a booth and takes pills and turns out to be Soulman. Comes out as a black man.

Who played Soulman?

Soulman is Herb Thomas, a cameraman who works here now. He was a young man at the time that was working in the print shop. He was, like, 19 years old when he started. Chuck came up with the idea of Soulman. And he was the white guy, Ed Tarbush, the mild reporter. When he would see bad things happening, he would turn into Soulman and save the day.

What do you think markets that don't have these kinds of shows have lost? What have they lost by losing their local personalities?

They lost the local flavor. Every city has their own local flavor, be it Milwaukee or Detroit or California— Berkeley or whatever. That's what they're losing: the local flavor of the city. We know the city, we know the people, and we know how to get around, the people to see and all that. That's what they're missing.

How much interaction do you get to have with the fans? Do they send stuff in? And have you seen that change over time?

Yes. As far as the fans sending stuff in, nobody writes anymore. Now they do email a little bit. But nobody takes time to send things in like they used to. We used to get a lot of mail. We used to get a lot of things sent to us—little gags and little things. Now you don't get that much interaction through the mail. You get some emails and that. But it's not like it was before.

What do you think has contributed to that? Are people just not interested in getting their stuff on TV anymore? Are there too many choices? They don't write. What do you think it is?

They don't write. They're tied to the computer. When was the last time anybody sent somebody a postcard? Or a letter? Computers now do everything. And if they don't get a response by computer ... (*shrugs*) We're old. Chuck and I are old. We like writing, calling on a phone. (*Laughs*)

What's the favorite sketch you've done?

I would say "Troglodyte." It was my favorite. And that goes way back. That was like my fourth skit we ever did. I damn near drowned in the thing. Chuck's son saved me. I can't swim a lick. That was one that I would say catapulted me.

"Troglodyte" is a Ray Stevens record. I played a caveman. And we had Bertha Butt, who was this big woman. So I mimicked the whole song, where I ran in the water to chase the women. And she was, believe me, a *big* woman. It was a fun thing to do. We were out at Hinckley Lake when we did it. It was just neat. I enjoyed that skit the most. I actually had muscles in that skit. So, if you ever watch it, my arm has a muscle.

There was another skit with you in a boat. But if you can't swim!

Well, Chuck writes me in all these things he knows I can't do. He knows I can't swim. So I'm always in the water. But it's always a thing where he ties a rope on me, so he can pull me back in. I'll tell you another thing; I don't go near the water unless I trust you 100%. I won't go near the water with my wife. But with Chuck, I've been out on Lake Erie in October, when it's been 30 degrees out, floating on a log! There was the one with the "Fish Finder," where they throw me in the water. And I go under the water and he pulls me back up.

And there was "Troglodyte," where I run in the water. I was supposed to be knee deep, but I was on a boat-launching ramp and—shoo!—I went right in. But then again, they paid us to scuba dive and I did that. (*Laughs*)

We're not as daring as we used to be when we were younger. (*Laughs*) We don't fall on concrete as easily as

COUPON
Lil John Rizoldi's Pizza
BIG SPECIAL
For a limited time only.
Purchase a Lil (12") Cheese Pizza for only
$4.99!
Delivery or Carry-out
NO LIMIT
Not valid with any other offer
Valid through 12/31/95

we did before. We've toned it down a little bit on the skits. I mean, it would be nothing for us. We have skits with us standing back-to-back four stories off the ground, walking along the ledge at the FOX 8 building here. Now we wouldn't even think of doing that.

Is there anything else we should have asked you?

I think the horror hosts, the hosts and their supporting players, are a dying breed. And like I said before, I think it's a shame, because people are losing the local flavor of the thing.

What is a horror host to you? What do they bring to the presentation of a movie?

What a host brings, I think, is the continuity of the movie and the breaks all together. It just brings everything together. In our instance, I think it adds to the movie. Especially when we have bad movies. It adds something, a continuity, to the whole show that makes the viewer see more things.

What does a horror host specifically do then? What does he add to the program?

I think he adds his wit, his wit and his humor. And with us, we have an audience. So, we add the interaction of the audience with the host. Horror hosts that try to emulate certain things, they have no creativity. I think this show is still creative. And that's due to Chuck. He's still fresh and creative and thinks of different things, and he stays up with the times and that.

You can see it from our earlier skits to the skits we have now. They're shorter; they're tighter. There's a lot of thought that goes in it. People don't realize it. When they see a skit, they think, "Oh boy, that's no big deal." For every minute that's on the air, it takes an hour to do. There's a lot of production done in our skits.

How much longer do you guys think you'll be doing this?

Well, I hope we do this for a long time. I'm in debt again and I have eight more years of house payments. (*Laughs*) I'd like to see this thing continue as long as we're both healthy and we're still having fun. And so far we are. I speak for myself—and I'm speaking for Chuck, too, because he's said he's having fun still—that we could do this forever. We tried work, we hated it. (*Laughs*)

Our Man in Flint
Christopher Coffin (Reed Farrell)
Interviewed by Sandy Clark and Michael Monahan (2003)

Venerable deejay and voiceover artist, Reed Farrell, worked as a major market radio disc jockey during some of the most turbulent and thrilling times in the country's history. In the course of his early career, Farrell reluctantly became the face of the anti–rock and roll movement with a staged "Rock and roll has got to go!" publicity stunt, even as he rubbed shoulders with cultural icons like Elvis Presley and John F. Kennedy. Of the latter, he recalled, "He glowed. The man had an inner glow."

Horror hungry fans in Flint, MI, knew him as Christopher Coffin, "Guardian of the Ghouls," on WJRT's *Theater of Thrills*. The show aired from early 1963 to the fall of 1967, remaining a ratings winner throughout its run. At the height of the program's popularity, Christopher Coffin was presenting two double-bill programs a week; one horror, the other sci-fi themed.

The hosting segments were creatively staged, with rear-projected castle photos adding production value and a murky otherworldliness to the show. Farrell's naturally resonant voice gave his host a grim gravitas. There was humor in the show, but Christopher Coffin's startling shifts from purring geniality to explosive threat invested the proceedings with an unsettling tension.

Reed Farrell was the commercial spokesman for many of the show's sponsors and designed the character of Christopher Coffin to mask his identity. He affected a costume beard and moustache, a hat to hide his hairline, dark glasses to shield his eyes, and most importantly, a wheelchair to disguise his height and body language. A blanket covered the lower half of his body, completing the transformation. Reed Farrell was virtually unrecognizable and Christopher Coffin was recognizably sinister as hell.

Following his reign as Christopher Coffin, Farrell continued commercial voice work, including a number of high-profile national ad campaigns. In later years he served multiple terms as president of the American Federation of Television and Radio Artists.

Sandy Clark: How did you come to be working for station WJRT?

I really wasn't at the station; I had a little advertising agency. In 1960, I was working in a radio station in St. Louis, WIL, which was a terrific powerhouse station. The station, in a market that was, I think 28 stations at that time, had a full solid one-third, which was a pretty strong audience. In fact, we had a station break saying, "Right now, it's hard to believe that two out of three people in St. Louis are *not* listening to WIL." At any rate, I was working at WIL in St. Louis. And all of a sudden, I was almost 30. I thought, I don't know too many 40-year-old disc jockeys, so maybe I'd better find me something else to do.

So I went to Flint, Michigan. I had been born there, but hadn't lived there since I was 11. I had a lot of friends and a few relatives. I went to a friend of mine in St. Louis and I said, "What do I need to know to open an ad agency?" He spent about an hour and a half with me and I went off to Flint. At that point, I was primarily interested in doing radio and television. I had a few clients.

One of them was in the furniture business. The station manager at WJRT tried to get me to buy the Saturday late-night horror movie for this client. I said I'd pitch him. So I was talking to the client, and I said, trying to sell him, I could even do a little (*sinister laugh*) Meh-heh-heh-heh! sort of intro, you know? He loved that idea. He says, "Oh that sounds great! Why don't you do that?"

I go back to the station, and I said, Jerry said he'll buy it. But he wants me to do a little intro thing. They were all in favor of it. So I came up with the *Theater of Thrills*. And we went from there. After the first week, it became an on-camera thing. And because my stage walk had always gotten a lot of laughs, we decided I wouldn't walk. So I was in a wheelchair. Then we decided it would be kind of neat to do part of it lying in a coffin.

Well, trying to buy a coffin is really tough. That is, unless you want to get in it. If you're willing to get into it and be buried, you can buy all the coffins you want. These things aren't built for opening and closing. They're built for put-somebody-in-it, close it and put it away. But finally we found, in Saginaw, Michigan, a company that was willing to sell us the coffin. It was the Opportunity Casket Company. Actually, we had to rebuild the coffin, because as I say, they're not built for everyday use. We put a piano hinge on it, so it would work better.

I would open the show with this eerie music that came from a Spike Jones album. Can you believe that? I can't remember the exact cut, but it was really weird as can be. *Spook-tacular* was the album, but I can't recall which cut (*The music was the instrumental organ prelude to* "I Only

Reed Farrell's urbanely sinister host, Christopher Coffin! Note that Farrell drops the "h" from the autographed "Cristopher," an affectation also utilized by Ernie Anderson who signed as "Goulardi."

Have Eyes for You," *which opens the album*). But it was so neat. The opening of the show would have the camera pan down the coffin, and finally show me lying there in repose. As the camera got to me, I would just come up and say, "Good evening!" Oh my gosh, the voiceover opening was really one of my favorites: "Ghost stories, tales of horror and suspense … even murder … hhnn… hnnn … HA! HA! HA! HA! HA! HA! HA!" That used to warm them up a little bit, you know?

The character was really very serious. I've seen some of the guys who've done horror-hosting shows, and they played it funny. I never played it funny. I played it very, very serious. And that's what made it funny. When we first started, I'm going on 11:30 at night. This was for adults, and though I wasn't looking to do a Howard Stern, there were a little double entendres used on several occasions … until I started getting these crayon fan letters. And then I figured I better clean up my act.

It was fun. Whenever stars came to town they came on the show. I remember locking Annette Funicello up in the prop closet. We'd have some fun with that. And the entire cast got into it. Actually, when I said the cast, I should have said "the crew." The camera guys, the floor guys, all came up with stuff to do. Fun stuff.

SC: Could you tell me a little more about the crew and the things they came up with? Do you remember any names?

Lytle Hoover was the main name I remember. Don something or other; he went on to work for CBS in New York as a cameraman. Everybody got into the act. I mean, they all came up with things. There was a staircase going up to a storage attic in the back of the studio, and Don would run up and down screaming and yelling, which sounded pretty wild. And I'd say, "That's one of my slaves…" That sort of thing. It was really a kick.

When we started running the sci-fi horror stuff on Friday nights, they'd use a lot of the Japanese product with the giant dinosaurs. One time I'll never forget, they had a miniature town built from kid's toys. It had wires strung like telephone wires and they had some sort of bug on the wire, a cricket, I think. And the way they'd shoot it, they could make it look like he was right outside my window. And they'd take the cricket and blow a little smoke on him. The smoke would really get him moving, you know?

There was also a show with a guinea pig, which was one of my favorites. One night I came in and they had this little guinea pig, a cute little white guinea pig. We had a prop syringe that would look like you were drawing blood. So I had the little guinea pig, and I take some blood from my arm and inject it into the guinea pig. I pet him a little bit, and then we go back to the movie. The next time we come back from the movie, the crew had taken the guinea pig and put him on a little piece of black velvet cloth somewhere else, shooting him with a different camera, making him appear bigger. Now, I'm petting the guinea pig like this (*gestures as if petting a large dog*). The next time they come back from the movie, they've still got the guinea pig over there, they've made him bigger, and now I'm looking over his back, petting him. And of course at the end of the show, he's standing next to me looking *down* at me. You can do so many neat things with black and white. Black and white television was so much fun. There were so many things you could do. Where with color—color's so damn real that you lose some of that fun effect, I think.

This was one of the real fun things of my life. I just had a great time doing it; it was a ball, a real kick. And we got great ratings. We got better ratings than *The Tonight Show* on Friday nights. Think about that, *The Tonight Show* was super strong at that point. I always looked forward to doing it. But you know that's been my whole life. I've never done anything for money that I wouldn't have done for free. I mean never.

SC: What came together that made a show like this happen? What made it possible, made it so much fun?

These things are a matter of chemistry. When you have a director working with some guys on the floor who are looking to have some fun, it's going to happen. You've got a bunch of guys who do the six o'clock news, the 10 o'clock news, and they do the same damn thing day in and day out. And then they go to the weather. Then the guy who does the sports stands up and does his thing.

Now they get a chance to do something that has no bounds. It's what you feel like doing, coming up with ideas. You know, everybody wants to write the great novel. We wrote it every week. It was a matter of the creative energy that came from these guys to me. They came up with most of the ideas. I tried to bring it off; I tried to bring their ideas to life. We had a chemistry among us that was just super. It was so much fun.

SC: How about some production details? What was the schedule like? When did you find out what movies you were showing?

It depended. As I remember, we would record Thursday afternoon at four o'clock. That was the normal recording schedule. So I would get the movie Monday or Tuesday, they would be bicycled in. Let me explain: In those days every station didn't have a complete library of films. So when station A got done using a film, they would send it to station B. And when station B got through using it, they sent it to station C. The films were constantly rotating around, and we referred to that as "bicycling" the product.

At any rate, when the movies came in, that were going to be used that week, I'd get a call, pick them up, take them home and throw them on my 16mm projector, and run the movies. I always enjoyed them. You know, those movies were short. All those Mummy things were never longer than an hour, you know? They're really short films. I'd go through them and mark where I wanted the commercial breaks to come. They'd tell me every eight or 10 minutes. So every eight or 10 minutes I'd stick a piece of paper in the reel, and when I rewound the film, that would tell them where it was. I'd also give them a little cue sheet. That way, I'd have some knowledge of what was happening in the scene before I came on, and what was going to happen when they went back.

SC: In your production, they always seemed to have a lot of inserts. There was one with the Frankenstein monster sweeping the stable.

Oh yeah. Sometimes those were the camera guys or floor guys you're seeing. Everybody got into the act, everybody, sometimes people driving by. When we did things outside, it didn't matter. Everybody got into the act. It was fun.

One year at Halloween I decided to take the coffin home. I set it up in my living room on a couple of sawhorses and draped it, you know? And I got a couple of the neighborhood kids to come by and be my doormen. All evening, I just stretched out in the coffin; I had some candy nearby. And when someone would come to the door, the kids would bring them in. I had on my dark glasses, so I could look up and see if I had four or five kids standing around. Then I'd sit up and say, "HAPPY HALLOWEEN! Heehhh, heeeehhh, heehhh!!!" Oh, it was really fun. I had a lot of fun with that character.

SC: What went in that character? When you first realized you were going to do this, what elements did you want to include?

I had an old smoking jacket. I think it belonged to my dad, one of those wild old satin-style smoking jackets. I had a white scarf, which I think was my dad's also. I wanted my character to look kind of formal, so I put on a hat. It was me (people finally figured out) because of the watch and the ring I was wearing at the time. If you look at the picture, the watch and the ring are prominent. And I wasn't smart enough to take them off.

I was doing commercials, on-camera commercials, while I was doing this show. So sometimes, I would come on and do my little shtick and throw it to commercial, and it would be me. So I would say, "We'll be back to the movie in a moment. But first here's a word from old baldy." You know, some derogatory remark about myself. But many finally figured out it was both the same person. But of course they couldn't figure out how I could get out of that wheelchair and do a dance so quickly.

SC: What kind of letters did you get?

Oh, gosh. I used to spend an hour or so every week going through the mail. And I had a gal at the station that would also go through and answer some of the mail for me. But anything she thought was of any consequence she would save for me. I used to send out little postcards, thanking people. I used to get a pretty good quantity of mail. I don't mean thousands, but a lot of mail every week. I never asked for mail, they would just send it

Reed Farrell discussing his career in TV and radio in 2003

automatically. I used to read some of the mail on the air, which was a kick.

SC: Let me ask you for a definition: What is a horror host? Why were these guys doing these shows, of which you were one?

Frankly, I never knew any of the other guys who did them, except for Ernie Anderson. I knew Ernie quite well. In fact, I was once driving back from dinner with a good friend of mine, who was also a friend of Ernie's. And we passed a placed where Ernie's wife used to have a store, some sort of a little shop. This fellow was recalling the fact that Ernie told him he'd made more money with one little thing that had happened there. They were building a new building across the street. And the people who were having the building across the street built paid Ernie to put a camera up in the loft of the store, facing across the street, so they could monitor what these guys were doing as they built the thing. He told my friend that he made more money on the camera than he did on the stuff his wife sold in the shop.

I've seen clips from a couple of the shows. But I didn't meet Ernie for years after he left Cleveland, and I was doing this in Flint. I knew him when he was doing voiceovers and I was doing promos around the country. You know, he was a very successful voiceover guy.

SC: Do you have any other Ernie Anderson stories?

All I can tell you about Ernie is that he was really dangerous when it came to the extermination of martinis. If it had been up to Ernie, I don't think there would been any martinis left. He might have destroyed the entire crop. He was pretty handy with a martini glass. He could handle that as well as anybody I've ever seen.

SC: When you first started Christopher Coffin, you were coming to it from advertising. Were you aware of any other shows like that around the country?

No, I'd never seen anything like that. But I felt most of the hosts did them funny. I never tried to do it funny. I always felt the horror movies that impressed me as a kid, the Mummy movies, Dracula and Frankenstein and those things, were done so seriously. And I tried to do it the same way. Let it be funny, but let it be funny because I'm being so damn serious. That was the mood that I tried to create. I just tried to be very, very serious.

The character was totally a figment of my imagination. And then, all the stuff he did came from a dedicated, elite group of fun guys who worked at that station at that time. I can remember one time—I can't remember the exact situation—but I had this mad professor who was pouring things into the beakers. And he was one of the cameramen. They would come in on a day they weren't working to help out with this thing. It was something we all just got a big kick from doing.

SC: You mentioned black and white before as an element of these shows. What would make it more difficult to produce something like that today?

Color would be one of the most difficult things. Because, how could you go from a bright, colorful human-looking thing and then go back to a black and white *Mummy's Tomb* (1942)? They don't jibe; they don't work together. When you see clips on awards shows of old black and white stuff, they look like "old black and white stuff." When we were broadcasting old black and white television, we didn't look old, because everything was the same. So the guy who did the news, and Christopher Coffin and Boris Karloff were all the same. I think that's one of the things. It would be pretty expensive to do it well. And I don't think local stations would do it. There have been a few examples of national characters. Like Vampira; she was a national character. But Christopher Coffin, the mood was dark. It really was dark. I mean (*lowers voice to menacing growl*), you have no idea how fearful it got.

MM: Christopher Coffin was on the air late into the 1960s. Did the show ever go to color?

No, no. Color came, but we kept the show in black and white. Some of the commercials were in color. I remember when we first got color. Oh, boy! I was handling advertising for a Jeep dealer and I had him bring a fire engine red Jeep into the studio. And I bought a red sport coat. I mean we did silly things. When we got the first special effects generator, it had 12 special effects. And man, you'd see those in every commercial, all 12! I mean, it was unbelievable, a big deal. We've come so far, but I think if I was to do Christopher Coffin again, I'd want to do it in black and white.

SC: Do you remember any of the other bits you used to do on the show, any bumpers or tag lines?

The opening was the primary thing. The rest was just the character talking. You could say anything you wanted to say and be a little nasty with it. And there were a lot of laughs. I used the crazy laugh, and when I went some place, people would say, "Oh do the laugh. We want to hear you laugh."

Michael Monahan: Coming back to the show for a bit. You said the ratings were always good. How fast did popularity come to the show?

Quickly, super-quick, it was one of those lucky things. To the best of my memory, it was one of those shows they didn't do a lot of promotion on. I think there were some promos that ran on the station, but there was no real promotion so to speak. But word of mouth on a thing like that, it just built like crazy. And in those days, television was still pretty new. The guy who had the 17-inch set, that was a big TV, you know? So there was not a lot of promotion. But it grew very, very quickly. And it stayed strong; it really did, throughout its run.

This was really a very cooperative effort. The crew came up with amazing stuff! I was in the advertising business and I was doing commercials. I mean, I had all kinds of stuff. On Thursday, I'd walk in there at three or three-thirty and we're going to tape at 4 pm. I'd go in this little dressing room and put on my moustache and beard and my smoking jacket, and they had all kinds of stuff set up.

They'd say, "This is what we've got," and then I could do anything I wanted with it. They didn't say, "You've got to do this," or "You've got to do that," or "This is what we're going to do in the first break, the second break." It would be, "This is what we set up for today. And do what you want with it." And man, we had more fun … and they were just so creative. They were just a fun group to work with, a really good bunch.

SC: Did Christopher Coffin ever make any personal appearances?

Occasionally. The manager of WRJT at that time was a man known as A. Donovan Faust, and Don Faust was quite a star in his day. In Detroit radio, he was the Green Hornet. That was one of my favorite radio shows as a kid, and Don was the Green Hornet. So one time there was some charity that wanted me to make an appearance with a bunch of young kids, and Don asked me if I would do this. I said, yes, if you'll push the wheelchair. And so he did. He pushed me into this room that was filled with young kids. I think the oldest was about 12 or 13, if that old. And as he pushed me in, they were all crowding around me and I said, sit down! And the little butts hit the floor so fast it was wonderful. You know, I created a very commanding personality, a very overbearing personality. You didn't want to cross this guy.

SC: With your background in radio, did anything from that medium influence or inspire aspects of the character of Christopher Coffin?

Oh sure, *The Shadow*. I loved these radio shows as a kid. I mean I was a big radio listener; I just loved radio. I think people who grew up without radio drama really missed something, because radio built images in your mind. "Who knows what evil lurks in the hearts of men?" It was neat when they did that. But when you see me do it, it doesn't have the same effect. If you hear it in a dark room with some eerie music going on behind…

The whole effect of radio drama had a big influence on me. *Inner Sanctum*, *Lights Out*, and *The Shadow*—all of those programs we had were just wonderful. When I first started in radio, some scripted shows that we did were really kind of funny. I remember I used to do a syndicated soap opera, *Second Spring*. "The true life radio story that asks the question: Can a woman who was once loved completely ever find her Second Spring?" Yeeee-rrgghh! But you know something? I got paid for it. Not all bad. It's not all bad.

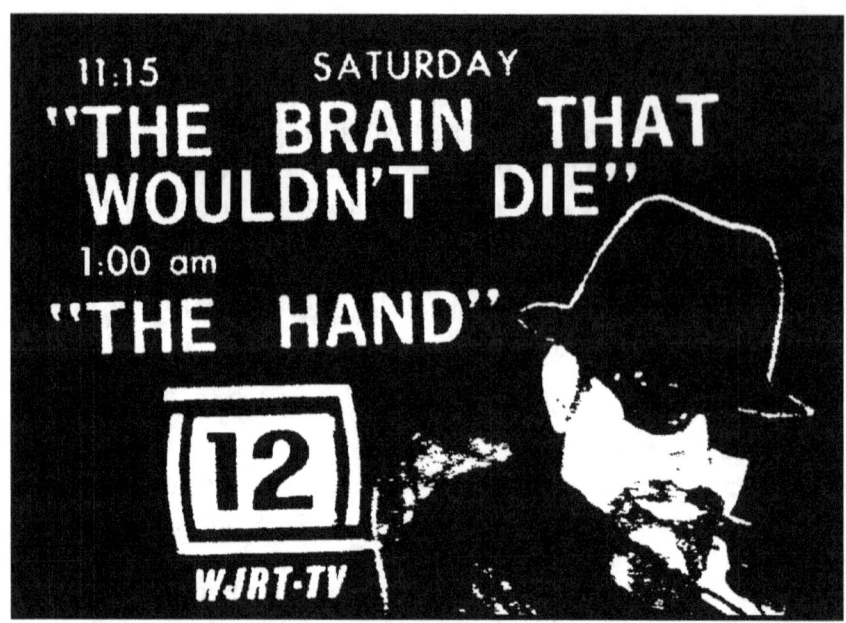

A classically bad double-feature on Christopher Coffin's *Theatre of Thrill*

SC: How did your show come to an end?

The Friday night ended because ABC put on *The Joey Bishop Show* against Jack Parr. And WJRT was obligated to carry it on Friday night, which eliminated the sci-fi stuff. And then I had an early mid-life crisis and decided to move to San Jose, Costa Rica for a while. I wasn't going to be there to do the show, so they took it off the air. That was the end of it. Chris Coffin moved to San Jose, Costa Rica! I drove to San Jose, Costa Rica. People always say, "How could you drive to that island?" Yeah, that island between Nicaragua and Panama...

MM: Back to your deejay career for a moment: Can you tell us the story of "Rock and roll has got to go"?

There's a bit of background I've got to tell you first. I was working in Chicago in 1955 at station WAIT. I was the big Elvis Presley disc jockey. I had emceed his show at the International Amphitheater when Presley came to Chicago for the first time. That was a kick. I met Presley several times, but this was the first time he'd come to Chicago. And this was the first time he'd be seen in the gold suit, with the gold shoes and all that jazz. And so I was chosen to emcee the show.

At any rate, I was the moderator at the press conference at the Stockyards Inn. That was while the first half of the show was going on, and Presley would go on after the intermission. So now, Tom Diskin, who worked for Col. Parker, introduced me and I went to the microphone; I had prepared about 25, 30 seconds. The audience wasn't there to see me; they wanted to see Presley. So as I walked to the microphone, Bill Black, the bass player, said, "He's not quite ready. Stall." Stall? There are 16 thousand people in this joint who came to see Elvis Presley, and he wants me to stall. I had no idea what to do. You have no idea how befuddling a thing like that is. So I said, "I just left Elvis." *YAAAAAAAHHHHHHHHHHHH!!!!* Anything I said, they screamed. My 30 seconds lasted eight minutes. And finally he said, "He's ready."

I was supposed to point up this ramp. I was supposed to stay at the bottom while he came down, shake hands with him, and leave. When I said to them, "Okay, ladies and gentlemen. Here he is ... Elvis Presley," and the spotlight hits him, these 16 thousand people started moving toward me. You've heard the expression, "a deafening roar"? Well, let me tell you, I heard it that night. A deafening roar builds to the point where you don't hear any sound; you just feel *bzzzzzzzzzz*! It's like a buzz, but it's vibrating off of your body. And it scared the living hell out of me. I jumped off the back of the stage and sprained my ankle and hobbled out of that place. I wasn't going to wait. It really frightened me. But at any rate, now I get into a battle with the guy that owned the station that I worked for. He was about to fire me. And I told him what he could do with his job, but before he got a chance, I left.

I went to New York. I was looking around the country, trying to find a place to go. I don't know if you remember the name Charlie Applewhite; he was a singer, a friend of mine. He and his wife lived in New York. So I was staying with them in New York, and suddenly I get a call to come to St. Louis to go work at a station, KWK. They had been looking for a morning guy, so they hired me. And I wasn't there two months before they decided to stop playing rhythm and blues, rock and roll. They were just going to play Guy Mitchell and Doris Day.

I went to a meeting of the staff, the jocks, the station management, and I said, you know, you're making a mistake. If you don't play what people want to hear, they'll find some place that does. The program director said, "Listen, if you don't play what they want, they'll want what you play." I said, really? They have a choice. You're making a mistake. Then they decided they were going to break records on the air. I said, you don't want to do that. You're insulting people's tastes. They said, "We'll get a lot of publicity." I said, that's not the point. You're going to make people really mad, because a lot of people like this music. If you want publicity, take the records and give them to a children's home. Or put them away. Maybe you'll start playing them again later. They said, "No, no, no. We're going to break records on the air."

Well, I was the only one to argue against it. Now I was the morning guy, the first guy on the air in the morning. They had a film crew there on the given morning, and I had to take a record and say, "Rock and roll has got to go!" and smash the record. Well that clip has been on every history of rock and roll. It's been an albatross around my neck. Everyone who knows me has kidded me for 100 years. And that was the whole story. I was the only one who didn't want to do it, and I got stuck with it. And you know the worst part of it is I haven't gotten paid for that! It was something that was considered news footage. But at any rate, that was the rock-and-roll-has-got-to-go story.

Then I got a call one day from a gal who does clip clearance here in LA. She clears things like that. And she says, "I have a recording artist who's thinking about using the audio part of that 'rock-and-roll-has-got-to-go' piece. I think that was your voice and he would love to arrange to use it on a record. And if you're willing, we'd be glad to send you $500 for a release." So I said, well, who is the recording artist? And she just sort of danced around. Finally, she said, "Well, it's Michael Jackson." I said, are you sure he can afford the $500? You don't want to do this for free? Anyway, I negotiated for considerably more money and six copies of the CD. And it got lost in the final cut. He didn't use it. He was going to use it on *Dangerous*. But it didn't make it. It was the only code A.F.T.R.A. (American Federation of Television and Radio Artists) doesn't have that I worked under—the phono code.

SC: Of all of these things that you've done, is horror hosting the most fun?

Probably. It's just fun to reminisce about some of the stupid things you do, these fun things. One night, when Jack Parr walked off the *Tonight Show*, I was doing a radio show on WIL in St. Louis. The news guy told me, "Jack Parr just walked off the *Tonight Show*." So I came on the air, and I said, "You just heard the news story that Jack Parr has walked off the *Tonight Show*. Well, I've gotten a number of phone calls asking if there is any truth to the rumor that Jack Parr is going to come here and do a show at WIL, I don't know. I've been trying to reach my boss to find out if there's any truth to that rumor. But to the best of my knowledge, I know nothing about it."

So then my boss calls. He says, "Fantastic! Milk it!" He was great. He was the most fun guy I ever worked for. So now I come on the air half an hour later, and I said, "Boy, I'm not sure what shift he's going to work … if he's coming here." You know, I just kept building the story. The next morning, there's a story in the paper about the possibility of Jack Parr coming to work for WIL. Oh, man…we used to do things like that.

We did it with records too. When I was a music disc jockey, I could take a record and make it a hit on a Saturday afternoon, sell 50,000 copies in Chicago. I mean, I couldn't if it wasn't in the grooves, you know? But if it was a halfway decent record … I would come on the air and say, in the next half hour, I'm going to play a brand new record by Joe Pizattz. And boy, this record is just fantastic! You're really going to like it. And now, in 15 minutes, I say, don't forget, in the next 15 minutes, you'll hear that new hit by Joe Pizattz. And by the time you play it, it's already a hit.

Now you put it on the air and you say, here it is, you know? And … nothing happens. So the minute the record ends, you say, "Folks, please stop calling the radio station. I will play that record again in the next 45 minutes. But please stop calling." So now, the phones start to ring. No one's called … But you could make a hit record that way. That was a kick too.

MM: At one point you were beginning to talk about a WJRT reunion…

Yeah, I went to a reunion there several years ago. They had a little clip of Christopher Coffin. But nobody even recognized me there in the group or asked if I would say a few words, because I would have. But it's different management and a whole different ownership. I don't know who owns it now. When I worked there, it was Knight-Ridder. It was WRJT Incorporated. One of the WJRT hierarchy bought it. They tried to hire me at one time to be program director there, but I was making a living. I really didn't want to do that. I didn't want to go to work for a station.

MM: They're an ABC affiliate now.

Well, they were an ABC affiliate then. But, they weren't an O&O (Owned and Operated), I'm sure. The ownership of stations changes, as you know, pretty rapidly.

MM: And of course, there's all this consolidation…Has that affected things?

Yeah, oh God. Pretty soon there'll be three people, three organizations in the whole world that we will work for, and that'll be it. And it'll probably all be Wal-Mart.

SC: You were talking earlier about the influence of radio during your childhood. When was the first time you got an inkling this is what I want to do?

Let me tell you something, it's strange you should ask. And it's strange I might have an answer for you. It'd be strange if I didn't, right? Okay. I remember one time when I was a kid. I think my voice changed early. I answered the phone one day and this friend of my mother's said, "Reed, you have such a nice voice. You should be on the radio." And I thought, yes, I should.

I then got involved in radio when I was in high school. I went to high school in West Lafayette, Indiana. And Perdue's radio station, WBBA, the voice of Perdue, West Lafayette, Indiana, had a lot of dramatic programming. They had a program called *Lady Story Teller*, they had *Mathematics Serves You, Yore Indiana*—Y-O-R-E Indiana—and they had a weekly debate program called *Citizens of Tomorrow Speak*. I was a regular member of the debating thing. They would give me one side or the other of an argument, and I would always think of something to say.

But I also did the dramatic stuff: *Lady Story Teller, Mathematics Serves You*—mathematics turned dramatic—which was really kind of neat. One time I was scheduled on *Lady Story Teller*, and as I remember that went on the air probably 8 a.m., 8:30 a.m. We had a blizzard in West Lafayette. The buses weren't running, but I had to be on the air. And man, I hiked through that snow … and I mean it was a good two or three miles to the Perdue Hall of Music, where WBBA had their studios.

I showed up, and I was the only cast member who showed up. And John Henderson, who was the educational director and the director of this particular show, said, "Do you want to try to do all the characters?" And there were five. I only remember there was a cook, a cowboy and an old man. I don't remember what the other characters were. So I said, well, I'll try John. I mean this was radio! This was the big time, man! And I'm 14! And I'm going to do my best.

At any rate, I remember when I was the cook; I'd lean back and pat my belly. And when I was cowboy, I'd bow my legs, and when I was the old man, I'd kind of hunch over. I would have given anything to get a copy of that show. There was no tape; there was no wire. If you recorded something in those days, it was shellac—a lathe cutting into shellac on an aluminum base. I got through it, and everyone in the control booth was laughing his or her fanny off. But I got through it, 15 minutes! Oh, man! That was really fun!

But that's how it started, and that's what I wanted to do. Radio was what I wanted to do. I enjoyed theater. But I really liked radio, because it was extemporaneous. I loved what I did in radio. I would always be able to do any damn thing that I wanted to do. A friend of mine would be sitting in the studio, and say work some word into the next commercial. They sold a lot of ad lib commercials with me. I'd work from fact sheets and I'd always enjoy that. So I would get a kick out of amusing my friends by working in whatever word, sometimes a word you weren't supposed to use on the radio. But somehow, I would work it in to the point it was there. At any rate, we had a lot of fun with that. I enjoyed it, and that's how it started.

MM: What other stations did you work at? Give us a little background.

First station I worked at was an accident. I went to visit a friend of mine. He and I had written songs together. He was living in Battle Creek, Michigan, and I went up to visit. This was just after I had returned from Los Angeles City College. My father had died. I had left the University of New Mexico, where I was on a football scholarship, as a drama major. So I went up to visit my friend, Warren Barnes. I was in Battle Creek, sitting at a bar. I wasn't old enough to drink, but I looked older. I didn't have to glue on a goatee or anything.

I sitting in a bar waiting for him, talking with the bartender. There was some other fellow sitting at the bar, and the bartender said to him, "Did they ever replace that announcer that left your station?" And the guy said, "No, they're still looking for somebody." Well, my ears perked up. So when the guy left, I asked do you know that guy that just left, he looked familiar to me. "Naw, you probably recognize his voice. He's on WELL. Next morning, I asked my friend where are the WELL studios? I get directions to the wrong studio—to WBCK—and I got a job. WBCK was in the Security National Bank building. It was the only bank in Battle Creek that wasn't on a corner. And their slogan was: "Make the bank in the middle of the block your bank." That was their marketable difference!

I used to do a telephone quiz show at that station called *Shaffer's Culturized Quiz*. And Jack Shaffer was a legend in Michigan, and still is. He was in the bakery business. *Such Crust* was one of his breads. He also had racing boats, and his racing boat was called *Such Crust*. At any rate, he sponsored this program, *Shaffer's Culturized Quiz*. I would make calls and give people prizes. One night I'm doing this show, and I'm doing a commercial for Shaffer's Old Style Potato Bread. I hadn't seen the commercial before. I just flipped the page, and there it is: Shaffer's Old Style Potato Bread.

As I'm about to do the commercial, the program director's waving at me from inside. I punch the phone, I pick up the phone, and I am now listening to him give me the score of the final game of the *ABC Little World Series*, which was like a little league something or other. I'm holding the phone, I'm listening to him, I'm writing down the score and I'm reading this commercial. So I said, "Ladies, the next time you're at the grocery store, be sure to pick up a loaf of Shaffer's Old Stale Potato Bread." I went, "Awww ..." Jack Shaffer called; he thought it was the funniest thing he'd heard in his life. He sent me the biggest fruit and nut cake I've ever seen. Shaffer's Old "Stale" Potato Bread" ... oh boy!

But we survive those things. I'm still here, somehow or another. I got my start in Battle Creek, moved to Saginaw, then Albuquerque, and from Albuquerque to Houston, then from Houston to Chicago, to St. Louis, back to Chicago. I went back to Flint, with the advertising business, and then San Jose, Costa Rica. I did a two-hour radio show in English in San Jose. There must have been 8,000 people who knew what I was saying down there. Retirees, a few people studying English, and they loved my show. People would call me with English questions. It was kind of interesting. Yeah, it was fun. Yeah, it was a bunch of fun!

MM: Was that type of nomadic existence typical of voice artists?

Not voice talent, but radio. You see, in those days voice talent lived in New York, Chicago or LA. That was it. I mean that was it. But to get ahead in radio, you worked in a small market, then a little bigger market. Then a little bigger market. Always looking to work in a market where you made more money. I started in radio for $40 a week. When I went to work in Battle Creek, I was making $40 a week. Now even then, $40 a week did not buy a lot.

It was always a matter of making a little more money. I remember I went to St. Louis and I had a contract that gave me union scale as a guarantee against 15% of all the commercials in my shows. I mean, I made more money than I ever dreamed of in radio there. It was a great station. The ownership of that station consisted of really wonderful people to work for. They were great. I went out with the salesmen pitching all the time, because it was money in my pocket too.

So yeah, the nomadic existence was pretty typical of the broadcast business. Not only disc jockeys, I think news people. You know, you worked *here* until you could find a better job. There were a lot of jobs that were stepping-stone jobs. I left out Galveston. I was working in Houston at a good music station, playing Guy Lombardo and hating it. I get a call one day from the owner of a station in Galveston saying, "How would you like to live a little closer to the water?" I said what kind of music do you play? He says, "Whatever you want." I told him I'll be there.

MM: So the moves weren't always based on purely financial considerations.

Oh yeah. You had to have money to live. But when someone said, "Look, Sunday night you can play jazz"... Sure, I'd love to work for you. I mean, that was the sort of thing we did, because you wanted to do something you liked. I guess you could say I was a pioneer of rock and roll. I remember working at the station in Houston, when I was playing a rock and roll record. The station manager came in and took the tone arm off the record. He said, "Play something else." I mean, it was tough in those days. It wasn't a matter of what people wanted to hear. They thought they could get away with imposing their taste on people and you couldn't.

I mean, I was playing T-Bone Walker and Ruth Brown on the pop record shows when that was unheard of. But that's what people wanted to hear, you know, some of the rhythm and blues singers: Winona Harris and T-Bone Walker, Ruthie Brown. They made really good music.

One of my best friends, who lives in Tucson now, is Phil Chess. He and his brother Leonard really started recording blues and rhythm and blues with Chess, Checker, Argo and Cadet Records. And they did jazz, too, with people like Ahmed Jamal and Ramsey Lewis. But I mean, they did Lightnin' Hopkins and Chuck Berry and people like that, when pop jocks wouldn't play stuff like that. Those were Doris Day and Guy Mitchell days…and Mitch Miller. I've got a picture somewhere of Mitch and me comparing beards.

MM: The local deejay or TV host plugged into the community.

When you take a Clear Channel—or you take some of the other conglomerates that format radio out of Dallas—to 600 stations around the country, they plug in

station breaks, and they think that makes it local. Jack Carney, who was one of the most creative guys I ever worked with, did crazy things. One afternoon on WIL in St. Louis, around the time all of the factories were letting out, he said, "I went to the parking lot of one of the factories today and I put my card with a special phone number underneath the hood of a car. And if the person who has that card calls that number within the next 15 minutes, you will win $5,000." And traffic on the highways around St. Louis stopped! Everybody got out and lifted their hoods, looking for this card.

One morning Gary Owens, who was the morning man on that station, kept saying, "When I wind up my show this morning at nine o'clock, I'm going to give you the secret words worth $25,000 at Mercantile Trust Bank." And he kept promoting that all morning long. And at nine o'clock, when he went off the air, he went, "Okay, here are the secret words worth $25,000 dollars today at Mercantile Trust. The secret words are "Stick 'em up!'" Yeah, everybody knew it was a joke. The police didn't think it was very funny.

It was unreal. But we did things like that. It was fun. And now that's the sort of thing shock jocks do, only they do it in more of a shocking way, you know? We never tried to offend anybody. We did try to cause a little problem here and there … We tried to be seen; we tried to be heard.

When I got stuck with the rock-and-roll-has-got-to-go that we talked about, I had to find a way to entertain my audience while I played things they didn't love. You may not remember, but the style at that time for women was the chemise, which was the big and baggy look. So I started campaigning against women wearing potato sacks. And one of our disc jockeys, a fella named Ed Wilson, wore a suit that was probably a size 56. He was a big, big guy. So I would make personal appearances wearing one of his suits. You did whatever you could to … in those days we called it "to make noise." That's all you could hope to do is make a little noise.

MM: Again, the focus is local.

It's local; it's local. I really hate what has happened. There are companies that buy almost every station in a town. So there's one newsroom. And does it have to stay on its toes? No, they have no competition. One newsroom feeds news to all stations. I'm not a big fan of Clear Channel. Radio lost the local connection. Look at the stations that carry Rush Limbaugh and Dr. Laura and Mike Savage. One after another, people who have no connection with the local market, none. And when they take phone calls, "Here's so-and-so from Peoria." It doesn't mean a damn thing to the people who live in Peoria. Who cares that somebody finally got through?

There was a Bozo show. I can't think of the guy's name. He had been doing it for many years, really nice fellow. And he did some other things at the station. I think he probably did some other programming. But the Bozo thing was quite popular. I know there was a time when your child was born, you had to make an appointment to get on the Bozo show. And now I'm sure those things have passed. We've lost the feeling that "this is my local station." I think I can better equate it with radio, than with TV, because TV always carried a lot of network programming.

It used to be *that* was your station, and here are your friends. When I was in radio there were times when I'd open a phone book and call people at random and ask them to listen to my show. I mean that's gone. There is no local connection anymore. I mean, we used to do remotes. We'd do a remote from the car dealer and that sort of thing. Or at WIL we'd do what we called "Splatter Platter Parties." We used to go to a public pool and play records. And kids would pay to come and swim and dance and listen to music. And the disc jockey got some money from that. It was a big deal. That's gone. As a deejay, you really wanted to get out and meet people, and have people know you, because that's how you build an audience. Not just by playing records. That was a very, very big part of it. I mean, we did a lot of things to "make noise."

But TV stations have really gotten away from that. It so happens that some local stations really do try. I think they try, but only with their news. They don't do anything that's creative, and all of the news runs at the same time. I think the local scene is gone. It's gone. Look at CBS, and everything they own. Viacom, you know? They compete with themselves. And that has become a problem. I really disagree with Michael Powell of the FCC, who would allow three people to own every station in the country. And I just think that's terrible.

It used to be that broadcasters owned broadcast stations. It used to be that a guy who started off working for the station wound up buying a piece of the station. And then when the owner died, he bought the rest of it. He was a broadcaster. He was somebody who grew up in the broadcasting business, and he continued. It may have been that he was in the seed business, or his father was in the seed business, and they bought a radio station to advertise their seed. But they became broadcasters. I don't want to say "mom and pop" operations, because that's not what I mean. They were broadcasters. They were professional broadcasters, because they wanted to bring the news. They wanted to bring entertainment to their market.

As we went through the contraction of ownership, and as we saw people bidding big bucks to buy out one station after another, and trying to figure out how to operate them more cheaply, this led to the Wal-Mart broadcasting system we have today. It's operated as cheaply as possible. And in many cases, these people don't even get benefits. They have no health care; they have nothing. They're there for a while, and then they leave. They haven't built any equity. Those of us that started in the broadcasting business really weren't doing it for the money, though we needed money to live. Those who were successful made some pretty good money. There are some people who have done very well. There are some others who get into for a while, and they do okay. But they never get past that bridge to where they're making a living. And they think, "Someday I may want to raise a family."

What would you do if you were in charge?

You'd have to ask the guy I would hire. I wouldn't want to do it the same way. I'd like to put together half a dozen creative people and brainstorm the thing. And we would put together some neat shtick. My job would be just to bring it together. And I'd love to do that. Boy, I'd do that tomorrow ... maybe even today!

Experiment in Chiller
Chilly Billy Cardille (Bill Cardille)
Interviewed by Sandy Clark (2004)

Bill Cardille's career as a professional broadcaster spans well over a half century, beginning at WDAD radio in Indiana, Pennsylvania. He soon moved into television, enjoying work as an announcer from the early 1950s. In 1957, Cardille was the first voice heard on WIIC-TV (later WPXI) Channel 11 in Pittsburgh as he signed on the air for its first broadcast day. He served as host and announcer for a number of programs including wrestling, news and the dance party program *The 6 O'Clock Hop*, earning a reputation as an suave jack-of-all-trades at the station.

In 1963 WIIC premiered *Chiller Theater*, with Cardille providing standard voiceover introductions for the movies. Within a year, he was in front of the camera as on-air host, where he remained until the final *Chiller Theater* broadcast on New Year's Eve 1983. Cardille's style straddled the worlds of the "straight" movie host and the more ghoulish standard of the familiar monster movie presenter. He generally dressed in a tuxedo or dress suit and played the role of chummy announcer. But he addressed his audience in front of a rear-projected laboratory or from within the confines of an elaborate castle set.

Over time, the show brought in a colorful cast of characters that added to the atmosphere of general weirdness you get whenever you mix monsters and ghouls with a guy dressed like a Las Vegas casino greeter. Terminal Stare (Donna Rae), Norman the Castle Keeper (Norman Elder), Stefan the Castle Prankster (Steve Luncinski), and Georgette the Fudgemaker (Bonnie Sue Barney) became regular members of the *Chiller* family in the late 1970s.

Cardille has been recognized as an influence on several celebrities, including Tom Savini, who practiced his monster make-up skills on the show, and Joe Flaherty, who credits *Chiller Theater* as the basis for Count Floyd and the popular "Monster Chiller Horror Theatre" skits on *SCTV*. But his most lasting cultural contribution was providing inspiration to Pittsburgh resident George Romero. A *Chiller* broadcast of *The Last Man on Earth* (1964) spurred Romero and his creative partners to make the horror movie game-changer, *Night of the Living Dead*, in 1968.

Chilly Billy returned to WPXI-TV 11 on October 28, 1998 for a Halloween special that doubled as his final farewell to television. He hosted *Night of the Living Dead*, with special guest George Romero joining him to reminisce about the landmark film and about Cardille's career.

Could you talk a little about the early days of Chiller Theater*?*

Chiller Theater first began on Saturday nights in 1963. WIIC television was the NBC affiliate in Pittsburgh. The call letters were changed years later to WPXI. I'm a staff announcer, always, having spent over 40 years at Channel 11. But when I started the show, I did wrestling every Saturday night live from 6:00 p.m. to 7:30 p.m. And then they would tear down the ring and set up for *Chiller Theater*. And I did the weather at 11:00 p.m.

I decided for *Chiller Theater* to wear a tuxedo. I was doing the Jerry Lewis Telethon every year. I thought people get tired of a character, but they don't get tired of a person. I mean, if I were to dress as a monster with all kinds of make-up, or as Ygor, or a hunchback, or Frankenstein, something similar to those, people would get tired of that. But if you appear as yourself…

So I went on as Bill Cardille. I wore a tuxedo. I eventually got a tuxedo sponsor. I would come out every Saturday night, and I would say, "Good evening, I'm Bill Cardille. Welcome to *Chiller Theater*." That would be right after I changed from doing the weather, and five minutes later I opened up *Chiller Theater*. Well, after the first three or four weeks, I came up with a different name. I always had alliteration. "This is Bill Cardille…" then I would string along seven words that began with "cill" and tie it in. One night the sportsman, Red Donnelly, said on the air, "Now stayed tuned for *Chiller Theater* and Chilly Billy." That night, we were on live till about three in the morning. We'd go to a restaurant after the show every Saturday night and a couple of people said to me, "Hey, Chilly Billy!"

And that week, I had about two people say to me, "Chilly Billy!" So I went to the sports director the next week and I said, listen, Red, would you mind calling me Chilly Billy? I know you have something for an introduction. But if you don't mind, I've had comments on that, and it sort of ties in—Chilly Billy with Chiller Theater. He said his son, who was 14 years old—Sean was his name, Sean Donnelly—came up with the idea Chilly

Billy. So it stuck and it became famous. People say, "I hate to call you 'Chilly'. I say hey, that's alright, it's better than mister. So I've had that name now, Chilly Billy, since 1963. I opened up a travel agency that went for 20 years, Chilly Billy Travel. I'm on radio, still. I'll always be Chilly Billy, and I don't find it offensive at all. I think it's great.

With all those folks calling you Chilly Billy, did you feel closer to your audience in the early days than you do now? How close are you to the audience?

You know, I've always been close with my audience. I have three children. And I remember my wife saying to me that I have a very difficult time, especially when I was younger, saying *no*. My wife said to me, "You know, Bill, you've been out for 33 straight nights. And guess what? You haven't brought in one cent. And we miss you." Now, I was working at the TV station maybe five or six days a week. It dawned on me I'm going everywhere, since I enjoy meeting people and I like what I'm doing. And at heart, I'm a ham, always have been. And anyway, I started to think my wife is right. So I cut back to maybe 15 nights a month.

I met a lot of people. And it's amazing how many people come back to you years later. I've been in communications now over 50 years. But it's amazing how many people come back and say, "Remember me? I met you in 1965 at the drive-in theater late at night." Or "I remember you when you spoke at a communion breakfast. Remember when you spoke at St. Agatha's?" You build up a following without even realizing it. There was no motive; I just like people. I couldn't say no and I went to a lot of places and did a lot of things.

Do any of those fans stand out for you? Do you remember anybody who's gone on to do something really special?

Oh, a lot of them. Tom Savini, the make-up man. Tom used to come up to our show. The director Jack Blayroe brought him up at the time. Tom was a 13-year-old kid and he hung around. Barry Sullivan, who did *Pyro* (1964) and many, many movies, turned out to be a good friend of mine. First of all he was a terrific guy. And there was a guy named Joe Balasco. I don't know if you know Joe Balasco, but he did make-up when he was a senior in high school. We had an annual parade. We had a big, big

display. The *Chiller* float was in it and I was in it. I sat in an electric chair. But Joe Balasco did a make-up of the *Pyro* monster; he started five in the morning. And Barry Sullivan came over to this 17-year-old kid and said, "Your make-up is better than what we had in the movie." And it was. That's amazing. And we're talking 1964, years ago. This make-up that he made for this kid had one straw that came out of his mouth. It was a miracle he could breathe through or drink through that make-up for seven hours. It was fantastic. Balasco later did make-up in Hollywood. He had a studio there. He did a lot of movies. And then, 15 years ago, I get this call. He has his own school in Florida. He's done very well. But there are a lot of stories like that.

George Romero and some of the boys at Carnegie-Mellon were watching *Chiller Theater*, and he said, "We can make a *Chiller* movie better than that!" He was watching Vincent Price in *The Last Man on Earth* (1964). And they wrote *Night of the Living Dead* (1968). George, and some of the people associated with the movie, called me. I said no, I don't want to make a movie. They had movie cameras. But finally they said, "It'll be fast, it'll

Voice announcer Bill Cardille signed on WIIC-TV 11 (later WPIX) on September 1, 1957.

be quick," you know? So I did the movie. And they got the idea from watching *Chiller Theater*.

George is a good friend. And my oldest daughter Lori starred in the third movie, *Day of the Dead* (1985). She's the only female in it, won several awards—best actress for science fiction in Spain and in France. And she's a very good friend of George Romero. And that's how some strange things happen. When he cast her, he didn't know she was my daughter.

Tell me about your family and friends. What do they think of all of this—the horror host part in particular?

My kids went to bed. They didn't stay up. But I had a movie projector and I'd take the movies home. I previewed every movie I ever ran. And that's for 21 years. I had my own index cards; they were 10-by-12. I had a screening room at the station and I would write where the cuts would be. And that turned out pretty well. The station let me schedule the movies, eventually.

We'd buy, like, 100 movies in a Warner Bros. package. Most stations would say you had to run all hundred to get your money back. You're allowed to run them three times, say, in two years, three years or four years, whatever the contracts said. But sometimes there'd be, say, 15 moves that were so bad, I'd say, I don't want to run them. And they'd say okay. I mean, that's good management. Mr. Sheldon Weaver and Mr. Bob Mortenson, Bob was the general manager; Sheldon Weaver was the program manager. They were nice to me and gave me a lot of freedom. So, it was nice.

Did you audition for this? Did you fall into it? Were you a host by accident?

That's a good question. You know, in the early days of television, the more versatile you were the more valuable you were. Luckily for me, I did everything. I did play-by-play sports on the education station in town, WQED. I did that for over 10 years; maybe 15 years. I did basketball, football and track. I did it all, because I went to college on an athletic scholarship. But the station permitted me to do that. I did wrestling; I did game shows. I did the news, the sign-off news. I did weather. I did everything except sing the national anthem. And the only reason I didn't sing the national anthem—they never asked.

I was in nightclubs and I was the opening act for, like, Jerry Vale at the Holiday House here in Pittsburgh, a big nightclub. I opened for Helen O'Connell too. I did all of that. I was on the air in Pittsburgh starting in 1957. And in about 1962 management came to me, because at that time I was doing wrestling, and it was very popular. And I was doing *The Money Movie*, and it was very popular. I was a staff announcer.

Ed Herlihy was one of my heroes. He was an NBC announcer and did *Movietone News*; he was a big man. I sat with him one time in New York when they were doing *Kraft Theater* live. And I said to him, "You do *Kraft*. Do you do any other shows?" He says, "I'm a staff announcer. Remember, NBC will always be here. But shows come and go. So always, if you can, be a staff announcer." So I was always a staff announcer.

But luckily, most of my shows didn't go away, they stayed on. I did *Chiller* a long time, wrestling a long time, *Money Movie* a long time. I was very, very fortunate. So when they wanted to do a late-night show at 11:30, what happened? This is a true story and … weird. When I was young, I took a lot of chances. But I didn't know I was taking chances. I just didn't like to do things on the air too straight. On Saturday afternoons, I'm in the booth. They had a pan of water; they had "Chiller Theater" lettering in the pan of water. They put a live camera on it. The water, disrupted with fingers, gave a rippling effect. And I opened the microphone in the booth and said over the picture, "It's Saturday afternoon and welcome to *Chiller Theater*. Today's feature is *Frankenstein* (1931), with Boris Karloff. Here's our movie." I did about three inserts. Next week: "Good afternoon, welcome to *Chiller Theater*. Here's *Dracula* (1931), with Bela Lugosi."

About the fourth week, with the temperature outside about 80 degrees, summertime, I assumed nobody was watching. There are three stations in Pittsburgh. I figured, who's watching? I'm going to have some fun. So the director is sitting in the other booth, with a couple of engineers. I said I want some reverb! When I say "Good afternoon," I'll raise my hand. They could see me, you know, through the glass. I'll go like this (*raises hand*) and cue them. And it was "Goooood afternoooooooon ... Welcome to ... CHILLER ... THEATER ... Today's feature is *Frankenstein*, starring Boris Karloff!"

Then I would say, "Sheldon Weaver—the boss—as a guest star. Tom Makowitz—the engineer on duty—has a feature role. This is the movie that defies description!" Or something like that. "Here, if you can hold your breath ... 10 seconds ... you did it ... here's *Frankenstein*!" I ad-libbed it. I did that for about three weeks. The guys would break up. They'd take a cut. I didn't know it at the time, but I got in the way of the movie. I'd say watch out! There's someone behind the tree! I found out people don't like to hear that.

So what happened after about three weeks, my boss, he was from Nashville, called me in. And he says (*Southern accent*), "Bill, I heard you on the *Chiller Theater* show for the last three weeks." (*Laughs*) "Yes, Mr. Weaver." I am thinking, oh here it comes. He says, "I like it. You know what? We got some ratings. That is really getting a rating." He was lovely. He says, "I get these movies for a hundred dollars. I just threw them on to fill time! Why don't you think of an idea? What could you do if we put it on Saturday night at 11:30 p.m.?" I said let me think about it. So I thought about it, and I thought a couple of the stations in town tried chiller movies. But they didn't last. One was an Igor, the other was a Doctor somebody, you know, and they didn't last at all. And I said I gotta be me. I've got to be myself. So that's where I came up with the concept.

They got an artist who was from Nashville who was working at the Pittsburgh Playhouse, and he designed a laboratory. So I got a smock, put a smock on. First of all, I did an introduction from a stool. I liked working on a stool. And I ad-libbed an introduction for a double feature. After I did that I got some dry ice, and I had some beakers, and I did a thing with water. It was just dry ice, but I put some dye in there, some food coloring. And I drank it saying (*mimes Jekyll and Hyde transformation*), "I'll be back!"

I did a couple of things, and I gave my conception of what the show should be. I don't want to make it too long now, but I did that. Now a couple of announcers were watching in the other studio. You know, when you're talking to a camera, you don't know how you're getting any response. So they leave and I leave and I figure, what the heck. If it happens, it happens. It didn't really bother

"Chilly Billy's Vamp" was used to close the *Chiller* show for many years. This picture sleeve 45 rpm was released on the Vampire label and backed with "Strange But True Tales," featuring vocals by John Yelland.

101

Chiller Theatre Family

Left to right: Terminal Stare, Sister Susie, Norman The Castle Keeper, Chilly Billy Cardille, Stefan The Castle Prankster

me, you know? I'm happy doing what I was doing. I figured it would last about 13 weeks. I didn't know what to expect. So I did the opening, did the show. And from day one it just built and built and built. And it lasted 21 years. I had a blast.

Eventually, after two years, they let me pick a cast. My first one was a guy I saw in the wrestling audience. If he had been born 20 years earlier, he would have been a star in science fiction movies. He had a birth defect. It was the deformed face with the bugged-out eyes. But he was the softest, nicest person. I said to him people might make fun of you. And he said, "That's alright. I'm a survivor. People make fun of me anyway." He came from Steubenville, which was about 60 miles away. He used to hitchhike to Pittsburgh to watch wrestling and hitchhike back. His name was Norman Elder.

I said, "Norman, I'm thinking of doing *Chiller Theater* and I'm going to put a cast together. You won't speak, but you'll be the Castle Keeper." He would take a bus every year to Hollywood to try to break into the movies, and he'd come back to Pittsburgh. He had nothing. It could be a movie in itself. But he would write scripts. He says, "I want to be a writer." And to be honest, I read the scripts and (*shrugs*) I told him to just keep writing. He always wrote a good part for himself. He was a nice kid. He died several years ago of a heart attack at 50.

Then I ran into a girl who ran a spa. Her name was Donna Dalinski. I made her Terminal Stare. She didn't say anything, but she had a body better than anybody you could think of. She dressed in a long gown. Her gimmick was she didn't say anything, but looked "terminal." She would wind up, and she would bump to the left and to the right—and we had flash powder at the time—a big flash powder explosion would happen. And sometimes the midget (Stevie, another guy I hired) would end up in a tree.

The way I hired Stevie was this. We were in Vegas, my wife and I. We were standing in line for a show and somebody tugged on my jacket. I turned around; I didn't see anyone. And he said, "Down here." He was 19 years old. He said, "Hi, Bill. Hi, Chilly! I'm Steve Luncinski." And I say hi. He says, "I watch you all the time on *Chiller*." Oh, nice seeing you, Steve. Call me sometime.

We see the show. Three o'clock in the morning, the phone rings. Three o'clock ... and I pick up the phone, figuring something's happened to the kids back in Pittsburgh. I think bad things. I pick it up and I hear, "Hi, Chilly! This is Steve. You told me to call you sometime." (*Laughs*) I didn't know what time it was. I say not at three in the morning! Anyway, when I had to put the cast together I thought of him as the Castle Prankster. He would appeal to the kids.

Then over the years I had two other cast members, two girls, the first of which was Georgette the Fudge Maker—she was Miss Pennsylvania and was very attractive, very nice and very young. She was for the younger men on the show. And she talked. We dressed her as a farmer—Georgette the farmer. She made fudge. Eventually she came out with her own fudge! She made good money, too. And then we had Sister Susie. She was sophisticated. She was very nice. My daughter picked her. She was probably the most successful model in Pittsburgh. So I put the family together. And rather than have them memorize anything I would set a situation. I'd say, "We'll do this, we'll do that, we'll do this." And they did it. It was just ... it was a lot of fun. And I used maybe a one-on-one insert. Then I used two on the next insert. I usually wrote for four inserts per movie, plus the opening, middle and a close.

And you learned the hard way that you don't get in the way of the movie. You don't make fun of your movies. If you don't like a product, you don't make fun of it.

I never made fun of my movies. Now somebody today said to me, "I remember you one time apologizing for the movie." And I did. I remember the movie. I can't think of the title right now, but it was a bad movie. It was one of those situations I got into late in the series. And I ran the movie. I said enjoy it, but it's not what you usually see.

Some nights the movies were so short, maybe 70 or 80 minutes, that they'd let me run three movies. And then sometimes I'd go on in prime time. When 3-D tried to make a comeback, there'd be a sponsor, a store, where you'd go pick up your 3-D glasses. You'd pick them up and put them on. We ran Vincent Price's *House of Horrors* (sic: *House of Wax, 1953*). I tried to stay current.

Also on my writing, I never made fun of individuals ... ever! I never made fun of individuals. Instead of saying, "Terry Bradshaw, the quarterback of the Steelers," I'd just say "The Steelers." I remember one time when the Steelers weren't any good, when they won maybe three games a year, I said I want to show you the highlights of the 1966 season for the Pittsburgh Steelers. Our *Chiller Theater* staff, crack staff that it is, put it together. Now, are you ready? I want to show you the highlights of the Steelers. Are you comfortable? Sit down, because here they are! The director punched black; punched back up. I said did you enjoy them? (*Laughs*) That's the highlights of this season. Now in case you missed it, here we go again! Boom, like that, and back up to wide. Terry Bradshaw, though, dated my daughter. (*Laughs*) She used to do the telethon with me.

I believe in what my dad believed in with me, to expose me to a lot of things in life as a child. So when you grow up you'll be able to make a better selection of what you want to do in life. And also, by being exposed to as many things as possible—going to a courtroom or going to a hospital, or things like that—you won't spin your wheels when you're in a position in life, as a late age teenager or something. You have an idea of what you want to do.

For instance, my oldest daughter, Lori Anne, was a runway model at 14. She was a model for the Earl Wheeler modeling school in Pittsburgh. She was tall. They used her picture for their ads. She did commercials at 16. So when she went to college at Carnegie-Mellon and majored in drama, she had all of that behind her and she wasn't frustrated. She graduated college at 20. When she went to New York, she wasn't wrapped up with being a model or doing the runway thing because she had already done that and been exposed to it. She wanted to be a serious actress and get on Broadway, which is what she did. So what my dad did worked for me and it worked for her.

How long were you broadcasting live? Or were you ever live, before you went to tape?

Tape wasn't invented when we started. It's an interesting story. In the early days, in the early 1960s, everything was live. I did wrestling 6:00 p.m. to 7:30 p.m. I went to church from 7:30 p.m. to 8:15 p.m. every Saturday night. It was only five minutes from our station. I came back, had a light dinner, maybe a sandwich and a cup of coffee. Nine o'clock they would let me— when tape did come out—tape two bits. That's it. They gave me an hour's tape to tape those two bits. And I had that tape, believe it or not, for a year. People will not know this, but *that* tape I used every Saturday for just two bits. And I'll tell you why. It had bullet holes in it! And I'd say I need another tape! But in those days you only had one tape machine, too!

I used to have characters, like Captain Bad—Doer of Dirt, Defender of Delinquents. I had long johns and I had stars painted on them. I had a YMCA towel for a cape. And I would come out and be the defender of delinquents, doer of dirt. Then we'd do a bit. And I'm the only announcer on duty. I was also running the announcer's

Skull in hand and dressed for the prom.

103

booth, answering the phone, you know, doing the show and doing it live.

I did Maurice the Magnificent, and it was a takeoff on Percy Dovetails (sic—*Percy Dovetonsils*), if you ever saw Ernie Kovacs. It was advice to the lovelorn. I painted a moustache, a fake moustache, and long sideburns. I had a silk top hat and had a cigarette holder. I used to smoke in those days. And I had all kinds of fake rings from the five and dime. And I go (*lisping*), "Well good evening, you silly savages! Welcome to *Chiller Theater*. Oh, my! I'm Maurice the Matchmaker." One fella says to me, "My brother's name is Maurice and you're ruining his love life!" (*Laughs*) I'll never forget that. I would write advice to the lovelorn. I'd write my own letters and answer 'em, you know.

And where I got the words "silly savage" was from Michael Landon on *Bonanza*. We did a telethon together. His partner Hoss (Dan Blocker) came in too. He was my kind of guy. He was a whack-o too, very funny guy. He had a good sense of humor. He said, "You know, what we do sometimes, the two of us, we go out and a critic will be interviewing us, and then we start, like you do …" He saw me do Maurice the Matchmaker. "He says (*lisping*), "We'd say, oh stop it, you silly savage!" So I picked up silly savage from him. He said they played the role, just to have fun. I mean, you know, in this business you have to have some fun … in any business. And then the critic wouldn't know they were just monkeying around.

So anyway, sometimes life imitates art and vice versa. We had a great time and management never stopped me. We had a big violin intro. We'd pan from the lilies over to me. And then I had the Love Book, a big book. And then I'd drop the book and you'd see silly Billy. And then I would do the bit and it was funny. But I'll tell you, honestly, it really took a lot of intestinal fortitude to do that. But I had fun.

And we were live. I did all the bits live, the easier ones. But I was allowed to do two inserts. I'd sit on a stool and interview somebody—Barbara Feldon, Johnny Carson or anyone. I'd interview them, you know. Or I would write a skit. For instance, once we had a girl on *Ironside*, and I did that skit in a wheelchair. But I didn't make fun of the wheelchair so much. My character was *Tin*side or something like that. And there was a pretty girl named Barbara on that show. I can't think of her last name. We did about two minutes. I didn't keep the bits long. I found in the beginning that when I did bits, like, Mr. Magnificent or the horoscopes, I did three or four minutes. It would be too long. I found out the best thing is short and to the point. And I'd try to do it two minutes.

What do think people liked about this? What made it so popular?

I had 30 different bits that I wrote from, and I didn't repeat the bits every week. I had a lot of trivia, Strange But True stories. I did Mr. Magnificent. I prognosticated the future. So here's what I would do—opening, middle and close. The close I would call Chiller-isms. People would write me mail and I would read mail or talk about things, interview Vic Damone, maybe. He'd have a late show or something like that.

I did eight bits all together, four in each show; I tried to mix it up. I had, like I say, 30 different inserts that I could do. It was easier that I didn't do the same thing every week, you know. You might see Mr. Magnificent twice a month. Then we had Chilly Billy Quickies. That would be quick jokes with a skull laughing in between. That could run 40 seconds. You don't wanna go long. I don't like mic hogs on radio, and I don't like camera hogs in television. Now, I'm guilty sometimes of going long. But it just turned out that way, you know.

What jumps out at you? What were some of the best movies you showed over the years?

The classics, without a doubt, stand out. *Circus of Horrors* (1960) is one that stands out. I don't know if you watched that one. It featured The Billy Smart Circus. And Anton Diffring was the star of it. He was a plastic surgeon. It's one of the best. And the theme song, "Wish On a Star," had an organ background. But because of our show, they re-released that record and sold, like, 10,000 records. It's a terrific movie, *Circus of Horrors*. But I liked all of the classics. I think the Wolf Man series was terrific. It's still good. *Frankenstein*, *Dracula*, Kevin McCarthy's *Invasion of the Body Snatchers* (1956), Barbra Steele. The English horror movies are great, too. Christopher Lee, Peter Cushing, Vincent Price. The black and white classics still work today. But the graphics are better today.

It works if you don't get in the way of your product and you don't knock your product; it helps if you have a dry sense of humor. You don't go for a Three Stooges style of humor. Once I started on my show and I had success, some of the other stations in town had *Charlie Chan Theater*. They did this; they did that. And they all fell by the wayside. What makes it successful … if you could bottle something, it would be great. But you can't bottle success. You hope for the best. And you grab it, ride it and enjoy it.

What interesting things did people send you?

Oh, I had so many. I had mail sent to me where they just drew a face and sent it to "TV 11." I had a lot of artists. Once a month I'd do different things on art. I started, for instance, Mess World. We did Miss America on NBC, and right after *Chiller Theater* came on. So I came up with the idea of the ugliest girl in the world—Mess World. And I did Mess World. The first year I did it, I did it with artwork, and the picture made international headlines! It was a drawing of a girl born in 1842; it was just a skeleton and straggly hair. It was Mess World of 1840 whatever, you know. And it was ugly! But I must have had 200 entries! That's a lot for a Pittsburgh station.

So anyway, I started putting in live people after that and I ran that for maybe eight weeks. Hot pants were in, so I'd get maybe four or eight girls and I would do the bit. "Here comes the four-bag girl; she comes from the lower Labonie area. She was born in 1917, formerly married to Count Dracula." I'd do bits tying in to our characters like that, just made up goofy stuff. "Her birth sign is Aquarius, she's a wet duck." And they would be nice. But you know what? We would draw on their face; this was with crayon, maybe a scar here. And you know, people complained. I didn't get a lot. I'm talking about the 1960s, early 1970s. But I stopped drawing. I just said, "Put a Band-aid on here, a piece of cloth here." You know, gauze. But we did that live.

When that became so popular, we went to a local racetrack called The Meadows. And we'd pick three fillies—win, place and show. And they'd be beautiful. There were about 20 girls in it. And I mean, they were really nice, hard to pick. I did Miss U.S.A. in Ohio, Pennsylvania, West Virginia. I never judged. I learned early in the career, you don't judge. I did baby contests when I didn't know any better. I judged beauty contests. Then I emceed or I had other people judge. I still won't judge anything. You can't win. It's like being an umpire. Safe! (*Laughs*)

Who were some of your early professional influences?

Ed Herlihy, he was just fabulous to me. I was 21 or 22 at the time. He

105

was terrific and he gave me some great advice. Did you ever hear of the name Bud Collier? He was Superman on the radio. Bud Collier had hosted the quiz show in early TV, *Beat the Clock*, I thought he was classic. He was great. He was really handsome and he had a good voice. And he was down to earth. When I first came to Pittsburgh in either 1957 or 1958, WQED, the public broadcasting station, needed a fundraiser. Our management was tight with them, so they got Bud Collier to come in. They got me; I was picked from Channel 11. And they also selected an up-and-coming guy who was doing a game show called *Who Do You Trust?* His name was Johnny Carson. So I go to the station. I don't know Johnny Carson. The three of us were there; we did a show together. Johnny was really nice. We were all young, same age, you know. We had some fun on that show. And it was great to meet Bud Collier. I told him, "I really respect what you've done." But he was humble. Most people I've met and known and respected in the business have been professional and humble.

I did a teenage show for years. People whose music I play now on radio, I interviewed many of them: Tony Bennett, Johnny Mathis, the list goes on and on. We were live then, and they'd come in and plug their records. Not to mention any names … one fella, in the middle of the song, he stopped and started picking his nose. And the director got off him. I didn't see him; I was waiting for the next act. So the director told his female manager to get out of the control room and take him with you and don't ever come back. Now he was only 19 or 20 years old at the time. Eight months later they came back and apologized, and we put him back on. I know he must have been having a bad day. But he sounded a lot like Johnny Mathis.

What were your feelings about doing a taped versus a live program?

You know, we eventually taped the show and I'll tell you why. In the Vietnam War, one of our directors went over there with NBC, to be a director and to set up a television station. After the Vietnam fiasco, he came back. His name was Lynn Covey. He was a good director and a nice person. He had a family, and there was nothing for him to do. So my boss came to me and says, "Listen, I'd like to bring Lynn back on our staff." He says, "But I don't have the budget for it. But if you will tape *Chiller Theater*... Bill, if you tape your show I can get the money ... I can put him back on the staff. It's up to you."

So I went to Lynn and I told him the set up. I liked him and I thought he was a great guy. He says, "Gee, that'd be nice. I can't get anything. I've been everywhere." So I went to Mr. Weaver, "That'd be fine, you know, we'll do it." So we did it. And in the meantime, six weeks later, he got a job offered him and he left. But we set up the taping and we stayed taping.

But you know what? It gave me freedom. It gave me a chance, on Saturday nights, to do nightclubs. So I worked at the V.I.P. clubs as a guest emcee every Saturday night for about four or five years. I did other things. It worked out real good. I mean, it gave me a break. I taped the shows Saturday night right after wrestling, usually. And then I would get out about nine, nine-thirty and I would head to the nightclub. I also had a chance to perform at nightclubs if I wanted and all that other stuff.

When you asked that question, I was thinking of a couple of wild stories. Every Halloween, I would have the people come up dressed in costumes. I never asked for permission. I just thought maybe six to eight people would come. We had one guard on duty; one cop. Well, it was like a telethon. They had to stay in the parking lot. We had bleachers left over from the wrestling show, and they sat in the bleachers. And every insert, I'd have maybe 10 or 12 people dressed in costume, and they'd stand behind me while I'd do a bit. Well, after about four years, we had to direct traffic. It just got out of hand.

One night a young kid was there dressed as Dracula, and I felt sorry for him. When I say young kid, I mean probably 24 or 25. And he seemed ... within himself. After you got on, you had to leave. Well, he got on and he went back up and sat down. But I didn't want to ask him to leave. We had to get everybody on, because, you know, that's the way I felt about it. Anyway, I put him on for two or three inserts, and he just stood there. I felt he was so lonely or forlorn. I said, you know, you've been on three times. I hate to say it, but you have to leave. Well, he left.

The next day I found out that when he left the station, he drove to downtown Pittsburgh; there's a sharp, blind curve, and he went over. And the car was in a spot you couldn't see, right in downtown Pittsburgh. And the next day they found him dead, with a broken neck, in a Dracula outfit. His parents called. That was tough, a very difficult situation. Who would have thought?

And also, we had Tiny Tim appear. Tiny Tim was a good guest. I felt sorry for Tiny. I really did. I thought,

you know, he was an unusual act. But he was just trying to make a living. So the police, they used to ride around the north side where the station is. They'd come in and watch me do some things, you know. Maybe grab a cup of coffee or something. So they're up there and here's Tiny Tim! It's about one-thirty in the morning. And I said, Tiny ... the next insert, I want you to play the ukulele. He couldn't play the ukulele, you know. And this was before he got married, too. But he was nice. He sits there, strumming. I've got a crew of about six. They're laughing; we're having a great time. He was a great guy.

So, one of the policemen came over to me. He says, "Hey, Bill. Do you think Tiny would come out?" I never told this story before. "Do you think he would go out to the parking lot? We'll put him on the police radio, and he'll sing 'Tiptoe Through the Tulips.'" So I said hey, yeah! What do you say, Tiny? He says (*high voice*), "Oh! I'd love to do it!" So we go out in the parking lot. It's a summer night, beautiful, about 70 degrees. They open up the police band ... they could have been fired. Oh! They

Bill Cardille, Sandy Clark and Michael Monahan swap stories of the joy of local television.

open up and they said, "Here's a special treat to all the police." And on the police band you hear (*singing à là Tiny Tim*) "Tiptoe Through the Tulips…" (*Laughs*) I still get comments on that. That was just so much. But I had a lot of good times like that. A lot of things happened, a lot of them funny. But you know I do want to say one thing with television: it's a powerful medium. So is radio. In radio, the difference is they listen to every word that you say. In television, they really don't know that you have a voice.

I started on radio in college and in high school. And after television, people say to me, "Gee, I didn't know you had such a good voice." It was because of the voice that my English teacher in high school encouraged me to get into radio. I had my heart broken enough, but I persevered. I remember the first time I auditioned. I've auditioned for ABC and NBC, and this audition was more difficult. For a disc jockey show, they gave me three names, like Prokofiev, and different operas. And they were playing pop songs. Anyway, I did my audition. I couldn't get in touch with the program director for two weeks. I was persistent. And my English teacher, Miss Deverio, said, "Bill, keep calling." So I called.

I got this man, the program director. I learned my lesson. I would never do this again. I auditioned other people and helped people audition. I would never do this, because of what happened to me. He said, "You have a lousy voice. Your diction is terrible. Get a job in the mill and stay there. You haven't got any future." I cried for … mmmm … a day and a half, on and off. I was so brokenhearted. I was so distraught. Miss Deverio said to me, "Billy, he may be right about some of those things. But you have a tremendous voice." And my dad cried for three days. We had a song and a dance act when I was a kid. We did minstrel shows and that, for the veterans. It was during World War II.

I gave up trying to do it; I will say that. I didn't think it was for me. When I got into college, and I was playing sports, I got into a radio club. I had an English teacher there, and the radio teacher, Dr. Bordman. I was a freshman. She said to me, "You have a *nice* voice." There were about 20 in the class. TV wasn't even around. She said to me, "I think you have a future in this business."

So we go to the local radio station, WDAD, in Indiana, and I asked a question from the back. Talk about luck and fortune and a divine intervention. The owner of the station, when I asked the question, said, "Who was that?" I'm in the back, way in the back. I raise my hand. "Can I see you and Dr. Bordman in my office?" I went in. He said, "You have a tremendous voice. Where did you work in radio?" I said I never worked in radio. I did high school plays. He introduced me to the program director. He said, "Within two weeks, you're going to have your own show." I had *Cardille's Campus Capers* every night from 11:15 to 12. I learned about radio. And I thank Dr. Bordman. I did a lot of things in school, too, through her; the vespers and everything.

But I met a lot of nice people. And I just want to tell anyone who's looking for a career in broadcasting, it's a tough business like any business. There are a lot of doors that exit the business, but there are few doors that let you in. So if you get the right advice, you get the right spot, the right time, and always tell the truth and believe in divine intervention, you definitely will be successful. I'm proud to be in the Pennsylvania Broadcaster's Hall of Fame. There are only three of us from Pittsburgh: Paul Long, Bill Burns and myself. I'm in the A.F.T.R.A. (American Federation of Television and Radio Artists) Hall of Fame. If you go to New York, at the Radio and TV Museum, in their hall up there, you can watch *Chiller Theater*. You can dial it in.

I've had many accolades and won many awards. But I owe it all to two women — my high school English teacher, Miss Caroline Deverio, who died. And Dr. Abigail Bordman and her husband, who believed in me when I was a teenager. And I just say, "It's been a great ride over 50 years and I enjoyed every moment."

"Watch Horror Films—Keep America Strong!"
Bob Wilkins and Bob Shaw
Interviewed by Sandy Clark and Michael Monahan (2003)

At first glance—and second and possibly third—Bob Wilkins was the least likely guide to the world of monsters and mayhem as you could imagine. Wilkins was an amiable pipsqueak with a desert-dry sense of humor that recalled the straitlaced, slightly surreal whimsy of Tim Conway or Bob Newhart. In contrast to the generation of hyperactive costumed vampires, slapstick mad scientists and frantic ghouls who came before him, Wilkins' placid, hip-to-be-square horror host dressed like a golfer's nightmare and projected a Zen-like calm.

Bob Wilkins earned his horror host stripes the old fashioned way: He stumbled into it. Working in the advertising department of KCRA-TV 3 in Sacramento, California during the early 1960s, Wilkins' quirky wit earned him the role of toastmaster for station birthdays, anniversaries and going-away parties.

In 1966, the station's owners decided to invest in late-night programming—at a time stations routinely signed off the air in the post-midnight hours—using a horror movie package of highly questionable quality as lure. Wilkins uniquely antithetical personality promised an offbeat camp appeal, and he was asked to develop the concept.

The show was a hit, and when KCRA program manager Tom Breen moved to KTVU-TV 2, he brought Bob Wilkins along to replicate the show's success in the much larger San Francisco market. Bob Wilkins' *Creature Features* became one of the most popular local programs in Bay Area broadcast history, and Wilkins emerged as a culturally influential personality. His tongue-in-cheek rallying cry: "Watch Horror Films—Keep America Strong!" is as famous today as when he introduced it back in 1971.

Wilkins remained active in both the San Francisco and Sacramento markets through the mid-1980s before retiring from television and returning to advertising. In later years, Wilkins was diagnosed with Alzheimer's disease. He continued to meet fans at local conventions and screenings until the advanced stages of the disease made public appearances impossible.

The following represents Bob Wilkins' final public interview. Although the disease had by this time taken much of his memory and robbed him of the capacity for a detailed analysis of his career, Wilkins remained cheerful and witty. His long-time friend and colleague, KTVU entertainment reporter, Bob Shaw, sat in and helped fill in some information.

Following a long illness, Bob Wilkins succumbed to the disease and died on January 7, 2009. Bob Shaw died in April of the same year from Crohn's disease.

Sandy Clark: First question I have to ask. Where did the cigar come from? How did it become such a trademark?

Bob Wilkins: Good question. Actually, when I first started the show, for some reason I was shaking out there a little bit. So rather than take a pencil or something, I chose the cigar. My dad was a cigar smoker. I don't know if it came from him or what. But I needed something to keep me from being nervous. And it became, from there on out, a trademark. People are curious. They want to know where this sucker came from. It was just one of those things. It was never lit, because we did get complaints about the … "Why is that young man smoking?" from everyone.

Quintessential Bob Wilkins—a mild mannered host and his iconic slogan

109

And we had a form letter we sent out. You know, "Mr. Wilkins *needs* that," and so forth.

SC: Were you influenced by radio as a kid? Did you listen to a lot of shows that had a host, like Inner Sanctum?

Bob Wilkins: Oh yeah, things of that nature. That started it all. I mean, I used to listen to them, *Lights Out,* things like that.

SC: What about the fans? What kind of stuff did you get from the fans? What did people send you?

Bob Wilkins: It was mostly favorable. I would ask them to pass it on. I would ask them, gee, how did you hear about this and they said, "Oh, our friends told us about it," and things of that nature. You must understand that, in those days, most radio stations and TV stations went off the air about 11 o'clock. After the 11 o'clock news, they went to black. Now of course, it's 24 hours a day. It's just one of those things.

SC: How do you think a show like this would play now?

Bob Wilkins: It's hard to say, because we've got all night broadcasting. I'm surprised someone hasn't gone back and gotten the old classic ones. Now, you know, at our house, we can pick up about 45 stations across the country. I may have looked up about a quarter of them today. It just mushroomed.

SC: I'm going to mention a few of names, people interviewed. And if you could recall anything about them from the interviews, any moments you remember. How about Ernie Fosselius, who did Hardware Wars?

Bob Wilkins: Ernie Fosselius! You picked a good guy. He came on the air, and it's one of the best interviews I ever had. He's a wild man, you know? And he talked about this and that. He has peculiar ... eye contact. He's almost like a rubber-faced guy, you know? I think he was one of the longest interviews I ever had before the movie started. And for some reason, he was nervous, but there's nothing wrong with that. But when it was over, I said you know, I could use you on the show once a month or something. I gave him an opportunity to do that, which I had never done before. And he showed some of the other things he did, that no one had seen. But he never came around.

SC: Do you think that the show influenced him doing those films, that he would have an audience, a place to show them?

Bob Wilkins: Yeah. No question about it.

SC: Ray Harryhausen?

Bob Wilkins: Yeah, very good interview.

SC: Ronald Reagan?

Bob Wilkins: Ron Reagan. Okay, Ronald Reagan. I did an interview with him. They called me in to shoot some footage of Ronald Reagan. It was for a commercial. He was running for office. And when he was through, he shook everyone's hand and so forth. And then he walked out, and that was it. But we used to play that on the air then. I would interrupt the program, "Here's a message from Ronald Reagan."

SC: What do remember about Night of the Living Dead *(1968)? You said previously it was one of your favorite films of the ones you'd shown.*

Bob Wilkins: Yeah, it was, because it looked real. It didn't look like actors filmed it. This one was black and white, I believe. It looked real, you know, as if someone just turned it on, trying to get the late news or something.

We did get a lot of letters. "What are you doing? Geez!"

SC: What was your favorite movie that you showed?

Bob Wilkins: *Attack of the Mushroom People* (1963). Yeah. I think we started off on that one, and we got a lot of letters on it right away. So we always pulled that one out of the bag. There are certain periods, rating periods, and we would run that one.

SC: What have your fans gone on to do?

Bob Wilkins: A lot of them are in jail … It's hard to say. I think a lot of them did perhaps get into the business of making commercials or … there would be scripts come in to me with notes: "Can we do this? Can you help us do this story?" and so forth.

SC: Did you ever appear in any of those?

Bob Wilkins: I might have, maybe two or three.

Michael Monahan: There was The Milpitas Monster (1975)…

Bob Wilkins: Right. Who could forget that one? I forgot it.

SC: How about George Lucas? I heard he was a fan.

Bob Wilkins: Yes, he was. He called me to his office. He had not started what he finally did with Lucasfilm. He wanted me to be president of his operation. Years later I bumped into him and he said, "I could have used you." It just didn't feel right for me at the time.

SC: Over the course of all those years, did you ever interview anyone you remember particularly well?

Bob Wilkins: I'd have to think that one over. It's been so long ago.

MM: Boris Karloff?

Bob Wilkins: Boris Karloff. (*Gestures to crew*) See, they know more … they're young.

SC: You wonder where the memory went; they took it.

Bob Wilkins: (*Laughs*) Arrest these two!

SC: Do you remember anything about the Boris Karloff interview?

Bob Wilkins: Karloff was a very gentle man. (*Turns to Bob Shaw*) Was that in Sacramento, Bob?

Bob Shaw: No. That was when Harry Martin was interviewing him for NBC on the set of *The Virginian*. You went down there, just jumped in.

Bob Wilkins: Did you get that?

SC: Would you say you had a guerilla style of producing this show? Did you just run in and grab what you could?

Bob Wilkins: No. I don't want you to think it was all put together at the last minute. If you're really going to do it right, you have to have breaks for the show that might tie in before the commercials. I think Bob Shaw helped me quite bit, right?

Bob Shaw: Well, I'd give you real information on the films and things like that. You're the one who came up with the comedy.

Bob Wilkins: But he (*Bob Shaw*) was the brains behind the whole operation. And I paid him well.

Bob Shaw: Twenty-five dollars a month.

You don't need a yellow submarine when you've got a yellow rocking chair. Bob Wilkins rocks his way through a psychedelic pop art wonderland at KCRA-TV 3.

Bob Wilkins: (*Laughs—points to crew*) They're laughing!

Bob Shaw: They think you're cute.

SC: If somebody backed a dump truck full of money up to you today...

Bob Wilkins: Yes, I'd take it.

SC: And if they said, "We'd like you to present a new program of horror and science fiction films," what would you do?

Bob Wilkins: I couldn't accept it. Maybe a dollar here, a dollar there, you know? You mean to go do it again?

SC: Yes. What kind of programming would you do? What kind of host?

Bob Wilkins: No. I would take Bob Shaw.

Bob Shaw: I'm getting too old for it.

Bob Wilkins: Yeah (*Laughs*). I mean, of course I'd get a cut out of it.

Bob Shaw: Twenty-five dollars a show.

Bob Wilkins: See, he was my biggest helper, because he knew *everything* about film. You could ask him right now about a so-and-so movie from 1946. He's just tremendous.

SC: How did Bob Shaw end up getting involved in your show?

Bob Wilkins: He was out of money. (*Laughs*) Now ... (*to Bob Shaw*) how did we meet?

Bob Shaw: I wrote you a letter in 1967 at Channel 3, and you read it on the air. And you would read some of my little film reviews on the air. And then you worked with Channel 40 and you had me on. And then you came to Channel 2, and here I am. One letter, that's all it took. Write Bob, that's my career advice.

Bob Wilkins: Yeah, I had no notion of which star was this way and so forth. He was the biggest helper.

SC: What things influenced you from your childhood? What sort of things did you remember when you were putting this together? Were there any specific radio programs, any specific TV shows?

Bob Wilkins: I wasn't even thinking about television. I think it started when I got into making commercials. Bob was in on that, I believe—when I came to one of those stations?

Bob Shaw: Just peripherally. I really didn't have that much to do with it.

Bob Wilkins: No, but I would ask you questions of various things. You know, can we get away with this? (*Laughs*) Stuff like that.

Bob Shaw: I was his legal department. I was 18 years old.

SC: How nervous were you on the first show?

Bob Wilkins: That's a good question, because that's where the cigar came from. One other thing I had that had something to do with being nervous—the rocking chair.

SC: What became of the rocking chair?

Bob Wilkins: It's still around. I think we have it at home. But we painted it because the color came out. I think that was repaired and re-stained and everything, and it's at our house.

SC: Where did the stuff on the set come from: the skull, the sign?

Bob Wilkins: People would send in things. With the skull, there no message attached. So I pulled it out that night and I said, gee, people are so messy. They just throw stuff in your yard, you know, when they're driving by.

Bob Shaw: One of them was a real skull, wasn't it?

Bob Wilkins: Yes.

SC: Someone sent you a real skull!?

Bob Wilkins: I can't say they sent it to me. Maybe an Italian guy just shot a guy and no one saw it. I don't know. Are any Italians here? It's all right.

SC: What were your favorite kinds of films? Do you have a specific one? Was horror your genre?

Bob Wilkins: No, no. I had no special thing about the films. They had to be cheap; they had to have action in it and so forth. People would send me in notes: "Hey, you should look at this one," and so forth. The fans, along with Bob, who really knew their stuff, were the areas I really looked for.

Bob Wilkins left KCRA-TV 3 in 1970 and moved his act over to KTLX-TV 40.

SC: We should talk about the Emmy you won for the weather, when you were the weatherman at KTVU.

Bob Shaw: You intercut the footage from a James Bond film (*On Her Majesty's Secret Service, 1969*), the skiing sequence, with a Tahoe ski report. Wasn't that the one you got nominated for?

Bob Wilkins: I think so, yeah, something like that.

SC: It was the same year where I think six Patty Hearst stories were up ... and one weather story. So how did that come about? How did the weather story come about?

Bob Wilkins: I don't know. I never asked on that one. When you win something, you don't go question it. (*Laughs*)

Bob Shaw: The thing about the weather ... you got to admit, you knew nothing about the weather.

Bob Wilkins: Absolutely.

Bob Shaw: You knew nothing about horror films.

Bob Wilkins: Exactly.

Bob Shaw: You just made it fun because, who cares about the weather, really?

Bob Wilkins: I guess. You know, there's nothing more boring ... if you live in an area where the temperatures are like here ... when was the last time it rained? And so, I'm not going to surprise them and say, hey, on August 5 it's going to snow here. Don't go away. And it's April when I say it. I just had fun with it.

Bob Shaw, Bob Wilkins' longtime friend, began providing Wilkins with horror movie trivia from the earliest days. Through Wilkins' mentoring, Shaw became KTVU'a first entertainment reporter, a position he held for 30 years.

SC: What other jobs did you end up doing in television?

Bob Wilkins: I strictly worked in the areas we talked about. I just sort of walked into everything I did. I had

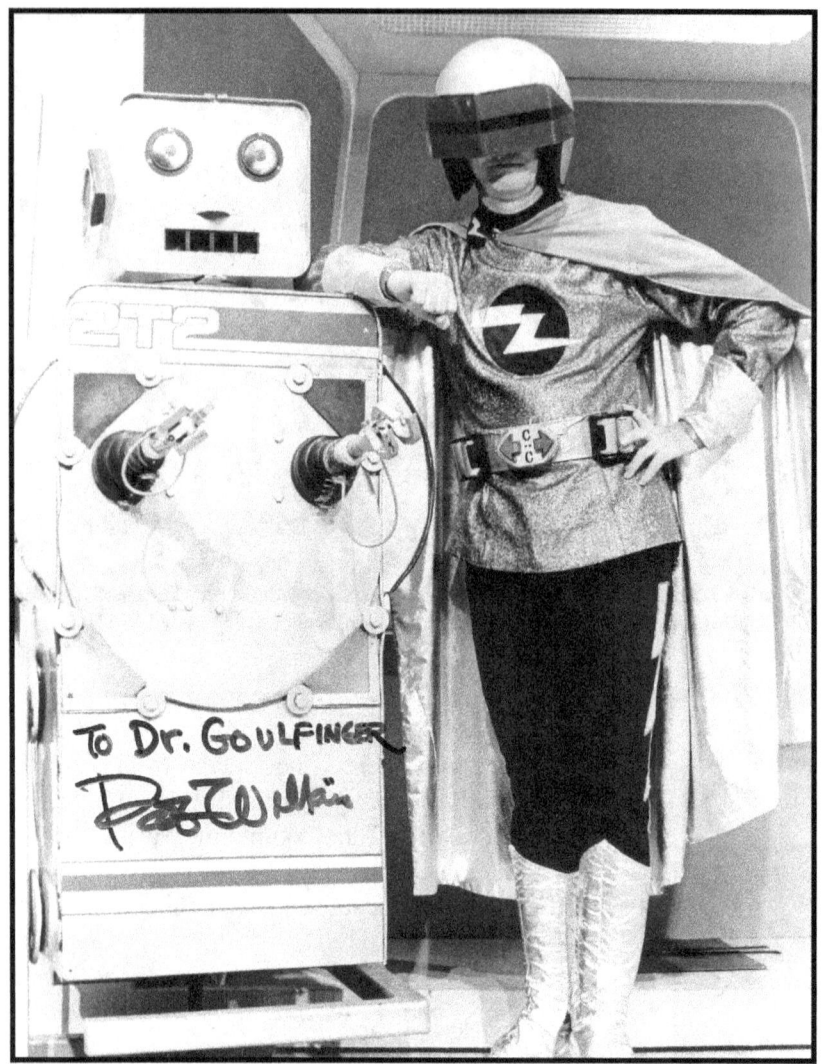

Like many horror hosts over the years, Bob Wilkins' personality proved eminently adaptable to kids' programming. Wilkins donned helmet, visor and cape to portray Captain Cosmic, a galactic emissary who showed sci-fi theme programming.

a job anyway, and this was just to see what I could do with the extra material. I never had to come in five days a week. (*To Bob Shaw*) Is that true?

Bob Shaw: Yeah. I patterned my life after yours.

Bob Wilkins: (*Laughs*) Here's a guy who could have gone the wrong way. You know, rob a grocery store or something? I took him away from all that.

Bob Shaw: And I went down the path of sloth. God bless you for that.

MM: *Bob, after you left television, didn't you handle advertising for casinos?*
Bob Wilkins: Yeah.

MM: *Your return to advertising, now, was that something you wanted to do, or was that just the first job that cropped up?*

Bob Wilkins: I don't think I got a lot of requests. But I was pretty much ... I had had enough of it. I may have done some special work for a special person or something like that. But that was the end of the TV years.

MM: *That prompted your move to Reno, then?*

Bob Wilkins: No, I had a job opportunity in Reno. (*To Bob Shaw*) What was it, Bob?

Bob Shaw: The Nugget.

Bob Wilkins: Oh yeah, The Nugget.

Bob Shaw: You didn't move for a while. You were still living in Oakland.

Bob Wilkins: Right. A fellow owed me a lot of money. And I didn't want to file Chapter 11 bankruptcy. Yeah. I think that's a terrible way. So I got a job in Reno. It was writing ... writing ... let's see ... (*to Bob Shaw*) ... what did I do, Robert?

Bob Shaw: Writing ad copy?

Bob Wilkins: Yeah, advertising for various products and things of that nature.

MM: *You know a current horror host out in Reno, Zomboo. Frank Leto plays him.*
Bob Wilkins: Yes.

MM: *Did you just meet him when you moved out there—someone from the industry?*

Bob Wilkins: Yeah, I think so, just bumped into him. If they're weird looking, why ... I always take a couple shots of them.

MM: *And you appeared on his show there one time, too.*
Bob Wilkins: That right?

MM: *Yep, in an electric chair.*
Bob Wilkins: See, I'm getting old, and I don't remember a lot of things.

From the Crypt to the 'Net
Count Gore De Vol (Dick Dyzel)
Interviewed by Sandy Clark (2003)

Dick Dyzel was a forward-looking broadcaster, keenly interested in new trends and technologies, from stereo television to the Internet. In 1998, he became the first horror host to jump firmly into the worldwide web, producing new, complete programs specifically for the burgeoning computer crowd, starring his alter ego, Count Gore De Vol. This full embrace of the digital future came after a long career in traditional local TV broadcasting.

He began in 1971, hosting the *Night of Terror* movie program on WDXY-TV 29 as M.T. Graves, in Paducah, Kentucky. In 1973, he relocated to WDCA-TV 20 in Washington, DC, where he first gave undead life to Count Gore De Vol. The Count is a classically dapper vampire with a comically inflated sense of his own sex appeal. The regally imperious stature and supernatural foundation, undercut by the clown-white make-up and rim-shot humor, distilled the image of the horror host to its purest form.

Creature Feature was first on the air between 1973 and 1979, and later revived for a second run from 1984 until 1987. In addition to portraying Count De Vol, Dyzel's on-camera duties at WDCA included stepping into the 83AAA-sized shoes of Bozo the Clown, and later donning Mr. Spock ears to play Captain 20, a popular kid-show host.

Count Gore De Vol returned to WDCA to host a one-shot special, *Countdown to the Millennium with the Count*, in which he presented two movies—one in 1999 and one in the year 2000. Dyzel inevitably extended his presence to the horror films themselves, appearing in *The Alien Factor* (1979), *Nightbeast* (1982), *Galaxy Invader* (1985), and direct-to-video features, like *Chainsaw Sally* and *Countess Dracula's Orgy of Blood* (both 2004).

I'm going to ask you some general questions...

I know nothing about generals, majors or anything military. So you can stop right there.

Did you have a horror host when you were a kid? Were you a fan of the host?

When I was growing up, I grew up in Chicago in the late 1950s. So Marvin, on *Shock Theater*, on WBKB— which no longer exists, since it's now WLS—was my horror host. And he was funny, and he was kind of naughty. And he had this wonderful female with him and we never saw her face. Joy, his wife, it turns out to be. It was great. I got my initiation into the horror classics, the Universal classics, when *Shock Theater* came out. Marvin was my host.

So what do you remember about his costume, his shtick, his set?

He was a beatnik! He was the beat generation, man. He was cool. I always wanted to be cool. I tried to be cool. I don't succeed too often. Unfortunately, I don't remember too much of his shtick. I know he was a beatnik, he was cool, we never saw the face of his wife, he had the band on the set. And I would love to see some of his stuff. I understand there may be some kinescopes still available. But, otherwise it's lost.

What films do you remember him hosting? Anything stick with you (that) you saw?

Well, there was *The Mummy* (1932), *Dracula* (1931). I mean the basic repertory. I remember the *Mummy* film in particular, even more so than *Dracula*, believe it or not. I'm a big Boris Karloff fan.

How old were you at the time?

Ten.

What else went with that? Were there any other childhood routines with watching horror then? Were there toys that you played with?

No. Actually, ironically, unlike a lot of other horror hosts, I wasn't into horror memorabilia, collecting. I mean, I never read *Famous Monsters*, you know. Before *Shock Theater*, I was really into sci-fi. I saw all the scary bug movies, and *(laughs)* if there was a space ship in it, I went to see it! *This Island Earth* (1955), *Earth vs. The Flying Saucers* (1956), and of course you can't forget ... which I just forgot the name of ... Gort! Um ... um ... *Day the Earth Stood Still* (1951)! *(Laughs)*

Where was the TV in your house, do you remember that? Were there any special procedures? Anything you had to do to get to watch it?

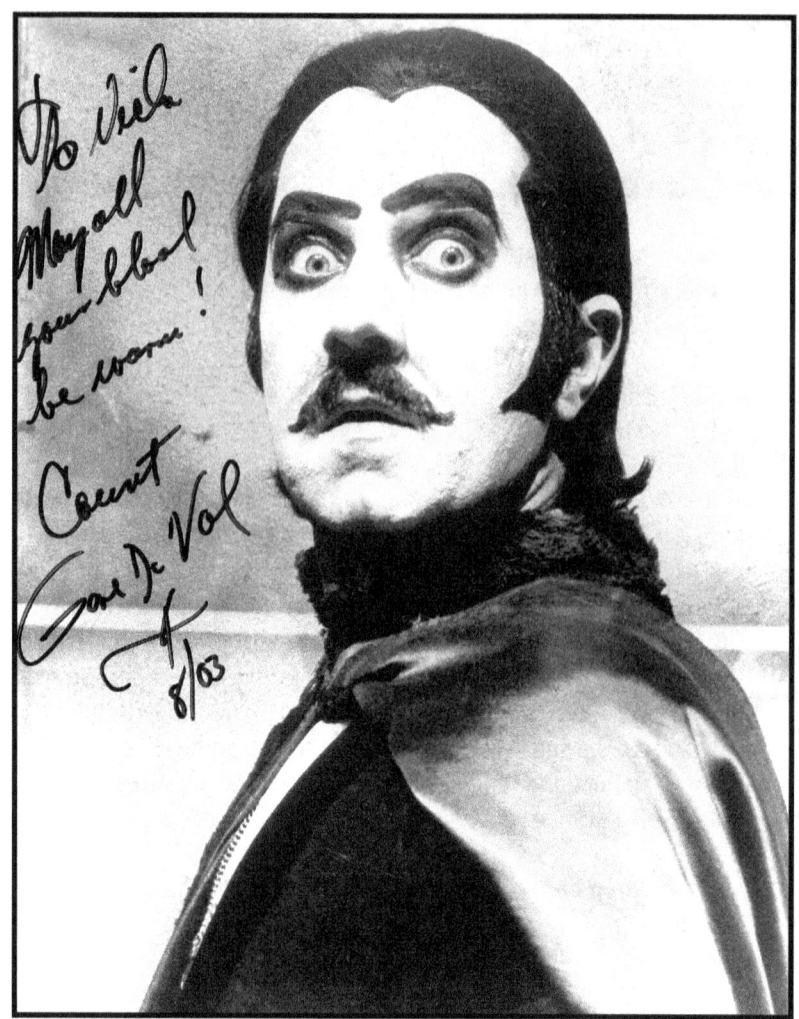

He is the very model of a modern monster movie host—Dick Dyzel as the smooth and goofy Count Gore De Vol.

It depends on which year you're talking about. When I was 18 months old, the television was in my bedroom and stayed there for the first years of my life. So I saw everything! Then we got a bigger place and the TV moved to the TV room. Actually, the TV stayed where it was and I moved out of the living room into the dining room, in a fold-out bed. It was … tight, you know? So I got to see a lot of early 1950s television.

Did you have any brothers or sisters, or anyone to share this TV with?

They tell me I had a sister. (*Laughs*) Gordilia … no, no, no, no, no! (*Laughs*) Actually, I did have a sister and she hates all of it.

So, when you were watching Marvin as a kid, did you have sense of what he was doing, or why he was doing it?

He was funny; it was just that simple. He made it palatable. He was humorous. He gave me a reason to watch the show other than just seeing a movie. I would watch the movie over again, because I was seeing something new besides the movie. I was seeing a new skit, and he did skits. And by the way, I do have a short collection of his actual scripts, which are kind of neat.

So, did Marvin influence you in any way?

No. Other than the fact that I knew that a horror host existed and that they were meant to be funny. I mean, obviously, do I look like a beatnik? (*Laughs*) I don't have shades!

Were there any other hosts in your childhood that you were aware of?

No. Again, because I didn't read *Famous Monsters*, I wasn't aware of Zacherley. I wasn't even aware of Forry Ackerman for a long time. It was not in my childhood group. No one was into it. *MAD* magazine was another story. I knew who Alfred E. Neumann was. And when it came to becoming a horror host, the only thing I could call upon was that I liked Bela Lugosi and I had a cape. Which is why I think I got the job—and don't ask me why I had the cape. I knew it had to be humorous. And that was the basis.

Let's talk about that. Were you a host by accident or design?

It's actually a little bit of both. This is the true story. I was working for a TV station, WDXR, Channel 29, in Paducah. That's Kentucky, by the way. It was the first UHF station in Western Kentucky and Southern Illinois, that whole Southern Illinois region, South East Missouri, Western Kentucky. It's one big market. And the station hadn't gone on the air yet. So we were still doing things like buying film openings for the movies that we bought, because we bought a lot of films. A lot of horror films, too. We had the Universal package. We owned it, and had a seven-year run on it.

Everyone at the station was involved. It was a small staff and we were involved in all the decision-making. And the general manager was 24 years old. He was a very sharp businessman, very good promoter. So we were all sitting around in the—I can still see it now—in the conference room, in the front corner of the building, watching reels and reels of 16mm sample opens for films, deciding which package you wanted to buy. And we had pizza and couple six packs and we're going till two, three o'clock in the morning. We're getting bleary-eyed. Up comes this thing: "*Night of Terror* with M.T. Graves." I said, yes, that's what we need! We need a horror host on Channel 29! Louis turned around and said, "You're hired." (*Laughs*) In shock I declared, what do I know about it? He said, "I don't know, but it sounded good. Work on it." And that's how it came to be.

What was your first film?

You know, I don't know. I was so scared I can barely remember the opening night. You have to understand; this is a small market and a small station. I was the news anchor. I was the news co-anchor. Ernie Mitchell and I were doing the news. News went from 10:00 p.m. to 10:30 p.m. *Night of Terror* started at 10:30 p.m. live. At the end we had sports. I had eight minutes to go from newscaster—get my microphone off, take off my jacket, *run* into the men's room, put on my cape, try to come up with some kind of make-up, run out to the other corner of the studio—and live, hit the air at 10:30 p.m. with *Night of Terror*! Now, am I worried about the title? No! I'm worried about whether I'm going to be there when they yell, "Roll it!" (*Laughs*) "Cue him!" And that was every Saturday night.

So what other jobs did you have: news anchor, horror host...?

I was Bozo the Clown. Bozo was the main reason for me being on-air talent. We did an hour, a live Bozo show five days a week. And then I did news at 10 o'clock. Then we did the horror showcase at 10:30 p.m. to 11:30 p.m. And weekends I did personal appearances as Bozo and was air shift director. I had an eight-hour shift where I actually switched things on the air on weekends. I was putting in about 100 hours a week. Welcome to small market television. And it was probably one of the most exciting times of my life, because I got to do everything. There was nothing I couldn't do. They wouldn't say, "You can't do that." Instead they would say, "You want to learn how to edit? There's a machine. See if you can make it work."

Who were your professional influences? Who were you drawing on, especially with horror hosts?

There were none. I had a degree in radio and television, and I knew the basics of how to put it together. I had some training as Bozo and how to produce the show, Bozo make-up—how to put on Bozo make-up—which was a good start. My girlfriend at the time had made me a cape, because this was the 1970s and capes were cool

... except in Paducah. (*Laughs*) The guys with the gun racks see you walking down the street with a cape, you know? It got a little bit touchy as times. I love Paducah, I really do. I go back every once in a while and it's like coming home. They treat me real well down there.

I basically had to make a decision though—to follow news or follow entertainment—because eventually I couldn't do both. And I got really tired of doing city council meetings and School Board meetings. I decided entertainment was more fun. Over the long term it was probably the wrong decision, because no one does entertainment anymore at the local level. End of discussion! That's why horror hosts on broadcast have disappeared, mainly. And locally produced kid shows, definitely, except for a few random markets here and there. But as far as professional influence goes, you made do. You invented things, you were creative; you bounced ideas off your cohorts. You know your cameraman and your director. "What do we do next?"

Do you think it would be possible to do a show like this today?

You could do it if they would *let* you. So the question is not can you do it but do you think there's someone who will let you do it? In Chicago, where I originate my web program, we still have Son of Svengoolie. He's on Channel 26. Actually, in 1998, I took a hard look at this, because I really wanted to do Gore. I wanted to be back because it's a lot of fun and I enjoy it. It's a creative outlet for me.

You look at the history of horror hosts, and hosting in general, local production. It started with V ... VHF TV, when they had lots of time to fill and kill. So they purchased movie packages. And to make the movies differentiated from the other station's movies, they added a movie host. Whether it be a horror host, a girl in a sleazy outfit who would host the 8 o'clock movie or a guy in a sport jacket who would give away money in a money movie program, or anything like this. So stations had these hosts when they were trying to fill time or differentiate themselves. When the networks became big, powerful, they dropped all that local stuff. They went to U ... UHF.

When the U's came along, they had to do the same thing that the V's did. They did the same thing; they got hosts. At one time at Channel 20 in Washington, I was hosting *Creature Feature*; I was hosting *Saturday Chiller*. We had a female host on the 8 o'clock movie; we had a midday host for the money movie. We had all these hosts. That worked fine until big corporate corporations bought the U's and had lots of programming. And they didn't need local production any longer. They could cut the producers,

the staff and the studio time. And they did away with that. So, you know, it was going to happen. But I looked back and said, "Where's it all going? I want to be at the edge of this." And I thought then, the Internet. When we can get enough broadband, enough streaming video, I could do it on the 'net. And I've been doing it for five [now 14] years (*since 1998, continuing to this day*) so far.

What do you think the host brings to the programming other than the local identification? What other services do you provide? What other ways do you accentuate the film or augment the film?

Humor, that's number one. Still is for me. You know, is it going to get a laugh, is it going to be funny? It doesn't have to be. I don't do the slapstick too often. I'm more what I would consider the old school. I don't do obnoxious jokes, I don't swear and curse and I'm not gross. I do more the classic deadpan double-take kind of humor. When we were in Washington we made a lot of fun of the politicians—a *lot* of material to work with there. (*Laughs*) And I still do, as a matter of fact. I just did a thing about the current not-elected president (*George W. Bush*), and at this point, why not? I've got the whole world to work with. I could make fun of the French too, only I don't want to lose that audience. Actually it's kind of funny. You look at where I'm getting viewers, my number one foreign market is the Netherlands and I have no idea why. I mean, a third of my audience is in the Netherlands.

I was just wondering what the host brought to the presentation, and has it changed over time?

No. I think that you have different varieties, and everyone has his or her own take on it. Like each comedian has his or her own style. And I never really considered myself a comedian, but I guess in many ways I am. But you've seen these movies … too many times! But there's some attraction to them. You watch them because now you're going to see a little different at the beginning, the middle and the end. That's basically a question to ask fans, rather than the host. I only know that I can deliver something and whatever I deliver seems to hit some kind of chord with a number of people.

What do your family and friends think about you doing this?

Most of them have … made accommodations. (*Laughs*) I was thinking of what would happen if I ran for political office. And I decided that's a non-starter. (*Laughs*) I'd be apologizing for everything. So I wouldn't do that. Actually my kids grew up with a relatively normal upbringing, and they think it's kind of cool now. During the teens it was kind of tacky. But basically, for a while there, my parents' friends would say, "Oh, your son's in television. What does he do?" "Oh, he's … in television." (*Laughs*) Actually, when I was doing Bozo it was a big thing to be Bozo, because my family was from Chicago. And the biggest Bozo show was in Chicago. So you'd say, "Bozo" and everyone would recognize it. Since I wore a lot of hats over the years they could point to that for name recognition.

Now it's a little more difficult, since it's primarily *Creature Feature*. I'm the only guy in Wheaton, Illinois with a coffin in his basement who has a dungeon. It was kind of funny when I had my house reappraised. We had to refinance my mortgage and the appraiser came in. "Do you have a finished basement?" Sort of… (*Laughs*) "Well, can I see it?" Are you sure? (*Laughs*) And I took her down and … "Is that a coffin?" Yes, it's very nice. Would you like to see? It's very nice, solid maple. It's very nice, a very expensive coffin. And see my dungeon here, and the shackles and all the rest? See, it's semi-finished. "Oh … okay. Can we leave now?" (*Laughs*)

Did she ask what kind of movies you made for the Internet?

No. You have to understand that Wheaton, Illinois is also the home of Billy Graham's Wheaton College, which, you know, is a very conservative area, a very Republican, conservative area. (*Laughs*) I don't think that I wanted to let it get out too much that I … (*Laughs*)

Tell me a little bit about where you think your show's going. Where are you going to take it next and what's the plan? How do you roll with it?

The show is going to evolve technically as we get more broadband and as the technology for streaming improves, although it's pretty decent right now. You have to have less than a 56k connection to *not* be able to enjoy what I'm putting on. From a technical standpoint, I will keep on the cutting edge. Right now my set is identical to what I had at Channel 20. It's actually a little bit bigger. The lighting is … well, I've got lower ceilings, so the lighting is not quite as good. But with the advent of digital video I have the capability to shoot, edit and present broadcast quality—*better* than broadcast quality—out of my computer, where before it took me a 10-million dollar studio. I don't need that anymore.

So that's not going to change a whole lot. From the content, it depends on the film I'm running, how I feel, who the President is, who the local politician is, etc. Right now what I really need to do is come up with a business plan, on how to make money on this, because this is not cheap. I've been putting this on, and basically funding it through sales of videos and t-shirts and things like this. But if I really want to keep this going long term, I need to come up with a business plan and/or merge or get some sort of corporate sponsorship or something like that.

No one has come up with a good business plan for the Internet, as we saw with the big bust of the big boom, because no one knows how to make money off it, at least in any new form. I mean, they're all traditional forms. So that's somewhat where I'm going. Also, how do I promote it? I mean, you have 35 billion websites out there. How do people find you? There's a lot of technology involved in that too. Right now I wet my finger, stick it up in the air and find out which way the wind's blowing and follow it.

What do you see as the technological milestones for horror hosts? From the beginning— the advent of television, the Shock Theater *package—to today?*

Well, the first impact was the idea of videotape. I mean, *Shock Theater* was live; there was no videotape, which is why we have no record of it. So videotape was the first milestone, then we had the capability to edit videotape. When we first started in Paducah, we had quad machines, but we couldn't edit with them. You needed a special machine to edit with. And frankly, I have been very strongly production-oriented all the way through. I've maintained very high production standards all the way through.

I mean, we had the very first stereo show in Washington. I sneaked it in because I was friends with the chief engineer and I found out we were actually capable of doing stereo. And a week before they were going to have the big premiere, I ran my show in stereo and made a big deal about it. And there was a lot that hit the fan the following Monday. But I said, It's too late. I'm already in the history books. *Creature Feature* with Gore De Vol was the first stereo show in Washington.

And when we got the one-inch machines, I was the first one to use them. As a matter of fact, with stereo, we had to re-wire the audio board to make it work. And this was the neat thing about *Creature Feature* and what we

119

were doing. And I don't know what the loyalty is. It wasn't to me, but it was to the concept. I got people to do things on their own time that they weren't paid to do, that they had no business doing, because they wanted to do it. And they did it. All I had to do was ask. Well … sometimes plead. (*Laughs*) A lot of times beg … sometimes bribe. But they did it.

So videotape, digital effects, all these were incremental. And I think now digital video and streams, and beyond that, DVDs—the ability to put digital content on DVD now where it won't deteriorate, and then to sell it. Hey, this is good stuff too. You never know where technology is going to go.

What about your fans?

I like the oscillating ones that go around. (*Laughs*) Oh! My viewers! (*Laughs*) Those kinds of fans!

Is there a difference between the TV fan and the Internet fan? How has your contact changed?

Let me tell you about the biggest similarity, which surprises me. With the Internet: you're on your computer, you can click on a link that will automatically open your email file and send it. I get as much response as when people had to put a stamp on an envelope and write a letter. That's the big surprise. I don't get as much instantaneous response as I expected. I don't know why. And I've talked to other people too. It's the mentality. People are on a TV mentality. Even if they're capable of doing it, they're not trained to feedback. And that's young, old, doesn't seem to make any difference. So that was the biggest surprise to me. I'd figured we'd have a lot more interaction, and I haven't got it. I tried to encourage it, but … you know.

I don't think there's any difference in the fans. When I see them at conventions—old fans, new fans—they like horror movies. They like the idea of a host for a variety of reasons, which you'd be better to ask them. The fans are there. They like this stuff. Some of them like more the classics, some the slasher. Some of them like the Japanese, some of them like the … pffff! They're all over the place. Some of them like the sci-fi. My favorite, my all-time scariest movie, the one that scared me the most was not horror, not strictly horror. It was *Alien* (1979). To this day I won't go to see it again, unless it's in a theater (*laughs*), because it's such a potentially scary film.

So have they ever sent you anything? Art work…?

Oh yeah. In 1984, when we had a new set built, and I asked for new props, people sent in all sorts of things. We had a human skull sent in from Johns Hopkins medical school. (*Laughs*) I had the complete Aurora classic monster collection, which I've now since donated to a guy who's my archivist. And he's had it refurbished. It's beautiful. Oh, all sorts of stuff. Matter of fact, we did the 13th anniversary show on *Creature Feature*; we were showing the movie, *House* (1986), which everyone has totally forgotten about. Anyway, it was free admission if you brought me a gift. You should see some of the stuff I got, from cards to over-sized glasses, to piles of plastic dog turds (*laughs*), non-use condoms. Things of blood—not real blood—all sorts of stuff. We haven't gotten a whole lot recently. Occasionally we'll get magazines and stuff, and pictures of people. I will get email, electronic pictures of people, files. "Here's what I look like." It's cool. I like that. I put it on the program. I like that kind of interaction.

Do you think they're more creative, the fans of these sorts of shows, than the general average viewer?

Well, the ones that respond obviously are. Again, you're asking me to generalize. And stereotypical is the guy who sits there with the beer and the pretzels and they don't move for six hours. Oh ... that's a sports fan ... wait ... (*Laughs*). So there's no interaction there. I don't know. I have never been on the other end. My guess is yes.

You talk about email and snail mail, but what about personal contact with your fans?

Occasionally you get the stalker. It's only happened a couple of times (*laughs*) and it hasn't happened recently. It never got serious, just people hanging around the station waiting for you to come in and out, dressed up in costume, trying to impress you. And occasionally at conventions people will try to impress you. Beyond that, not really.

What about the promotional aspects? You mentioned the conventions, you mentioned hosting some live stuff. What other sorts of appearances have you been involved in?

Well, with the advent of direct-to-DVD films, I've appeared in a number of films as a horror host, which I like. There was, let's see, *Stakes* (2002), done by Timewarp Films—the current Don Dohler/Joe Ripple production company. Then there was—soon to be released—*Countess Dracula's Orgy of Blood* (2004). It's a Don Glut film starring Glori Anne Gilbert. Actually I'm hosting the ... what-cha-ma-call-it ... the outtakes on that one. And I can't talk about it, but there's a series of independent short films that I'm going to be hosting. Hopefully, it's going to pan out. We're just in the process of doing the first one. I'm not involved with the production. *Cremains* (2001) is another one. That was out of Alabama, Mobile.

Let's talk about your program, to just fill some holes here. What format do you go with? It sounds like you use some interviews. Tell me what goes into a show.

Well, you see, the web program offers me a lot of flexibility that I didn't have on the TV show. The TV

"Yes, capes are cool!" says Dick Dyzel. "I've had one since 1970 ... that's before Gore!"

show had two different formats, four and seven inserts. Open, close and either two in middle inserts or five in middle inserts, depending on the era and what the program director and sales department wanted. You could do interviews within that, and we did. We had Forry Ackerman on the show and it was a very good interview we conducted over four segments. But you're also limited by the time frame you had. Fortunately, most of the time I had a 120-minute slot. So I usually had plenty of time unless we had a very long movie. And I would tell the film department to cut it. (*Laughs*)

But the web program is both video and text. So I can do a variety of things. For example, yes, I do have streaming video of the movies. I do host the movies and I do it in a three-segment—open, intermission, close. Okay? And I do it for broadband and dial-up. That's one thing. Interviews are a separate thing altogether, separate page. That's "On the Rack." If I have someone "On the Rack," I interview them there. I have movie reviews. I do the theatrical movie reviews. We have video reviews. I have three people who review the videos for me. One is actually an independent producer/director, who goes unnamed, just as far as his real name goes. And we have another person who is just a contributor, who does a very good job.

We have other guests. We have other things. We have expanded beyond film. We get into books. J.L. Como, the horror writer, she's my Tomb Keeper, and she does two mini-book reviews every week. And she also interviews. When we got to the conventions together, she interviews the authors. And she has "The Vault" where she will interview directors in the vault. So we can bring in the horror writing community into the program. So now we have the horror film and the writers.

So we have text, we have streaming, we've got contests. Oh, contests, can't forget contests! Now we've got tied in to some of the major distributors who are provid-

ing us with prizes and material for contests. We had a big thing with *Underworld* (2003); we got a new thing with new Lon Chaney DVDs coming out. We're going to do something with *Freddy vs. Jason* (2003) on that release coming up. So we've got lots of tie-ins. So from that standpoint, I'm building relationships with the promoters from the studios. They are now aware of *Creature Feature* on the air. We've been on the air for more than five years. I am the *first* horror host on the Internet. So I did grab that claim to fame.

Channel 20 attempted to try to do a local production for New Years Eve, 1999. This was big. They invited me back; I was the returning hero. I got flown in—coach—put up in a nice room. Not a suite, but they put me up. I had basically carte blanche to a wrap around for two movies, to take us from 1999 to 2000. Other than the fact that they gave me too much budget—and I kept telling them it was too much budget; they were spending way too much money—it worked out pretty well. And it was fun. But frankly, even though the production staff really tried,

they were not used to doing a program. The idea of having three cameras going in a studio at the same time without editing was just, like, I was from Mars. So I brought in my old lighting director, who now works for ABC. We brought him in my audio person, who now works for Fox; we brought him in freelance. The director did have experience with multi-cameras. It turned out pretty good.

How about charities? Do you remember doing any work with charities?

No. The only charity that I, Count Gore De Vol, have ever been asked to participate in was the Red Cross, for a blood drive. And actually, I gave blood on-air. It was very successful.

That leads me into my last question regarding your costume, something you already touched on briefly. What made you decide, "Okay, this is the outfit I'm going to use, this is the character"?

I like Bela. I could roll my r's. I had a cape. I had a tuxedo. It was the simplest thing to do. It has evolved since. This is, like, the third set of tails that I've had. This is only my second cape; it's well done. Gingis Formal Wear just managed to dig up a couple of ruffled shirts, and they hand-made a new tie for me. I told them I want a butterfly tie from the 1970s. (*Laughs*) I ran into one of the guys, he said, "Sure, I'll make one up for you." So, they've been very good to me. They said, "Who knows … you may come back." But that's pretty much it, you know. I mean, it's like I'm suave. I'm debonair. I'm the sex symbol of Washington, and now the Internet. I've got to be smooth and cool. And when I'm bad, I've got to be so bad that I'm good. Or good at being bad or something like that. So the ladies love me, and I always like to put the bite on them. And all I can say is—"May all your blood be warm."

Rubber Chickens, Rim Shots and "Rumble"
Svengoolie (Jerry G. Bishop)
Interviewed by Sandy Clark (2004)

Jerry G. Bishop was a hip, flip radio deejay in Cleveland during the mid-1960s, a period he termed "the second golden age of AM radio." His preeminence in the market even earned him his own soul-pop single, "She's Gone," released in 1966. By 1967 he was in Chicago, at WCFL radio, where station advertising declared, "If Jerry can't make you laugh, you lose!"

Bishop was doing booth announcing at television station WFLD-TV 32 when *Screaming Yellow Theater* premiered. Initially the show was un-hosted, with movies introduced in voiceover under title cards. Bishop couldn't resist goofing around, adding a burlesque Bela Lugosi accent and inserting off-script jokes. Viewer reaction was positive and Bishop was elevated to on-camera host.

Dipping into his memories of Cleveland, Bishop repurposed elements of Ernie Anderson's Ghoulardi, creating an updated hippie variant called Svengoolie. *Screaming Yellow Theater* became the vehicle for a broad range of crackpot humor, from vaudeville to cutting edge to topical, quickly establishing Svengoolie as the hippest host in town. Where else were you going to find rubber chickens punctuating Watergate jokes?

Each week Svengoolie burst forth from his coffin, spewing some sort of jabberwocky intro to the evening's movie, often assisted by celebrity guests like Rudy Vallee, Bette Midler and Mort Sahl. The balance of the show featured the usual assortment of skits and commercial parodies—though done with a higher degree of skill than usual, thanks to Bishop's exceptional creative team.

Svengoolie remained on the air from 1970 to 1973, when Kaiser broadcasting replaced his show with a syndicated version of Cleveland's host, The Ghoul. Bishop continued to work in Chicago until he was offered a daily live talk show in California, *Sun Up San Diego*, which he hosted from 1978-1990, winning three Emmys. In 1980, Bishop opened a popular restaurant in San Diego's Seaport Village called "Jerry G. Bishop's Greek Island Café."

Like many TV announcers, you got your start in radio. And you were acquainted with one of the most famous announcers of all, Ernie Anderson.

He was great. I knew him in Cleveland. I did a morning radio show in Cleveland and he was Ghoulardi. I stole the name from him, in a way. When I was working at the station in Chicago, Channel 32, they were doing horror movies on Friday nights. I was doing some booth announcing, along with a talk show and a couple other things. And I started, just for fun, in the voiceovers, from the booth (*Bela Lugosi accent*) "And now, back to our movie!" And little by little, I just had more fun. Sitting in a booth in a TV studio's the deadly job in life. Little by little it grew. We took some still pictures and I created this costume, the one that we'd still use, with a red sweatshirt. And I had some guy paint the character. We called it Svengoolie. Where'd I get the name? I remembered Ernie Anderson as Ghoulardi in Cleveland. And it worked!

Had you been in the Cleveland market? Did you see him there?

Oh yeah, I was in radio. In fact, I traveled with The Beatles for two years as a reporter, from that station in Cleveland. So, everybody knew Ernie. In fact, one of his shticks involved a town called Parma, which is outside of Cleveland. And every time he'd say Parma, everybody off camera would say "Parma?!?" Well, I stole that. There's a town called Berwyn outside of Chicago. It's a working class neighborhood, kinda like Parma, okay? Blue collar. So every time I'd say Berwyn, everyone would say, "Berwyn?!?" and throw rubber chickens.

So again, he was kind of an inspiration. But I never watched him in Cleveland and said I wanna grow up and be a horror movie host. It just happened synergistically. And it was a great … two … three years, really. Of all the things I've done—and I've interviewed presidents and kings and The Beatles, and you name it—this was probably the most fun period of my life, doing the horror movie stuff.

If we ever did a horror host family tree, you'd be this distant Ghoulardi branch…

Son of Ghoulardi

There's a guy (Ron Sweed) who did The Ghoul, who was on his show….

123

Svengoolie promo card featuring Jerry G. Bishop and Zelda the skull

I remember. They syndicated him to our station when I left.

The Son of Ghoul came on after that in Cleveland. He's been on for 15 years now and he's still on the air.
You're kidding. Why would you want to do that for 15 years?

Big Chuck Schodowski used to work with Ghoulardi...
Sure, Big Chuck! I'll be dipped.

He kept that same time slot. We just interviewed him and he's still doing the show in the same slot [The Big Chuck and Lil' John Show *went off the air in June of 2007*]. *Forty years...*

Oh, my god. I had a neighbor in the suburb of Chicago where we lived, named Bob Bell. Bob Bell was the original Bozo in Chicago on Channel 9, WGN. He was a really nice guy. He hated being Bozo because he was a regular staff announcer; he did voiceovers and news. But in the morning, they would put him in the Bozo costume, with the nose and the whole thing. And he was great! He told me one time that if at any time somebody found out who he was, he would run the other way. He couldn't stand it because he was *Bozo*! He was a 50-something-year-old guy, with kids yelling Bozo at him. He hated it.

I wasn't too thrilled myself when I was doing Svengoolie. I'll tell you a good story. I had done an appearance. I was, in those days, getting $5,000 for a personal appearance at a shopping center—to do nothing. Just to go up there and yell "Hello kids! How are you?" And then I'd sign some autographs. I had to have police protection a couple of times. The show was that big. It was scary. I was afraid for my life. One time, I came home from one of those and my son—who is at this moment in Czechoslovakia playing hockey—was, like, two. He wouldn't let me in the house since I had the horror movie costume on. He was terrified of me. He was not happy that Svengooli was his dad. They didn't know.

How does being a horror host compare to other things you've done? What are the advantages of being a host?

It's pure fun, just over the top craziness. We throw rubber chickens around and make fun of everything in society. That was once a week. There was the horror movie on Friday nights; we'd tape it Friday afternoons. But at the same time I was doing that, I was doing a serious talk show, a regular face-to-face "How long you been a ghetto priest?" kind of talk show. And I was doing some news. I was hosting an afternoon movie in my mufti, you know, my regular life costume … clothes.

And once a week, you get to be this maniac. It was the early '70s, a lot going on. I know a lot of kids from the various colleges around, and probably high schools as well, would light up on Friday nights. They just smoke joints, watch Svengoolie and get happy … and eat the munchies. It was a way of life.

But to get back to your original question: Yes, the most fun, pure fun that I've ever had. When you do a regular talk show, like the one I did here in San Diego for 13 years, a morning talk show, kind of like Regis. It was called *Sun Up San Diego*. You can't be crazy. You've got to ask questions. A guy's written a book is there and you've got to ask him six questions. He gives you six answers and you've got to say, "We'll be right back." And that's pretty much it. But doing this kind of thing, we just spoofed everything. We took shots at everything.

Ernie Anderson said that having the beard gave him a license to say things he could never say as Ernie. Talk a little bit to that. What things could you get away with?

Well, it was the Nixon years, and we loved making fun of Nixon and Watergate. It was the liberal point of view, which is what I have, liberal views. The one that springs to mind most is the Watergate hearings. We would do regular skits. It wasn't just the horror host talking to the camera.

I had guests. I had mystery guest coffin openers every week. We'd open the show. I'd be in a standup coffin. The top came off. The show would open on a shot of somebody signing the guest book. We had Bette Midler a couple of times, and Barry Manilow, who was her piano player then. He loved the show. In fact, he wore a Svengoolie sweatshirt on one of the TV specials in the 1970s, which freaked me out.

They would shoot the guest signing in; they would walk over to the coffin. He'd sign the coffin and knock on the door. I'd open the door and do this little opening poem every week. *(Svengoolie voice)* "The time has come for scary things/Like monsters, ghosts and vampire wings/With horrible movies, all drippy and drooly/And horrible jokes, with me, Svengoolie!" By the way, you want to know where I got the accent? My uncle, Hymie, Hyman Leibo, God rest his soul, came from Russia. He had a very thick Jewish accent. That's the way he talked. So, it was easy for me to pick that up.

Your show was on at a time when you could put horror on TV and it was a family event, anybody could watch this. Talk to that a bit. What kind of audience did you have?

It was family, some. But mostly it was an 18 to 28, 29, 34-year-old audiences ... kids. It was on 10:30 at night. Don't forget, 10:30 in Chicago is like 11:30 on both coasts. The news comes on 10:00, and at 10:30 people would go to sleep. So if kids stayed up—on Friday nights they were allowed to stay up—they skewed younger and younger. I get emails from people all the time who say, "Hey, I saw you on the Internet and we used to watch your show. I was only six years old and my mom would let me stay up." Those kinds of things are kind of cool, you know? They're fun. But I think the bulk of the audience was college age.

Did you get things sent in? Did they send you things they'd draw?

Yeah. I've got one at home, in fact, in the bathroom. Somebody crocheted a portrait of Svengoolie, and it's in a frame. People are amazing. Most of the stuff I frankly didn't keep. I'm not a saver. An example that doesn't relate to Svengoolie: When I was doing a radio show in Cleveland, there was a big teen audience. The station had asked me when I started, *don't* talk about the fact you're married. I had just gotten married. They said don't mention that because the audience consisted of young girls.

We had this stupid philosophy from management. But I said okay. I never said I wasn't married. But I never said anything about it. And then my wife had a baby, a daughter. My wife calls me from the hospital and she says, "There's a reporter here from *The Cleveland Plain Dealer*. He's downstairs in the lobby and he wants to come up and interview me."

I said, well, do you want to? She said, "No." So I said well, tell him not to come up. They got her picture. They broke into the station and took her picture off my desk. And there was an article on the front page in Cleveland. The story said "Deejay Jerry G. married, wed, and a father." And then they had a story about my wife, Elizabeth, and her picture was in there. She gave birth to a little girl. The station had asked me to keep it quiet because they were afraid of offending my teenage girl audience.

That radio station was a 50,000 watt—and AM was all it was in those days—Clear Channel station. It covered the whole Middle West and into the East. I got booties and little stuffed animals. I'm talking thousands of them, not 10. And people did that with Svengoolie. It wasn't the emotional thing of awww, a baby. But I got a lot of … junk, pardon the expression.

There was a strong connection to radio for a lot of the early horror hosts. Talk about what you got out of radio, and what prepared you to do live television. Was it live or tape?

It was taped. We had to tape it in the afternoon, because they didn't want to pay a crew to stay at night. But it was live in the sense that we never did anything over. Anything that would go wrong we kept. If they'd throw a rubber chicken at me—that was a big shtick with us, rubber chickens—if they would hit me with a rubber chicken and it hurt me, it stayed. Once I had a nosebleed. But I had

a green beard. You couldn't tell, but I could. I left it in. And eventually, I just took a rag and said, "Look at that, folks!" We got a tight shot of the hand with the bloody handkerchief. Anybody who sees anything on television believes that's what the personality meant to do. Nobody thinks that anything ever goes wrong. So when it goes wrong, it's fine. That's the way it is.

So, how did the show come about? Surely you didn't go in and audition.

As I was telling you, I was doing booth announcing, and I started doing voiceover. "And now, back to the movie!" It was just a voice. People started writing. Who is that guy? And little by little, it expanded. I thought, hey, maybe we got something here. Let's just have fun with it. I came up with the name Svengoolie, stolen from Ghoulardi. A friend of mine, an artist, did a sweatshirt that had a caricature of a character. We didn't even know what it was going to look like. And so I said we can do that.

Somebody got me some of that spirit gum and crepe hair, and we made a moustache and beard. And I wore shades. I had the headband and a shoulder-length green wig that a friend of mine dyed. It was a blonde wig that they dyed Kelly green. And that was the character. Finally, the station said, "We're starting getting a lot of mail. Why don't we see if we can go live with this thing?" We did. We started taping on Friday afternoons, and they'd run our bits in the breaks, just like all horror movies do. Always run it up to the back-to-the-movie part. That was always the finish, And now, back to the movie! So, it developed. And developed, frankly, into, if you'll pardon the expression, a monster. It got very big. I had no idea…

It was not a planned career move. You can't plan that kind of a thing. There had been horror movie hosts in Chicago before, Marvin, for example. He was big. I remember his name when I was a kid. But I never watched it, frankly. So, that was not a role model for me. And I hope to God Svengoolie wasn't a role model for any kids watching then, either.

Why do you think a host was so popular? They had them all over the country. Why would you need a host to host a horror movie?

Once of the reasons, I think, is that most of the movies that we showed were garbage! They were so bad that they were good, you know? We're talking pure camp. We had a whole package of Yugoslavian horror movies: *Vampires of Blood* (sic), and all those things. All the soundtracks were dubbed in English, and they were never on the mark. You can't make it perfect, Yugoslavian to English, anyway. The movies were bad. The hosts were just … I don't know. That's a hard question. I don't know why you needed a host. But, you did.

But on the other side of that, our competition on Friday nights, on Channel 9 Chicago, WGN, ran *Creature Features*. Ours was called *Screaming Yellow Theater*, for some reason. Some guy in the PR office thought that up. But WGN—which carries the Cubs, by the way—was *Creature Features*. They had done that before I did Svengoolie and they did it afterwards. It was just a slide, a vampire or something, and the booth announcer: "And now back to tonight's *Creature Features*." That was all it was. It did well; it got good ratings.

We became a phenomenon. But none could ever last. I'm astounded when you tell me that some of these guys are still doing this, horror movie hosting, and have been doing it for 30 years. I would kill myself if I had to do that for 30 years. It was like I said, pure fun. But the kind of fun that was of the moment and you knew it could never last. It wouldn't be fun 10 years later. I can't imagine they're still having fun. I hope they are. But I doubt it.

That brings us to: Why did you eventually leave? What drew you away from Svengoolie?

Well, it was time, I think. I was working at Channel 32, doing this Svengoolie thing. I had done it about three years. And I was offered a really good opportunity at an NBC owned and operated radio and TV station in Chicago, WNAQ. I did a morning radio show, which is really my background. I'm still doing radio and a once a week television show on channel 5 in Chicago, for triple the money. So, it was not a hard decision to make. Plus, I was thrilled, because I knew I didn't want to do this forever. I remember Bob Bell told me, "Man, don't be Bozo for the rest of your life." In my case, I would have been Svengoolie for the rest of my life. Not what I wanted to be.

So you passed Svengoolie off to someone else, someone else came along.

At the height of the Svengoolie mania—it almost was in Chicago—I started getting letters from a guy who was at Northwestern University, a broadcast major named Rich Koz. And he would send me jokes and shtick and bits. I started using them. And after a couple weeks, I called him and I said, "Rich, come on down to the studio." So he would be off camera, along with a bunch of other people, whoever was hanging around, throwing rubber chickens and yelling voices and all. He ended up writing most of the show with me. I would write the whole show, script the whole thing, but the show never really followed the script anyway, But that's okay. He ended up writing a lot of the stuff. Turned out to be very talented, had a tremendous stable of voices. He could do anybody. He'd do voices, off camera stuff. Then he'd come on camera and do some things.

When I left, I went to the management. And I said if you want to continue this show, Rich should do it. He couldn't do it as Svengoolie, because it would be too obvious a change. Physically he didn't look at all like me. And so he called himself Son of Svengoolie. And he had a picture of me on the wall of the set. They kept the same set. It was like a grotto, with a dungeon-looking thing. He had a big picture of me, and it said "Dad." And then he played himself as Son of Svengoolie for a long time. He wore a different outfit. In fact, one time I came back to Chicago for something—I was living here in San Diego by then—and I went on the show, we did some bits together. Then he asked me for permission, "Can I just call myself Svengoolie?" I said, yeah, why not? It didn't cost me anything. So that's who he is now. He's been very successful. He's won a couple of Emmys and is very popular in Chicago.

What are you doing now?

I came here to San Diego after five years at NBC—that job I told you about—to do a morning talk show. A kind of Regis and Kathy Lee, Kelly, whatever her name is, show. It was kind of the local version of it. Every city had one: An *AM Pittsburgh* and a *Good Morning Detroit*, and *Get the Hell Out of Bed, Muncie*. This was *Sun Up San Diego*. And I did that for 13 years. Three Emmys … but who counts? We interviewed everybody in the world. Presidents and big stars, whoever was in San Diego. That's the show.

And when that ended I had some back surgery. I took two years off, and just did nothing. A local radio station called and asked me to come in and do a morning radio show. They knew about my radio background. That's really my first love. You're in total control. You're not counting on the cameraman or the director cutting to the right shot, any of that, which I never minded on Svengoolie.

With radio you're in total control. So I went back to radio, and I've been doing that ever since, working at one of the Clear Channel radio stations. Aren't they all? But that's another story. I'm doing the middle of the day, from 10 to 2. That's big bands and Sinatra and music I grew up with. I also grew up with do-wop. There's a station in Chicago, also owned by Clear Channel, coincidentally, where I do a show from here in San Diego by satellite, every weekend. It's an oldies show, real oldies: Dion and the Belmonts and The Crests, those kinds of songs. Songs I really love, songs with soul, balls. So I'm playing a lot of music I like. And I talk in between, and that's basically what I'm doing now. Plus I'm in the restaurant business, a little Greek café. That's our

Jerry G. Bishop, signing a chicken! Now there's a sentence you don't read often!

major source of livelihood. My wife is at the register right now, taking people's money and giving them food. So if you're ever in San Diego, The Greek Island's Café at Seaport Village. Thank you very much. This has been a paid political announcement.

What kind of things did you do then that you couldn't get away with now? How has television changed?

Well, in the current environment in this country, where conversation is being recorded, you probably couldn't get away with a lot. The media right now is full of people like Howard Stern, who represents obscenity on the airwaves. We were never obscene, but we were irreverent. And that's, I think, the difference. Irreverence is hopefully acceptable. Obscenity is not my call. Somebody in Washington, though, thinks the things that Howard Stern says—and Bubba the Love Sponge and Janet Jackson's breast—are obscene and should not be seen in the home. Children, all that stuff.

Do you think there were things in your show—particularly since you were poking fun at the administration at that time—that you couldn't get away with in today's climate?

I'd like to think not. But I don't have an insight into what the FCC's thinking anymore. I don't know. Again, to me, irreverence is fine. Obscenity is a question mark. I don't want my grandchildren exposed to a lot of obscenity. But the best censorship is the dial, period. That's all you need. You don't need somebody in Washington to say, "That's not acceptable." Turn it off, period.

The Ghoul, Ron Sweed, worked for a Clear Channel station.

At one point Channel 32 brought in that syndicated *The Ghoul Show*, which I saw a few times when I was in Chicago. It was the worst thing I'd ever seen, between us girls. No offense, Ghoul, but it was garbage. What we aimed at was pure satire, just making fun of the stupid world we live in. It would probably be a little tougher today, since it's a pretty scary world, a much scarier world now than it was then. Don't forget, we were in between *Ozzie and Harriet* and *All in the Family*. It was swinging to the left in terms of irreverence. But I doubt very much we would be censored for anything we did at that point. It was all meant in fun ... although I hated Nixon.

Do you have any feelings or any thoughts about the changing nature of horror films? Maybe it's something to do with the scarier world, but horror films have become more violent and bloody and we really don't have horror films where you can sit down with a 10 or 11 year old and watch anymore.

It's "We have to top the last guy. We've got to have more violence and more explosions, more stabbings…"

But you never had good films on your show either...

Well, we had *Night of the Living Dead* (1968), and that's a classic. But that doesn't mean it's good. Those are two different things. I mean, it wasn't *To Kill a Mockingbird* (1962) or *The Caine Mutiny (1954)* or *Citizen Kane* (1941). It wasn't that. But in its genre, it was great. But again, you had to accept it as this could never happen.

Have you seen any of the other hosts at all, aside from The Ghoul?

I knew Ernie (*Anderson*), met him in Cleveland several times. I wasn't doing the horror movie thing then. I was a radio deejay and TV host. But he was the only guy I'd ever watch. If I would be home and he was on, I'd watch him, because he had an edge to him. He was tongue-in-cheek and you always knew he was ready to burst out laughing.

He and Tim Conway worked together. They did an album...

Oh yeah, they were great together. You ever hear that album? It was funny stuff. Tim is a genius. There was a guy named John Mashita, who was sort of popular. He's now the off-camera announcer on *Hollywood Squares*. But back when I was doing the TV talk show here, he had done a TV commercial for somebody where he talked so fast and he could say more words in a minute than anyone in the world. He was in the Guinness record book. He just had a talent for talking fast. So we had him on the show; he was plugging something or another. And at the same time, we had Tim Conway as a guest. Not together, they were doing two different segments. I wondered what could I do to put these two together, because we always tried to do that. And I said, how about a fast-talking contest? And they both loved it. So I gave them each ... I forget what it was, *War and Peace* or something. And I said, when I count to three, each of you just read as fast as you can. And Conway yells..."Oh, I can do that." I go one, two, three ... bang. And this guy just goes off a mile a minute ranting bludda-bludda-bludda, blaaaa.

Conway goes, "In ... the ..." He lapses into the old man character he used to do on the *Carol Burnett Show*. It was hysterical. You can't re-tell it. I've got video of it at home. It was so funny. And after it was over, we dinged the

bell, and he had gone, like, four words. The guy had read six full pages. I said, "We'll be back with the decision of the judges, right after this."

He (*Conway*) worked at the same station as I did. He was gone by the time I got to Cleveland. But he was at Channel 3, and he was a legend then. I think he did some directing, and I forget what else. He was a stagehand, became a director or something. This guy's always funny. That kind of a mind, I guess. He's a genius.

Working on the set must have been playtime. The crew had to be the crew's favorite time.

They loved it, because most of what television does is canned. It either comes down the network line, or it's a video show, or a film or something. So guys that work in TV studios, they don't have a lot to do that's creative. It's either push the buttons or roll the tapes. The only thing in local television these days is the news. That's not very creative. They've got remote cameras. They don't even have cameramen in the studios in most cases. So when this horror movie show came up, and we started taping this on Friday afternoons, guys were fighting to get on the crew on that day. Whoever was on was assigned. After a few months, I insisted, because I got power, that we use certain guys who could run audio. They were always dropping in little sound effects and voices. And certain guys were better than others. But I was getting the luck of the draw. So yeah, it became a plum. Everybody looked forward to it. "Who you gonna have on this week?" This from the guys at the station, I wish I could remember all of them.

But we had guest coffin openers. It got to be a plum for them. I would get calls from their managers, saying, "Neil Sedaka's going to be doing a concert. Can we get him on Svengoolie to plug the concert?" Yeah, sure. So he was a coffin opener. And I would say (*Svengoolie voice*): "And here he is, aging rock star, Neil Sedaka!" Things like that that are priceless and you can't script. You can't create that character.

Ghoul Power!
The Ghoul (Ron Sweed)
Interviewed by Sandy Clark (2003)

In 1963, the airwaves in Northeast Ohio were warped beyond recognition by the arrival of Ernie Anderson's cracked creation, Ghoulardi, the host of *Shock Theater* on WJW-TV 8. Anderson's libertarian beatnik grabbed young viewers by the scruff of their minds and shook them with a potent combination of cheap horror, unchained rebellion and cryptic hipster gobbledygook. Some half a century later, Ghoulardi arguably remains the single most influential television personality in Cleveland broadcast history.

In 1970, following a failed attempt to talk Anderson into reviving the character, a young Ron Sweed secured permission to create an offshoot dubbed The Ghoul. The earliest incarnation was a note-for-note recreation of Ghoulardi. But as he grew comfortable in the role, Sweed unleashed a wilder, rougher version of the character more in tune with the modern spirit of rebellion. In many ways, The Ghoul's brand of low-rent anarchy, exaltation of trash and abrasive antisocial posturing offered a prescient vision of the coming punk aesthetic.

The Ghoul first aired on the local Kaiser affiliate, WKBF-TV 61 in Cleveland. He later enjoyed expansion to several national markets as part of a syndication experiment by the parent company. He was off the air entirely by the mid-70s, resurfaced briefly in the mid-80s and disappeared with seeming finality in 2004, after a rocky six-year run on WBNX-TV 55.

In 1986, WOAC-TV 67, a local Akron, Ohio station, began broadcasting a horror movie program hosted by Keven Scarpino as The Son of Ghoul. The name and the look—a manic character sporting a suspiciously familiar Ghoulardi-style phony beard—were in Sweed's mind ample reason to sue Scarpino and the station for half a million dollars. The case went to court and the judge ruled in Keven Scarpino's favor, sparking the sort of fierce multi-decade horror host feud that could only happen in Cleveland.

Can you tell which markets you've been in over the years?

I have been on Cleveland television, Detroit television, Philadelphia, Chicago, LA, San Francisco and Boston. They put me on prime time in Boston back in the 1970s, the same year *Bob Newhart* and *All in the Family* started. I had to run against them with cheap, cheesy movies—like Michael Jackson dangling his baby from a balcony. We had them all, even way back then. But we've been doing it since 1971, which if we do the math is about 32 or 33 years. It just doesn't seem like 33 years.

Let's go back in time, before The Ghoul took over your life. Can we talk a bit about Ernie Anderson, Mad Daddy and any other early influences?

Yeah. We'll start with Mad Daddy, because he was first. He was Pete Meyers. He was a deejay in Cleveland at WHK radio, which is still going strong. And he worked at the same time Ernie Anderson was at WHK radio. Pretty cool. Now, I was about eight or nine years old, and it was the first time I saw the Frankenstein monster, because Mad Daddy—in addition to his radio job—became a horror host on Channel 8, which was the same station that Ghoulardi was on, Ernie Anderson.

I didn't realize he was on. But late one night, my mom and dad were ... somewhere. So I could stay up late. That's when I saw the Frankenstein monster. And when they went back to the station, there was Mad Daddy. He wore a death's cowl and had, like, bat wings on it and everything. And he was saying, "Hang loose, mother goose!" and ... wait, I better not do that one, it's not clean. "Little Jimmy, peachy keen/Built himself a time machine/Twisted a dial, pushed a button/Poof, and there was nuttin.'" He'd do stuff like that. It was all in rhyme. It was just absolutely fantastic. And I was so taken with Mad Daddy. My mom's friend was a seamstress. And so that Halloween, I was Mad Daddy for Halloween! So not only was I The Ghoul and worked for Ghoulardi, but I was Lil' Daddy too! Got a lot of candy, too, that year. Then Pete Meyers, I believe, went to the West Coast or New York.

At that time, the whole face of radio was changing and he just wasn't accepted the way he was in Cleveland. And unfortunately, he took his own life. That was the demise of Pete Meyers. But when he was doing Mad Daddy in Cleveland, I believe that was the first run of the Universal *Shock Theater* movie package, back in 1958. At that same time, I think that's when Zacherley popped up in Philadelphia, and you had Vampira—who Elvira's been ripping off shamelessly ever since—Manila (*sic*) Nurmi, I think her name is, on the West Coast. And Morgus, I think, was around. And Chilly Billy Cardille in the Pittsburgh area. So you had a lot of cool people in 1958.

Then in 1963, the package came around again. There were looking for someone at Channel 8, the same station Mad Daddy was at, to fill the bill as the local host. Ernie Anderson was a staff announcer and also a freelance announcer. In fact, he was Cleveland's highest paid announcer. He was doing work for the Ford Motor company and all kinds of national spots. They asked him if he would do the fill-ins on Friday night. So he came up with the beard and moustache and the fright wig and everything. Because he didn't want to be recognized playing the fool, as John Lennon says they sometimes do.

So he took the guise of "Ghoulardio." There was a contest and the name Ghoulardio was the winner. Well, he dropped the "O" and just called himself Ghoulardi. And in 1963 a Cleveland legend was born. I think Mad Daddy was somewhat big. But nothing like Ernie Anderson, nothing like Ghoulardi. Cleveland police maintain to this day that from 1963 to 1966, the crime rate on Friday nights at 11:30 would go down drastically because people were watching Ghoulardi.

I for one can tell you we would go on dates on Friday night. We would go to the show, and I would always meet my girlfriend inside. Why should I pay for you? I'll meet you inside by the pop machine! That way she would have to pay for her own admission. But by 11:00, the movies would still be going. All the guys would look at each other and, "See ya, girls! It's time for Ghoulardi!" We'd head back home and be in front of the TV set by 11:30.

Ernie Anderson had been on the air for about six months and he was making an appearance at an amusement park called Euclid Beach. I thought, well, I'm going to meet him one way or another. The way I orchestrated this meeting was this. I had a gorilla suit, which I had obtained about three months earlier. We'd been to see "Dr Silkini and His Live Stage Show of Horrors!" Five great ... well ... five *bad* horror movies! King Kong live

Ron Sweed in his wigged-glory as The Ghoul. Photo by Bob Paulin

on stage! The Frankenstein Monster! Dracula! After the five movies were over, everyone saw the live monsters stumble up and down the aisle. These were the same guys who would come home with me to watch Ghoulardi on Friday nights. We took the short cut through the back alley. Well, Dr. Silkini started packing up. Unfortunately, he left his truck unattended, and I became the proud owner of a gorilla suit! Hey look at that! And I grabbed it and went on home with it.

And that is how I met Ghoulardi. I figured if I wore my gorilla suit to Euclid Beach, he's gotta notice a gorilla, and I'll get his autograph. You see, I figured the chances of getting an autograph were slim to none when you have that huge a crowd. But if you're a gorilla, you got to get some sort of special treatment. By this time, Ghoulardi was not only on Friday night, he was on Saturday evening and Monday through Friday 4:30 p.m. to 5:00 p.m. with a show called *Laurel, Ghoulardi and Hardy*. So I took the bus, because I was only in 9th grade. I took the bus wearing my gorilla suit. My buddy had confiscated a dog chain and collar from his dog and had it around me. And the bus driver, who had no sense of humor, said, "Hey! You gonna ride on this bus, you got to take the head off!" All right, so I take my head off. We get to Euclid Beach,

One of the Ghoulardi postcards with Ron Sweed's forged Ghoulardi autograph on the back

I put the head back on. A lot of people thought it was Ghoulardi in the gorilla suit. So we didn't deny it, you know? So we had a huge crowd around us.

Ernie Anderson did three shows that day: two in the afternoon, one in the evening. So he came on stage. I was pretty close to center stage, a couple of rows back. He comes out, "Hey group! Cool it ove'day!" All of a sudden he stops. "I don't believe that! A gorilla! Come on up here, baby!" And so I got to go onstage with Ghoulardi. I'm just mugging along with him. He's going, "Ghoulardi ain't afraid of no gorilla." The stage was about five feet high, six feet high. Bam! He hits me in the chest and I stumble back. Unfortunately, I stumble back too far and suddenly I'm laying on my back at the bottom of the stage, like Gamera the turtle. I couldn't get up in this thing.

Suddenly I see him peer over. "Hey, you okay, baby?" I give him a thumbs-up. "Come on back up here! See that? That's a tough gorilla, nothing can hurt him!"

So I did that show. And afterwards he took me to his backstage, which was behind the Laugh In the Dark, the back part of it, with all the greasy gears and everything. He's taking his stuff off. I asked for an autograph and he obliged me with an autograph. Then he went back to the station to do *Laurel, Ghoulardi and Hardy*. All this stuff was live at the time. We'd seen a cameraman there. So we rush home. And sure enough on *Laurel, Ghoulardi and Hardy*, he showed films from a couple hours before at Euclid Beach. And there was the gorilla! All right! As soon as *Laurel, Ghoulardi and Hardy* was over, back on the bus! Back to Euclid Beach! Back for one more show. And we all knew the routine by now. "Hey, Ghoulardi ain't afraid of no gorilla!" And I knew enough not to stumble back too far, so I stayed on stage this round.

This was the same day the Manners—which is what we call the Big Boy franchise out here—came out with the Manners Big Ghoulardi. They were these orange freezes with blue whipped cream. Ghoulardi said, "If they don't make you sick, you got a bad one!" In real life he hated junk food. He said, "I'm not drinking that crap." But he showed it on each and every commercial. Well, I asked him if I could come down to the station with my gorilla suit the next day. He goes, "I don't care. You wanna come down, come down." So I came down and he put me on the air the next day, on the Saturday show. Each week, I'd have my dad drive me there and I'd sit in the lobby waiting for him to come in. He didn't care if I came or not. Eventually the guard, who was old Mr. Vickers, about 92 years old, would say, "Ah, you may as well go into his office and wait for him there." This was after about a month and a half.

And his office was piled high with props. Obviously he wasn't keeping a neat inventory of stuff. I figured I'd make myself useful. So basically, I'd put everything in order. I found checks of his for freelance work, hundreds of dollars, that weren't open yet. "Oh, there's where that check is! I thought they stiffed me!" So I did make myself useful. Eventually I was able to go into the studio and get his props ready for him; he counted on me to do that. And that's what I did. I graduated from his gorilla. You can only get so much mileage out of a gorilla suit, running around. But I did all his mail on a weekly basis. Probably 75% of people in town who figure, "Hey, I got Ghoulardi's autograph," from the early 1960s," that's actually me signing the photo. He showed me how to write it and he said, "There ya go. Send everybody an autographed picture." And I can do his signature, Ernie Anderson, or Ghoulardi, exactly. All of a sudden the price of Ghoulardi autographs dropped drastically after people heard this. "I got Sweed's autograph, not Ernie Anderson's! Shit!"

I stayed with him till 1966, when Tim Conway, who was his best friend, lured him out to Hollywood. He'd lived in Chagrin Falls and he'd come back every summer and visit his mom and dad, with his kids and stuff. And I'd be able to go to Tim Conway's house with Mr. Anderson. That was pretty cool, got to hang around with Tim Conway. They'd go to restaurants and take turns breaking each other up. It was like being on the *Carol Burnett Show,* almost, just fantastic. After *McHale's Navy*, Tim Conway started a new show called *Rango*. It lasted 13 weeks, but they didn't know how long it was going to last. He had Mr. Anderson as the sheriff. So Ernie just gave up everything. He was the highest paid announcer, plus double for Ghoulardi. I think it was little over $100,000 a year, in the 1960s.

He just said, "So long, Cleveland." He always minimized Ghoulardi. He just thought it was some stupid little thing he was going to do briefly. He never realized the impact it had on so many people. *Rango* lasted 13 weeks, but it didn't take him long to establish himself as the second or third highest paid announcer in the United States. I think Ed McMahon is first; Casey Kasem came in second, or, tied with Ernie Anderson. He'd do national accounts, like "Cougar ... A man's car!" Not many people realize that was *his* voice in all those commercials, or, "The Loooooove Boat!" That was his voice. He became the voice of ABC, right up to his death a couple years ago.

After he left in '66, a fella who was sort of like my big brother, Big Chuck Shodowski, started a show called *The Hoolihan and Big Chuck Show*, with our local weatherman Hoolihan. So basically I went from being a gopher to where I'm writing segments now. I was still in high school. In fact, Chuck gave me the producer credits on the show. But then all the old timers at the station went, "Geez, the kid isn't even out of high school, but you put him in as producer?!" He got so much flak; I had to take my name off. I think I got production assistant or something.

In 1967 I started going to Bowling Green University. I would come home on weekends and do *The Hoolihan and Big Chuck Show*, then go back for Mondays. Eventu-

ally—nothing against Chuck—but comparing Big Chuck and Hoolihan would be like comparing Herman's Hermits to Ghoulardi and The Ghoul being the Rolling Stones. I was actually getting bored with the kind of mundane material. The Smothers Brothers was out at that time and there was a lot of good topical political humor going on. I was writing some good stuff for Chuck and it was, "Ohhhh, it's too offensive! We don't want to offend anybody out there." "Chuck, look at your mail. We're offending a lot of people. You can't get everyone to like you."

Ernie Anderson came back with a guy called Chuck McCann to do a special, only on Channel 5, not Channel 8. A guy called Herman Spiro asked him to come out. Chuck McCann was the guy from the Rite Guard commercials. You know, the guy on the other side of the medicine cabinet. "Hey guy, one shot and I'm good for the whole day." Let's see, what year was that? That was 1970. He was going to do a couple Ghoulardi segments on the show. He called me from the West Coast, because he had left all the Ghoulardi props with me. He said,

"Bring all the stuff down. Just set up for me like you used to do at Channel 8. Bring it by to Channel 5 Saturday morning; we'll be in Saturday afternoon. I'll do a couple of Ghoulardi segments, and then we'll do a couple other comedy segments, too." All right!

So I got all the stuff down there and set up. My plan was to ask him to come back once a month to Cleveland to tape four shows. I knew by now he loved the West Coast, and he wasn't going to re-relocate to Cleveland. So that was my plan. So after we had done the show at Channel 5—it was mid evening—he and his wife at the time, Edwina Gough, who was Paul Thomas Anderson's mom, and myself went out to a restaurant we used to go to that was two doors down from Channel 8. They had killer cheeseburgers and all the beer and martinis Ernie could drink. I hit him with that idea and he says, "Naw. I done it. I don't plan getting into that Ghoulardi stuff again. That three I did today was just, you know, for fun."

I had a backup plan. "How about you let *me* recreate the role as Ghoulardi?" And he goes, "*Why?*" I told him I'm getting bored with Chuck's show. And that was the wrong thing to say since Chuck and him were pretty good friends, and remained so until his death. He looked at me. He goes, "Chuck's boring, huh? You've been in college three whole years and you know it all, huh?" "No! No! No! I'm not saying that! I'm just saying that everyone would love to see Ghoulardi again, including me. And I would love to do the show. I'd be your producer and have it all set up. But if you don't want to, I would like to try and recreate it."

He said, "You know, you're a nice quiet Dick Cavett kinda guy. Why don't you do something that is more in tune with your personality?" I said there's another side to me that you never saw. But I'm not going to go goofing around. I've always been in awe of you. You've been like a second father or an uncle. I said, I really think I could pull it off. And he looked at me again, and I'm thinking, uh oh … he's gonna give to me again. But luckily, and to my surprise, he says, "Storer Broadcasting owns the name Ghoulardi, I own the character. So knock off the 'ardi' and call yourself The Ghoul, or whatever the fuck you want." Ernie had very salty language. I'm cleaning up a lot of this stuff. So he gave me permission to do it.

The first place I look was Kaiser Broadcasting. I brought them a pilot I did at Channel 8. In 1971 the only local TV stations were 3, 5 and 8—ABC, NBC and CBS. And then you had two UHF stations. United Artists was 43 here in Cleveland and Channel 61 was Kaiser. So I took it to them and the sales department there loved it. They said, "We got something here, we can make some dough with it." The first four weeks I did a dead on impression of Ernie Anderson doing Ghoulardi. After that, the 5th week, I incorporated my personality. I strapped on a pair of roller skates and went skating into the studio, crashing into sets and then falling over. The crew's laughing, I'm laughing. It was all one take stuff, whereas Ernie Anderson basically was more laid back on the stool. But that was the nature of comedy then. You still had Bob Newhart and Shelley Berman doing more laid back comedy. By then heavy metal was just coming in, people like Alice Cooper. You had to go some to put on more of a show. So that's what I did.

I knew I couldn't do laid back appearances anymore. Right from the beginning, back in 1971, I tried some great cerebral material and killer stuff that I wrote. And these metal heads were sitting there, basically wrecked, be it alcohol or whatever, they're just staring at me. So I'm thinking, okay, now, what can I do? So I take a garbage can with some scrap film I brought with me. "Hey gang;

Just as Ghoulardi was a spokesman for Manners burger chain in the early 1960s, The Ghoul advertised for the local Love's restaurants.

this is next week's movie! I'm going to see it never gets on the air." I threw an M-80 into the garbage can and *BAM!* Garbage is all over the place and suddenly I'm getting a standing ovation! "Heeeey! He's a genius! Whooooa!" Okay, that's the way it's going. So that's the way I had to go with it.

As I said, two of the cities I was in were LA and San Francisco. Big Chuck would go out to California and do periodic interviews catching up on what Ernie Anderson was doing for the Cleveland fans. He came back after one of those interviews and said, "I have a message from Ernie." I said, what? He said, "Tell the kid he fuckin' did it." He was watching me in LA on Channel 44 KBHK (*KBHK Ch 44 was the San Francisco station, the Los Angeles station was KBSC TV-52*). You can't get better praise than that. He acknowledged it and he liked it. So that was great. So that's what happened. I've been doing it ever since 1971. And now it is 2003.

We're going to go way back to the beginning of that question. What elements of Mad Daddy do you think Ernie Anderson used and that you inherited from the Ernie days?

To me, they always seemed like two separate entities. Ernie Anderson himself said he used a lot of Jackie Mason in his delivery and voice. I'll tell you the biggest difference. With Mad Daddy, there was an insistence that he never wrote a script, that all of his rhyme came off the top of his head. And I have no reason not to believe that, because he was considered a very intelligent guy. He was in the armed forces and was in charge of security or something. But, and I don't want this to sound the wrong way, the rhymes are contrived rhymes. You had to think about what you were going to rhyme about and everything. Whereas Ghoulardi was just very sarcastic and caustic and honest, you know? It was the first time you heard a host anywhere go, "Man, this show is a turkey tonight gang! You got something better to do, I urge you to do it. I wouldn't sit around and watch this garbage even if they paid me. And they are paying me!"

What kind of effect did that have on you? What age were you and what effect did this irreverence toward the material have?

I was 13 and it was just beautiful to see an adult doing this, since I was quite irreverent myself. Here I was 13 and getting kicked out of school quite a bit, just because I would tell teachers what I thought of them. Even from the time I was five, parents were calling my mom up saying I beat up their kid or ... whatever. I caused my parents a lot of trouble because of my irreverence and this was just amazing: an adult ... being honest ... all right! I couldn't get enough of it.

At 14 I set two goals for myself, and I achieved both of them. Number one, I was going to meet Ernie Anderson. And then after I met him in 1964, The Beatles broke, and I said, that's my next goal. The next goal I'm going to achieve is to meet The Beatles. And I did. And again, it was the irreverence of John Lennon, more so John than Paul and George and Ringo, that impressed me. In fact, I make that comparison. They were very similar people, John Lennon and Ernie Anderson. As far as I'm concerned they were both geniuses, they were both irreverent and tolerated pomposity *not* at all.

I remember John Lennon at the first press conference we were at. Joel Daly was our news anchor at the time. "Mr. Lennon, what do you think about all these psychologists who psychoanalyze your fans and say they scream because of this, that or the other? What do you think of them?" And he said, "Well, they probably have nothing better to do." He made Joel Daly a laughingstock in front of his peers there. But, you know, that was John and that was Ernie Anderson. Anybody who had an ego problem, and who encountered John or Ernie Anderson, left feeling awfully foolish.

So tell me what elements you kept from Ernie. What Ghoulardi elements did you keep and what were added? You touched on it a little earlier with the roller skates.

I tried to keep all of Ernie Anderson's act, because you can't improve upon perfection really. So I tried to keep all of that. Plus then I had to add just a, what would you call it, just a wave of lunacy and insanity that Ghoulardi didn't have. As I said, it was just more of a laid back time for humor in the original Ghoulardi days. I blow up a lot more stuff than he did. He used to blow up models and stuff. I blow up garbage cans and toilets. On one show in Detroit a guy said, "Hey, put a pack of firecrackers in my back pocket and light 'em!" So we did that. I blew up a person. Well, *just* his jeans...

Oh yeah, and Froggy. He didn't have Froggy then. Froggy was just supposed to be a one-time bit. I was walking through Toys 'R' Us during the first year of *The Ghoul Show* and there's a rack of these Froggys. I remember Froggy as a kid from *The Buster Brown Show*. Andy Devine was the host, and before that it was Smiling Ed McConnell. And Froggy would usually give those two guys grief, rather than the host giving Froggy grief. So I figured that would be a funny bit. I'd bring Froggy on going, "Hi ya! Hi ya!" Anyone my age or older is going to remember this. Those that don't remember it would

As a devoted Beatles fanatic, Sweed regularly worked references to the Fab Four into his act.

then remember the end result of the bit—whacking him to death with a baseball bat. So it was going to be a one-time bit.

Well, the next week Froggy got more mail than The Ghoul did. Go figure. So I figured, all right, we'll do him another week or two. He just became very popular and I thought of more ways to blow him up. We blew him up a lot of times. He's helped me cut the lawn and I run over him with a power lawn mower. He felt sick one time, so we pulled his tongue out to check it out and his tongue got to be 9 feet long. We kept pulling it as he's screaming, "Ow, my little Froggy tongue!"

I mean, just stupid bits, you know? This was many years before the Mr. Bill thing came out. In fact, I wouldn't be surprised if Mr. Bill came from Froggy, because a lot of the *Saturday Night Live* writers from the Gilda Radner days in the 1970s were from Michigan, mainly the Detroit area. You can have one coincidence, two coincidences. But after a whole year, say in 1974, where you're seeing the same bits that you're doing on *Saturday Night Live*, you know someone's watching. They say imitation is a measurement of success. But I'd like some of that *Saturday Night Live* money, too! So we added Froggy and did a lot of blowups. I would say the whole thing just became a hundred times more maniacal and insane.

You mentioned one instance where you were mistaken for Ghoulardi that very first time you were in the gorilla suit, with people thinking, "Maybe that's him. Maybe that's him." Have people walked up to you since and mistaken you for Ghoulardi? How does that make you feel?

Oh yeah. In Cleveland, it's maybe 30% of the people. "Hey Ghoulardi, how are ya?!" It's a good trick if he could be here, I'll tell you that. It would be a big long distance drive from all the way up there to here. But that's happened from day one. In fact, that's how I changed from Ernie Anderson's Ghoulardi to The Ghoul. The front page of the *Cleveland Press*, the big daily afternoon paper, used to have a thing called "Action Tab," where people used to write in with a question, and it would be answered. That would be one whole column to the left on the front page. The letter I remember was, "My wife and I have a steak dinner bet on this. She says it's Ernie Anderson [*who plays The Ghoul*] and I say it's not." And that was the first time, after the fourth show, that the *Cleveland Press* said, "Looks like you win the steak dinner, because it's Ron Sweed, who used to work for Ernie Anderson … blah, blah, blah, blah." And that's when we started doing The Ghoul, rather than my imitation of Ghoulardi.

Still, to this day, I do appearances and basically people older than myself go, "Hey, Ghoulardi!" And it's interesting, because you'll also see people who blur the line of The Ghoul and Ghoulardi. "Oh yeah, I used to see Froggy. Ghoulardi used to do Froggy all the time." But that never happened. Or they'll make references to music that wasn't even out when Ernie Anderson was doing Ghoulardi, music that I picked out for my show. "Oh yeah, I love that piece of music. Ghoulardi played it all the time!" At first, I guess it bothered me. Because that's Ghoulardi, I'm The Ghoul! But after 33 years of it, if you're going to get mixed up with somebody, who better to be mixed up with?

Why do you think Ohio attracts so many horror hosts? Was it just Ernie Anderson? His spirit was so powerful it just moved through the state?

I think so, I really do. People saw the value. I mean station managers, program directors, they saw the value in what happened in Cleveland. But that's an odd thing. When Ernie Anderson was doing Ghoulardi in Cleveland, they took him to another station in Toledo and it didn't work. The ratings weren't very good, and after 13 weeks, they dropped the show. So who knows? Cleveland and Detroit are very similar, first of all. Maybe it's the working class ethic. They're blue collar and just really like to have a good time, and they like their entertainment crazy. It's just difficult to say. I know in Detroit, you multiply my popularity a hundred times, and it's just insane. They never had their Ghoulardi; they never had Ernie Anderson. They had a few minor hosts, but I'm their Ernie Anderson.

I told my crew when we came out with the Ghoul book (The Ghoul Scrapbook, *by Ron Sweed and Mike Olszewski, Grey & Company 1998.*) a couple of years ago.

The Ghoul's rock 'n' roll roots show in this cover for *Scene* newspaper in 1973.

"When we go to the malls and do book signings, you aren't going to believe the crowds we generate." They're used to the crowds here, which aren't shabby. So we go, say, to the Westland Mall. We get there about seven o'clock for a book signing. They closed the mall at nine, and we still had a three-hour line that they let out a little at a time. Five or six hour lines, you know, to see The Ghoul. Whenever we do a club, we pack the club. They have to have a cut off because only "x" amount of people are allowed in the club.

A guy from the *TV Guide*—on the newsstand, not your local one—did a thing on me about three Halloweens ago ("The Best and The Frightest" Oct 28-Nov 3 2000 issue. *The article includes profiles of Zacherley, Svengoolie, Stella, The Ghoul and Count Floyd*.), and he said, "I'm sorry I've never had a chance to see your show. But I was in the Village with a girlfriend of mine who was from Detroit." They had some Ghoul memorabilia at some shop there. His girlfriend said, "If you're doing hosts, you've got to do The Ghoul!" "Well, what's so great about The Ghoul?" "He's the best!" So he got my number and we sent him out some tapes. He did a nice little piece on us in *TV Guide*.

Tell us about the ups and downs of your show. How many stations were you on at one time, how far across the country? What's that like, moving from station to station? And talk about the competition from cable and syndication, as well as from Saturday Night Live. *You were right there in the crunch when they were just squeezing hosts off the air.*

It was pretty cool. *Saturday Night Live*, in its heyday, would be on Friday nights in Detroit. And we would either tie *Saturday Night Live* or beat them in the ratings. And that's a UHF beating NBC, which was unheard of at that

137

The Ghoul's "Stay Sick Spew Sack," designed by local artist Joel Wilheim. One version of the sack came with Big Chuck and Lil' John's mailing address pre-printed on the back.

time. Also when I was on Friday nights, we would tie Carson or, during some 15-minute periods, beat him. So I was pretty proud of that.

In Detroit, let's see. I got kicked off just about every channel there except the PBS station. And I'm darn proud of it, too! I was on about four or five stations, I think, in Detroit including The Kaiser and some non-network stations. I know the numbers; I can't recall what they were at the time. In Cleveland, on Channel 61, a Kaiser station where I originally appeared, I had the honor of knocking the station off the air not once but *twice*. The first time they went to home shopping. So that was it for Kaiser. And then home shopping went off the air and another company brought it back in the 1980s and called me in Detroit and asked if I'd bring it on the air, which I did. Then we knocked that off the air totally. So it was fuzz for a while. Let's see, what is it now? It's the Spanish station. So I'm taking lessons. "Hola, Froggy! Como estas?" See, I'm taking the whole course. We'll be on the Spanish station before you know it.

Let's see, Boston. As I said, they put me on in prime time in the 1970s, against *Bob Newhart*, *All in the Family*, *Mary Tyler Moore*. I forgot what the fourth one was. But it was that whole two-hour block. "Hey, The Ghoul's not getting very good ratings here in Boston!" Nooooo … you know? So Boston was our first Kaiser station we lost. Eventually, Kaiser was getting rid of their broadcasting because it was Kaiser Industries, and then they went into broadcasting. Eventually they were letting go of each of their stations, one by one. As soon as they got rid of a station, so went The Ghoul, too. The amazing thing is I never realized the impact The Ghoul had up until the advent of on-line and emails. Our website is *theghoul.com* and we realistically get 10,000 hits a month. And it's amazing. People remember the show from the 1970s in Boston, Philly and Chicago. I just had no concept of the impact the show was having at the time. I just figured it was extra money from Kaiser. Channel 61 and Detroit were our two big markets.

And now a lot of these people have relocated to Japan and Australia. So now I'm getting email from people in Australia and Japan who have never even seen a regular show. But friends of theirs have given them tapes. "Blimey, Ghoul, we've got nothing like you Down Under. Wish you had a show down here." And I know once we hit national syndication, which I have no doubts we will—it's taken me longer than I would have liked—it's going to be a killer. In Japan, they're going to eat The Ghoul up. "Ah, Ghouli-san!" We'll blow up sushi, all sorts of good stuff.

Talk about being a fan and seeing your stuff on air, and what fans send you, what you receive from them and what you do for them. How important are fans to your program?

Hmmm…it's just amazing. Prop departments built none of our sets. They're all viewer-generated. Two guys came out of an appearance at Cedar Point dressed as The Ghoul with a big boom box with a skull on it. When you hit the button, it's the Papa-Oo-Mow-Mow Boom Box. The song "Papa-Oo-Mow-Mow" comes on and the skull's mouth goes up and down and the eyes pop out and light up. And it's got two speakers on it. So to this day, I walk in the 'hood and I defy any of the brothers to beat my Papa-Oo-Mow-Mow Boom Box!

Speaking of Japan, a Japanese lady, I guess her husband's an American from Detroit, won second place in a quilting contest with a huge tapestry of my head. And they sent a picture of it. Go figure that one out. And just this week a fan sent in a huge white sock, around six foot tall, that I use as Santa Ghoul for my bag of toys and my bag of kielbasa and Cheez Whiz. I enter and exit the studio on one of those huge bounce balls that kids use that a fan sent in to me. Someone found one that has a Froggy cover on it. So they sent that in a couple weeks ago. We get all kinds of different Froggys and stuff. And a lot of the things we blow up everybody generates. We do a couple blow-ups per show of models. The letters go, "Hey Ghoul, I spent two weeks making this. Blow it up for me." And we'll eradicate it in 20 seconds.

What brings that out of people? Is it just the ability to get something on TV? Or do you think it's something about seeing somebody else do it and it gives you permission?

I think people just really like to let loose and be nuts. And it gets harder and harder as things get more "politically correct," you know? Don't say this, don't say it like that, act normally. Another skit I do that Ernie Anderson hadn't done is "The Galloping Ghoulmet," where I'll take all kinds of food, throw it in the bowls and take whipped cream and put it all over me. "Hey, gotta have Cheez Whiz in this recipe, gang!" And I'd take a glop of Cheez Whiz up my nose. "Hey not bad, it clears up your sinuses, too!" "Hey, it's better than Vicks VapoRub!" And I'd put it all over my chest. "Hey, Tuck's Deodorant Pads!" … and into my armpits. Then I'm covered with Cheez Whiz, covered with whipped cream. I've got this bowl of glop and I throw an M-80 in it. BAM! It's all over the set and everything else. And people wish, I think, that they could do that. You see it in *Animal House*—food fight! You see it in cafeterias, if the monitors aren't looking—food fight! People just love to go nuts, you know? And I think, since they can't, I provide them with an outlet. Or shows of my ilk do, of which there aren't many.

Do you think this trend in corporate homogenized television is killing this sense of fun?

They really don't seem to give a rat's rear anymore, because of the nature of television now. You used to send out your sales department and they'd generate a lot of bucks by saying, "We've got this local personality or that local personality." But now, without even having to leave their sales office, an infomercial in Detroit brings in six thousand bucks! In Cleveland, an infomercial brings in three thousand bucks. So what do they care, really? The corporate heads are not in it for philanthropy. They're in it for the bottom line, to make money.

It's amazing. I'm surprised Howard Stern is still on. I like Howard Stern a lot. In fact, he did an interview with me before he moved out to New York, out of Detroit. And it was one of the most literate interviews I've ever had done. I just like the guy immensely. And I'm so surprised. They keep on boxing things out and I hope he can keep it going forever. But yeah, if you take a look at entertainment, especially the situation comedies, they're pretty bland. And to me, they just don't have much to offer.

You know, The Smothers Brothers, if you ever get a chance to catch their show in repeats, said a lot more. Letterman, I think, he's able to maintain it. But Letter-

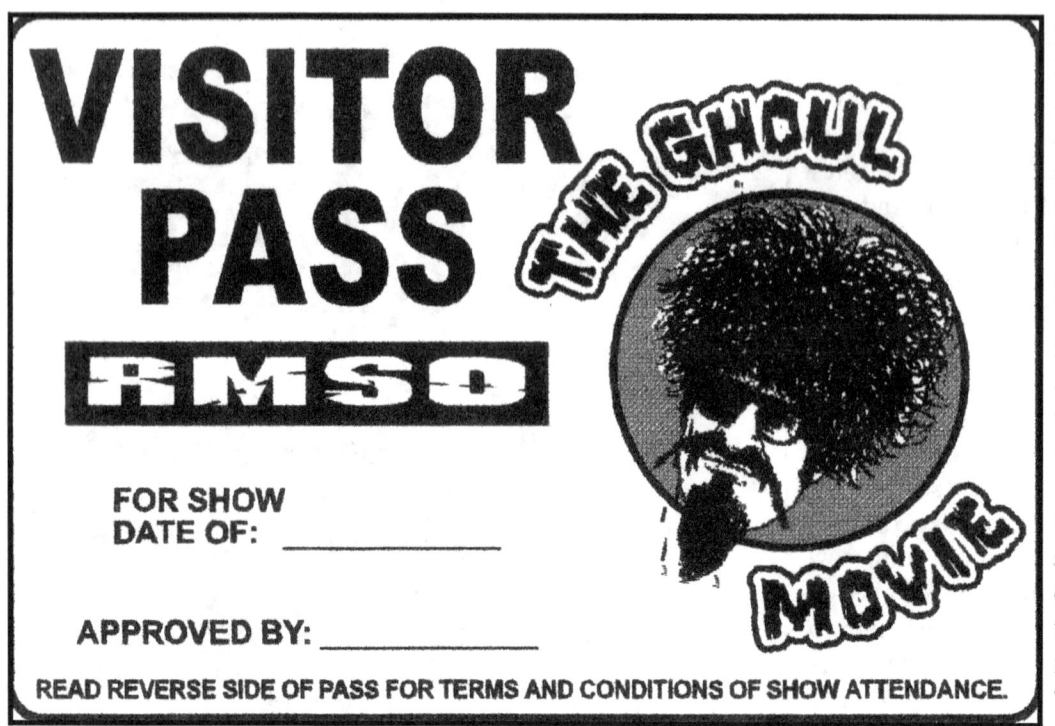

man and Jay Leno, when they got their network shows, you could see how drastically they had to pull in a little bit. They weren't as caustic and they weren't as irreverent as they were when they were guests on other shows. And again, it's the corporate thing. I'm sure it happens to everybody. I'm sure Elvis Presley had to modify some of his stuff a little bit, and that's back in the 1950s. The Beatles, for instance—Brian Epstein put them in the suits first, rather than their leather stage gear. So maybe it just happens everywhere. I do believe, though, the corporate thing is killing real good spontaneous entertainment, both on the radio and on TV.

I worked at a radio station here, WNCX 98.5, classic rock station. And we used to play anything we wanted to. The show I did was called "All Request House Party." You would call in with your request and we'd play 'em. Once Infinity took us over about two, three years ago, they gave us a play list. Our program director, a great guy, well, this is killing him; he's a rocker. He said, "Look, a lot of you have been straying from the play list here and there. They audit 24 hours a day and they're not happy that the play list isn't being adhered to. They said if I can't get you guys to stick by it, they'll get someone who can. So I'm telling you right now, start sticking by that play list."

Now John Lennon, in his vast catalog, has one hundred something songs. If somebody wants a John Lennon song, the only one we could play was "Imagine." That's it. Now take that scenario from East Coast to West Coast, with all Infinity stations. Suppose you turn on an Infinity station on a cross-country trip. All you're gonna here is "Imagine." since it's the same play list across the USA. Imagine how boring and dull that gets. Again, 230- something songs in The Beatles catalog, as a group, but they cut us down to 13 Beatles songs.

I did the show with a partner. And again, talk about irreverence. I don't care if the audience knows or not, but this guy's real "company." Throw it to me over on the microphone, "That's right the "All Request House Party" ... no longer do you give us a title. You pick the artist and we'll pick the titles for you!" We went into commercial and he says, "You can't say that!" I go, why not? It's absolutely true. "Yeah, but you're not supposed to let it be known it happens behind the scenes here." I go, I don't give a rat's rear. That's the situation. Four hours now seems like an eternity playing the same damn song, week after week, day after day.

I left WNCX, and it's too bad, and joined a new station that came on, an on-line station called Cleveland Hits.Com. Not only did they have the audio but also state of the art digital studios. It was right up the block from the Rock and Roll Hall of Fame. And they had, like, four cameras mounted in the studio. Not only could you hear me, but also I wore the stuff. You could see me too. For some reason, advertisers didn't sustain it. So last year, just before Thanksgiving, they closed their doors, which was too bad, because we were right back to what radio should be. We would play what we wanted. In fact, every hour, there would be 10 songs that you would be able to go to. And the three songs that got the most votes were included in the next hour's play, in addition to the ones I picked. So it was the best of both worlds, listeners got to pick 'em, I got to pick 'em. You could call me, email me and it would be instantaneous feedback. So now I go back to WNCX and do a little specialty stuff on the afternoon thing, a little café thing we do. And that's too bad. Luckily on the TV show, they haven't sanctioned me yet.

Let's talk a little about family and friends and what they think of all of this. Also, is this a part of the family tree that they want to acknowledge.

Actually my wife doesn't, since she's a mental health counselor. Plus she's a counselor at Catholic schools. She has a private practice and then during the week she's plugged into a couple of schools. *Cleveland Magazine*, two Valentine's ago, featured local personalities and their spouses. She said, "That's okay. I'll be in it, but I wouldn't have my face to the camera." So all our five pictures were her back to the camera and I'm hugging her, or my arm's in front of her face, or something. She's got a killer sense of humor, you know. But we figured it wouldn't do business all that good.

What was the first film you ever showed, and what were some of your personal favorites?

The first film I ever showed was probably *House on Haunted Hill* (1959), and after that, the perennial favorite, *Psychomania* (1973). The personal favorites, as far as the ones I've had on were *The Screaming Skull* (1958), *I Was a Teenage Werewolf* (1957) and *How to Make a Monster* (1958). It gives you not only one monster but two, the Teenage Werewolf and the Teenage Frankenstein. Oh, and *Invasion of the Saucermen* (1957). Those are the four I like. And then whatever Boris Karloff movies I've had on. You can't go wrong with Karloff. No matter how bad the material is, Karloff elevates it about five or six notches.

One last thing, if we could run through some of the charities you have helped out.

Sure. From Kaiser Broadcasting, I have sweated my pirogues off in the hot sun for Muscular Dystrophy at the fishbowl outside Channel 61. Those Labor Days can be *hot*, gang. We did those for probably five or six years. And I just did a Muscular Dystrophy telethon this year. WB55, my station, has now picked it up. I walked on and presented a check for five thousand dollars that we raised at a bar on the West Side called Ghoulardi's. Ghoulardi, the name, is now public domain. So a guy who has become a good friend now just opened up a very nice tribute bar to Ghoulardi. I appear there about every three months. We did a go-cart race that raised in excess of $5,000, and the owner presented that to Muscular Dystrophy.

Sickle Cell Anemia, with the Cleveland Browns, I've done. Naturally here in Cleveland, I wouldn't be doing it in Pittsburgh with the Cleveland Browns. Soupy Sales, before he became ill, did a telethon every summer in Detroit for retarded children and I would always participate in that. In fact, I scared Soupy the first year he was on. He had his back to the orchestra, and I blew up a bag with Froggy in it with an M-80. And he said a naughty word. It wasn't on camera, but … still. In Parma we do the animal shelter every year and raise money for the distressed dogs and cats and whatever else they have at the time. And remember, Parma spelled backwards is Amrap.

Any final words you want to say?

Final words? Stay sick! Turn blue! Scratch glass! Climb walls! But most importantly of all, boys and girls, do it while you can, but don't get caught!

Ho-Ha-HA!
Dr. Creep (Barry Hobart)
Interviewed by Sandy Clark (2003)

Barry Hobart came from a family of spook show performers, paranormal investigators and horror moviemakers. So the evolution from TV staff technician to late-night horror host seemed the outcome of natural selection. As Dr. Creep, Hobart hosted *Shock Theater* on Dayton, Ohio's WKEF-TV 22 from 1972 to 1985. But this host was more Captain Kangaroo than Crypt Keeper. Clad in black, with raccoon eyes, Amish beard and infectious laugh, the rotund Dr. Creep was far too jolly to be terrifying.

The bawdy late-night antics of Dr. Creep and company delighted hormone-happy teens, and Hobart's naturally sweet nature and puppet companion, the plush pinheaded alien, Obieyoyo, tickled the younger crowd. For a time, Dr. Creep moonlighted as the co-host of the weekday afternoon kid show, *Clubhouse 22*. This in turn inspired the station to give *Shock Theater* a shot with the kiddy crowd by moving it to a Saturday afternoon slot. But the show couldn't shake its sexy late-night edge, leading to conflict with management and eventual cancellation.

Dr. Creep continued to appear at various Halloween and charity events in and around Dayton over the years. In 1999, Dr. Creep returned to the airwaves with *The New Shock Theater*, made independently and broadcast on a local public access station. The show lacked the bounce of the original and only appeared sporadically through 2005.

Charity work was always important to Barry Hobart. In 1973, he joined with Linda Gabbard in creating Project Smiles, an organization that collects toys at Christmas for local children in need. He was also a regular and welcome figure at MDA fundraisers.

In December of 2010, following a series of massive heart attacks, Barry Hobart slipped into a coma. He died January 14, 2011 at the age of 68.

It seems the roots of the TV horror host spring from the old Spook Shows.

Barry Hobart in the guise of Dr. Creep

Live monsters on stage were a big attraction. There was this one show with Frankenstein, okay? The Wolf Man comes in and there's this fight sequence between the werewolf and Frankenstein onstage. Now the guy that did the Frankenstein was a fella by the name of Don Henry. He's actually a cousin. He put on the stilted boots and everything. The thing is, every time he put that costume on he thought he was Frankenstein, and he was a strong man. He would come out in the audience and do all this stuff. The way it ends is the werewolf kills Frankenstein somehow. My uncle, Doug Hobart, played Dr. Frankenstein. He has long hair and he pulls him offstage and he's screaming. And you hear the howling and everything in the background. Then the final death knell and he screams. The curtains close, you know? This was live.

I've got a book (Ghostmasters—Mark Walker, 1991, Cool Hand Communications, Inc.) *that makes the mistake of not including him.*

They didn't include my uncle. And a couple of those people who are included in that book hated my uncle, because he had a better show than they did. And the audiences would go see his show rather than theirs. When I read that particular book—somebody gave it to me for my birthday—I'm going, "Where's my uncle?" My uncle had one of the most fantastic shows around. In fact, he got the audience so engrossed one time, the stage curtain caught on fire in one of the small towns he was playing—it was burning pretty good—and he stopped the panic in the theater by making that part of the show. They were able to get the fire out. But there probably would have been some people killed if it wasn't for my uncle. He just convinced them it was part of the act and went on with the show, you know, and the theater was burning.

Your character name…

Dr. Creep. It was very interesting, because we drew it out of a hat. There were other names, like Frank N. Stein and a few other weird names. But I drew out Dr. Creep. But when we did the show, we thought the name would be spelled K-R-E-E-P. It came in as C-R-E-E-P. We were on the air for 13 years on commercial television. Then I got out of the business for a little bit, came back, did some videotapes (*Best of Shock Theater Vol. 1 & 2*). Then I came back with some friends—Andy Copp, who's an independent filmmaker, and my other friend, Rick Martin. We started on cable access, been there almost five years.

Did you ever see a horror host on television yourself, before you did your show?

Actually, my mentor was one of the first horror hosts, and his name was Zacherley. In fact, I've got his private telephone number. (*Laughs*) Someone told him that I patterned myself after him. Zacherley was the one I was influenced by. And there was a fella down in New Orleans named Dr. Morgus. He had a sidekick, a hangman or a hatchet man or whatever. I forget exactly what his sidekick was. So there's been a lot of horror hosts over the years. I've traveled the country, seen them all. But I think Zacherley was my first and the only one that I was really influenced by.

I'll tell you something interesting. We did a live show on cable access once. We did *Blood Feast* (1963), and we also had a second feature, *The Brainiac (El Baron del Terror, 1962)*. See, I work for an alcohol and drug rehabilitation and release program. So they were watching the show that night and I had one of these cups (*a clear plastic cup*) on air. One of the guys called up. He called me The Big Kahuna. He says, "Big Kahuna, what's in the cup?" Nothing, just water. "Yeah, I believe that!" It was a live call-in, and a lot of the guys from the facility called in that night with all kinds of strange things.

I've done it for 33 years, but the first three years on commercial television my show was a thing called *Science Shock Theater* and I just did bumpers and things going into the movie. Then they came to me and said, "Would you like to audition?" I had approached them the year before, but they must have forgotten about it. They said, "Well, we would like to have a live horror host. Would you like to audition?" Sure, that's a great idea. Actually it was my idea a year before. We really only had David Frost on that night, on Saturday nights, and his show wasn't doing that well. They wanted to do a *Shock Theater* thing.

What station did you get started on?

Hosting? It was Channel 22, Dayton, Ohio. It was WKEF-TV. And I was on at 11 o'clock. That was when we were first on, 11 o'clock. Then we moved to 12. I was on Friday night, a *Friday Night Madness* thing. I was probably the only horror host who had two women guest hosting with me, okay? One was called Firma, and the other was Terra. One was indeed firma. The other was just a small little girl. We called her Terra. It was a joke. And the thing is, they kept asking me, "Can I bring my friend on the show?" And I said yeah, fine, it's okay with me. We'll work them in somehow. We were live for about three years, until they got wind that it was actually a party. Then they moved me down and we taped. We were on Saturdays and Sundays in the afternoons. And then we went back to following *Saturday Night Live*. We were *Saturday Night Dead*. It was taped, but it was still like a live show. We had a lot of fun with that show, we really did.

How did SNL affect you?

Saturday Night Live? I liked them. I liked them. I really liked the first four or five years of *Saturday Night Live*. They had some fantastic comedians. I think it affected us a lot. We did a lot of comedy bits. What we did was we built our show around the motion picture. Then there was a time when things just fell into place, you know. The thing was, when we first started out, I tried to make it like one of my uncle's Spook Shows, make it very eerie. We had a lot of special effects in the first few days of *Shock Theater*. But a lot of the sound effects and things didn't go off as planned. So it became a comedy. And for 13 years it was nothing but a spoof on a lot of the horror hosts around the nation. And we're still doing it that way.

So how did the show get started? Was it by accident or design?

Well, probably by accident and probably by design. I was an engineer at the station. I was an operational engineer. But the year before, we were not getting the ratings that we should with the *David Frost Show* on Saturday nights. We were going to play it really straight. The name was going to be Dr. Death instead of Dr. Creep. I was going to be in a monk outfit and things like that. But I drew the name out of a hat, Dr. Creep, and it stuck. We went on the air 11 o'clock, January 1, 1972. I figure my audience was hung over. And we got the highest ratings they ever had in that particular slot. And we went for 13 years. We went until 1985, 1986.

Do you remember your first film?

Yes. The first film was *Black Sabbath* (*I Tre Volti della Paura*, 1963); it was one of *my* favorite motion pictures. I remember that well, because we did a telephone bit in it that ran long. Actually, since we were live for about three or four years, if we only had a 60-minute movie, let's do three hours! (*Laughs*) We were the only thing on. So basically, that's exactly what happened. We did almost three hours with a 60-minute movie! (*Laughs*)

We had a lot of fun. We brought people on, and we did a freakers' ball. We did a lot of strangeness. I had a lot of magicians and illusionist friends of mine who came on the show. We almost got kicked off the air by doing, on Mother's Day, a song called "Fifty Ways to Kill Your Mother," and things like that. I thought it was funny. They didn't. They were in the studio that next Mother's Day, 'cause I was looking for that hook. I said, "We're going to do a tribute to Mother," and this same guy was on that did "Fifty Ways to Kill Your Mother." His name is Dow Thomas. He's a national comedian, and he goes around the United States to the different comedy clubs. He did a lot of things. We did a lot of things together.

He was on the show the next Mother's Day and they were right there in the studio—the station director, the program director. I was looking for the hook, since I was known as a rebel. I would have played the song the second time in a row, when they told not to do it ever again. Thomas did the strumming of the guitar. We didn't do the chorus or anything like that, just strumming the guitar to "Fifty Ways to Kill Your Mother." And I saw them coming my way, man. And Dow Thomas goes, "A tribute to Mother ..." and then we just did a poem. But the thing is, they were coming for me! Oh, were they coming for me!

We had a gay Frankenstein one time. I just did the Jerry Lewis Muscular Dystrophy Telethon in Dayton, Ohio at Hare Arena on Channel 22, and they had Ronald McDonald on there. So we were talking, and he and I have a mutual friend, Mike Martin. He was my Uncle Creepy. And he says, "Don't you recognize me?" And I said, no, I don't recognize you. He says, "Remember that gay Frankenstein you had on your show? I was the gay Frankenstein." He's doing Ronald McDonald now! (*Laughs*) I said would you like to come back on and do the gay Frankie again? He cracked me up.

I went back to the movies. I was just reading off what we were going to be having for the following weeks, and he was seated on the chair next to me. And we got to *The Million Eyes of Su Maru* (1967), and he says, "By the way, you have beautiful eyes. Those were the most beautiful eyes I've ever seen." And he just totally cracked me up and we went back to the movie. I couldn't go on any more. He just cracked me up. It was really fun.

We had a lot of things go wrong on the show. But everybody thought, well, it's just part of the show, you know. I had some of the most bizarre people on. We had a gay Dracula. That was funny, see, because one of the salesmen said to me, "There's going to be a children's show at the Victory Theater in Dayton, Ohio. And it's going to involve some superheroes and a villain. The villain's going to be Count Dracula and we would like you to promote it on the air." I told him, okay, fine. Bring him on. So he came on, and I knew I was in trouble, because his cape lining was pink.

So they were going to have Rocky the Flying Squirrel and Bullwinkle, Wonder Woman

Dr. Creep co-hosted the weekday kid show, Clubhouse 22, in the early 1970s.

and Superman, and everything. The plot of the thing is—and he (*Dracula*) says it in his beautiful voice—"I steal Rocky's nuts and they chase me around the stage." I'm thinking I'm going to kill the salesman who had me have this guy on." He's saying, "Rocky gets his nuts back at the end of the show." And I'm saying I'm glad! (*Laughs*)

Things like that would happen to me all the time. I almost got thrown off the air because this guy flashed the camera. They brought on the Northmount Jaycees. I was friends with the Northmount Jaycees. I always did their haunted house and I always promoted it on the air. And they were all in costume, except this one guy. He had a top hat on and a trench coat. I was wondering, where the heck's his costume, man? And I had to ask him. I shouldn't have done that, because he flashed the girl in the back. They started laughing. And then he turned around, flashed the camera. And he had … you know what he had. It was just funnier than heck.

I had a thing called Victim of the Week. It was kind of like write in and tell me if you want your girlfriend to be Victim of the Week. I had several different torture devices. Well, I ran out of all the torture devices, and I was getting to the last Victim of the Week, and my crew said, "We have got the girl for you. You're not going to have to solicit someone to write in for the last Victim of the Week. We've got the girl for you." So they brought her on the show. And the thing is, she was in a black sheath, right? Nice cleavage, gloves and everything. I said, here's the way we're going to do this, since we're out of torture items. When we come up on the Victim of the Week segment, we'll play David Rose's "The Stripper," and all you have to do is a few bumps and grinds.

So when I was talking with her, she said, "I don't dance. I don't bump and grind, okay?" I'll tell you what. We'll come up on me, Victim of the Week, yadada, yadada. And then, we'll play David Rose's "The Stripper" and I'll say, I'm going to take care of this myself. I'll pick you up and we'll go to black as I carry you off. And let them think whatever they want to. So we get into Victim of the Week. The crew set me up, because she was a professional stripper. We came up on Victim of the Week, here she is, our last Victim of the Week." And she went *BOOM* … when the David Rose music came in … *BOOM-BOOMPA-BOOM-BOOMPA-BOOM!* She started pulling off the gloves and everything … and I saw my life go before me.

What I did is I took off my cape, since she was going for the zipper and everything. I hear the crew laughing, and I'm going, we've got children watching! I go over with my cape and throw my cape on the camera lens. So nobody could see what was *really* happening. But she was a professional stripper. And when we went back into the movies, I said, yeah, you really got me boy. Yeah, she was a professional stripper … I'm going … I could just see myself in the program manager's office the next week, "Why did you have that girl on your show?!" "Well, I didn't know she was a professional stripper." (*Laughs*) We had a lot of things like that happen on *Shock Theater*. That's really what's made it popular over the years, because things just happened. And I have to react with whatever's going on, you know?

Do you like live or tape better?

I kind of like live. I'll tell you why. We had an orange creature by the name of Gorsh on the show. He was kind of like a Sid and Marty Kroft puppet, like their Sweet'ums. The fellow who was the puppeteer on my show loved and worked with Sid and Marty Kroft. He loved Sweet'ums, so he built his monster similar to that. We called him Gorsh. A couple incidents happened in regard to Gorsh. We were going to do *Cat People* (1942), and a friend of mine had a mountain lion by the name of Wendy. So I said, well, since we're going to do the original *Cat People*, I'd like to have Wendy on the show, and then she can be seen at my feet. So he says, "Fine." What they forgot to tell me was they play with this particular mountain lion wearing a couple of orange felt gloves. Now, Gorsh was orange, okay? So he walks out on the set. We're live, there's nothing you can do about it.

So … Wendy's ears perk up. She broke the chain and started chasing Gorsh. I had a coffin that sat upright, okay? Now, Gorsh is a big creature. He's not going to get in that coffin, so he's part way in and part way out. And you hear over the air, "Heeeelp! Heeeelp! Get this thing off me!" And the mountain lion's going (*swinging arm in a striking motion*) tish! tish!—trying to get the coffin all the way open, man! He's striking the coffin tish! tish! He wants to get to his plaything, which is Gorsh! And he actually chased my two co-hosts up a light ladder. (*Laughs*) And they were yelling the same type of thing, you know? Gorsh was one of my more fantastic people to work with me. He came on the show quite a lot. We did a lot of pantomimes with him and everything else. But things like that happened with *Shock Theater* all the time, you know? It was a lot of fun

And we were showing a movie—I think was something they did in Morocco—and there were blind vampires and all this. So we decided to do "Ahab the Arab," the Ray Stevens song. I found this one girl to do the show. She was dressed in this harem costume. Okay, we're on the air,

PUT A CREEP IN THE WHITEHOUSE
VOTE THE DR. CREEP - DOW THOMAS TICKET
Copyright 1996 EIA, Inc.

and we're doing "Ahab the Arab." Someone grabs the girl up, and he swings her. The camera cuts and you've got a full crotch shot. You can't take it back, man. Her mother never let her back on the show again! But the swing he made with her was there, the camera went—bing—full crotch shot of that harem costume. (*Laughs*) And you couldn't take it back. (*Laughs*) As I said, things like that happened to me all the time.

What kind of thinking went into your show? What did you decide about costumes, sets, style, the format?

I always told the cast, we don't go with a script, okay? Give me some kind of leeway. So, we would go with a script, a semi-script, and everyone would have to follow us. That was basically the way it worked. We would give the people a semi-script. I actually took down the owner of the comedy club in Dayton, Ohio, who was leaning over a desk. He was right next to the bell that was on the desk. And I took him like this (*mimes grabbing him*) and I brought him down on the bell and said, "Your face looks familiar, but it doesn't ring a bell with me." I pulled him down a couple times and hit him with that bell ringing.

The fellow who played one of my puppets, he was with a group called Night Vision Puppets. We had Obieyoyo, who looked like an orange-squeezer from outer space, you know, with eyes, okay? The thing is he was good. I love double entendres. What we would do is this. We would say something and you could take it either way. And we would ad-lib around that.

We used a lot of blackouts, too. But that got me in trouble one time, because they didn't have the monitor where they were supposed to have it. It was moved over. One of the girls brought one of her girlfriends on. She wanted her on the show, and she was a really buxom girl, really beautiful. I say she can be sitting on my lap. I would say, "I was never good with geography. But I was always good with facts and figures." And I went like this (*gestures with hands*) and the talcum powder came out of the old book, and I just threw the book away. And she kissed me, but she *French* kissed me. So I French kissed her back.

I'm saying, "Ooooo, well, hey, okay!" We went to black.

But the monitor wasn't there with my mic light, and the floor director was off to one side. I couldn't see him. But then he came into my view and went (*gestures with hands, pointing to chest*) like, my mic's on. Now this is what came over in black before we went back to the movies, she says (*in high voice*), "Oh, my God! I hope my mother wasn't watching!" That's because the monitor was not where it was supposed to have been, so I couldn't see my mic light. I didn't know my mic was still on. And the following week I went to different places in the community, and people were saying, "I really enjoyed your show. Especially when the girl said (*in high voice*): "Oh my God! I hope my mother wasn't watching!" (*Laughs*)

No replacement for live television.

No, there isn't, man. Once it's there, man, it's there. You can't take it back.

Do you think it's even possible to get away with something like this on a commercial station these days?

Not on commercial stations. You can do it on cable access, and that's why I like cable access. And anyway, now with each TV station being the way they are, most of them are affiliated with a network of some kind, and there's no time. If you do a *Shock Theater* of some kind, you'd be doing it at two, three, four in the morning, where they have the infomercials, okay? So seriously, cable access can give you a better time, and they give you more leeway. There's not much censorship. See, we've been talking about going back on commercial television. But I don't want to lose my director, Andy Copp. I don't want to lose control of the show. If you go back to commercial television, you're going to lose control, because there'll be a censorship type thing. Or you'll have a different director you're not really familiar with. I mean, they'll want to see the script or whatever before you do the show. And most of my shows over the years have been ad-libbed.

You don't have poetic license to do certain things, and I don't want to be on two, three, four in the morning. Only those people who are night owls are going to be watching you at that time. I'd like to be on midnight or something there. But you still have a lot of syndication, a few other things, on at that particular time. Count Gore De Vol is on the Internet. We've been thinking very seriously about going on the Internet, too.

I want a relaxed atmosphere. I don't want anyone looking over my shoulder saying, "You can do this and you can't do this." Like, I had a lot of problems with an executive producer on my show, since he and I never saw eye-to-eye on what a laugh is, okay? I had one thing that he took off the show. I used to bring on these bizarre bands. (*Laughs*) Oh ho, really some bizarre bands, too! I had one group on called The Creeping Unknown. And they remained The Creeping *Unknown*...

But then I had this thing that one of the engineers came up with; it was called Cheap Puppets. No puppets were used. It was basically things like this (*gestures with right hand, talking motion*) and things like that (*gestures the same with left hand*), and you'd have dialogue between them. And they were walking and this sort of other stuff. It was, like, about a two-minute bit or something. And the thing is, I thought it was really funny. But the producer took it off the air for me. But that was one of the funniest things we had. People really enjoyed it. But he killed the bands, he killed this and that and what have you. And towards the very end of *Shock Theater* on commercial television, it wasn't the same. I liked the ad-libbing, I liked playing with people, and we just didn't have it. We went off the air in 1986. I think, July. I got out of the business for a while; I was kind of burnt out. Then I came back with a company called Expressions in Animation and we put out *The Best of Shock Theater*. It's now called the ERHM Agency, and we put out a couple of other things.

Then we went back on. Andy Copp and Rick Martin approached me. "Would you like to do another *Shock Theater*?" I told them "yeah, fine." He says, "Well, we've been talking with the people at the cable access and they'd love to a show." I said I'd love to do a show, too. So we started on cable access, and that's where we are now. I've been a horror host for 33 years. I think Gore De Vol and I are the oldest horror hosts around, because he's been on the air for over 30 years. But the thing is, yeah, I've been a horror host for 33 years. I've enjoyed every minute of it.

My uncle did movies, had a horror show, traveled around with my dad. That was an influence. But my biggest influence was Zacherley, since I loved everything he did. We've covered the gamut regarding radio, television, and also stage shows. I'd love to rebuild a stage show. My uncle used to take packages, film packages from, say, Mexico. He'd go into drive-in theaters, have a blood mobile and all this other gimmicks such as being buried alive, things like that.

I was buried alive at a drive-in theater. I used to do a lot of crazy things. I lost my swimming trucks at one of those major hydroplane events in Dayton, Ohio. I came around one corner and I lost them going for home. This big wave hit my swimming trunks. I was Dr. Creep; I had on the black outfit and everything. And it pulled the trunks off my body. I almost was going to be nude. I got 'em back on. They brought the boat out saying, "You in trouble?" I tell them, yes, I'll be in trouble because there's tens of thousands of people along that doggone shoreline and my trailer is about five hundred yards up the shoreline!" I can see me walking out of this place half-naked, going up to get my clothes on, you know? (*Laughs*)

So we had a lot of fun. Over the years I've done a lot of things. I've raced cars the wrong way; I've been in wet bike competitions, all kinds of stuff. They always say, "Dr. Creep *will* do it!" (*Laughs*) And that's exactly right: I *will* do it!

So, radio. Let's talk a bit about radio. What did you listen to on the radio back in the era?

Oh, I liked all these different things, like *Inner Sanctum* and *CBS Mystery Theater*, *The Shadow*. I used to listen to all those different things on radio over the years. But *Inner Sanctum* was probably one of my favorite radio shows. See, I was with the Armed Forces Broadcasting Service, and I did a thing called *Nightmare Theater* in the Far East. We would grab these different scripts. The one that I remember that scared even me was a thing called *Crickets*. You hear these crickets chirping and this guy is saying, "They're coming to get me ... because I learned what they're doing. They're chirping the names of the dead. And the thing is, they know that I know, and they're coming for me."

We did a lot of different things. The fellow working with me was Rick Flickinger, and we had a pretty good audience for *Nightmare Theater*. *Inner Sanctum* and these other things, I used to play on the air. But an order came down that they were too old, and that they wanted them all destroyed. I had someone standing behind me because I was wondering how could I ship these home. Okay? I didn't want to break these things. These are things that I have treasured over the years, you know? But I had to take an axe to these 16-inch discs of *Inner Sanctum*. And I'm going, what a waste. And some of the other shows they had too, that you've heard on radio. I had to take this axe. The United States government is telling me to destroy them, and I'm hacking them up. And I'm going, these are shows that I loved!

Do you think that the host on Inner Sanctum *influenced the horror hosts?*

I think so. You can tell by some of the things that they do. I always tried to copy my uncle's laugh, that "Hoo-ha-ha!" type of thing. But I never did copy his laugh. You hear it a lot from the horror hosts. They've got something like that going for 'em. So yeah, I would say yes. The fellow who hosted *Inner Sanctum* had a lot to do with a lot of horror hosts over the years.

Tell us, this horror bug, how far in your family does it run?

Well, it runs to my uncle. My dad's dead, he died in 1980. I've been involved in a lot of different things over the years. I was a psychic investigator. I did a thing for the Fairfield Jaycees in Hamilton, Ohio. They had a haunted house at the top of High Street in a place they used to call Poor House Hill. And they used to have an asylum up there, or a medical center. When they said they were going to do a haunted house in there, they were going to run two lines—one for people who like to be grossed out, the other for people who can't stand too much blood. And a friend of mine from one of the radio stations was going to be buried there. I came up one of the nights, and I'm saying, do you know that in this particular house, several times a night, nobody would venture out of their rooms. There would be strange noises in there. I says. You're actually in a real haunted house. And I'm going to predict that sometime during this haunted house visit that they're going to see something that can't be explained.

So one of the weekends, these people come out of the haunted house saying, "Man, that was a fantastic illusion of green eyes floating down the hallway!" Now they closed up the house and they're all talking together, all the different Jaycees, and they're saying, "Who put the green eye illusion in the house?" And there was no green eye illusion in the house. It was actually what I said, that they were going to experience something in that house. They closed it down for about a week, trying to find if somebody had rigged something there. But they never found it. But these people were going out, "Man, that's fantastic, those green eyes floating down the hallway!" I said you really picked a good area anyway. Just up the street there's a cemetery.

At certain times of the year, when it's a full moon, you'll find a girl, or a woman, with or without a dog, actually thumbing down High Street. If you pick her up, by the time you get down to the bottom of the hill, she's no longer in the car. And if you don't pick her up, you feel, like, icy fingers on your throat. Even a mile up the road there's the ghost tracks. So I'm saying you guys picked a really fantastic place to have a haunted house. It was really great that my prediction came true.

I lived in a haunted house. Yeah, the haunted house I had in Middletown, Ohio with Tintin Gerard. We had seven to eight different entities that would enter my dad's mother. She was an automatic hand writer. And there would be angels and sometimes a swarthy man in a black outfit. My dad called them guardians. There was also a woman dressed in black. She was also a guardian of the house. The evil influence of the house was a woman named Bela. She was an Arabian tent girl. But there were several other entities in the house. I actually saw swirling clouds and things like that. There would be the smell of roses in the dead of winter and not a single flower in the house. You could walk in that house and actually be melancholy the moment you stepped in. You could be happy. The moment you stepped through the door, there would be a sense of melancholy in the house.

Yeah, I lived through a lot of different things. As I said, I was also a paranormal investigator. I also investigated the U.F.O.s. There were a couple of them that were supposed to come out of the river in my hometown, Middletown, and they got it on film. In the Dayton area, we were going to build something like the A.R.E. (Association for Research and Enlightenment), you know, the Edgar Cayce organization? And one was going to be built in the pyramid style in Dayton. But they never brought it off.

What do you remember about your uncle?

I was always aware of my uncle, Doug Hobart. He's been in a couple magazines where they've featured him. That monster show was one of my favorites. I really enjoyed that show. And my dad was involved with it as Doug Hobart was his brother. The funny part about the Hobart clan—and I kind of researched somewhat the Hobart clan—one of the major judges at the Salem witch trials was a Hobart. That was one of our kinfolk. It seems like the Hobart clan was cut down the middle. There were those people that were involved in the occult and loved the supernatural. The others were judges and things. They actually persecuted the other side of the family.

So the thing is, my uncle, I'm amazed at him. He's fantastic with make-up. He was involved with a group called Star down in Florida, where he does special effects make-up. And also he does special effects. Around about Halloween, he was known as "The Monster of

Curtis Street." He would actually put on the werewolf make-up. It took him about two and half hours to do it—the rubber hosing up the nose, the crepe and everything. He didn't use a mask. He built himself up. He had an overhang on his house. And the thing is, on trick or treat night, or Beggar's Night, he would jump down. You could see all the beggars running down the street. He loved to do that. And also, in the back, he would have little markers for tombstones and things like that.

I'll tell you the funniest story about that werewolf thing. There was a bar down the street. It was called The Kingpin Tavern or something. He knew everybody in there. So one night he decided that he'd dress up as the werewolf and go into the bar. It's kind of dimly lit, and there's smoke all over the place. He sets next to the drunkest guy at the bar, and the guy's slung over the bar. My uncle is in the werewolf outfit. And so he punches him and goes "*Grrr-rrr-rrr.*" The guy thinks he wants a light for a cigarette. So he just turns around and he goes (*gestures with hand*) "click." And then my uncle goes, "*RRRaaRRAH!*" You could hear the scream about two or three blocks down the street. He ran out of that bar. And they said they probably lost their best customer. He never came back in again. That trick probably scared him sober, I don't know. But the thing is, my uncle just walked casually out of the bar and walked home.

When he did the horror shows, he actually had the F.B.I. come into one of the theaters. People said—and I think he leaked it himself, but no one really knows for sure—that the mummy in that coffin was actually a dead body, that he was a gravedigger and that he had actually dug that body up. They had him un-wrap that entire mummy there in the theater because they thought that he was a body snatcher. He would do things like that to draw attention.

What films have stuck with you? What were your favorites?

I'm probably one of those old school people. I don't want to see all these hacker flicks and all that other stuff. Okay, I think my favorite motion picture of all time is the original *Dracula*, the gray image and everything. And the women, the soft focus and things like that. And the entire

set, you know. *Dracula* with Bela Lugosi is one of my favorite motion pictures. One of the science fiction ones that scared the daylights out of me was *Invasion of the Body Snatchers* (1956), the original. I don't mean the other two remakes, okay? The original *Invasion of the Body Snatchers*, when they started to foam up and form the human body and everything. Scared the daylights out of me, man! Now, I like Freddy Krueger, because of a lot of the different things he did, and the comedy. But I also like *Hellraiser* (1987). And every time I see a *Hellraiser* movie, I cringe. I'm feeling the pain of the guy who's got barbed wire wrapped around him, you know?

So over the years, there's a lot of different ones. I'll tell you one of the ones I enjoyed. They couldn't get a distribution for it until we did the premiere for it. It was called *Dead Alive (Braindead, 1992)*, made down in New Zealand. Yeah, that was one of my favorite films of all time. It took truckloads and truckloads of blood to do that motion picture—especially the scene where a lead character says, "Let's party!" and goes crazy with that lawnmower. Everybody's running around, and the little baby escapes. I enjoyed that movie.

Actually, we premiered that movie in Dayton, Ohio, and that was a lot of fun. We had zombies coming out the aisles during the motion picture and things like that, you know? Yeah, *Dead Alive* was one of my favorite motion pictures. Besides that, I like Freddy Krueger. I like Jason in the first one. But the thing is, after a while I thought the franchise got boring. But this last one with Freddy and Jason, it's pretty good, yeah. But yeah, there were a lot of good movies over the years.

Plus, my uncle would shoot me if I didn't say I liked *Death Curse of Tartu* (1966) or *The Sting of Death* (1965).

Now, *The Sting of Death* is an interesting one, where he's a human-jellyfish. When he was doing this particular motion picture, the girl victim wouldn't scream right. So he took her off the set and he said to her, "Honey," he says. "I've always wanted to kill somebody on film and have it recorded. And you're it. I'm sorry, but you're it." So they got into the scene. He's stalking her as the human-jellyfish. And you hear this blood-curdling scream. And he's, like, "Cut." That's what they wanted, for her to scream. But he had convinced her that he was actually going to kill her in that film. That's how he got the reaction from her when he went towards her in *The Sting of Death*. Yeah.

Doug Hobart in the jellyfish monster suit from *The Sting of Death*.

So what kind of relationship do you have with your fans?

Right now I've got my own site: *www.drcreep.com*. People correspond with me; they send me a few things from time to time. I have great rapport with my fans. I'm a people person and I really enjoy conventions like this and meeting everybody. It's fun for me, it really is. It could be considered therapy. (*Laughs*) Some people think I'm nuts, but I don't know. I'll tell you what I laugh about more than anything. I chuckle every time someone calls me "The legend." Even though I've done it for 33 years, I don't consider myself a legend. I just consider myself Dr. Creep having a lot of fun, okay? And I'm hoping to do more years, you know. And as I've said, I'm really thinking of getting on the Internet. That's a new field, which would be nice.

I have a foundation called Project Smiles. At Christmas time it's called Project Christmas Smiles. And one of my benefits actually is Horror-Rama, which is the last weekend in October. For the last several years, it's been, like, 45 to 65 thousand kids in a nine-county radius that we've been able to help with Christmas. I enjoy doing that. Project Smiles is 31 years old this year. I've worked with Muscular Dystrophy. My mom says I'm a yes man. I guess I am. If someone comes to me and says, "Dr. Creep, can you be at this charity or this charity," I usually say yes.

I think the biggest coup I ever had was when Vincent Price appeared on my show in Dayton, Ohio. I thought to myself, I'm going to be doing an interview with Vincent Price, and he's going to say, who the heck is this guy? When I talked to Vincent Price, he was down to earth. I only did a 10-or 15-minute interview with him. But we sat down there and talked and laughed. And he told me a lot of different things over the years, the people he's worked with, how he rated all the different Draculas, and other things. He actually rated Christopher Lee as the greatest Dracula. He said, "I worked with Bela Lugosi. But I really think Christopher Lee was the best Dracula."

I'm in awe of a lot of people. And they're probably in awe of me, okay? And I'm not trying to get an ego thing going here, because there's no ego. The thing is, you don't have to be in awe of me. We'll sit down, if you want to sit down and talk or whatever. I'm there. I'm not going to say, "Who the heck are you? I've been around this industry for 33 years." I've done radio; I've done television. I did a motion picture. I got a couple things. But as I said, I'm the same way as Vincent Price was. He was a star, but he was down to earth.

Do you have that Vincent Price interview on tape anywhere?

You know something? I've lost that interview and I don't know where it is. I've moved several different places, and somewhere down the line that Vincent Price thing is no longer there. We had a nice talk. I asked him if he was going to do another Dr. Phibes movie. He said, "No. I won't be doing that unless my wife is in the picture." But yeah, I would love to have that footage. But I don't know where it is. I'd like to know what happened to it.

Over the years, I've lost a lot of footage. But then I've also got a lot of footage, too. There were two of my friends who were with me on the show that have some footage that *I* don't have. I've been trying to find somewhere to dub two-inch videotape; I've got six to seven two-inch videotapes with a lot of material on it. But most of the TV stations no longer have two-inch tapes. They only have one-inch, okay? And sometimes even three-quarters and things like that. And the thing is, there's material recorded and I don't know what's on it And the thing is, yeah, I'd love to get it dubbed over.

Barry Hobart passed away January 14, 2011.

Nite Owl Blues
Fritz the Nite Owl (Frank Peerenboom)
Interviewed by Michael Monahan (2010)

In 1963, John Haldi, the program director at WBNS-TV 10 in Columbus, Ohio, brought radio deejay Frank Peerenboom into the medium of television as the station announcer. He discovered Peerenboom's talent extended to writing and assigned him to the late-night *Armchair Theater* movie. When the program's name was changed to *Nite Owl Theatre*, staff artist Dave Wagstaff created a "Nite Owl" mascot for the show. The character appeared on title cards between commercial breaks, with Peerenboom providing voiceover transitions back to the movie.

Viewers married the disembodied voice to the cartoon bird and began writing letters to "Fritz the Nite Owl," and Peerenboom soon evolved into an on-camera host. Once they had a flesh and blood Fritz to play with, the show began to develop a strong visual component, from Fritz's garish Elton John–era sunglasses to clever camera trickery that put the host into the movies and title cards. But it was the smooth, ingratiating qualities of *that voice* that really sold the show, creating a conversational intimacy familiar to FM radio in the wee hours, but rare on late-night television.

Double Chiller Theatre was the Friday night edition of the station's nightly *Nite Owl Movie*. The other six nights of the week, Peerenboom presented films from every genre: classic comedy, gangsters, Westerns, musicals, etc. But Friday nights were reserved for horror, and this earned Fritz his official horror host credentials. *Nite Owl Theatre* and *Double Chiller Theatre* ran on WBNS-TV 10 between 1974 and 1991, garnering Frank Peerenboom five Emmys. Both shows remained popular. But as national trends ran toward syndication, the show inevitably disappeared from local airwaves.

As with all deejays, radio remained his first love, and this is where he returned. As Fritz the Nite Owl, Peerenboom hosted a jazz music program for many years, first on WWCD 101.1 FM and later on WJZA 103.5. Fritz lost his job at WJZA in August 2010 when the station abruptly dropped its smooth-jazz format. In October of that same year, Fritz returned to hosting horror movies in a series of live events at the Grandview Theatre in Columbus, Ohio.

What are your feelings when you look back on the movie programs you hosted over the years? Do you approach your work with a sense of pride?

In all of these years, I have never, ever seen a complete tape of one of my shows. I kept very little of the tapes I made. All of the voiceover stuff was live. I was actually sitting there. But the video was pre-taped. We would do a week's worth of stuff in one session—three breaks or four breaks per movie. And then they would run that for the week. Then the station would reuse that tape to record the new segments. They were always getting erased. I would just save the best segments for my Emmy submission. Somewhere there's a tape that this guy, Rome Maynard, made that actually won me my fifth Emmy. I won the Emmy in 1991 and 1992.

And this is for local personality?

No, I won for on-air performance—four for on-air performance and one for producer. But you could only submit a half hour. And I won my award in 1992 for the work that got me fired in 1993. It's like getting voted "Most Valuable Player" and getting kicked off the team. It was kind of good in the sense that it was the only Emmy that the Channel 10 programming department won that year. And as I say, it was my fifth. I've got five sons; the oldest is 52. So I said, "When I die, you cremate me and hollow out the Emmys. And each of you will have an Emmy with ol' daddy-o sitting on the mantel somewhere.

You got your start working part-time at WMNI in 1959. That was your first broadcasting gig. What attracted you to broadcasting and how did you get your start? And what was radio like at that time?

Actually, being a child of the 1930s, I grew up with radio and movies, which was our only form of entertainment. We had shows like *Sam Spade* and *Michael Shayne* and *Superman* and *Buck Rodgers* and *Terry and the Pirates* and *Hop Harrigan*. And we listened to these serials every day. My voice changed in, maybe, seventh grade. I sounded then like I sound now. And I was the only kid on the planet who could do, in Bob Collier's voice, Superman. "This is a job for … (*deeply*) Superman." That voice coming out of a seven year old was quite … interesting.

Then in high school I was a movie usher for two years. So I would see six movies a week, two or three times per shot. And of course, as I say, I was growing up in the 1930s and the 1940s. There was no TV to speak

Frank Peerenboom, sporting his signature specs

of until the early '50s. So movies were still a very strong influence on people of that age. I always had an interest in that. We only had to usher twice. Once for *At War With the Army* (1950), starring Martin and Lewis, we actually had to show people to their seats. And *An American in Paris* (1951), we had to show people to their seats. The rest of the time we stood in the aisle. We'd relieve the popcorn girl; we'd relieve the ticket taker. The rest of the time we'd stand on the aisle and watch the movie. I'm thinking, jeez, I'm getting paid to do this? We got our jobs if you fit the uniform. I got my job because a guy my size quit. I applied for the job and voila. The uniform fit me and, boom, I'm a movie theater usher.

I went to college at Ohio State; I went there in '52, then I was a radio and TV, theater and English major. And I got a secondary education degree. I was going to be a schoolteacher. And my plan was I'd get enough credits so I could qualify to teach in California or New York. My idea was I would go to whoever gave me a job — California or New York — teach for two years, learn the lay of the land, save all my money, and then just spend the next two years going out looking for acting or narrating jobs.

Meantime, the Army drafted me. I graduated in 1957 and was going to go to California, take a teaching job in Catalina. But I got drafted. Well, fortunately the Army had a thing at that time called "Get Choice, Not Chance." So rather than wait to get drafted, I enlisted. And they gave me an MOS (Military Occupational Specialties). I had worked in college for three years as a TV production assistant. No on-camera stuff, no voiceovers, nothing — but holding up cue boards, getting props, setting up commercials, setting up the sets for the newscasters and weather people. In those days, you would set up a set, then the guy would do the news and you would tear it down. Then you'd set up the weather or set up the Stroh's beer commercial. It was done all live, and so they had a full crew of guys. And that's what I did for three years. Plus the fact that I was a radio, TV, theater major did not hurt at all.

So they gave me an MOS of a "TV production specialist." They sent me to the Signal Corps Pictorial Center in New York City, where for two years I narrated, wrote and produced training films for the Army. Now the Army Pictorial Center was the old Paramount Studios in New York. It's now the Hoffman Astoria. They shot *Fort Apache: the Bronx* (1981) there; they shot *The Wiz* (1978) there as well. That's the old Army Pictorial. And when I see a movie that was shot there, or parts of it, I know exactly where on the main stage they got that shot. And for me, the two years in the Army were like a Master's Ph.D. in TV and film production. All we did was make films for the Army. We made the training films for the Army; we made the promotional films for TV and movies. I tell people I put more GIs to sleep with my movie than any guy playing Taps.

Anyway, those two years in the Army allowed me access to all the special effects equipment, which was brand new at the time. And the only guys on television using that stuff were Ernie Kovacs and Steve Allen. I got to learn all of this stuff in the two years in the Army. So when I ultimately got *Nite Owl Theatre*, no one else was doing it that way. Every horror host would either come out of a coffin, or they had a castle or did the undertaker thing.

I'm going to use the special effects and tie everything into the movie— visuals, music, blah-blah-blah.

So, there were the two years in the Army. Got out of the Army, went to work as an ad agency writer/artist and got a part-time job at WMNI as a deejay. I would do sign-off on Saturday night and I would babysit with the Saturday night music remotes. If something went wrong, I would play records and be a deejay. I'd sleep on the couch till six o'clock in the morning, put the station on the air and babysit for all the preachers and the remote religious shows. And again, if something went wrong, I would deejay in there. They were a rock station. My picks were, like, Charlie Mingus, Miles Davis, Ella Fitzgerald, Frank Sinatra, all that jazz. They figured, "Well, you know, for 75 cents an hour, let the kid play whatever music he wants, because, you know, some preacher's going to follow him." But ultimately I got a job part time there doing rock.

And from there, I went to WBNS AM and FM. I had to audition at 'BNS AM and FM eight times, and they would say, "Well, we like your voice and we like your style. But you've never had commercial experience. So we won't hire you." And I'd say, well, if you won't hire me without commercial experience, how do I get commercial experience if no one will hire me? And they would just go, "Catch-22." After that—no audition at 'BNS—they just called me and they said, "Look, we're starting up. We need someone to put FM stereo live on the air. Do you want to be the announcer?"

What year was this that they started stereo broadcasting?

Let's see, '59 to '61, I was at 'MNI. I was doing part time at 'BNS ... so about '63 they started the stereo. And in those days you had to have an AM and an FM radio turned on to get the stereo effect. So I would broadcast on WBNS and they would duplicate it on FM. People at home would have the AM and FM on and get the stereo effect from the music. So I was the first live AM-FM stereo announcer in Columbus. But the question was, how did I get interested? I just grew up with it and I always wanted to do it. Early on I had the voice for it, and I thought I'd give it a shot.

It also sounds like you developed that appreciation for jazz at an early age. Where did that come from?

When I was growing up in the 1940s, and the popular music of the day was the Big Bands—Benny Goodman, Duke Ellington, Count Basie, Artie Shaw. And just about any teenager on the planet at that time, you'd ask them, "Who's the lead saxophonist for Artie Shaw?" and they could tell you. I mean, we just knew that music. And guys like Sinatra always had the jazz influence. Frankie Laine, Johnny Ray, plus blues....

Then I moved to Baltimore, Maryland for a couple of years—it was a real good jazz town. So there was a lot of live jazz we heard on the radio. And like some many of these other things, you're not aware of it, it just sort of seeps into you. You absorb it without realizing you are absorbing it. You begin to get a little leaning toward, "I'd rather hear Count Basie than, say, Lawrence Welk." There are people who say, "Hey, I'd rather hear Lawrence Welk, I don't want to hear Count Basie." The thing is, you kind of absorb it without really realizing that you're setting a taste. But you are setting a taste.

Many of the early television hosts and booth announcers came out of radio. How did you make the transition to television, and what were the primary differences between radio and TV?

I was an afternoon primetime deejay from 1969 through about 1974. In the old days, when I started in radio, it was play what you want, say what you want. If you could have Miles Davis follow Kate Smith and put it together, they could have cared less. We later got this program director that had this 20-song play list. When I would go into work, I would hear what song was playing and know what song my show was going to start with, what it was going to end with. Our air shifts were four hours a day, six days a week and we would play the same 20 songs twice a day, six days in a row.

A booth announcing job came up at Channel 10 (WBNS), and this tight format was so boring that I thought, I'd rather sit on my duff and watch television—and every half hour get up and do a station break, a voiceover commercial, or read a commercial on-camera, whatever. And the rest of the time just sit there and watch TV. It had to be a lot more interesting than these same 20 songs. So the opening just came up and I said I want this opening. They gave it to me, and I started to be a booth announcer. The booth announcers had to be able to go on and sub for the weatherman, the sports guy. They would bring a guy in for anchor. But you would have to do subs, and you might have to do live commercials during the course of your shift.

How did it differ from radio? It was a lot easier. Radio was more relaxed in the sense that physically it didn't make much difference what you looked like. It didn't make any difference what you wore. Whereas with television, you had to be concerned with, okay, how do I look as well as how do I sound? I had theater training. So as

Footman Rip Offs!, a project described by Peerenboom as, "Just another creative cement zeppelin in which I was involved."

Most of the deejays I've spoken with who made a transition to television, pretty uniformly have a preference for radio. It's their first love. They all point to the intimacy of it and the freedoms that come from it.

Absolutely. And again, that goes back to those shows like *Sam Spade*, *Buck Rodgers*, *Superman*. *Inner Sanctum* where I got my interest in chillers. That *Inner Sanctum* was always a chiller-horror thing. The host was a guy named Raymond. Raymond would open that squeaking door. And at the end of the show he would say, "Gooood niiiight, pleasant dreeeeams..." and that squeaking door would slam. And you're eight years old … your hair is standing straight up, you know.

And that clearly became the format for horror hosts when they first appeared on television. The earliest shows on TV were essentially visual radio. It was slap some grease paint on a guy and say, "Do Raymond."

I was thinking the other great horror show on radio was called *Lights Out*.

Oh yeah, Arch Obler.

Yeah, yeah. I'd forgotten Arch. I'm glad you're mindful of the historical information on top of it. As kids, we would listen to that stuff every bloody week. You didn't miss Raymond; you didn't miss *Lights Out*. That was one of the places I got my intrigue in horror from. And in those days, when you would go to the movies, and you would see *Frankenstein* (1931), *Dracula* (1931) or *The Wolf Man* (1941), you'd see these things on a *full screen*! Again, you're nine years old, eight years old. It's much more intimidating than watching it on a 12-inch screen where you're bigger than Frankenstein. And then of course, in those days, after you'd see that movie, you'd have to walk home in the dark from the theater. Believe me; you'd get a medal for bravery!

I was in a small town in central Wisconsin. In those days, a kid could only go to the movies Friday night or Saturday night. We saw them for the first time and they were infinitely larger than life. So that put a fear factor in us early on. It wasn't that these movies were geared for kids. It was just that in the small towns that I grew up in, it was the only film showing in town that week. So kids and adults and everybody went to the movies on Friday or

a new announcer I wasn't as nervous as people who just came from radio into television. So I'd say radio was more relaxing and conversational. Television, there was very little room to ad-lib anything, for the booth announcer. You know, they'd have a 25-second movie preview. You come on, "Starts tomorrow at these theaters." "Try it now at your favorite Kroger supermarket." "On sale through Thursday." That type of thing appeared. It was more formal, originally, to be an announcer on television than it was on radio.

Saturday night. I mean Nekoosa, Wisconsin, population 2,212. Aurora, Minnesota, north of Duluth, had about two thousand people. And everybody went to the movies two or three times a week. Regardless of what kind of movie it was, you just went.

Can you talk a little about becoming the host of Armchair Theater, *and how you developed the style?*

It was kind of accidental. I just got assigned to do the night-time show, and at that time they were running *Armchair Theater* Monday through Thursday. Friday was *Chiller Theater* with Dan Himmel, who sat in an armchair with a movie projector. Dan wore a suit, well-dressed; he was just a straight guy. Friday was *Chiller* night and he would introduce the chiller feature. Saturday night was *The Saturday Night Movie* and Sunday night was *The Sunday Night Movie*. Well, I took it over. Dan Himmel was the *live* host. You'd see him three times, but the rest of the time only the booth announcer was doing voiceovers.

It always bothered me with voiceover announcers, it was always, "We'll be right back with *Ride Out for Revenge* (1957) with Mike McGrainer after these words," and this guy never seemed to be watching the movie. So I'm watching *Ride Out for Revenge*, starring Rory Calhoun. Early on, Rory robs a bank, slips around this corner in old Mexico. And there on the side of the building, big as life, is this huge Coca-Cola sign. We fade to black, and without thinking of it, I say, "Well, why didn't Rory stop for a Coke? After a dusty bank job like that, even Rory Calhoun gets thirsty." Nobody said anything; there was no calls from the program director. So every break I started to make some comment about how Rory Calhoun was one of the first big stars to get nailed by *Confidential* magazine, just various and sundry details.

The program director John Haldi, very creative guy, didn't seem to bother. I was the host of the *Nite Owl*, and they had these cartoons. And I just started commenting on the movies. Well, since my voice was so well known to radio, people started writing in to "Fritz the Nite Owl." The Nite Owl cartoons would show, oh, the Nite Owl putting the cat out, what people would be doing at that time of the night. He'd be fixing a late-night snack; he'd be necking on the couch, getting ready for bed, setting the alarm clock. If it was a war picture, the Nite Owl was in a foxhole, and shells bursting.

I'd be doing these ad-lib comments on the breaks and people started writing to Fritz the Nite Owl. There was no Fritz the Nite Owl, they just knew my voice from radio. They assigned it to that still cartoon picture by David Wagstaff. And the mail was so good. John Haldey said, "Let's create a Fritz the Nite Owl." At first they were talking about an owl suit like the San Diego Chicken. In those days, the announcer also had to be able to do commercials. They said, "Look, a guy in an owl suit might be able to sell hamburgers or a soft drink. But you can't put a guy in an owl suit next to a refrigerator or a car or a high-priced ticket item. So fortunately, the owl suit was dinged.

At that time Cher and Elton John were both popular, massively popular. And Haldi and Dave Wagstaff said, "Let's try the glasses. Because a guy in owl glasses next to a refrigerator isn't going to be that much of a stretch. So they went to Revco, which is a drug chain—now CVS—and they bought a pair of over-sized sunglasses off the rack. Dave Wagstaff created these horns, and smashed a mirror and glued the mirror bits onto the horns. They could put a star burst filter on the camera. So when the Owl turns his head, and the light catches these odd-shaped pieces of mirror, it'll throw a star burst back into the camera for a more unique visual effect. So, it just kind of grew.

So Fritz first became established as a voiceover character. Then when they put me on camera they did the glasses business. Every other horror host I'd seen up to that point either came out of a coffin or was sitting in a projection room or a castle. That's when I said, okay, I want to do it unlike anybody else has ever done it. This was way before *Mystery Science Theater 3000*, and I'd never seen Ghoulardi. So I just decided everything is going to be a visual. And since no one was using special effects, other than Ernie Kovacs and Steve Allen, I would do a visual presentation that tied into the movie.

And then I wanted to try to find music that was tied in. There was a lot of good jazz that was *Chiller* oriented: Al Di Meola, Eric Truffaz, a killer trumpet player. Even Miles Davis, an album of his called *Aura*, has a chiller feel to it. For the other movies, six nights a week, I just used, like, a nice loping easy kind of jazz, and it worked. I would integrate the voice with the music I was playing. So again, it was radio on television. Every movie had an on-camera open, a mid-break on-camera and a close on-camera. Breaks number one, two and three were just Nite Owl cartoon slides, music and voiceover. And break number four would be the on-camera mid-break. Five and six were voiceovers, and then the close was pre-taped on-camera. So every movie was a combination of on-camera and voiceover.

The voiceover was live?

The voiceover was live. The on-camera stuff was pre-taped.

An atmospheric portrait of The Nite Owl

The voiceover continues to call back to that intimacy of radio. There is a more intimate quality in just hearing the voiceover a graphic than having the host talk directly to you into camera.

That was done by design, because I often describe my show as "radio on television."

On the visual side: You mentioned Ernie Kovacs. His name comes up a lot, particularly with people on the East Coast, as a major inspiration in what they were doing.

Well, he was the only guy doing crazy visuals on television at that time. And he did that even before Steve Allen. But then Steve Allen started. Among the things I remember is he would be playing the piano and they would "key" a dancer on top of the piano. Then Steve would reach over and squash the dancer. That was one of the first things that I saw. But Kovacs was really the first guy to ever use special effects in the television medium as part of his shtick. The thing was I never used the visuals or the effects as a gimmick. Everything I did tied into that specific film in one way or another. That was one of the challenges I had in doing the thing. It was one of the things I enjoyed about it.

The selections, at least on the shows that I've seen, were predominantly horror. But there were things that crossed over to other genres.

Six nights a week, we did all types of movies: the Westerns, the Martin and Lewis, the MGM musicals, the 20th Century Fox dramas, the love pictures, the *Casablanca* (1942) intrigues, the classics, the Warner Bros. Our program director, John Haldi, was a movie buff and he had a good budget. And the best packages that were available, he would get. One night a week was *Chiller* night. And on that, our version of "chiller" would include horror, science fiction, psychodrama. We even got into, where, as a *Chiller* feature, we showed *Helter Skelter* (1976) part one and two as *Chiller* one and two. And *In Cold Blood* (1967)—we would show that as a *Chiller*. We'd show films like, say, a Buck Rogers, Tarzan, a fantasy. Spider-Man—they made some films out of that first TV series. So even superheroes and sword-and-sandals were also a part of *Chiller* genre at Channel 10. *Hercules* (*Le Fatiche di Ercole, 1958*), *Colossus of Rhodes* (*Il Colosso di Rodi*, 1961) fell under the Channel 10, *Chiller Theatre* version of a chiller feature. Nobody complained.

Nationally, you're usually recognized as a horror movie host. But locally is it more generic? Are you recognized more as a general movie host? Or do people tend to lean more toward the horror?

When I was doing it people leaned towards me as a movie host who did horror on the Friday night *Double Chiller*. But some of the fan magazines, like *Scary Mon-*

sters, would start to do articles. So nationally, I got to be known as a horror host. People didn't know that I hosted movies like *Diary of Anne Frank* (1959), *An American in Paris*, Martin and Lewis or Frankie and Annette, Abbott and Costello. They didn't realize that I hosted all kinds of movies six nights a week. So locally people knew me as a movie host. The horror thing is the thing that got me national attention.

When *TV Bloopers* did their thing they introduced as: "Last week, we did all the people who did horror. This week we're going to show you some people who host just the regular movies." And the selections they used of mine were a combination of non-horror and horror films. So when I got to be known nationally it was only as a horror host. But locally, through most of my career, it was just as a movie host. The *Chiller Theater* was the most popular night of the week. Now I've been gone since 1991, I did a couple of low-power television things. But not many people saw them, because you had to disconnect your cable to see it, you know. Since *Chiller* was the most popular, more people remember me for that now, rather than for showing them *Casablanca*, *Diary of Anne Frank*, *At War With the Army*, *Annie Hall*, etc. etc....

And maybe some of the visual elements—dropping yourself into the photos and postcards, the animations—connected more with a fantasy movie audience.

Right! And a lot of people have told me, "I really realized I was starting to be able to be considered a grownup when I could stay up Friday night at 11:30 with the old man or old lady or my boyfriend watching *Double Chiller*." But the thing is, I would show movies of all kinds. The audience would stay with me. I don't know how many second shifters I got. I was prime time stuff for the second shift people.

Did you always do double-bills with the Chiller?

Chiller was always a double-feature called *Nite Owl Double Chiller*. Originally, when Dan Himmel was doing it, it was just called *Chiller Theatre*. Then when they made the *Nite Owl Theatre* seven nights of the week, it became *Nite Owl Double Chiller* on Friday nights, whereas the other six nights were just a single feature.

What type of direct feedback did you get from your audience? Did people send things in? Did you get artwork and fan letters?

People would send in artwork—whether it was *Chiller* artwork or Owl artwork. A lot of people would draw their version of me, or they would draw just Owl pictures, paintings. Some of them were oil paintings. And they'd send in tons of letters. *Chiller* pulled the most mail. There were kids—I could tell they were seventh or eighth grade—that would send me, like, four pages of loose leaf paper, folded up, into this huge compact block. And I'd open it up and there'd be: "Dear Mr. Nite Owl: Please show..." and every horror film ever made was listed on this four page thing in this minute handwriting. That was funny. But take a guess as to who were the two most requested performers in the 17 years I was doing *Nite Owl*. These two performers were the most requested.

Bela Lugosi and Karloff?

Nice try. The two most requested were Godzilla and Elvis.

A lot of times we would do a weekly theme. You know, we'd have all Elvis movies, Bogart films. We did an Elvis week once and I thought the people were going to elevate me to sainthood. And the Elvis package ... you know those distributors, how they'd sell a package and there are six Elvis movies in there. And there are 44 other movies. For six Elvis Presley films you bought the whole package. So I ran this Elvis week, and we ran four of his movies. I mean to say, the letters ... "Do it again! When are you going to have another Elvis week?" And they knew they were going to see the same four or six movies. And it was the same way with Godzilla. We never had a Godzilla week, but every time we would show a Godzilla movie, the mail would just mushroom. When I would go to do personal appearances or speak at schools, Elvis and Godzilla were the most requested. They beat out John Wayne, Dean Martin, Errol Flynn. They didn't stand a chance against Elvis and Godzilla. The Big E and The Big G.

But what is it about horror that connects with children?

I think the Godzilla movies weren't scary like *Frankenstein* and *Dracula*. They were more fantasy. And a lot of times the later ones—which I liked less—would actually have kids as leads in them. Kids could kind of relate to that. I was an adult, or a late teenager, when the first Godzilla came out. When I first saw *Godzilla* I thought it was corny. It wasn't like when I first saw *Frankenstein* or *Dracula* or *The Wolf Man*. I don't know if the producers meant them to be this way. But they just weren't as scary, or as threatening, as the other ones.

They have the sort of epic fantasy quality that the Ray Harryhausen films do, even if the special effects are of a totally different type. Godzilla appeals to that destructive

side of kids who don't want to put away their toys. They'd rather stomp them and kick them around the room.

Speaking of the Harryhausen again, that type of movie was grist for our *Chiller* at Channel 10. It was just part of the big umbrella we had. It wasn't just all monsters or horrors or people coming out of graves. It was really a wide range of sci-fi, fantasy, psychodrama. We even showed *The Red House* (1947), the Edward G. Robinson film, one night. We showed a Hitchcock film one time as part of *Chiller*, *Shadow of a Doubt* (1943), the one about the evil uncle. We showed that as a *Chiller*. Suspense was also a genre that fit into our version of *Chiller*.

What are your own tastes in film? Outside of fantasy and horror, what type of films do you like?

It depends on what time of day you ask me what are my top-five favorite films. But always in my top-five are *Casablanca (1941)*, *Annie Hall* (1977), *Play It Again, Sam* (1972), *From Here to Eternity* (1953*)*, *All About Eve* (1950) and *The Red House*. I've always liked *The Red House* because of the Theremin music in there. And again, that was a psychodrama. It's a little bit dated now, but for some reason it holds up with me. It's just that I grew up with so many. I like the Westerns; I like the musicals. I like Betty Grable and Marilyn Monroe. Oh, Jane Russell. I fell in love with Jane Russell. She set my taste in voluptuaries. After Jane Russell, if you're less than a size-8 ... there were a couple of very buxom ladies who were horror stars. Hazel Court, for instance.

Going back to music for a moment: Did you view the television show as an opportunity to showcase some of the music that you enjoyed and played on the radio?

Absolutely. In addition to warping their minds with the visuals, I was also going to brainwash them in giving them an appreciation of jazz, the saxophone, Miles Davis and Dave Brubeck, just all of it. I'd done a jazz show on the air in Columbus since 1959. From 1961, when I started at 'BNS AM-FM, through 1970, when the new program director came on, all of the music I played on radio was either jazz or jazz-influenced. So I did always use the music, yes. And it is kind of interesting, since I would get a lot of mail and comments on the music from the *Chiller* fans. There was an Al Di Meola track I used ("*Alien Chase on Arabian Desert*") and then Bob James had a great version of *Night on Bald Mountain* that I used a lot. And Eric Truffaz! There were about three or four albums that are just great. And there's this Miles Davis *Aura* album. And then there was this electronic guy by the name of Tomika that had some great chiller-sci-fi music, which also had a jazz influence to it.

Yeah, I was propagandizing with jazz on the movie and I did use it as a platform to help spread the word. As I say, check out this trumpet player, Eric Truffaz. I think he records for Blue Note or Columbia. It's a big label. Eric Truffaz also has some great haunting electronic trumpet stuff. Miles Davis' album, *Aura*, I think you might like.

Please talk a bit about your relation with superheroes. You're featured in an issue of The Power of Shazam, *and were the voice of the Green Lantern in an animated project.*

I was actually in about six issues of *The Power of Shazam*. Again, when I was a kid, in terms of entertainment, comic books were huge. And my favorite was

Captain Marvel, the best-selling comic book of the Golden Age. I also liked Superman, Batmen, Bugs Bunny, Donald Duck. At age, maybe 41, I started reading Captain Marvel again, the original Captain Marvel. I must have been seven years old when I sent away to be a member of the Captain Marvel fan club. And as part of that he would send you a letter every month. In 1994, DC published a hardcover book titled *The Power of Shazam*, written, drawn and hand-painted by Jerry Ordway. It was superb!

So, I wrote a letter to Mr. Ordway, complementing him on his marvelous book. He wrote back, and after an exchange of letters, he asked if I'd mind being included as an occasional supporting character in the book as an associate of Billy Batson, Captain Marvel's alter ego, who worked at a radio-TV station. I said I'd be honored. So he began dropping me in now and then, either seen or mentioned. In *The Power of Shazam* #20, I gave a minor assist to Captain Marvel and Supes (*Superman*) in saving the Earth. It was the least I could do.

The Green Lantern was included, with 10 or so other DC titles for a pilot TV show called *Warner Video Comics*, produced by our local Warner Cable, very early after they came to Columbus, around 1980 or a bit later. For the series, DC provided blowups of the original black and white art and lettering used in the actual comic books, hand-painted them and sent them to the series producer-director, a very talented lady named Pat Arthur. The camera would select an individual picture from the page and zoom in or out, pan or tilt as needed. And we the actors would do the dialogue through balloons and boxed descriptive narratives as needed for each individual pic, panel, splash page, whatever. Later, she added the necessary sound effects. Thus, the audience could read along with the dialogue printed in the comics and hear the sound effects, enjoy the art, etc. Really a creative concept and one never before used. Even though the pictures were still, her creative camera work gave an incredible amount of motion to the series. And the colored, original comic book art far surpassed all of the animation art currently being used on animated TV shows.

I did 13 episodes of *Green Lantern* comics, providing the voice for GL and his alter-ego, Hal Jordon. I saved the universe 13 times. No other deejay, horror host or TV personality can make such a claim. I also did numerous character voices in other titles such as *Superman*, *Batman*, *Flash*, *Mystery in Space* and others. All the books in the series were shown for a short while on our local Warner Cable, which at that time was interactive with the audience, but this was another project that, sadly, didn't last too long. The finished tapes were sent off to the power elite at Warner Bros. and that was the last anyone ever heard of them or the project.

When I was younger, I actually wanted to be a comic book artist, a superhero artist. But in those days to say you wanted to be a comic book artist was like one f-stop away from being a pornographer. I could never understand why the newspaper cartoonists like Al Capp, Milton Caniff and Hal Foster, all those greats, were lionized, respected—and yet the comic book artists were regarded as junk. I never understood that. I'm delighted that now you can learn comic book art in all the prestigious art schools, like CCAD. They teach courses in drawing comics. I only wish it had existed when I was ready to go to school. I always just liked the superhero genre. In those days we would trade comic books. I grew up with *Captain Marvel*, *Spy Smasher*, *Superman*, *Batman*, *The Green Lantern*, *The Flash*, *Tarzan*.

Of course, Berne Hogarth drawing Tarzan was a feast for the eyes. Berne Hogarth was one of my artistic influences. But comics were just a part of a young adolescent's life in the 1940s. It was kind of interesting that, in those days, if you were caught reading a comic book after age 13, you were instantly put into the wimp class. I used to go into the drug store and I would read the comic books in the rack and hope that nobody saw me reading them. Today you find adults really enjoy comic books and the graphic novels.

The sort of visual tableau you were doing on Nite Owl *looked like comic book panels.*

Again, that was David Wagstaff, who was the station artist. He was a terrific artist, could do everything. This was in the days before computer art. Those were all original paintings done on 14 x 20 cards. They would make a 35mm slide out of those and show the slides. Every TV station had a couple of 35mm slide projectors.

But you would also insert yourself into a Frank Frazetta painting, or that type of thing.

Frank Frazetta was a god to me. He passed on. Rest in peace, Frank. Not only was he great, but in his early days, when I first discovered him, sometime before '46, he used to sign his early drawings "Fritz." And the way he made his "F" was the way I started to do it. And to this day, the way I sign my name is with a variation of the Frank Frazetta "F" that he used when he would sign his drawings, "Fritz."

Did you pick up the Fritz moniker from him? Or was that a happy accident?

"Morganna and the Owl"

A promotional photo for an unsold TV pilot, circa 1993, featuring Fritz and Morganna, the Kissing Bandit. The program was structured as a Siskel and Ebert home video review show.

No, I was Fritz. My Sicilian godfather was known as Fred. And so just to keep us apart, he was Fred, I was Fritz. Plus, my mother always thought, as a little kid, I looked like Fritz in the *Katzenjammer Kids*. I got double-teamed there from my Sicilian godfather and the Katzenjammer Kids, Hans and Fritz.

Fritz was on the air during a key transitional period in broadcasting. The changes in the duopoly rules sounded the death knell to independent stations and a lot of local broadcasting. Were you involved with one of these stations that transitioned to a WB or something of that type?

WBNS AM-FM and TV were all locally owned. And at that time, those were the only radio, TV and newspapers that they owned. Through my radio career, I always worked for locally owned stations. 'MNI was locally owned, 'BNS was locally owned. And I worked for WOSU, but that was Ohio State University owned. It was part of PBS. But again, OSU owned it. And then 'BBY was locally-owned, 101 was locally owned and 'JZA was locally owned, until about three or four years ago when they became a part of a group called Sega Communications. Most of my career was at one-ownership local stations, so I was never really affected by the duopoly. Not to any great degree. Not at all, in fact, until just recently. Apparently the power elite came out of wherever the hell they are, the ones that decided that WJZA should no longer play jazz. Their new format sounds like a bucketful of doorknobs bouncing off a tin roof. Miles Davis and Charlie Parker and Houston Person and so many great players, replaced by this ... crap.

When did you finally go off the air and what led to that?

I went off the air in late July of 2010. On July 25 I did my Sunday night show. "Thanks for listening. See you next week, same time, same megaplex, blah, blah, blah ..." The following Friday at 4:30 in the afternoon, I got a got a call from the station, "We changed our format at 4:30 this afternoon. There will no longer be any jazz on the station. Thank you, it was nice having you. Goodbye." The end of July 2010 is when *Nite Owl Jazz* went off the air.

Why did you decide to revive the character of Fritz the Night Owl with an Internet series?

Well, I always had fun doing it. And in addition to enjoying it, I feel The Nite Owl can still be a commercially viable product and make the cash register ring. Ol' Gordon Gekko—"Greed is good." Right now my income ... I'm on the public dole. That's about it, you know. I could use the dough.

And it's fun for you to get back to this?

It's fun and it's challenging. At age 75, you know, I still swim good. But other than that, there's a lot of other stuff I can't do. Things I quit 10, 15 years ago. I still paint; I still draw. But this is kinda mentally challenging. Mike McGraner, the show's director, and I are talking about what kind of visuals we're going to use for *Plan*

9 from Outer Space (1958). What are going to use for *Santa Claus Conquers the Martians* (1964)? What are we going to use for *The Outlaw* (1943) when we show that? So just having that mental activity … My mental challenges these days are pretty much the morning crossword puzzle. Like Bette Davis said, "Getting old ain't for sissies." So it's a bit of that, and I just want to see where it will go. We'll do two or three, and if it catches on, great. And if it bombs, well, I've created some lead zeppelins in my life. Why not now? But I think it's going to succeed.

Fritz The Night Owl overtop a sequence from *Night of the Living Dead*

There does seem to be a revival of just general interest in local TV and local horror hosts. And this is across the country. People like yourself, who've established a character within their community. I'm hearing back from people and they're saying, "I put this character away for 20 years. Now I've got conventions coming up." People are genuinely excited at the prospect of seeing you again.

Maybe because of the radio show. I've done personal appearances with the glasses ever since 1974 when *Nite Owl Theatre* started. But I still do, like, school talks, personal appearances, things like that, in the Nite Owl glasses. The character has not been off the scene as much as, say, some of the other people that did similar shows. I do a lot of school talks about careers in radio and TV. Writing, so forth and like that. I've been lucky in the sense that I still have the glasses, I still wear the glasses. Before Mike wanted to do the Internet TV show, I was at a senior center, where they were giving out awards, and I was the host for that. I've got 10 granddaughters, so I've been doing the high school shows for as long as I can remember.

What's the reaction from kids who never saw the television show?

It's generally good, because before I do the thing today for audiences who haven't seen it, I ask them to run a portion of that half hour tape Rome Maynard put together for me of Fritz highlights. I'm talking about the one I won my fifth Emmy for. And it was the one I was using for my audition tape-CD. The tape won me my fifth Emmy in 1992. The only difference is that I added the TV Bloopers segment to it. So I have them show that, so people can get an idea of what I did. And then I come on, and we're off and running.

Is there still a sort of romance to television, to appearing on television, for a younger crowd? Does that still sound cool to them?

Oh yeah! For all of my granddaughters, who range in age from second grade up through age 32, their teachers would find out they were my granddaughters, and in class they would say, "Well, we've got a celebrity here. Alice's grandfather was on television and is currently a deejay on radio." Then everyone was interested, and it was a big deal. So I'm delighted for that. Most of the teachers today, if they grew up in Columbus, remember growing up with me. One of my granddaughters, just going into second grade, remembered when her teacher saw her last name and said, "Oh, are you any relation to Fritz the Nite Owl?" Then the teacher proceeded to tell the class just how terrific I was.

There's a special kind of enthusiasm for these kinds of shows you grew up with. It's exactly the same sort of thing you were talking about in terms of jazz, radio, film and comic books. You connect with something at a certain age, and it's with you for a lifetime.

I was amazed when I got my first computer, and I went on the Internet and typed in Fritz the Nite Owl—N-i-t-e—in the search. Five pages of stuff came up. I thought, holy shit, there are people out there who know more about my life and career than I do. And the strange part is, when I was doing it, I never realized, or even conceived, that anybody beyond next week was going to care one way or another. I always thought that they regarded me as the sprinkles on the meringue that was on the pie. It's nice that it's there, but it's going to be gone tomorrow. And I had no idea.

Bob Marvin and I used to talk about this, after we were off the air. He played Flippo the Clown. When we were doing it, we knew people liked it. We knew we were popular, and we knew there was always a good crowd at our personal appearances. We never thought that five years after we were off anybody would care. You know, maybe a few hardcore fans, we thought. Flippo—now passed on—was probably our biggest local non-news celebrity on television. But he had been off the air as Flippo the Clown for 15, 20 [years]. And I mean to say, you say, "Flippo the Clown" to anybody in Columbus, Ohio, of any age, and they will know instantly who he is, what he did, what he looked like. After he had retired, and I was sort of between TV shows, we would talk about how amazed we were that people still hung on to it and still remembered us. People will tell me about movies I hosted. I haven't the vaguest recollection. But at the time, we just didn't figure there was any longevity. I mean, we knew we would keep going until the ratings fell or something like that. We just didn't think that anybody, 20 [years] afterward, would care one way or the other. I'm grateful that I'm remembered.

When Mike McGraner approached me for a documentary, my first reaction was who's going to be interested. My wife and my sons and granddaughters convinced me to do it. And literally, my reaction was, who the hell's gonna want to see this other than, say, family or real hardcore fanatics? But we're doing it.

There are a lot of local people in other areas of the country, doing the same thing. The technology is much more readily available. What I picture is eventually we'll have a quilt of oral histories of local television that the fans themselves, the people who grew up with them, are generating. They're taking back the history and documenting their own backyards.

There was a book; it was longer than it was wide, on TV horror hosts ... it had a lot of the horror posters in it. The back of the book is devoted to horror hosts.

Oh, the Shock *book* (SHOCK! Theater: An Illustrated History *published by* Monsters From the Vault). *They reprinted the original SHOCK! promo book. Yeah, that's wonderful.*

The guy who wrote about me in there, Mark Miller, also put out award-winning books on Peter Cushing and Christopher Lee, and he actually interviewed these guys for the books. Mark Miller is a horror fan, and you'd be interested in reading some of the books he has. Christopher Lee and Peter Cushing were two of the people that he actually went to see, and they talked to him at length about each of the movies. So, a name to jot down as a horror host fan—Mark Miller.

Do you have any final thoughts about Fritz or your career?

It's been fun. And I've always had this thing about how terrific it is somebody is paying me to do this. I never considered it work. I think that's one of the reasons why, at age 76, my health is pretty good. It was never a stress to do it; it was never a job. I looked forward to go to work. Haldi, as I say, would buy these terrific packages. And then there was a lady who would schedule the films, by the name of Betty Dixon. If there was a Mike Monahan film starring Mike Monahan, and there was a Mike Monahan celebration day, she would make sure that the Mike Monahan film played on Mike Monahan Day. Like *Groundhog Day* (1993), she made sure that film played on Groundhog Day.

That Channel 10 crew, when I was there, from about 1974 up through 1990, when Haldi retired and the new guy came in—and fired 14 of us the same day—it was just golden. It was never work. It was fun and just a great ride all the way.

Sven Again
Son of Svengoolie (Rich Koz)
Interviewed by Michael Monahan (2010)

Rich Koz was a student at Northwest University in the early 1970s, doing what most college kids in Chicago were doing at the time—digging Svengoolie. Koz was a fan of cinematic slapstick veterans like The Marx Brothers and The Three Stooges and saw a similar vaudeville spirit in Svengoolie's TV antics. Eventually Koz sent Jerry G. Bishop some jokes for the show. Bishop was impressed and Koz soon found himself a regular writer and crew member on *Screaming Yellow Theater*.

The show was cancelled in 1973, but Koz and Bishop continued their creative alliance on radio. Years later, WFLD-TV 32 decided to revive the spirit of Svengoolie in late-night. The original Svengoolie had relocated to San Diego. But he had left Koz with permission to use the character in any future projects. In 1979, Koz picked up the twisted thread of his mentor and wove it into The Son of Svengoolie.

The *Son of Svengoolie* show had a popular run, garnering a number of local Emmys. In 1986, the station was acquired by FOX/News Corp., who felt locally produced programming somehow demeaned their brand, and the show was cancelled. Three years later, management experienced a change of heart, due in part to press coverage of what should have been The Son of Svengoolie's tenth anniversary. They invited Rich Koz to return for another hosting gig in 1989 with *The KOZ Zone*. The show began in late-night, offering movies like *Astro-Zombies* (1968), *Hell Night* (1981) and *The Return of Count Yorga* (1971), before briefly morphing into a Monday through Friday afternoon kid show featuring Three Stooges shorts. Cancellation followed soon thereafter.

At the stroke of midnight 1995, Rich Koz signed on WCIU-TV 26 with a special all-night preview schedule of shows that would be part of the station's regular line-up. He appeared in the familiar form of Son of Svengoolie. But Jerry G. Bishop, noting he was all grown up now, had given him permission to drop the "Son of" and present himself henceforth simply as "Svengoolie."

Can we start by talking a little about your background? Did you grow up in Chicago?

I pretty much spent my whole life here in the Chicago area; born in the city. We moved out to the suburbs when I was, like, four years old. As a very young child, I remember a couple of times getting a few quick looks at *Shock Theater* with Marvin, which was the big seminal horror show here, when Universal let out the *Shock* package. Marvin was Terry Bennett, who also did kid shows. His show was very popular. I was very young at the time and wasn't allowed to stay up late. So I only saw a little bit of it. But I remember my older cousins and such always talking about it. "*Shock Theater*? Yeah, we watch that every week!"

I grew up out in the Northern suburbs of Chicago and eventually worked my way into a brief stint at Northwest University. During that time period is when Jerry G. Bishop started his Svengoolie show. I was a fan of that and started sending jokes to him. He responded and said, "Can you send me some more stuff?" Then he said to me, "Can you write a bit about such and such a thing?" Eventually he volunteered to come down to do a radio show I was doing at the college radio station, then invited me to come watch them tape his Svengoolie show. That worked into me working for him, coming down to the studio every week and doing off-camera voices and artwork, and writing very specific bits for him.

What original elements did you bring to the show? Did you add characters or concepts and running gags to the program?

There were a few things along the way. He was doing parody commercials. I pretty much did those for him, and parody songs. His whole thing was, "You know, it was lucky you came along when you did, because by that time I'd pretty much done everything I knew, and I didn't know what else to do." We did a *Sesame Street* parody that I came up with for him. It was called "Svengoolie Street." I just kinda built on some of the bits that he already had going.

What were some of those bits? What were the elements of Svengoolie that were so attractive to you?

I liked his sense of humor. I was a fan of his radio show. He was on the radio at the time and had been for several years previous to that. As an overall fan of his I appreciated his sense of humor, more than anything

Son of Svengoolie circa 1980. Rich Koz dropped the paste-on moustache when it caused an allergic reaction, opting for a drawn-on version.

else, and the horror movies, which I enjoyed. There was a Golden Goolie Award, which was a punch line to a bit. It was presented to this woman because she didn't want to wake the kids, so she shot her husband with a bow and arrow. We'd just pick some old joke and build it into the bit. And there were so many of those cheap Ronco-type commercials back then. So we'd always come up with parodies of those. Jerry played the guitar. He knew only a few chords, it turned out. But I'd try to write parody songs for him; things that made sense with the movies and such.

Did you contribute some technical aspects as well? I remember one of those bits where Svengoolie is interviewing himself, for instance.

Well, I kind of suggested some stuff. It's hard to remember which stuff he suggested and which stuff I suggested this far down the road. But he did that with a split screen and pre-taping the interview part of that. I'm pretty sure that I wrote that bit for him.

Ghoulardi had done something similar, where Ernie Anderson interviewed his alter ego. Did Jerry G. ever talk about the Cleveland origins of some of the music and audio drop-ins he was using?

A little bit about it, yeah. I learned more about that after Svengoolie was done when we were working in radio together. He would tell me stories about Ernie Anderson and such. Tim Conway, who was also working out there. So I knew a little bit about some of the stuff, and how he had borrowed the sound effect of the door with the bell that he always used, like a shop door, from some other morning team that was in Cleveland at the time.

The Kaiser network bumped Svengoolie in Chicago for its own host—ironically from Cleveland—The Ghoul. What was your perspective on the reaction of Chicago audiences?

He was not very well received. I think the show The Ghoul did—replacing a bunch of hosts in the various cities where Kaiser was broadcasting at the time—was, "Well, we took care of *him!*" I don't think that set well. That and the fact that I think the quality of the humor was a little better with what Jerry did. It was a little more clever stuff. Here's a guy whose main talent is blowing up stuff.

It's the difference between satire and slapstick.

Yeah. I know people for the most part were not fans of it. It lasted, I believe, less than six months here. It got such a bad reaction.

At some point the station decided to revive the Svengoolie brand. What were the circumstances behind the resurrection and your audition for the spot?

It actually started a little before that, because someone here had talked to Jerry about doing Svengoolie as just a summer fill-in type thing on a local station. And at the time he said, "You know, I don't really think that I would want to do that." One of the reasons being—and I always thought this was funny—was that Jerry was very civic minded. And I'm sure he still is. He actually thought that he might want to run for local office. He said, "I think it would be terrible if I run for office and they could hold up a picture of me as Svengoolie and say, 'This is what my opponent is trying to do!'"

I was very flattered that he had enough confidence in me that he felt, "You could play the part. You could be Son of Svengoolie and I'll just produce and work with you on writing it." We had some false starts, nothing really happened. Then when Jerry was preparing to leave for San Diego, he asked what I was going to be doing. One of the guys I had worked with was Dick Orkin, famous radio and commercial name. He had already gone to Los Angeles and now Jerry was going to San Diego. I said, "I'm not quite sure. But I thought I might see if I could talk some local station into letting me do some TV." And he said, "I'll tell you what. If you want to try doing the Svengoolie thing, you've got my blessing. Go ahead and do it," which was very nice of him.

Like I said, first of all, I was very flattered that he had the confidence in me that I could pull it off. And secondly, the generosity of saying, "Here, you can go ahead and do it." I called a bunch of local stations here and got very little response from them. One, when I talked to the program director and told him what I wanted to do, he laughed at me and hung up, which was very enjoyable. But then I pitched it to WFLD, where Jerry had worked, I went in to talk to them, came in with a full-blown concept, examples and everything. The program director said, "Yeah, ya know, that's a great idea. We've been thinking of doing something like this. But I'll tell ya what. Why don't we make this a bake off and let everybody audition who wants to do this?" And I was like, "Yeah, okay. But I've just brought you this full-blown thing." He said, "Yeah, I know. You can audition first." And so I did.

A bunch of other people auditioned, including a local radio host who was gaining popularity at the time. And some other folks that I never knew. The funny thing was that originally the guy who was the program director ended up being fired by the time I auditioned. Now it was a different program director who didn't care for what I did, which is always nice. He decided he wanted some friends of mine, who had auditioned as a couple getting ready to go out for the evening but who were distracted by the movie, to be the hosts. I think he was voted down by higher-ups who said, "No, no, no. We want the traditional-type thing."

It seems like a one-shot concept.

I don't think it would have stood up. So then I guess it fell to me as the guy coming out of the coffin. Anyway, I ended up getting the job.

You painted the coffin, didn't you?

I actually designed it, the original design when Jerry had it. Then I painted on my face and changed a few other things to reflect things that had changed on the show. When I did my original audition, I looked exactly the same as Jerry G's Svengoolie. They felt that was a very dated early '70s look. You know, a hippie type thing. "We'd like you to look different." So I made some changes and they weren't quite sure. I made some *more* changes and they weren't quite sure. Finally I just said, "You see the way I'm dressed now? This is it. Take it or leave it." It was close to the way I look now.

Were there any specific influences that went into the final design?

Part of it was some stuff I had at home. (*Laughs*) It was funny, I had actually checked out theatrical wigs. They were all so expensive that I ended up going to a K-Mart, where they sold the women's wigs for like $29.99. I picked up one of those, and it's the same one that I'm still using. I'd love to get a new one, but they don't make that sort of Jaclyn Smith style anymore.

You brought a wide range of comedy influences into the show. Can you talk about some of them?

Oh geez, I really love doing impressions. So I bring in other characters and voices like that. The Tombstone character, the talking skull, was actually based on the character that Jerry had, a female skull named Zelda. His full name was Zalman T. Tombstone, Jr. It was play off the Raymond J. Johnson character comedian Bill Saluga was doing at the time. "You don't have to call me Ray..." At first Tombstone had his own kind of litany of the same sort of thing he would go through. It changed every week, of course. It was never the same. He was pretty much a nemesis and we still use him in the shows.

I was into so many things. I loved the old style comics, like Jack Benny, the Marx Brothers and Laurel and Hardy. Then the more contemporary ones like George Carlin and Albert Brooks. I guess all that just kind of worked in. And Jerry G, he was an influence on me as well, because I listened to him and watched him do stuff for so long. I adapted some of the things that he did.

Was he doing something similar on the radio, in terms of the style of humor he was doing as Svengoolie?

Svengoolie returned to Chicago TV in 1995. At Jerry G. Bishop's suggestion, Rich Koz dropped the "Son" from his title and fully embraced the legacy of his mentor.

appearances and got a great reaction. I think we were very lucky at that time, because the show was a little before cable hit really big here. So people were still really married to the handful of stations they could get locally.

What sort of film package did you have at the time? You eventually got hold of the Universals. Was that there for you from the beginning?

Pretty close to it, yeah. And also they had the American-International stuff, the Roger Corman stuff and a lot of the bizarre side stuff like *The Mad Doctor of Blood Island* (1968). I remember one of the shows. We had already worked it out and one of the guys in charge said, "Why do we have him do that crap? Let's have him do more of the Universal stuff. It kind of made me mad, because they pulled it at the last minute. We had just done all the work on it. It was funny, because we were doing some sort of *Star Trek* parody. I was dressed as Captain Kirk, and even had my hair sprayed with coloring stuff so it was lighter. I got word they were pulling the movie after we'd done all the work, and I remember storming into this program director's office dressed as Captain Kirk. "What are you guys doing?!" He just kind of stared at me. (*Laughs*) Yeah, that was amusing.

Stations had a real interesting mix of film packages at that time.

He used a lot of the same sort of gags. The sound effects were the exact same ones that he used in radio. He did the same thing. He did little songs and things on the radio. He was a great radio personality.

When did you first go on the air? Was it a hit with fans from the get-go, or did it develop its base over time?

It caught on pretty quickly. I went on in June of 1979. It was only a couple of months when I noticed it really started taking off. We were getting a lot of mail and requests for autographs. I went out and did some public

So much was available! Now of course it's so difficult for a station like ours, which is still an independent station, to get this stuff. Most of the distributors would rather make money by selling it to a cable outlet.

Right. So what's your leverage for something like that? Recently (2010) *it looks like you've been getting some terrific films. You've had the Ray Harryhausen movies,* The Birds *(1963)...*

Yeah, it's great. All the credit goes to our vice-president here, Neil Saban, who is the one who put together these stations. He has really just done an outstanding job in getting this stuff for our show. I don't know who else was running Universal stuff before we got it.

I thought Ted Turner had it all locked up.

Yeah, and he managed to make the deal for that. He got Sony-Columbia to give us some stuff for a while. He just works very hard, and I appreciate that he makes the effort, and doesn't just consider this a throwaway. He wants us to have good stuff for the show to be worthwhile to both us and the viewers.

How is the show doing these days, ratings-wise?

Well, we're doing very well. I'm often very pleased to see that we're still holding our own here in prime time on a Saturday. The show's still on at nine o'clock on Saturdays and again at one in the morning on our sister station, MeTV, which is more a nostalgia-based station.

Can you talk a bit about some of the special shows you've done on your program, like Son of Sven's Hot Rods to Gila *and the more recent "Out of the Woodwork" Ed Wood special?*

The *Hot Rods to Gila* movie was actually the idea of Michael J. Smith, a late film editor friend of mine who worked there and was in charge of the films. We had the usual *Giant Gila Monster* (1959) and also this awful film called *The Ghost of Dragstrip Hollow* (1959). They both had a lot of stuff with these young kids with jalopies running around like crazy. And we were both also fans of the attitude of the old *Hot Rods to Hell* (1967) movie. So Smith said, "What if we put these together?" So we did. We made our own credits for it that looked like 1950s-type credits. I think it only ran once.

I think so. Didn't you have to deconstruct the film afterwards? You were working with film prints.

Yes, we would bicycle films from station to station, so we had to take it apart and put the two prints back together afterwards. It was so funny. One of my favorite things is, at one point, a journalist from *The Ghost of Dragstrip Hollow* says, "Yeah, I'm writing a story about these kids. I think I'm going to call it..." And he had some title like "Youth In Trouble." "What do you think?" Then our edi-

tor cut in a shot of a theater full of people bringing their hands up and holding their noses." (*Laughs*) That was fun.

The "Out of the Woodwork" was the result of us getting a load of Ed Wood movies. We were all pretty fascinated. That was before Tim Burton's *Ed Wood* (1994) movie even came out. We were all just fascinated by the story of this guy. A lot of his stuff we had not seen before. We worked out the whole special on that to try and educate people about it. We were very proud of the end result.

So that was prior to airing the movies on your show? Plan 9 *and* Bride of the Monster *showed later?*

We might have already aired a couple of them. But we then used all the footage to then illustrate the story.

You were syndicated to various cities in the early 1980s. Did you create specific material for each market?

What we were doing most of the time was we would do specific opens and closes and mail segments for each city. Then we did promos and bumpers for those that wanted them.

Was it the same film package from city to city?

No. That was one of the things that made it so much work. It ended up some of them had the same film packages we did, but they didn't schedule them the same. How much brain power would it have taken to say, "Okay, let's schedule this movie the same week as the Chicago station or the Philadelphia station"? No one stepped up to do that. I always got the feeling, quite honestly, that other stations felt the Field Communications people forced the show on them. That was reflected in a lot of their reactions. I'd call and say, "How's the show going?" "Okay..." "Are you getting any mail or anything?" "I think we did. I'll send it to you if we can find it."

Now years later, in the time that I've been here at WCIU, with the advent of the Internet, I've heard from so many people. "Oh, you went to Chicago after you left..." Name the city, Boston, whatever. And I said, no, I was always in Chicago. And they were like, "Oh, we used to all love to watch the show." People would get together in the college dorms every week to watch it. I've heard so

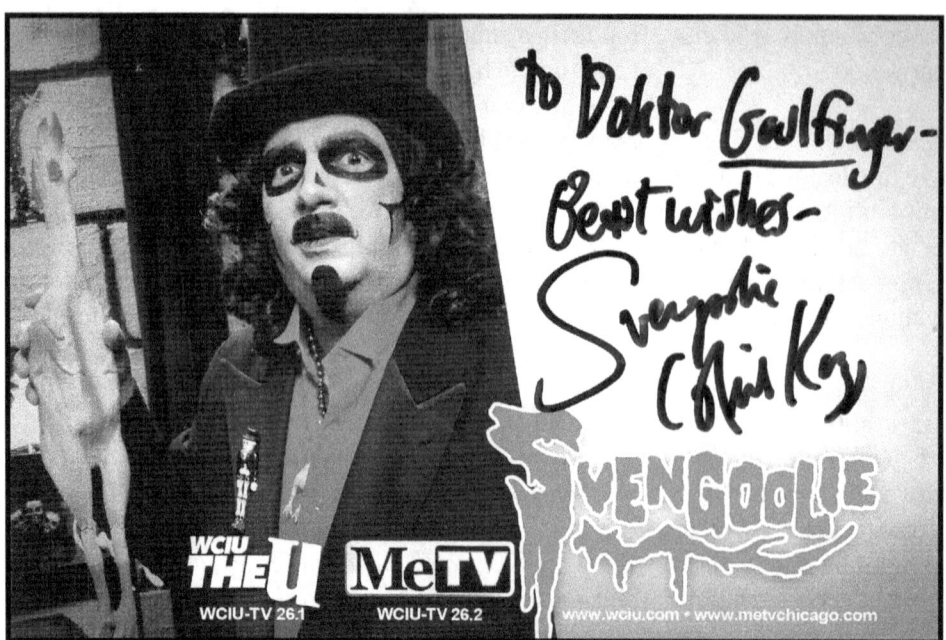

The Svengoolie look gets a slight overhaul for the new millennium. The red turtleneck is dropped in favor of an open neck shirt and rubber chicken bolo tie. The show was again syndicated nation-wide by MeTV beginning on April 4, 2011.

many stories of how people loved to watch the show in other cities, which was never conveyed to me by the stations themselves. Because they felt, I guess, that (*Droopy Dog voice*), "They were making us run this..." And they never put much effort behind it.

Did it change the way you produced your shows? I'm guessing you had to create more generic comedy that wasn't attached to a specific movie.

More and more it just had to be generic bits, not necessarily playing off the movie. And we had to lose some of the Chicago-based comedy, except in the local opens and closes. We had to make the specifics disappear in the middle of it, so it would play in all the other cities.

It must have been strange to lose some of that identity, which so key to doing a local show.

Yeah, that kind of bothered me. In a way, the reason we were doing the opens and closes that way was to establish a sort of local identity. Each one of the stations was told to have somebody send me a little information packet with, like, who's a goofy local weatherman I could make fun of, a car dealer? Different places in town to make fun of people or businesses. It was funny to see the reaction from these different cities. In San Francisco we had no problem, because Tom Spitz, who was from Chicago, was involved. He provided me with a lot of information about that area. I remember the people in Boston being very enthusiastic and giving me a lot of information.

I can't remember which other city it was; they sent me one little memo paper. Handwritten, some of it illegible, but very little information I could use. Again it was reflective of this attitude of "they're making us do this," like it was homework or something. So we just had to do whatever we could for some cities, because we didn't have as much information.

Did you air for longer in some cities than others?

Yeah. Quite honestly, I think San Francisco was the one we stayed in the longest. Early on we lost Detroit or Boston. I can't recall which went first, but I think the last two were Philadelphia and San Francisco. They just gradually fell off. They were given some option when they could opt out. It wasn't like it was a big deal to them. It just took a little extra work to opt on. And yet, it was too much for them, you know.

It seems pretty easy. They were receiving the content. There was nothing to produce...

Right, and yet the work was too much for them because the content was not married to the film. The way we do it now is, we have all the bits tied onto the movie segments. We couldn't do it back then. Even at my station we couldn't do it that way, just because they had the separate film chains and we were on videotape. So we would just send them a reel of our bits and they were supposed to insert them at certain points. And it was too much work for them. (*Laughs*) What can I tell ya?

What was the gap between the syndication dropping off and the cancellation in Chicago?

I think the syndication dropped off, at the latest, in 1984. And then the show was cancelled very early in January of 1986. The reason for the cancellation was the fact that we were becoming FOX stations and they felt the show was not a suitable sort of product for a FOX station, which still makes me laugh. That wasn't suitable, but the Joan Rivers late show *was*.

The funny thing is, the guy who's always done my music, Doug Sharff, who plays the Doug Grave character on the show, had a friend who was involved in the band on the Joan Rivers late-night show, and Sharff got him a job playing trumpet in that band. He moved his family out to Los Angeles and played for the short time the show was on the air. After that he was stuck freelancing and eventually decided to move back here.

You also worked in radio. Were you doing that during the Son of Svengoolie run? Or did you begin after it went off the air?

I did it on and off then, because I did mostly fill-in stuff. I didn't really have the time to have a full-time shift. Although there were times had it presented itself, I probably would have jumped at it. But I worked at a couple different stations. I had a long run, on and off, with the WGN radio, which was a real powerhouse.

Were you taking inspiration from Jerry G. in that as well?

I think a lot of it was pretty much my own, but there were things that Jerry did that I liked. For example, he played around with the sound effects carts. I liked using that. Although when I was doing things at WGN they had a very popular, very famous morning man who was the guy who built the station, really, through the '60s all the way up through the end of the '80s. Wally Phillips was a very important guy in Chicago radio. He used a lot of drop-in sound effect type things. And when I was there, I remember one of the management people saying, "Well you know, you really shouldn't do that, because people will think you're imitating Wally." I said, well, wait a minute. Disc jockeys have always done that. He said, "Yes, but for a lot of our listeners, the only person they heard do it is Wally."

In other words, "Wally owns this."

Yeah. People had listened to him for so many years and that was all they knew. And most WGN listeners at that time would not switch around to other stations. They stayed on that station all the time they were listening. So they had no idea there were other deejays that did bits with pre-recorded old sound effects.

Were you doing this as Rich Koz or as Son of Svengoolie?

Most of the time I was doing it as Rich Koz. Occasionally Svengoolie would show up as a character. But for the most part I was fronting as myself. When I went back on TV doing my *Koz Zone* program in 1989, one of the local radio stations hired me to do mornings for a short time. One of the things they wanted was that I would have to play the Son of Svengoolie character also. So he was on every morning with me, on pre-recorded tracks, to make it sound like there were two separate people and such.

So even though you were off the air on television, radio provided a bridge for Son of Svengoolie?

That was the funny thing. At the time the show was cancelled I was still doing guest shots on radio and TV as Son of Svengoolie. And I was doing public appearances as him. So he was still around, more or less, no matter what else I was doing.

What about The Koz Zone? *How did that come about?*

It was actually thanks to a local TV columnist, Rob Feder. He wrote an article in *The Chicago-Sun* in 1989 noting it was about the time of my anniversary as Son of Svengoolie. At the time I was still freelancing and trying to find another gig. He had called me up and said, "I want to write an article talking about what a loss it is that you're not on the air currently, as Son of Svengoolie or something else."

And I was felling kind of funny about it, because I don't want it to be a "Oh poor him" kind of a thing. I had also had a daughter born who had some medical problems and I said, I don't want this to turn into the Jerry Lewis Telethon or something. He said, "No, just let me write something. I'll make sure that it doesn't come off that way." And he did, which was very nice. He just wrote a little thing that said, "This would have been the tenth anniversary of Rich Koz as Son of Svengoolie and it's something that's lacking." He was very kind to

The Son of Svengoolie in an early publicity still. Photo by Rich Koz

say, "He's a very talented guy who is not working and it's a shame that broadcasting doesn't have room for him."

It was funny since the people back at WFLD felt that this was something that might give them bad publicity. So they decided, "Let's bring him back doing something else."

And they called me. "We would like you to do something. We don't want you doing Son of Svengoolie, but we would like you to host a movie." One of the promotion guys said, "Here's what we want you to do. We want you to be like an old guy who lives down in the basement of the station, some weird character that will show some of these old horror movies." I said, that would be great, except one of the country music cable stations was doing that.

Oh yeah, Sir Cecil Creape on The Nashville Network. They had a show called Phantom of the Opry, *where he lived under the Grand Ol' Opry house.*

So I said, "I don't really want to do that. There had been an actual incident where somebody had stolen a remote truck, or borrowed one, and broke into programming on both Channel 9 and Channel 11 here. So I said, "Here's what I want to do ... pretend that we're breaking into the broadcast when we do this movie thing. We can use some of the reality of the situation. A guy was fired from the station and is going back on the air. So they went, "Well ... I guess so."

We made these spots that actually started off as a Bill Cosby or Phil Donahue promo. It would suddenly break into static and then you'd see me working with this electronic stuff. There would be a fuzzy picture, and in the background was a sign that read "Friday Night At 10:30." Then it would fade out and go back to the regular promo. People started to think that it was for real. The head engineer even got a call from the FCC. "You know, we can send a truck and find out who's doing this ..." He told them, "No, it's actually just something we're doing as a promo." They were not very pleased.

And that carried over to the first show, where The Astro-Zombies *apparently broke into a Lassie movie. What was the reaction to that?*

A lot of people caught on. "Oh, it's the same guy who used to be Son of Svengoolie." It was actually pretty well received. And I created a character that was supposedly the head of the board of directors at the station, who then became my nemesis. He kept trying to capture me while I was breaking into the signal. Eventually we had a thing where he hired me just so he could make my life a living hell.

How long was Koz Zone *on the air?*

It was on from the summer of 1989 into March of 1990. At that point, that was when FOX started doing all their kids' shows, and they demanded each one of the stations have a live host to promote their FOX Kid's Club to give a local sort of feel to everything. Our general manager decided that I would be the perfect person for it. He said, "You're not someone who's going to be talking down to the kids and you'll be doing the shtick." He was a big supporter of what I did. So he said, "We'd like to take you off that late-night show and have you be a kid's host." I was thinking, "I don't know necessarily that I want to be a kid's host. Couldn't I just continue with what I'm doing?' He said, "Well, there's no guarantee that show will still be around," which seemed to be the writing on the wall. So it was, okay *The Koz Zone* will now become the daily kid show.

So that was a daily weekday show?

It was Monday through Friday. I was in between the cartoons doing all these bits and such. We were live three or four days a week and one day a week was pre-recorded.

Were you showing Three Stooges on the kid show? The late-night version aired them at some point, correct?

Yeah, the nighttime *Koz Zone* had gone from showing movies to showing Three Stooges shorts. That was, I think, from about January to when the show ended in March.

What were the circumstances behind the resurrection of Svengoolie on WCIU?

Basically, I had left FOX. In 1994 I was freelancing, trying to get another gig. Some friends of mine, who worked at WGN radio doing the overnights, had a yearly food drive that they did right at Halloween. They asked, "Would you mind dressing up as Son of Svengoolie this year and come out and help us?" I said, "Yeah, sure. I'll do that." When I went out to do it they mentioned to me that a friend of theirs, Neil Saban, who they had worked with in radio, had gotten into TV and was about to take over the programming at WCIU. He was going to try to turn it from what it had been, an ethnic station, a brokered station and a Univision station, into an independent. They said, "You really should talk to him."

I said, well, I have to tell you. The guy who's the program director at FOX always told me that Neil Saban absolutely hated me. He was working on the opposite station, Channel 50, at the time. He was running that. They said, "I don't know if that's true or not. Why don't you talk to him?" And it turns out that that was the story this program director at FOX had made up, because they wanted to make sure I didn't try to go to another station during the time they had me on the air. Or use it for leverage or whatever.

So I met up with Neil and talked to him. We hit it off right away. We watched the same programming growing up and had a shared appreciation for a number of things, including the Three Stooges. He said, "I'd love to have you be here on the ground floor when we start this station." And so I did. He said, "Do you want to do Son of Svengoolie again?" And I said, sure! I mean there had never been a time when somebody didn't recognize me and say, "You know, I used to love that show. I wish you could do it again." I said there's so much interest. I'd be happy to do it. And we did.

Weren't you the very first personality on the air with the new WCIU? They did an all-night marathon of classic TV shows and you were the host..

Yeah, they did an unannounced preview that started just after midnight, because the station went on January 1, 1995. And the night before we went on I did little hosted elements that were lead-ins for the whole thing. Then the first full day we were on, January 1, we did a *Munsters* marathon hosted by Morton Downey, Jr. and me. That was quite an adventure.

Big Chuck Schodowski had a theory about the longevity of his career in Cleveland, saying the region had a static population, leading to multi-generational fans. Would you say the same is true in Chicago?

I think so. One of the things I always hear from people when I do public appearances is, "I used to watch you as a kid and now I watch you with my kids," which I think is a really big compliment. The fact that it's not something that people outgrew, that it's still something they have an appreciation for. I see such a wide range when I do appearances. People bring these little kids up and talk about how they watched the show every week. And then there are the teenagers and young adults. It just blows me away. Seventy-five year olds come over to say hello. It's very impressive to me.

And I think that's it. Somebody else brought up that the longer you're on the air, the more people are used to you being on the air. It does get passed along from generation to generation, because the parents are watching and the kids watch, and they grow up and continue to watch.

How has television changed since you started, and what do you hope to give to the next generation of viewers?

In a lot of ways we've lost this locally hosted type thing. If a local station is doing local programming, for the most part they're putting all their efforts behind news and public affairs and sports. If you're lucky, they'll do some magazine type show, which everybody does to death. "We'll show you where to find the best pizza in the city!" I think we're bringing them something they don't see, which is the host who is talking directly to you. It's the one-on-one thing that all the good kid show hosts

Rich Koz: "One of my first PR photos. Notice the coffin still has the *Jerry G. Sven* picture. I had to paint my face over it!" Photo courtesy Rich Koz

and local hosts did. You got the feeling they were talking to you and that they were your friend. That's exactly what you're aiming for. You're not talking to a whole big audience. You're talking to that one person. I think you connect by establishing that and by doing this sort of local shtick type stuff. One of the local writers was very kind in writing something about me. He said, "It shows you don't have to be in Los Angeles to be writing good comedy for TV."

I'm not sure people who've grown up with syndicated programming fully appreciate how local shows represent control of the creativity. It's not something processed and delivered from far away. Local people are making art.

Right, yeah. I've seen the same thing here. There are so many guys and gals on cable access now, doing their hosted movie type things. Several of them said to me, "I saw you doing it and that inspired me to do it myself. The whole idea that you've got these people who see this *American Idol* type stuff ... You're not going to walk the street tomorrow and run into someone from those shows, whereas, if you see this local host here, you have a chance to actually interact and see him at a local event. You might even accidentally run into him on the street somewhere.

It's an achievable level of celebrity status as well. Seeing the celebrity on the street takes it out of the abstract.

Yeah, exactly. That was the amazing thing for me when I was in high school, and the high school had an actual FM station. That just amazed me, because I loved hearing guys on the radio. I even thought, I wonder if there's ever some way of doing it. Wow, yes, there is a way to do it. That graduated to the fact that you can actually get a job doing this. It is possible. When I was first sending information and jokes and stuff to Jerry, quite honestly I was just thrilled that, hey, I'm in contact with this guy! I never thought that this is going to build into a job for me. It was so cool to know this guy and be in touch with him and talk to him. And of course, the flattering thing that he wanted me to write stuff for him. That was just so cool. Never was I sitting there calculating, okay, this is how I'm going to get a job and get into this business.

There was certainly a lot of luck tied in with this. I've always told people, for all I know, I could have sent the stuff to Jerry and he could have said, "Thanks a lot, kid," and that would have been it. He was, first of all, a very honorable man, and a very generous man. He felt that I had talent. And not only did he feel that he could benefit from it, but that I could benefit from it.

Why do you think horror hosts continue to appeal to an audience?

I think part of it is just the ongoing appeal of horror movies themselves. But there seems to be a tradition tied

Rich Koz, alongside his alter-ego, Son of Svengoolie, holding the inevitable rubber chicken, circa 1980. Photo courtesy Rich Koz

in with this as far as local broadcasting. Whereas most stations nowadays feel that they have to have a news show and a public affairs show, with independent stations it seems like a lot of people remember one of things they enjoyed was the hosted show and the horror hosted type thing. I think there are people now in charge who've grown up, who remember that. And when they have a station where they can actually do something like that, that isn't tied in with some network and they actually have the leeway to do these types of shows, it seems part of the tradition for these stations. It's part of the background.

And I think you have people who flock to these things, because again it's that sort of local connection. You've got that sort of one-on-one appeal people don't necessarily get in other shows that they've seen. The one thing that I always touch on is that the show means something to people. I don't think I'd be doing it if it didn't. As I said, when people would recognize me on the street, when I wasn't doing the show, they'd say, "Wow, when are you going to do that again?" Even today, the fact that it means so much to them, that it creates some happiness in their life, blows me away. I'm just doing silly, stupid things. But it means something to these people and they enjoy it. There couldn't be a greater compliment.

There's real color in a horror host, as opposed to someone in a sweater hosting a Dialing For Dollars *movie.*

It depends on the person more than anything else. It depends on the talent of the person doing it.

And it gives you a lot of leeway, doesn't it? With the Svengoolie and Son of Svengoolie shows, you've been basically doing a comedy variety show.

Exactly, it was basically an excuse for me to be an entertainer. It was the hook to hang it all on. Of course, I'm a fan of horror movies. So that made it a little easier. But the whole point was finding a place for me to do shtick, and that's what happened to come along.

And I think the fantastic element allows you to experiment a lot more visually, like playing all three Marx Brothers in one skit. And just interacting with puppets!

You're right, exactly. It's that basic suspension of disbelief. Sure, the guy's talking to a sock.

And more importantly, it's talking back.

Exactly, that just adds to the whole unreality that is our reality.

A number of horror hosts point to Ernie Kovacs as an inspiration for some of their visual gags. Would that be the same with you?

Oh certainly, I remember seeing his stuff as a kid and really liking it. Then we were fortunate when they broadcast him on the PBS stations. They ran a lot of his stuff. It was just great to see that. He was definitely an inspiration. There were so many things you could do, and this guy was doing them. He'd come up with some strange idea and make it happen. That's something to aim for. There were little things here and there that I would notice and think, that's something we could do. It was definitely something that fired your imagination and gave you some momentum.

Television used to be entertainment in a more playful way.

Sure, I agree with that. I never went on with the attitude of the shock jock people—oh, I'm going to go on today and talk about this guy and I'm really going to *get* him! It's about having fun, not going out to shock or really upset people. You're hoping to make them laugh.

There's a community aspect to that as well—being a good neighbor, not being rude.

I think that's part of it. I think a lot of us that have that old school view of it. You're a guest in somebody's home when they turn on your show. And you're not going to do something that's going to be out of line. I remember one guy coming up to me and saying, "One of the other guys on the radio really pushes the envelope. How come you're not more like him?" I said, because that's not my act. That's not what I'm aiming for. That's part of what he's aiming for. But I'm not looking to shock people and upset them.

Along those lines of "old school," what other shows do you remember watching growing up? You mentioned seeing Marvin a handful of times. What were some of the other local programs and hosts you were seeing?

One of the guys who did a lot of stuff here in town was Ray Rayner. He worked at Channel 2 here and then worked at Channel 9 for years and years. Another person that I've gotten to know, fortunately, was Bill Jackson. He did the *Gigglesnort Hotel* show but was very big here in Chicago on WFLD doing *BJ and Dirty Dragon*. He was another very talented man who did this stuff. There was Frasier Thomas, who again was doing that sort of one-on-one stuff talking with puppets. He did *The Garfield Goose Show*. And then, of course, Bozo, which was broadcast here. I think it was the last city where Bozo was on the air. And little local record type shows, things like that. That was what I saw. I enjoyed that kind of stuff.

Being a local station, particularly at that time, there was still a lot of creative freedom. One of the highlights in talking to people who've been in television from the 1950s onward has been hearing about the Wild West quality of local TV stations.

Oh yeah, and people were not as litigious as they are these days, and as apt to say, "You used our footage without permission or not in the way it was intended," and all that kind of stuff. So that was cool.

Speaking of local programming, you've won a number of local Emmys.

I'm up to eight at this point (*Laughs*). Also, I was inducted into the Silver Circle of the Television Academy. I actually have a plaque here that has the date. Wow, it was in 2004. You had to be in television for 25 years. And, as they put it, "For outstanding contributions to Chicago television." It's like, you sometimes feel you don't belong somewhere ... Boy, I sure *did*. You hear all these different names, and it was people I grew up watching on TV, very honored people. It was just amazing to be pulled into that. I don't remember who I was doing an interview with, but he said, "You know, you're the most legitimately decorated horror host, because you got all these Emmys." (*Laughs*) I don't know if that's true or not.

Finally, and this is perhaps the most important question: Curly or Shemp?

I have to say I'm with Curly. But I have a great, great appreciation of Shemp. I've always thought he was very underrated. I love some of the stuff where it's obvious he's ad-libbing and he comes up with the damnedest, funniest stuff.

Kansas City Haunt-fidential
Crematia Mortem (Roberta Solomon)
Interviewed by Sandy Clark (2004)

Roberta Solomon had over a decade of radio experience behind her when, in 1980, she successfully auditioned for the role of host on *All Night Live*, a movie program on KSHB-TV Channel 41 in Kansas City. The show featured horror films, with Solomon performing unrelated comedy skits at the breaks. Though fairly popular in its time, Solomon recognized the limitations of a standard comedy skit format in a monster movie setting and developed a new guiding host more in tune with the films offered on the show.

Solomon's creation, Crematia Mortem, was an endearing Gothic goofball, a theatrical vamp with a Bette Davis accent and twittery mother-hen protectiveness. Although her costume corset, courtesy of Frederick's of Hollywood, proffered a healthy *décolletage*, she maintained a family friendly atmosphere, making her a perfect monster host for kids. Solomon had a genuine zest for comedy and her hosting segments were infectious fun, always brimming with playful puns and creative visual gags.

Crematia's *Creature Feature* ran its course in 1988, but Roberta Solomon has remained active in radio, notably as a cast member of the comedy program, *Right Between the Ears*. She also continues as a multi-media voice artist, working on both local and national commercial campaigns, documentary narration and station promos.

So, let's start off by talking a little bit about how Crematia Mortem was born.

In 1979, while I was still in college, I started working at the "Beautiful Music" station here in Kansas City, the old KMBR. I was on the air from seven to midnight, and across the hall was the "Dean of Kansas City Radio," a guy named Walt Bodine. Walt is still on the air now; he's just an amazing talk show host. He had all of these people from the industry who sort of came to learn at his feet. And one of the guys who came in fairly regularly was Rob Forsythe, a producer at KSHB-TV. Rob went on to become the Creative Services Director at the station.

KSHB at that time was an independent station here in Kansas City. And they were doing all sorts of interesting things. They had a show running every weeknight called *All Night Live*, which was sort of a local version of *Nick at Night*. It was live, every night, Monday through Friday. They played bad Westerns and old comedies, sit-coms like *Leave It To Beaver* and stuff like that. The host who was on during the week, "Uncle Ed" (*Ed Muscari, later the horror host, Edmus, in Phoenix, AZ*), had created quite a stir in Kansas City. KSHB decided, because the show was so successful, that they wanted to expand it to Saturday night. And they had this whole library of monster flicks they wanted to play.

So one night Rob Forsythe—who was the Creative Services Director at KSHB by then—came to the radio station to visit Walt, walked into the studio while I was on the air and said, "Hey, you know, we're holding auditions for the Saturday night host or hostess of this *All Night Live* thing that we're going to do, and you oughta audition." I said, but I don't have any experience. And he said, "That's okay. That'll make it even better." So I went over to KSHB and auditioned for the job. And got it … which was so weird, because I truly had no experience other than a couple of college TV classes. And a week or so later I went on the air, live, as "Sally Roberts." The people at the radio station made me change my name because they were worried I was going to embarrass them on TV.

I hosted these monster shows as Sally for about eight months. I'd created this whole repertory company of goofy characters I played, and the show was doing pretty well, but my comedy bits just weren't really working with the monster movies. So we decided it would be easier to change me than to change a whole library of movies, so

Roberta Solomon during her 2004 interview with Sandy Clark

I grew up in St. Louis. We had this horror host, but I can't remember the guy's name.

But they used to play monster movies on both Channel 11 and Channel 30 and I loved them. I'd get together with my best friend every Saturday night and we would drag out our sleeping bags, go down in her basement and turn on the TV and watch these inane monster movies. And we'd sit there and tell jokes, like, look, the monster has a zipper up his back! So I grew up watching those movies. It was only after I was doing Crematia that I realized, oh my God, this is just a continuation of my childhood, hosting this show.

Can you remember anything about that host whose name you can't remember? Can you remember anything about his shtick or his routine? Was he a vampire or a ghoul?

He was just your sort of generic monster guy, you know? He sort of hid in the shadows. I don't remember much about him, because I don't think he was on very long. But I remember *the movies*. They played *Day of the Triffids* (1962) and all the classically bad Japanese monster movies—Godzilla, Ghidrah, Gamera, Mothra. *Destroy All Monsters* (*Kaijû sôshingeki*, 1968)—you know, where all the monsters are in the movie at the same time. And they would play the classic Universal movies—*Frankenstein* (1931) and *Dracula* (1931) and *Creature from the Black Lagoon* (1954). It was heaven. I don't remember the host, but I remember the movies.

we came up with the concept of a horror host. My last weekend as Sally, I went on the air and I said, "Well, you guys, I've been fired. I have no idea who your host is going to be next week. And they won't tell me anything about her. I guess they just dug her up somewhere." And the following week, Crematia Mortem made her debut.

My radio pal Walt Bodine helped me come up with that name. I had decided I wanted her to be called Crematia and told him about it in his studio one night. But I couldn't come up with a last name for her. And Walt said, "Well, of course! Her last name needs to be Mortem." So that's how she was born.

Growing up, did you see a host? Was there a host on in the market you grew up in?

Are there any of those movies that you think still stand up today, that are good to you as an adult? And what were some of your favorites as a kid?

Well, I thought they were retarded when I was a kid! (*Laughs*) *Day of the Triffids* scared the heck out of me. I just watched it again a couple of months ago. The dialogue is pretty stilted, but it holds up pretty well! And the first time I saw *The Thing* (*The Thing From Another World*, 1952), the original *Thing*, oh my gosh! That just flipped me out. It was so scary. But mostly I remember the Japanese monster movies—Godzilla, Ghidrah, Mothra and all of those. They were just awful and fun.

What were your favorites to host when you got to host movies? What worked best for you?

The worse the movies were, the better the show was… because there was more material to work with! For a while at Channel 41, I don't know what happened, we got, like, these Mexican and Filipino monster flicks. And then we got those movies with the wrestlers in them, you know? The lucha libre monster flicks. Those worked really well, because all you have to do is watch and laugh and you've got your show, you've got your material!

But I think one of the funniest moments came when for a brief period we were doing the show live. We were playing *Destroy All Monsters*. And the director said, "Now this'll be fun. I'm going to drop you into a little box down at the bottom of the screen as the credits are rolling. And all you have to do is just *read* the actor's names as they roll by." And they were names like Tashiko Akiashi, George Guskashurawa, all these really complicated and hard-to-pronounce Japanese names. And they were going by really, really fast! I just started laughing and my mascara started to run, because it was totally impossible to keep up with those names.

Did you do any other inserts into movies? Did they key you into films or anything like that?

We did that a lot when I was live, just because we could. But the show was taped most of the time, which I actually liked much better. Doing the show live didn't work for me, creatively, because Crematia had this little world she lived in, you know? It was much funnier when she could control the flow, rather than "breaking the wall" to take a live call from some guy working the counter at a 7-Eleven in Topeka. And interjecting myself into the movie live never seemed to be as funny as when we taped it.

You had no trouble mocking the films when they deserved it. What kind of things would you come up with? How did that start? Did you know from the very beginning that would be part of the movie presentation?

No, it kind of grew. Initially, when we first started the show, I was just this generically creepy lady who would show up and say creepy things. But over time, I sort of grew into the character. Crematia became kind of a loopy nut-ball. I began to play her as always one step away from really "getting it." She never really quite understood what was going on.

I remember as we screened those movies—I would screen them on a Movieola every week—there were so many inconsistencies in them. The monster would turn and you would see the zipper up the back of his costume, you know? Or people would be talking to each other, and in the next scene, they'd be reversed. So there were all these cinematic mistakes that would pop up. And that was the material we built the show around. You had to comment on the mistakes—because that's what people were doing at home! And later on, that's exactly what *Mystery Science Theater* did so beautifully. I felt part of a grand tradition. Monster movie hosts and hostesses had been doing that across the country for years.

Talk a little bit about Mystery Science Theater 3000.

When I first saw *Mystery Science Theater*, it was sort of toward the end of my tenure as Crematia. And watching it, I thought, oh my gosh! That's what I've been doing for 10 years! They're doing exactly what we had been doing. And I thought it was wonderful because it was a completely novel take on it, having these little people sitting down in the theater, just riffing on the movie.

What about working from outlines instead of scripts? You probably didn't script a lot.

No. I would go in on Tuesday and, with my director, screen the movie. It had already been cut up, so we knew when the breaks would fall and what would happen in each section of the film. So I would write notes for myself. The next day, I'd meet with the director and we'd go, okay, now in this scene, the monster turns around and he picks up the heroine and tosses her out the window. And then we cut to commercial. So we would build our bits to reflect what was happening in the movie. I worked from an outline. That was easiest for me, because of my background is in theater and comedy. So as long as I knew I had to get from point A to point B to point C, I could sort of figure out a way to get there. We'd rehearse the break a couple of times, and then we'd shoot. We worked very fast, and when I made mistakes, we'd just work that into the bit.

Tell me a little bit about the lifespan of Crematia Mortem. Did the show change over time? What got better about it, what got worse? And what finally drove it off the air?

I started doing the *Creature Feature* in 1981, and my last show was in January of 1990. So I did it for about nine years. Initially, Crematia was not as endearing as she became over time. I really had to settle into the character and become ... *bold* with her. I realized there was this love affair developing between the audience and Crematia. I mean they adored her! When I began to understand what was going on, I started playing around with that. Crematia became much more playful, funny and goofy. So we grew in that direction. It was the most exquisite experience of my life to do that show. And especially to have kids watching, because it turned into this thing that moms and dads, grandmas and grandpas, babysitters, college kids, whoever—could do together. They could sit down on a Saturday night together and watch that show. I knew it was unusual, and how precious that was. We were family friendly before anybody even thought of that term.

We did fall into the quagmire of bad taste, you know, the cesspool of bad taste, pretty regularly! But I don't think we ever got dirty or mean-spirited. We were racy. I mean, you can't be parading around every Saturday night in a corset with your cleavage hanging out and not get a *little* racy. But I always understood there were kids watching, and I wanted it to be appropriate for them. If there was something icky or really scary coming up in the movie, I'd say, "Now boys and girls it's time. Cover your eyes." Or I'd say, "Parents, make certain the little ones are down the hall, because there's something that you might not want them to see." So I would warn them, you know, if there was something weird coming up.

The thing that started to happen was, as KSHB's commitment to programming from the FOX network grew—going from being an independent station to a FOX affiliate—network programs started to push out the local late-night programs the station had carried. It was happening all over the country. FOX had *The Joan Rivers Show*, and they started placing other shows in late-night. The *Creature Feature* got pushed back later and later, until finally it wasn't starting until midnight. And I just didn't want to do it anymore, because it's a lot different to do a show that comes on at 10:00 or 10:30 on a Friday night or a Saturday night, then it is to do a show that goes on 12:30. Kids are going to be asleep. And as much as I love the guys at Leavenworth, as much as I love the guys working overnight at 7-Eleven, I didn't want to do a show that was just for them—because it was always about the kids. So it just seemed like an appropriate time to step back and to move on to something else.

Tell me a little about your outfit, about your set, and maybe a little about how that evolved, too. Were they your choices, somebody else's choices? How did they come about?

There were no choices! (*Laughs*) It was just what we got. The week before Crematia went on, I think the station gave us $500 to go out and buy junk for a set and buy my outfit. And I think I also kicked in for the outfit as well. I had this Frederick's of Hollywood blue corset. It was like one of those satin Victorian corset things. And this black peignoir I got at ... I don't know where, K-Mart or something like that. There was a place out in Independence called Wild Woody's, which was kind of a weird general store that was a point of kitschy historical interest for a long time. And somebody told me about this Korean couple there that ran the wig department. So I went out to Wild Woody's and got this long black wig from the Koreans. It was really bad quality, so every couple of months I would start going bald. (*Laughs*) So I'd have to go back out to Wild Woody's for another wig. And the Korean lady would go, "Oh, here come that funny lady on TV again. She's buying some more hair."

I went out with my director to garage sales and thrift stores a week or two before the "Creature Feature" debuted. We got this terrible lamp, this mangy-looking stuffed bird, an ugly wicker chair and that was the set. And we hung up some cobwebs. But the thing that was very cool concerned my husband at the time. He was friends with an undertaker at the Federal pen at Leavenworth, and he gave us a coffin. It had, like, a door on the top and a door on the bottom ... it was a transport coffin. We chained it up in the corner of the studio, which contained basically concrete block walls with this casket in the corner and cobwebs. We lit it with these strange lights and that was the set. So there really wasn't any artistic choices that went into it. It was, "Oh, we got a coffin. Great, we got a show."

Do you still have any props from the show? Do you still have the ugly lamp?

The ugly lamp is actually in my mother's bedroom now! (*Laughs*) We put a pretty shade on it. So she's got the lamp. The bird ... I think it finally fell apart. The costume got screwed up on one of my last shows, when I was out at the Renaissance Festival. One of the performers there, a guy, was part of a jousting and comedy duo called Puke and Snot, and he threw me over his shoulder and the corset ripped. So I knew it was time for me to stop doing the show. A lot of stuff from the set stayed at Channel 41 when I left. Apparently, the coffin is still propped up in a corner of the studio. And it was so funny, because a couple of years later, KSHB became an NBC affiliate and they brought Tom Brokaw to Kansas City to anchor one of the first newscasts of the new NBC 41. The news set was in the corner of the studio where I used to do my show. I happened to be driving by the station that night, just as he went on the air, and I thought, I wonder if Tom Brokaw realizes there's a casket behind him right now? It made me feel kinda good that the spirit of Crematia was tainting the *NBC Nightly News*.

*The Elena Watson book (*TV Horror Movie Hosts, *McFarland & Company, Inc., Publishers) mentions you doing* *something as kid, reading a horror story from inside a trash can or something...*

You bet. My best friend and I watched those monster movies on TV back in St. Louis. We were into theater and plays and stuff. We had a little Panasonic cassette recorder, and we used to make up monster shows, radio shows, on this cassette recorder, and we would play all the parts. One time I was over at her house, down in the basement, and I was playing the part of the monster. I wanted it to sound big and scary. So I picked up this metal trash can she had, and I put it over my head, going "roar!" You know, making horrible noises. Her mother must have wondered what the heck we were doing down there, because she came downstairs to check on us. When I took the trash can off my head, all I can remember is the look on her face, like, "Oh my God. My child and her friend are insane." I really do think that was the beginning of it all, because it was so much fun putting the stories together.

What were monster movies like in your house? Did you have to sneak in and watch them, were your parents cool? Did you have a TV in your room; did you have to go downstairs in the living room? What about special toys or the Aurora model kits?

No. That was something boys were into, you know? Not girls! My parents wouldn't buy any of them for me. But I thought it was so cool, because the kid across the street had the Aurora Frankenstein and Creature from the Black Lagoon, with the big claws and stuff. I helped him put them together. And I wanted them. But of course, my mother totally didn't get the monster thing. Barbie was okay, not Dracula! But the monsters always fascinated me.

A promotional postcard from Crematia's heyday on KSHB-TV 41, circa 1981

I remember seeing *Day of the Triffids* on a black and white TV in my room, which I only had for a short time. It was mostly over at my friend's house that I watched monster movies, usually with a sleeping bag up around my face, hiding. Or making fun of them! Watching those movies was just precious. It was always in the context of being with a friend, watching in her basement or somebody else's living room.

I remember these people who lived up the street from us. They had about six kids, and theirs was the house where all of us hung out. They had this big, big black and white TV set in the middle of the den, surrounded by baskets of laundry. The baby was usually asleep in one of the laundry baskets, while their big brother was practicing a tuba down the hall while their sister twirled a baton in the back yard. There was always an open bag of bread and a jar of peanut butter on the kitchen table, socks and underwear everywhere, Tom Lehrer or PDQ Bach playing in the other room on the record player, and it always seemed like they had another batch of kittens. I remember sitting there with the neighbor kids on Saturday afternoons watching all those wonderful old Universal movies. So it was kind of a neighborhood thing that we did.

On the subject of neighbors, in a larger sense, tell me some of the charities Crematia got to work with.

I never wanted Crematia to be making appearances at used car lots or doing for-profit appearances. Every time I went out in public as that character, it was always for a non-profit organization, because it just seemed like that's what she should be doing. I wanted her to be doing good things in the community. Whenever I would go out, it would be like to the Trick or Treat Village at the local mall, where we would give money to a shelter for battered or homeless children. Every year, I used to have this writing contest. I was really big into literacy at the time, and want to encourage the kids to write and read. So we would have a scary story contest every year. But the big thing was, I never wanted to use that character to be selling things. I wanted her to be doing good things and popping up and delighting people. That was really important to me.

Roberta Solomon happily displays her Ghoulardi mug as she recalls meeting his counterpart, Ernie Anderson, at a promotions convention in the late 1990s, shortly before his death.

Did you ever have guests appear on your show?

I did, I had guests on the show pretty regularly. But the regular characters on the show, for the most part, you never saw them. Every week, I had a conversation with The Man in the Wall. We would record some shtick with KSHB's booth announcer Paul Murphy. He did the voice of The Man in the Wall, and Crematia's sidekick, Rasputin. And later on he became the voice of her other sidekick, Dweeb. He was a nut. The deal was—The Man in the Wall—we never did figure out what his story was. We never really made concrete sense why he was in the wall. He had just done something really bad way back when, and Crematia had walled him up inside the bricks. We would talk every week. He would give her advice.

Paul also did the voice of Crematia's mother for a while. I would commune with her from the beyond, because, of course, she had passed on. Crematia had this weird family. And around Halloween, for several years in a row, they would all show up. Katy Chucking played Remora, Crematia's sister; she was a morning radio star here for years. Katy's my best friend, a really fun comedic actress and one of those people I could just drag onto the show. I would rant, c'mon, I want you to put on a monster outfit and be my sister!

There were two guys who played Crematia's mother Desiree, on-camera—a local comic named C. Wayne Owens and later on Katy's husband, John Woolam. Steve Bell, another radio announcer, played Crematia's weird cousin Henry. He was wonderful. He would walk around in a lab coat doing these weird experiments ... and just sort of not really be there. And we had this other character that was an insane inventor, Professor Pete Moss. Andy Fugal, a very funny guy that I'd done theater with in high school, played him. So the whole family and all of Crematia's friends were played by local radio and TV people in town and whoever I could drag onto the show who was willing to work for free.

What was the atmosphere like at these shows when you had all these people together?

Oh, it was a total gas! Because we would sit down ... you know we actually *worked* on those shows! All these funny people would kind of improv and build each scene. I would go, okay, here's what I want Remora to do. Mother is showing up for the annual Halloween gathering and we're going to carve pumpkins with a chain saw. And we would sort of create it together, build a script that way and lock it in. It was so wonderful.

Were there any advantages, do you think, about doing this kind of show and being a woman—as opposed to being a male host?

I knew there were monster hosts all around the country. But I wasn't really aware of how precious it was at the time. I just knew I was having a blast. The thing that was so remarkable about that character is that, when I was doing the show for those eight months, hosting the monster movies as Sally Roberts, the viewers would write in and call and make horrible comments about my hair, my clothes—my make-up was bad, I said something stupid, whatever. But as soon as I became Crematia, the audience was so reverent! I could get away with things as Crematia that I could never get away with as Sally. I could say raucous things, make fun of stuff, comment on local characters; Crematia could say practically anything and the audience just loved her.

What keeps a show like this off the air these days? What are the obstacles?

Well, there are logistical obstacles now that didn't exist then. At the time, stations filled their late-night slots with whatever they could get that was the cheapest; it was assumed that nobody was watching then. They didn't have commitments to networks, and people didn't have access to the movies except when their local stations played them. I mean, the whole culture was really different. The late-night slot on local TV was where they put all the stuff that wasn't good enough to air during the day. They had a whole basement full of movies that they owned, which they weren't going to show during the day, because these movies were so dreadful.

So the space existed for *Creature Feature* shows, but not now, because you have network programming all day long and syndicated shows and infomercials all night. I think one of the things that worked against the hosts at that time was the rise of slasher films—really violent horror films. The movies we showed were just campy. But those movies became very popular, and it was hard to promote them because they weren't films that little kids could watch. I never liked slasher films. But it seems now, there is no horror film that doesn't show people getting killed in gross, terrible, awful, messy ways.

There was a kind of innocence to movies that we played and to the way that we went about presenting them. I think there's certainly room for that now in our consciousness, because a lot of people are, I think, sick of too much violence, too much graphic everything. But such films became very popular, and that became a challenge for me on the show because I didn't want my littlest viewers to go see them! Also, it's very easy now for people to find the movies. You can rent it somewhere, or find it online and watch it at home. We have access to everything. At that time, the only way to see those movies was to watch them on Saturday night on the *Creature Feature*.

Looking at your make-up, your costume, your shtick, were you influenced by The Addams Family *at all?*

Oh god, I loved *The Addams Family*! *The Addams Family* and *The Munsters* were two shows that I just absolutely had to watch when I was growing up. I thought Gomez was so sexy! (*Laughs*) And Morticia, she was just so beautiful. When I was putting that character together, I wasn't thinking, "Oh, I really want to look like her." But of course, when you think of a goofy, wonderful, sexy monster lady, it's going to be Morticia Addams, so I'm sure the connection was there. The thing I loved about *The Addams Family* was, like, Cousin It and Thing. I loved the hand just appearing out of nowhere, in little boxes, *helping*.

I wanted to have characters like that on the show. Of course, we weren't low budget—we were *no* budget! But what I really wanted to do was to have creepy puppets. There was a host, a children's show host on Channel 41, Mary Lou Anderson, who did *41 Tree House Lane*, who had all these puppets. I really wanted her to make a worm, the videotape worm, which would come out of the wall. Or create some creepy monster puppet that would drop from the ceiling. But we never had enough money to pay her, so we ultimately decided just to use a voice. That was what we could afford, you know?

Would you do this again? If someone came to you and asked if you'd host a feature film, "We'll do it in prime time, maybe just for the holiday." Is this something you'd do again?

Absolutely, I'd do it again in a heartbeat. I would love to do it again.

What would draw you to it?

When I stopped doing Crematia, there were a lot of things going on. Not only was the show getting pushed back later and later at night because of the commitment to other programming, but also I was at a different place in my life. My voiceover business was expanding. So it was just time for me to move on. But I always understood when I stepped away from that show that, at some point the time, it might be appropriate for Crematia to resurrect herself and foist herself on the public once again.

I think that time has come, because the people who grew up with that show, who were eight, nine, 10 years old, now have children of their own. And everybody is looking for things to do with their families that are acceptable. You want to be able to sit down and watch a movie with your kids, have a good time, share an experience together. So the people who watched that show now are

Fan art created for Crematia's *Creature Feature* TV series

parents, looking for cool things to do with their own kids. And it would be wonderful to be able to provide that. Selfishly, the reason I would want to do it is that it was the most wonderful experience that I had in my life as a performer. To have that audience, with those kids, doing that particular show, was really, really a treasure. And I would love to have that again.

What sort of show would you do if asked? What kind of movies would you program? I guess you'd bring Crematia back.

Of course. But I'd have to get Crematia's corset online now, because Fredrick's of Hollywood went out of business! You know, I would be playing the same movies we were before. I loved those Hammer films, the Christopher Lee, Peter Cushing movies. There was fake blood everywhere! Those were so wonderful; I'd want to bring them back. I'd want to play the Japanese monster movies, because they're just so terrible.

Cult films, if you could get your hands on them, like *Attack of the Killer Tomatoes* (1978) and dreadfully bad ones, like *Plan 9 from Outer Space* (1958). The wrestler movies, that's a whole genre. You don't get an opportunity to see those at all anymore. That would be really fun to bring those back. And spice it up with some really good classic horror films. To be culturally literate you got to have those films in your arsenal.

What about the cast? Are there people in town who you think would crowd together to do this again?

I think I'd have a line down the street. I know that the original people would come back and do those characters again. And in the meantime, Crematia's been gone for a long time now. The last time she was here, George Bush, Sr. was president, and she's been asleep. So if she would pop out, she would think only a day had gone by! She totally wouldn't get that there had been *another* George Bush in office. And the whole Internet thing would be an incredible phenomenon to her. I can hear her now, "Ooooh! A worldwide web! How dreadfully brilliant."

So there would certainly be all sorts of comic territory to explore. And I don't think I'd have any problem finding other actors! One of the things I wound up doing after the *Creature Feature* ended, I joined a radio comedy troupe called *Right Between the Ears*. We're broadcast on about 150 NPR stations around the country now and it's carried every week on Sirius/XM's Laugh USA Channel. It's a ghoulishly talented cast, and I'm sure I would want to press them into service, to create some new characters. That would be a lot of fun.

You were talking about the radio shows you did as a kid. Did you ever get to hear any of the old radio shows, like Inner Sanctum?

Sure ... "*Liiights Ouuut!*" (*Laughs*) I heard of those shows because of my parents. They grew up listening to those shows on the radio. My dad used to tell me, on Friday and Saturday nights, only one person would have a car. So everybody would pile into the car, and they would go to Forest Park in St. Louis, sit around the car and turn on the radio and listen to *Lights Out* or *Inner Sanctum*. I was so fascinated by that whole idea of going out and lying out on a summer night, listening to radio. It seemed so cool that people would gather around the radio like that, that when I got to UMKC (University of Missouri Kansas City) — and they have a wonderful sound library—I pulled all those old recordings out and listened to them on cassette. They're just marvelous.

And that certainly informed what I was doing as Crematia. It's logical that, after I left Crematia, I would continue on in a radio comedy show. Radio has always been my roots. Everything I did really grew out of that experience. Listening to those shows, creating those characters. How did they make those sound effects, what did the actors' voices sound like? I think I used a lot of that when we were creating the *Creature Feature*. Now, doing a radio comedy show, we listen to those things all the time. So it continues, it continues.

Everything I did as Crematia really grew out of my work in radio. I started in radio in '79, while I was still in college. Because there weren't many women on the air at the time, we just drew attention to ourselves. I started doing commercials and corporate voiceovers, that kind of thing, and built a whole voiceover career out of that radio experience. Those people I met at the radio station were the ones who encouraged me to audition for *All Night Live* and then create *Creature Feature* and do the Crematia thing. And out of those experiences, I grew into a voiceover career that now includes work in film, television, documentaries, commercials, and TV and radio stations all over the world. It's just sort of grown, but radio was the root of it.

Could you talk about your meeting with Ghoulardi/Ernie Anderson?

Sure. After I left the radio station and started as a freelance voice performer, I joined a number of professional organizations, one of which was Promax, an international organization of Promotion Directors for TV stations, production companies and networks. I went to a Promax convention in Los Angeles. This would be in, I guess, about '96, '97. I can't exactly remember the date, but they were doing a tribute to Ernie Anderson. First of all, he was like God in the announcing world. His voice, everybody knew his voice—"The Loooooove Boat"—even if you didn't know who he was. He was one of the first voiceover superstars.

But the fact that he was also Ghoulardi ... my gosh! I was all a twitter! They brought him out on stage, and he was already in a wheelchair. He was quite thin. He was really ill at the time and it was not too long before he passed away. I went up to him to introduce myself and I was so nervous. Really, meeting him was the only time that I ever just got goofy in front of a celebrity. I just wanted to touch the hem of his garment, because he was ... *Ghoulardi*! Oh, my God. It was very, very exciting meeting him.

Have you gotten to see any of the other hosts around the country? Were you even aware of them?

I didn't even know it was going on. Honestly, I wasn't even aware of it until after the fact. Of course Elvira came into Kansas City for a few years before I stopped doing the show. And I was always proud of the fact that we consistently beat her in the ratings! But I really wasn't aware of the other local hosts and hostesses around the country until after the fact. I started seeing video of them, and I thought, "Oh my gosh, I was part of this, like, wave!" (*Laughs*)

What do you think about the timing of that? What made this precious moment in broadcasting a time where hosts could exist?

Well, there was space for them. The movies weren't readily available elsewhere. Stations were looking for cheap ways to fill the time. And it was way before even the advent of the cable superstations. KSHB was kind of a mini-superstation. We were carried in Missouri, Kansas, Arkansas, Nebraska, Oklahoma, and parts of Texas. I think we got into Illinois a little bit—Iowa. It was about six or eight states. So there was that kind of thing going on, where a local station with a silly, creepy nighttime program could suddenly be reaching outside of its home community.

How do feel about the timing, personally, about getting to be inside this window?

Oh, I'm incredibly grateful for it! I didn't even realize at the time what was going on. I just knew that every Saturday I got to dress up in a corset and long black wig and tell stupid jokes about bad movies. How cool is that? But I didn't realize until after the fact that this was a really specific and precious time in television history that we will never see again. There are some venues for monster hosts and hostesses that exist now that didn't exist before. The Internet is very cool, doing work on public access TV stations, local access channels. That wasn't around then. But it was a really, really special time in television.

What do you see for the present and future?

I've always thought that Crematia is like my ace in the hole. If everything else goes to hell, I can always trot Crematia back out, and know I'll find a warm welcome! (*Laughs*) And I would love to do that show again, but only

Crematia Mortem once did an Easter-themed episode of her show.

if it was right. I'd love to bring Crematia out to help raise some money for our local PBS affiliate. That would be very cool. I don't know that I would want to do it every week. I'd have to figure out a way to do this with some mondo taping sessions four times a year, something like that. I couldn't commit to doing a show every week again. Because even though it looked like garbage, it was a lot of work to make the *Creature Feature* look that bad! (*Laughs*)

That was Dr. Paul Bearer's routine. He would tape once every six months. They would do it assembly line over a long weekend. He would spend the rest of the time going around doing promotions. He was on Hee Haw *once.*

See, I just didn't stick around long enough. I could have been on *Hee Haw*!

Did you meet people doing this show, connections that you've carried forward? Was it good for your career?

To this day—and Crematia's been off the air a long time—I cannot go out into the community without somebody recognizing me or asking me about the show. Sometimes I'll see somebody in the grocery store looking at me with "the look," you know? And I'll just smile and say, "Crematia Mortem." And their face just lights up. Or they laugh. That's really wonderful.

I don't know that it helped or hurt my career. But it's really, really a treasure, just a wonderful thing, to have Crematia tucked in my belt. I love looking back on that show, thinking, "I did that." I love the idea that I'm part of Kansas City broadcast lore. I met a bunch of wonderful people I've stayed in contact with. And I still get emails every week from people who are now all over the country, who grew up watching that show. That is really neat, all these years later to be getting these letters from CEOs of companies who were kids in the Midwest, who say, "By far, the coolest thing I ever did in my life was meeting you when I was 10!" That's really remarkable.

I remember some things that happened on that show that were so hysterical. The aspect that I really, really liked was when the kids would *make* things. And they would bring them on the show, monster sculptures and creepy drawings, Lincoln Log creatures, fantastic animals made out of chicken bones. There was this one kid who lived in a small community out north of the river, and he had spent almost a year creating a monster out of papier-mâché. Every day when he would come home from school—he kept this thing in his garage—he would add a little more papier-mâché, and then he painted it. He had stilts in the legs, and it was in three sections. He sent me a picture of the monster and said, "Dear Crematia: I want to be on your show." He was a darling kid.

So we built a whole show around this monster, because it was *huge*. It was, like, 12 feet tall. He got on the stilts inside the costume, and the head was up over him. And the setup was—Crematia had been looking for the man of her dreams, and she finally sees him! And, oh my gosh, this creature is the love of her life! And we were going to play "Afternoon of a Fawn," as love music. We were going to have them run together across the room in slow motion, and then she was going to wrap her arms around his … boot, because he was such a giant.

And he came walking across the set, and that big boot of that 12-foot-tall costume snagged on the edge of the rug. I heard this creak, this "*errerrerr*," and suddenly, he's falling over in slow motion. And when he hit the ground it was like … boom!!! This big cloud of dust went up in the studio, and I just went, oh my God, that kid's dead inside there. As the dust settled, it was absolutely silent. And from inside the costume, I hear this little 10-year-old voice go, "Would somebody please get me out of here?" He was fine, but he didn't want to finish the show. (*Laughs*) It was so great, you know? Those kinds of things happened all the time. Things would just go horribly wrong.

What was it about these shows that inspired this kind of creative feedback? Why did people get so inspired to send you stuff?

Well, it was a whole fantasy world, a whole weird world that you didn't have access to any other time of year except Halloween. But with Crematia you had it every week. And I think it was safe. It was an outlet for people to express themselves with creepy things. You don't get an opportunity to do that kind of stuff. If you're drawing pictures of creepy monsters, your mother is going to go, "What are you doing drawings of monsters for? Why don't you draw a picture of a dog or a kitty or of a cute little whatever?" In Crematia's world, it was safe and cool for a kid to be creepy.

Tell me a little about that contest you had, "Win an Evening With Crematia."

I was seriously into literacy. I love to read, I love to write. A really big influence for me when I was a kid was reading Edgar Allan Poe stories, creepy stories. And I wanted to turn kids on to that. One of the things I did every year was sponsor a Write a Scary Story contest, and we gave prizes. We had kindergarteners and below, K through three and categories for older kids. We gave different prizes in the age groups. But the grand prize-winner got a night on the town with Crematia in a limo, going around to haunted houses. The deal was you had to take a friend and your parents, or two guardians, with you. It was two adults, two kids and me, with dinner in a limo going to haunted houses.

I remember one year a kid won, who was about maybe, 11. He looked kind of like Larry Mondello from *Leave It To Beaver*. Kind of a funny pudgy kid, you know, and he was just real cute. We had dinner at the station—Happy Meals from McDonald's—and I took them on the set and they got to have their picture taken. We shot some video on the set with Crematia that they got to take home. And then, we loaded them into the limo and went down to the Main St. Morgue Haunted House and to The Edge of Hell and we got to be first in line. Of course, we were celebrities. And the kids were so thrilled. I remember, at that time nobody had cell phones, but the limo had a phone in the back seat. This little Larry Mondello kid got on the phone, called his best friend, and went, "You're not going to believe where I am!" And then he stood up and stuck his head out of the moon roof and went, "I'm driving down Ward Parkway in a limo with Crematia!" He yelled it out as loud as he could and I know he'll remember it for the rest of his life. It was very, very cool.

The Maneater from Manayunk
Stella (Karen Scioli)
Interviewed by Michael Monahan (2009)

The flagrantly trashy, infectiously tacky Stella (aka "The Maneater from Manayunk") hosted *Saturday Night Dead* on Philadelphia's KYW-TV from 1984 through 1990. Joined by her faithful butler, Hives (Bob Billbrough), Cousin Mel (Glenn Davish), various wacko relatives and visiting guest stars (John Zacherle and Rip Taylor among them), Stella and company offset the entertainment value of their often dire movie package with macabre bedroom farce once aptly described as "Carol Burnett with cobwebs."

Set in Stella's haunted condo, the show's serial storylines regularly centered on supernatural themes—séances, sentient furniture, reincarnation and spiritual entrapment inside a Mrs. Butterworth's syrup bottle were common. But cultural icons like James Bond also came in for elaborate ribbing in a multi-show thread featuring Bob Billbrough doubling as arrogant nitwit spy, James Blond, pitted against Scioli's Jersey girl super-villain, Blowfish.

In 1987, horror host legend John Zacherle returned to Philadelphia to celebrate the 30th anniversary of his debut as Roland. The following year he returned once again to appear on *Saturday Night Dead*, where he joined Stella in hosting a pair of episodes from the Hammer House of Horror television series.

Scioli credits Stella's resemblance to a drag queen for her popularity among Philly's gay population. "The gay community embraced Stella," she recalled. "And it was close to my heart, too. I did a lot of AIDS benefits."

Karen Scioli's post-Stella career includes starring in an "old dark house" stage comedy called *Bats!* (which she also co-authored) and she turned in a touching performance in the independent film *Postcards from Paradise Park* (1998). In 2010, Stella reemerged at the Blob Fest convention in Philadelphia and the Chiller Theater Expo in New Jersey, and has made numerous convention appearances since, with the ever-faithful Hives the Butler in tow.

The station conceived Stella as competition for Elvira, and they had an open audition. What had you been doing up to that point that gave you an edge at the audition and got you the part?

For a year or two, or a couple years prior to getting the part, I was doing standup comedy in New York, originally in Philly, but then in New York, and a little in Los Angeles. But mostly back in New York, though. So that helped. Somebody who could write comedy, or attempted to perform it, was a plus.

So they were looking for a writer as well, someone to essentially create the whole show?

Well, that was probably pushed. I was not the only standup who came in, but I did write my audition specifically for it, and they must have liked what I wrote. When I made the finals—they had 10 finalists out of 150—I went back and the audition script was something I wrote for the first one. They stole my material for the finals. I remember looking at it and thinking, oh, wait a minute. This is what *I* wrote. So I looked at the producer and I said, uhhhh … I see you've … ummm … used my material! And he was joking around, he said, "Yeah, well you should be flattered." I said I will if I get the part! (*Laughs*) Fortunately, I got the part.

I seem to recall somewhere you said that the producer wrote the first few shows and that you finally thought, "Forget it, I should do this myself."

No, that was further into it, within the first 10 shows. He wrote one and I thought, oh, boy… I didn't know I was going to have to write the shows when I first got the part. I didn't realize that. But they said, "Yes, one of the things we like about you is that you write comedy." And of course, you use all your ideas up in the first show! So it was a challenge. I probably bitched about it, and the producer said, "Okay, let me write one!" Then I went, okay, that'll never happen again. I know the humor is supposed to bad, but … (*Laughs*). Steve Bronstein was my first producer. I'm joking about him being a bad writer. We actually had fun together. It's always a collaboration you know. I guess they liked me because I didn't audition as a ghoul. I didn't come in looking like the Bride of Frankenstein or a witch, or something. I came in as a human being with weird relatives. That's how I auditioned for the part. That appealed to them.

So, that repertory company quality of the show was part of the original concept?

No, that developed. I used safe people at the audition. I used a severed hand as a character. I was given one actor who wasn't really on camera that much. He was mostly, like, a voiceover person. He played Iggy, who was my monster projectionist and different things. The doorman … we started out was a sort of *Rhoda* thing, the way that Rhoda had that doorman, Carlton, or whoever that was. But eventually I built up the company of characters. I had the one guy who was on steady, Jeff DeHart. He was a standup comic, and he did all the voices. And then starting with the second show, we brought in Glenn Davish; he became a regular. We didn't know he was going to be on every single show after that, but he came on as a character for the second show and just kind of stayed.

He became Cousin Mel.

Cousin Mel. His first appearance was as Dr. Schuylkill; Schuylkill is the river here. He was a mad scientist. He played it like an old Jewish doctor, but he was a mad scientist, Dr. Schuylkill. And yeah, he did Cousin Mel, who was Stella's cousin, who just cried all the time. He never stopped crying, wore a raincoat all the time. And he did Mario Aldente, who was, like, a spaghetti Western–type director from Italy. He always wanted to put Stella in the movies, and try to do horror movies. He was horrible. They were his main characters, repeated characters. And then he played about 5,000 other characters at the same time.

Steve Bronstein was my producer for less than the first year. He got it started in the fall, October 1984, we went on the air, and then he left in May. He moved to California and became a producer out there. The second guy was Ray Giuliani, who does a lot of producing now. I think the last time I saw him was on *Joe the Millionaire* show, or one of those reality shows. I think that's what he's doing. He did a lot of daytime talk shows, etc. And he was on for a year. Then Stan Gibell took over and he finished out. So he was there about three years. We had the most fun with Stan. He let us be as insane as we dared. By that time the show was real popular, and he came into it at a good time, because we had all found our groove as these crazy people. So Stan let us do whatever the heck we wanted to do, which was real fun for him. We had different directors that came and went.

Brassy, bawdy and beautiful, Karen Scioli gets glamorous as Stella, The Daughter of Desire.

Didn't a couple of the guys on your crew work on the Ernie Kovacs show?

They used to tell me how much fun it was to do *Saturday Night Dead*, because they finally got to do goofy things the way they used to do with Ernie Kovacs. We had about the same budget. I think Kovacs actually had a bigger budget. They'd take old scraps of lumber from the machine shop and build me a Western set. The bar would be slightly slanted, so when we put down a drink it slid. You know, all kinds of goofy stuff, whatever we wanted to do. And they had a ball doing that. All the old guys loved doing that. After Ernie Kovacs, it was *The Mike Douglas Show* in Philadelphia. We shared the same green room and all that stuff that Mike Douglas had. That was fun. My directors were much younger, of course. So was the crew. In television, the directors certainly have an input. But it's the producers who are more like directors, in a television situation.

As far as guiding the show itself...

Yes. The directors in television are more technical. They give the camera angles and shots and stuff. But it's the producer who puts together the big picture, in terms of visuals and stuff like that.

Along those lines, did the idea of story arcs and story lines develop over time as well, or was that built in pretty early as the structure for introducing the films?

It did change. It definitely changed and grew, if you want to call it growing. We found a rhythm. In the beginning, it was little vignettes. We had a scene for the evening. We tried to do little plot lines for the whole evening, so that it carried through the half hour we were on. We came on between the movie bits, of course, just like Elvira. So we had a story line for that night. We would throw gags specifically to the movie. But the movie was more influential to what my bits were when I first started. By the time I got to my second producer, which was less than a year, I refused to watch any of the movies anymore. I said, "Okay, that's it. I don't want to see another stupid horror movie for as long as I live. These are so bad; I can't stand it. These are not inspirational at all."

The movies, mind you, once we got past the expensive ones—the House of Hammer, the Vincent Price, all those good ones—after we got through there, which was my first season—the rest were really, really bad. I never heard of these movies before in my life. They look like they were made in somebody's back yard. I'm sure they were, they were so ridiculous. Occasionally we had a good movie, but these went beyond campy. They were horrible. I just refused to watch them. So I said, if you want my skits to be about the movie, give me a synopsis of what the movie's going to be about, because I can't bear it anymore. We didn't really stick to the movie. I made more and more fun of the movies as I went on. Eventually, over the years, I saw the Stella side of it as its own entity. So that was fun, because we got to do little serials that would continue the next week.

You've mentioned Carol Burnett as an influence. But the story lines themselves, with the strange cast of characters who would pop up in various settings, actually reminded me as much of Rocky and Bullwinkle.

It's sort of like *Rocky and Bullwinkle* meet Harvey Korman and Carol Burnett. She had two sidekicks, Harvey Korman and Tim Conway. Well, I had Glenn Davish and Bob Billbrough. So we used to pretend we were them … in a cartoon. So there's where Rocky and Bullwinkle come in. I'm telling you, I think Glenn and Bob are just as talented as Harvey Korman and Tim Conway. We used to crack ourselves up all the time. It was amazing what you could do on a dollar and 32 cents budget. The costumes would come up, and the props fell down. It was ridiculous.

And the energy! Everyone seemed, not just invested, but so loyal *to each other. That really came across.*

Well, we realized how lucky we were to be working actors. So yeah, we were very loyal to each other, since we wanted to keep working! But we had a blast. We knew when we were doing *Saturday Night Dead* that we were never going to have so much fun in the creative world ever again. It was ridiculous.

It seemed you had that freedom, too. Once you took the reins on the writing, all bets were off, right?

Again, the big bosses changed so frequently over and over during our six years. I had three or four bosses on two different levels. So after a while, they just stopped watching the show when we were on the air. I really can't imagine anyone sitting there watching my taped bits, since we taped them ahead of time. We taped on a Monday for the upcoming Saturday night. So during the course of that time, the executive producer and the program director are supposed to look at them and say, "Okay, this is fine." They did that in the beginning, as they would question some of the stuff. And I'd go, oh, I can't say that? But later they stopped watching completely.

There was one show that we were amazed that we did. We didn't know what to do. The plot line was dragging on for week after week. What would happen was, during Stan Gibell's days, we would only do new shows during the sweeps months. So we did them in May, and we did them in July—which was a little sweeps month. Then we would start in the fall and do, like, mid-September through the end of November. We'd go off and come back again in February. So we had four or five new shows in February. They would all follow each other; there would be a plot line. So that was fine. But sometimes it became challenging. We would run out of steam and go, okay, where are we going to take this stupid … plot line? Whose idea was this anyway? That would lead us to things where we'd have to fill in and, you know …

Stella wound up in a Gypsy camp one time, looking for her dog. This was weird anyway, since she hated animals. But she went off to find her dog and came into a camp of Gypsies who all talked like Zsa Zsa Gabor. She was Hungarian, so we made all the Gypsies Zsa Zsa. So we had a Queen-Off, a Gypsy Queen-Off in the camp, to see who would be Queen. It was three actors and me. There was Bob, Glen and Donna Ryan. We had Donna Ryan; she was an actual woman. But Glen and Bob dressed as Zsa Zsa Gabor, drag queen Gypsies having a Queen-Off; I couldn't believe we got away with that.

No wonder you guys had such a big following in the local gay community.

Oh yeah, yeah. We had to redecorate the campsite. That was one of the challenges. (*Laughs*) We had a Broadway song sing-off that we came up with. It was very gay—very, very, very gay. And I know nobody watched that because that got on the air and nobody questioned anything. I thought, man, no one is *watching* our show! Great, nobody cares! Put on whatever we want! And the only letters I ever received, in complaint of going too far over the edge—we did come on at one o'clock in the morning—was when a couple of parents wrote to me because their kids would sneak off and watch *Saturday Night Dead*. That was a big thing with kids, to sneak off, when their parents were sound asleep at one in the morning, to watch *Saturday Night Dead*.

And it was different back then. We didn't have as many restrictions. I think you couldn't say as many things, but it seems like we weren't as worried about being politically correct back then. But I did get a letter from … I don't remember the name of the official organization, but it was something like The Institute of Mental Health in Philadelphia. Stella went on the *Dating Game*, and one of the guys—they have bachelor one, two and three, you know—was a schizophrenic. So it made the whole thing confusing. She couldn't see, so she thought there were a whole lot more people back there than there was. And we got a card about that—"You should not make fun of schizophrenics … And they're not really schizophrenics; they're split-personality people." We apologized, and a year later we got a letter from them again when we showed a rerun. But I didn't know we re-ran it. They said, (*sternly*) "I thought that we ..." Oops, sorry. That was the only time I got a complaint letter.

"You put cleavage on the TV. Word is going to get around!" Scioli explains the popularity of Stella.

You had Roland (John Zacherle) *on your show at one point.*

That was huge for us, really, really big! And I just saw him in May of this year. I now belong to Broadcast Pioneers here in Pennsylvania. They wanted to do a tribute to Stella! And Roland was going to be there. They invited him down. And it was *great*! He drove down from New York, John Zacherle. Actually, it was so fun, because I was there with my sister. There he was, John Zacherle, and of course he remembered me. I took Bob Billbrough—Hives—with me, and my husband. We went and we had a blast. I saw some old crew guys that I haven't seen in years. And Sally Starr, a big icon here, she was there. She was on when *t* was a kid. And she was retiring, so they were honoring her. There were all these old TV icons that were there that day. It was just amazing. I was actually the youngest of them. It was strange. And I remember John Zacherle was there, and he was in his 80s. I think he was

86. And I'm sitting there, and I remember turning to my sister and saying, am I crazy, or is he kind of sexy? She said, "Please! I was thinking the same thing! He is—he's kind of sexy!"

He's got those sparkling eyes and that devilish smile.

Duke Ellington's "The Mooch" perfectly captured the woozy hoochie coochie atmosphere of Stella's *Saturday Night Dead*.

He does! And he didn't look any older than he did, because he played his character with that "old" make-up. So I'm going, okay, this is really freaky. He's tall and he's slim, and he wore a suit. And he was funny. It was amazing; he was just amazing! I was so happy to see him, and we did get some pictures with him again, too.

So he was on my show. It was a huge, huge thing when he was on my show. The PR department did a lot of publicity for it, because he is a special icon in the city. He was so incredibly popular! Nobody knew how popular. I don't even think they had Nielson's back then. They did a publicity day one time, "Meet Roland," and thousands of people flocked WCAU, this station. They couldn't believe it. There were so many people; they couldn't handle them all. Thousands of people showed up that day.

I think his show came on 11 o'clock at night. I was a little kid, and I remember that was really late. I always thought he was really, really scary. Like, occasionally, if we did get to see him, my sister and I thought that it was terrifying. We absolutely loved it! We didn't see it that much, and his show was live! So he was on one year, he was extremely popular, and then he left and went to New York. He became Zacherley, used his real name, and then went on to do all the other stuff that he did. My understanding is that he is only the second horror host in the country, the first being Vampira. And Roland said he did fly out to California for a publicity thing and met with her one time. There is some photo of the two of them together somewhere. At least, that's what I remember him telling me. I might be wrong about that.

I think there was a period where Zacherley was syndicated in Los Angeles for a short period of time. So they must have been using kinescopes. In fact, Maila Nurmi—Vampira—they had done something similar for her. The station, KABC, produced a number of kinescopes and they were going to syndicate her out to the New York market.

She had a weird life. So really, Roland was the second of that ilk here in Philly. That's from my understanding, anyway—that he was the second one to do something like that. Just in Philly alone, he started the whole history off.

Did they have any others on in Philly between you and Roland?

There was one. There was Dr. Shock. He was on a long time.

Of course, right. That was Joe Zawislak.

He actually asked John Zacherle if he could take his character, or use his character. If you look at the two of them, his character was very, very, very similar to Roland. And Roland didn't care. John Zacherle said that was fine. Joe was a very nice man. I never met him, though. He was on more like four in the afternoon, so he was, like, a kid-oriented type of thing. He did pass away.

Yeah, he had a heart attack, very young. My wife actually met him at her high school once, back in Philly, which is great. He just seemed like a genuinely nice person, very colorful and playful.

Everybody loved him. I don't think he was as scary as Roland, but I was younger when Roland was on, too. Roland was more adult.

Dr. Shock actually started as a late-night host with a scarier demeanor that was more like Zacherley's. After 13 weeks the station was ready to cancel, but they got a lot of letters and brought him back. And that's when he started to develop the more kid friendly version of the character.

That's what I remember. How about that? Very interesting. And then there was me.

So how did Stella do in the ratings over the years?

She did great; my show did great. We were very fortunate because that format is real popular. I mean that everybody loved it. We followed *Saturday Night Live*, so we were called *Saturday Night Dead*, of course. It was such a great lead-in for us with that generation in the 1980s, because everybody watched *Saturday Night Live*.

I think they only charted my ratings for the first hour. After that the Nielson's stopped. I think they only went from one until two o'clock in the morning, and we were on till three. They didn't even go past one-thirty or something, so the ratings were based on my first half hour or my first hour. So it was tremendous, because of *Saturday Night Live*. I used to do better than the news. I got better ratings than the local news. The news department was not happy about it, but the sales department absolutely loved me. They made a lot of money off of the show; they were able to make deals. "Well, if you buy a really expensive spot on the *Eleven O'Clock News*, we'll throw in on Stella's shows." And they'd go "Okay, okay! Yeah, that's great!" So I went from local yokel type of advertising to Coca-Cola, Nike ... I had all these big sponsors.

Why was the show eventually cancelled? Did the ratings begin to taper off?

No, the ratings stayed strong. I was on for six years. The year I went off the air they fired, I think, a 130 people from Channel 3. It was just that programming drastically changed. Everything was becoming syndication, and they really couldn't afford the locally made shows anymore. There were other shows that bit the dust, too, that were really expensive, though my show wasn't that expensive. *Evening Magazine* was one of those magazine format shows, like *A Current Affair* or something. In the beginning there were five *Evening Magazine*s on Westinghouse stations across the country—San Francisco, Philly, Boston, Baltimore and one other. So that was a show that went because it was Westinghouse actually producing those, not the network. So everything was changing drastically, and they were getting rid of a lot of local programming.

I gave them an opportunity to get rid of the show. They let me go from my show because of something I said in the press, believe it or not. They fired me. It was ridiculous. It wasn't that bad in retrospect. It doesn't bother me. But at the time it was like, "Oh my god!" I think they were looking for an out. It was crazy! Protests and everything erupted in front of the show. It was really silly. Not me, I didn't protest.

That sounds about right, that they would be looking for any excuse to drop a local program.

Channel 3, my station, had the lowest-rated news. They were trying to put more money into the news department and sacrificing local programming and entertainment. So there wasn't anything like that anymore. It was the end of an era, that's all. It was the end of an era. Nobody really does that anymore. Someone might do it on some kooky cable shows, but not on the network affiliates ...You don't really see that anymore.

I think the only current horror hosts working in the country right now are The Son of Ghoul in Cleveland, and that's on a very, very small station. Svengoolie in Chicago and Rich Koz who's on a UHF station. And then there's a guy named Zomboo out in Reno, Nevada. He's on an independent station. For Zomboo and Son of Ghoul, it's skin-of-the-teeth time with the switch to digital in 2009.

That's it, too. When I went on the air, my whole family went out a week before and bought a VHS machine. They were extremely expensive, too. They were, like, four hundred and fifty bucks to purchase. And they were top-loaders where the top would pop up. They were brand new. We went out to get one because my show was airing. Remember how complicated it was trying to figure out how to tape it and hook it up? Today, you can go out and rent a DVD of what whatever movie they want. Audiences don't have to look at the commercials. They don't care too much about horror movies that are on television.

I've got kinescope footage of old hosts from the 1950s and 1960s—Zacherley, and other hosts. Because of the

John Zacherle, who started out in Philadelphia as Roland, returned to his home turf for a 30th-year anniversary appearance on *Saturday Night Dead* in 1987.

quality of the lighting, how flat it is, because of the quality of the tape to film transfer, these old shows seem more immediate than something that was filmed last week. They still feel like they're in your house after 50 years.

Yes, very immediate, exactly, exactly. Half the time we had bad lighting on my show. Everybody was complaining about it, or this or that. "Oh, my God! How come there are so many shadows this way? Whoever reset the lights?" It just really did look real. People thought they knew me. They thought Stella lived in your neighborhood, and they felt that they knew her. And that added, I think, a scary element to it. It added the sense that this person lived near you. It's like, "This is scary; she's local. Whew! Stay out of that neighborhood!" There was something. Kids just ate that stuff up.

My nephew married a girl—they're getting older now—but she'd say, "I used to be so scared!" She can't believe she married Stella's nephew! She said, "I was so terrified of you, I didn't even want to date Julian. I thought you were so scary." Of course, I didn't think Stella was scary. I thought she was ridiculous. But the kids, they were terrified!

There must be something where they're connecting the feeling from the movie into the Stella thing. And maybe there's a level of hysteria in the Stella stuff, that bedroom farce quality, with people running in and out of doors. It was simply weird.

Yes, the weirdo factor. That was it. But it is different today. So that's something that's gone.

What did you do after the show? You wrote and performed in a play called Bats!, *and you were in some independent films...*

Yeah. I did, you know, a whole bunch of different stuff. I also earned my living as a production coordinator. I worked on the show, *Cops*, the TV show, for a few years. That was interesting. I would go from city to city for about two years. That was pretty much right after I left *Saturday Night Dead*. When I came back from my two-year stint with *Cops*, I did the show, *Bats!* with Robert Dunbar. And while I was doing *Bats!* I got the independent movie, *Postcards From Paradise Park* (2000). And I'm doing things here and there—personal appearances, murder mysteries, all kinds of fun things.

And now I've been doing—for about four years—a character called Ree Ree DaNucci. She's a South Philly hairdresser. I'm on an oldies station here, WOGO. I'm on every Monday and Friday, live appearances with Ree Ree from a remote in South Philly. Ree Ree, my character, has lots of make-up and hair and jewelry. Who was the Mike Meyers character, "Can we talk?" It's sort of like an Italian version of that. She has her own hair shop. So I'm on twice a week. I do all the writing for that. It's been a lot of fun. So I continue to do that.

It is strange that now I have this second long-lasting character in Philadelphia. Ree Ree has been on at least four years, maybe five. I know it's weird. It happened through my connections at Channel 3. I used to do a lot of different characters. It was on *Evening Magazine*. I would sometimes, for fun, do cross-promotion. And they would say, "Oh, can you come on as Ree Ree, the hairdresser?" I'd say, sure, and I would do something.

So Nancy Glass, I don't know if you know that name, she was on *Evening Magazine*. She left to go on and do bigger and better things. Eventually she had her own morning drive radio show here in the Delaware Valley. She called me and said, "I want to do something different. Why don't we have Ree Ree call in?" And it started by doing *Ally McBeal* recaps. That's when I started, when *Ally McBeal* was on. That was a long time ago. So that's when I started recording every Tuesday, doing the *Ally McBeal* recaps.

That went away. Her station went away and the producer went to the oldies station and said, "Oh, this is perfect for Ree Ree. It's your demographics." I said great, and Ree Ree's been on ever since then. I just call up and complain about my family or whatever stupid thing. There's always bookies involved, and mob shit, you know. It's Italian, lots of Italian things. We talk about how to watch *The Sopranos*. She lives in these tiny row homes in South Philly. She had to have the whole bay window taken out so you could get the big screen TV into the house so she could watch *The Sopranos*. I mean, it's just, like, ridiculous. It's fun. But I have an appearance tomorrow at 5:30 in the morning. I can't believe it.

Comedian Rip Taylor joins Stella in 1990 to host *Scorpion With Two Tails*.

I'm curious. You were in that TV Guide article (The Best and The Frightest *by Frank DeCaro, issue # 2483, October 28, 2000) with a number of other hosts. Stella seemed a bit of an oddball choice. I didn't picture her as having any national recognition, as the others included Zacherley, The Ghoul and Elvira.*

The person who was writing the article came from New York City. But he had lived in Philly, or went to school in Philly, during my Stella days, and he was a big fan. I think that's how it went. So when they decided to put this article together, he wanted to include her. Now, I reached up all the way to North Jersey, all the way down to Atlantic City. So it was a really big area. If you were on the East Coast, anywhere between Washington and New York, you could conceivably have seen Stella.

It was also the size of the signal and it was the beginning of cable. Some people out between Philly and New York, up in North Jersey and stuff, they started getting cable. I remember getting fan mail from some people in Virginia who picked it up on their satellite system. That was at the beginning of satellite and cable and stuff. People would pick it up on satellite. We did put out a very strong signal, being in a big market. And again, I was on the network affiliate station, so it wasn't a really weak station. So coming through NBC, I don't know, I guess the signal would be strong. I think that's what was happening. People would pick me up on satellite.

Was there anything else about the show or the people you worked with that you'd like to mention?

Just that I'm still very close with Glenn Davish and Bob Billbrough, real close friends. We spent our holidays together all the time; we're like family. It's interesting that we're still good friends after all that. It's definitely during such an important time in our lives that we became such good friends.

Glenn, he was a producer on *The View* for five years. Then he did some stuff with *Court TV*. He's been a bigshot producer for a long time. He's out in Chicago, he just moved to Chicago. He's working on an NBC show called *I Village*. It's an NBC show, not a syndicated show. It's a typical noon show for women, just like *The View*. They have three hosts. Two of the hosts, I think, are ex-winners of *The Apprentice*, Donald Trump's show. But they gave Glenn a lot of money to go there. Bob's done great, too. Bob's an actor; he does a lot of wonderful Poe. He does Poe one-man shows. And Mark Twain … he just finished a whole gig of Mark Twain. He's excellent.

He's such a good actor. You can see his range on your old show, flipping from Hives to doing a James Bond parody.

Oh my God, we used to laugh all the time! We used to make ourselves laugh. We still laugh at it! That's why we're such good friends.

Legion of Decency—Retired!
Commander USA (Jim Hendricks)
Interviewed by Sandy Clark (2004)

Jim Hendricks was driving a hack when he auditioned for an opening to host movies on the USA cable network. Hendricks came in with a character he'd created as the graveyard shift rock and roll deejay in Junction City, Kansas, a jolly sleaze, Uncle Willie. The producer didn't care for the raincoat-wearing Willie but saw possibilities in sliding the avuncular personality into red spandex and a cape.

The result was Commander USA ("Soaring super hero! Legion of Decency, retired"), the wacky host of *Commander USA's Groovie Movies*, from 1985 through 1989. A slightly seedy but relentlessly chummy stogie-chompin' comic book hero, Commander USA beamed his show from a secret headquarters located under a teeming shopping mall in New Jersey, aided by his "right hand man," Lefty, a literal hand puppet created by drawing a face on his palm with cigar ash.

The Commander was unfailingly enthusiastic about the films he introduced, be it *Inframan* (1975), *Mako, Jaws of Death* (1976), *A Polish Vampire in Burbank* (1985) or any other number of low-to-no-rent celluloid oddities. Hendricks has always expressed a special affection for the horror movies produced in Mexico—*The Brainiac* (*El Baron del Terror*, 1962), *Doctor of Doom* (*Las Luchadoras Contra el Médico Asesino*, 1963) and the films of German Robles.

When the program aired as a double feature, action-packed kung fu movies were often added to the mix, compounding the already volatile psychotronic energy of the show. One only has to contemplate an afternoon spent absorbing both *The Man with the Synthetic Brain* (1972) and *Shanghai Massacre* (*Shang Hai Tan da ye*, 1982) to appreciate the cheerfully scurvy atmosphere of the Commander's super-secret subterranean grindhouse.

Following the run of the show, Jim Hendricks continued to perform, mostly on stage, where his credits include *Tony 'n' Tina's Wedding* and *The Big Vig*. He also contributed to another syndicated host horror show, *Horrible Night at the Movies*, where a dead 1950s biker, Eddie Frame (Frank Kane), introduced the films.

How did you get into acting? Pre-Commander USA, how did you get into the business?

Before Commander USA ... Well, I studied acting at college in the 1960s, the late '60s. Then I was a schoolteacher for a little while, up in the Bronx. Then I became a radio disc jockey, up in Kansas, Vermont, working for a couple of stations up there. Then I decided to move back to the city (New York) in 1979. I was doing plays, showcase and things, until I read they were auditioning for the Commander. Originally, he was called Captain. But just before we went on, they found out the name was taken, Captain USA. So we switched it to Commander. The first three takes I came out and said, "Captain USA here!" "Cut" But it went from there, it went from there.

How much input did you have on the look and style of the show?

It was an open audition, basically. They had an idea that they wanted to have a super hero, but they weren't quite sure what it was going to be like. And I went in and auditioned as a character I used to do called Uncle Willie, who wore the raincoat up to the neck. He was a little sleazy. So I went in and auditioned with that, and then it kind of became a blend. So he became a superhero who's retired and has no powers. They finally took away his pilot's license. A little inner ear problem affected the balance when I was flying. So I got grounded. And then there were insurance problems. You break through a wall, who's going to pay for that?

How much material did you just come up with on the fly?

We did a lot of improv on that show; we did a lot of improv. I would usually get the movies beforehand. I'd get to know what I was going to show. But sometimes I didn't, and we would just go by the seat of our pants and do what came naturally.

What was the production schedule like? Was there any rehearsal at all?

We had no rehearsal whatsoever. We would go in, two days a month, three days a month, and tape anywhere from four to six different programs. When we started out, I think we ran five hours. We ran from noon until five in the afternoon the first year. We'd show two serials and two films—*Zorro's Black Whip* (1944) and *Undersea Kingdom* (1936), that kind of thing. But we'd just go in and tape, tape, tape. We wouldn't do any take two's.

Were you aware of any of this material beforehand? Had you seen horror hosts?

I was a Zacherley fan, growing up in New York City. What I always remembered, and it's haunted me for a long time, was he had that Jello. And it looked like it had coconut all over the outside. And it scared me unbelievably when I was a kid. Zacherley was my guy.

What was the routine for watching Zacherley's show? Did you have to sneak down to see it?

It wasn't too bad. My brother was a little older, so he'd be out of the house. My sister was a baby, and my mother was busy with that. So I got to watch a lot of TV. And that was really what I liked, watching a lot of TV—Sandy Becker, the kid shows, Chuck McCann. He would do all of those characters. I'd liked those kinds of things. So, I think that set me on.

How about movies and serials? Were you a big fan?

When I first started, I didn't know too much about them. Some of the horror cult classics I loved, but what really opened up for me were the Mexican horror films. Those huge bats, you know? They were three feet wide! Abel Salazar was the director on many of those. And many starred German Robles. That was the actor, German Robles. They were great. I loved those, especially the bats. It was so ... ridiculous! But they were fun. The zombie movies I liked a lot. Of course, *White Zombie* (1932), that was a classic. *Return of the Cat People* (*sic: Curse of the Cat People*, 1944) was a new one for me. So I got into that one, too. It always struck me funny that she was wearing a fur coat.

Did you have much say in what they were programming?

As far as the movies went? No, it was whatever was in the public domain or whatever came in that week. So I'd get them and we'd program for that. But they were all terrific. You can't go wrong with a ship of zombies and those types of 1950s babes. It was a lot of fun.

How many people did it take to produce the show?

Commander USA (Jim Hendricks) flashes the photo of a perceived look-a-like. Some note his resemblance to The Comedian, a fascist costumed hero in the dystopian graphic novel, *The Watchmen*, by author Alan Moore and artist Dave Gibbons.

It was probably ... I'd say 15 people on the set at any one time. We didn't use a lot of extra characters, you know. Friends of mine, friends of the producer, the cameraman would come on and do a bit if we needed something. The director would come on and do a bit. But that was pretty much it, friends and anyone we could talk into doing it for free. That was the important thing.

Was it a pretty fun set?

Oh yeah, oh yeah! We would do just one take. You could tell how you were doing by how the crew reacted. So if they were laughing and thought it was funny, that worked.

What about the rest of the audience feedback? Did you get letters?

Oh yeah, we got lots of mail. Of course we were sending out the Commander USA membership cards, which showed that you were able to be committed. Or you should have been. Actually we got quite a bit of mail from prisons, the guys that were into the movies—and from bars, where people would hang out on Saturday afternoon. If there wasn't a big game or something broadcast, they'd watch Commander and Lefty for a while.

You were on in the afternoon. Do you think that changed the character of the audience you got?

I suppose. I always thought it would have been cool to do the show at midnight and go with the older crowd.

But something about the kids watching, with mom, you know, we had a good range. There were such good letters, especially from little kids, like eight, nine, 10 years old, who swore that they heard Lefty talking. That was always kind of sweet. I liked that.

Did you ever show off any of their artwork?

Oh sure! They would send in pictures, lots of pictures of Lefty. And people sent some pictures of me flying, which you didn't see very often. I guess that was kind of an expensive thing to do. But, oh yeah, they would send all kinds of wonderful stuff.

Tell us a little more about your radio career. How did that experience influence your movie hosting?

That was Hy Brown, right, who did all of those old radio serials? You know, I was a big fan of Jean Shepherd when I was a kid. I mean, when he broadcast three hours a night and would just talk. That fascinated me, you know? I would just listen to him all the time. I started getting into his books. And eventually they made the movie based upon his writing, *A Christmas Story* (1983), and they used all of his stories and stuff. But he was really the person I liked and got interested in radio. You know, being able to talk. Though at the time it was mostly pop records, rock and roll was going on.

Do you think there's a similarity in the intimacy you get with a hosted program and radio?

Oh sure. There has to be, since you're really only talking to that one person. Oh yeah, with radio you felt that. But the Commander did too. He knew he was just talking to you.

We need to touch on how the show ended. What killed it off?

I don't know. I don't think it's dead. I think there's room for this. They're trying to do different things now, such as cooking dinner during the movie; they do different kinds of things. I think the time is right for another good, you know, fun host—especially with the Internet opening up. Though I'm very low-tech. I don't understand too much of it. I can basically get my email and that's about as far as I go. But I think there's a lot of room for this kind of thing. The movies don't get old, they already are. I mean, they're not going to get older. You know, I like them.

If someone asks you what's a horror host, how would you define it?

I just felt like I was in 8th grade again for a second. I got scared. I felt like I didn't do my homework. Ahhh ... a horror host! I always looked at the Commander as loving these movies. I mean, he was waiting for the next scene to happen! You know, "Ward Bond's gonna come out and get hit by a beer bottle! Whoa! You'll see this happen!" I would get myself excited about seeing the next part. Maybe that's the essence—to show, to remind people how good these movies were and what to anticipate coming up.

What about how bad they were?

(*Laughs*) I think that was obvious! Who was the atomic turtle, the Japanese movie where ... Gamera! Oooo! Look you can see the string if you look real close, you know? That's what the director has given us as a gift, you know, to let the viewer know how these things are made. Yeah, action, lights, *Gamera*! Those were great! Yeah...

Later, did you see Mystery Science Theater 3000?

Yeah I did, I did. I liked that. I liked that they could watch the whole movie live and comment, because that's sittin' around with your friends, right? Just having a good time watching these things.

Can you remember the first time you saw it? Did you see it as a progression of what you used to do?

Yeah, that's what it looked like, because they got to see the whole movie. You know, the two ... the three of them. Yeah, maybe I was a little jealous. I don't know. I don't know. I could have been. Because that's the fun part, making up your own lines, going along with what's going on in the movie and having a good time. Yeah, I like that.

So, how did your show come to an end? What finally killed it off on the USA Network?

Oh, probably age, numbers. I guess it just ran its course after a while. The original producer was a fellow named Hillary Shackner, and he was a real rock and roll guy from I don't know when. And he really wanted to do cutting edge kind of stuff, if that's what you called it back then. And we did try to push things a little bit. And then he kind of left the show and other people took over. Somebody wanted it to be, you know, more of a children's program and that kind of thing. I think that had something to do with it.

Did you ever have any strange moments on the show, get any weird mail, or ever just wondered what the hell happened?

Oh yeah, a lot of times. With the mail, they'd often just give it to me and I'd start to read the letter and not know where I was going with it. I remember this one: It was such a simple letter; it must have been a seven-year-old kid or something. And she said, "Dear Commander. How come we don't see you fly?" And I said, "That's easy, darling. I don't have one, a fly." Well, I guess it was funnier back then.

What's the best bit you remember about the show?
Well, the best all-over bit had to be my pal, Lefty, and the invention of him. I had gone to the audition and did the character. I was home that night, and they gave me a sheet with suggestions about what to do. The producer basically said, "Throw that away and come up with something else." So I'm sitting in my La-Z-Boy, with the ashtray on the side. I say, eh, we need something. I dip my figure in the ashes ... (*draws on hand*). Ah, here's my pal, Lefty, uh? He was born. I always tell people I met him when I

Commander USA's fan club card ... the Commander shares the card with his pal. Lefty.

was 14, up in the Finger Lakes. He's been my right hand man ever since. The show got cancelled; he went down to Palm Beach, the little knucklehead. But Lefty, he became another character on the show. So, he was my favorite.

So, a lot of improvisation was going on. How about props, things around the set?

We had some good people working props, you know, cutting things out and building things all the time. I always enjoyed our "Groovie Man Dinners." Whatever was around the studio, we'd put in half a peanut butter and jelly sandwich, half of an apple. And we'd throw in a dollar. You know, go out and get yourself an ice cream bar after you're finished. I think they sold for $14.95 too. You could only find them in the research and development section of the super market. My acting teacher, of course, was Uda Hagen-daas. She wrote that book, *The Rocky Road to Success*. I always admired her. Then there was Dr. Ruth Wisenheimer. She was a horticulturalist. She ran a couple of beds downtown. Tulips, I believe.

God, I miss the 1980s. What do you think has changed about the nature of television since you started? Do you see what USA was doing somewhat more like what the local stations were doing—using that type of programming to generate an identity?

USA, it was national. But it always had that local feel. Yeah, that's the feeling it had. Today, I don't know. I'm still fascinated by television. I love television. And with cable and all the choices that we have, yeah, I dig it. I still dig TV.

This certifies that the bearer is an official member of the COMMANDER USA FAN CLUB, and pledges to remain an All Around Good Guy forever. SURE!

_____
(Member's Signature)

The back of the Commander USA fan club card, espousing his simple motto for leading a good life.

Anything jump out at you? Iron Chef ... any opinions?

Ah, *Iron Chef*! *Iron Chef* is all right. I know a guy who's really into the show because he's a chef. I go more for Emeril; I like him. I learned to make a hell of a Hollandaise sauce from Julia Child, watching her. Now that's going back a ways. But yeah, I like the cooking shows. The History Channel is fun. I watch a lot of reruns, you know, the old stuff, when I was a kid. You know, if it's *Leave It To Beaver* or *Sex in the City*, I might go with the Beav. Nostalgic, yeah, I like that kind of stuff.

Compare the Commander to some of your other roles. Does he stand out as one of those really great moments? Or is he just one of many?

Oh no, the Commander, for me, is unique ... was unique ... is unique. There was so much about him. It was such a nice concept for me that you had this super hero who can't *do* anything. And his disguise is a raincoat left open. You can see the costume. He had suspenders. He wore glasses as a disguise but also for reading. You know, he needed these things. He had bad knees from landing on the concrete all the time. That kills you. You can't do that for too long. And of course when they put that embargo around Cuba, he had to smoke those cheap cigars. Just didn't work as well. Commander always liked top shelf.

If someone were to come to you today and said they like to put the Commander back on, and give you somewhat of a free rein to program, the kind of show you want to do. What kind of show would you put together?

We have to start with a bigger suit. I would love to do the same kind of show, I'll tell ya, I had a good time with that. And if you get the right movie, and you're enjoying it, and you know what's coming up, you could probably show the same movie every week and just have different shtick! And for me, that would still be funny. I would do the same kind of show.

Were there any embarrassing flubs on the show? Was there anything that got you into trouble?

Oh geez, I guess when we had the electrical transformer on. She-He was an electrician who used to dress up as a Spanish dancer, with the fan in front of Her-Him ... and then take it down and had a huge moustache. I think we got in trouble for that a little bit. Some people objected to the cigar. But I actually never smoked that cigar. I would buy them pre-smoked from this Cuban guy on the West Side. So I ever actually lit that up. I wouldn't want to give the kids a bad influence there, a bad role model. Well, I really didn't care.

I liked it, I liked the show ... I mean, but the whole thing was embarrassing. I mean, as a grown man, putting on red tights and blue shorts and my super mask. If that's not embarrassing enough, what is? That's about the most embarrassing thing that ever happened to me.

You blew the slide whistle to activate the Psychotronic Screen...

Oh that was amazing! There's a piece of technology, the Psychotronic Screen, my God. I mean, we had some good engineers on that show. The screen would get stuck every once in a while. The Tele-Psychotronic Screen ... wow, I hadn't thought about that in a long time. But don't touch the red button! Uh oh! Things would happen.

Do you remember what the ratings were like? I mean, how you stacked up with the rest of the USA Network's schedule?

I think we did pretty well. I mean, for our time slot, for a Saturday afternoon. They weren't too forward with that information. I guess they didn't want my agent hearing about it. But I think we did all right. They always said if we got, you know ... what is it ... a one, or anything above a one, we were doing great! So I remember a couple of times we might have got up to a four-something. That was always fun.

Were there any comic books or real life characters that you drew on for Commander USA? There are things that just feel familiar about…

Well, one of my favorites was Ernie Kovacs, of course. I mean he was such an innovator, and so funny, that I think I drew on him a lot. And really the guys that I watched as a real young kid, even Buffalo Bob and Howdy Doody, and those kinds of shows. I dug those, and I liked the guys on them. So that's probably the influence there.

What was your feeling coming up to the audition? I mean when you said, "Wow, this would be the chance to do that kind of show." How worked up did you get about that audition compared to others?

When I first got there, it was up in the office, up in on 6th Avenue in an office building. They had just moved in. The producer I was auditioning for was locked out of his office. So we had to meet in the hallway. So I really didn't have any idea this was going to be a class operation at all. You know, I had big doubts about that. But then when I was told what we were going to do and it was going to be happening, yeah, it was very heady, very exciting. This was really what I had wanted to be doing for a long, long time. Have something funny, having a TV show, and maybe having something I could right a good part of. So, yeah, it was exciting.

Does anyone recognize you these days? Does anyone ever stop you in the street?

Every once in a while, yes. It doesn't happen too much anymore. This is a long time ago now, right? Fifteen, 20 years ago. People do tend to remember you when you're wearing tights. But it starts to fade after a while.

You mentioned Zacherley as one of your favorites. Did you ever get to meet him?

I never did, no. No.

What would you say to Zach? I mean if you could say something to Zach about what he did for you, as inspiration?

Commander USA proudly displays his fan club card.

He did give me a lot of fun, Zacherley. He was the guy that I would watch that you probably weren't supposed to be watching. I mean that Mom didn't know about or … even my older brother didn't know about. I mean he was the guy we would go into school the next day and talk about. He would just crack us up. I guess later on, maybe when I was in high school, Steve Allen came on late at night, and he was that kind of innovative artist. I mean, I'm not comparing Zacherley and Steve Allen, but I felt that way about both of them. Watching it, it was, well … he gave me good things. He made me laugh and that's all I was ever looking for with Zacherley. And he could do it.

Did you ever see any other hosts, other than Zach?

Not really. We had Zacherley here in the New York area, and I grew up here. And I never really left until it was time, until I was 17 or so. I don't think I'd been further west of the Hudson River more than a couple miles. So Zacherley, that was about it for me, although I've heard about them a lot, of course, in my travels around the country. I've gotten to meet a couple of guys.

Public appearances … Did they ever ship the Commander around the country?

Not too any conventions. They would send me out to some of the affiliates. Yeah, I'd do that, go out to Indiana, you know, out to Seattle, and California a couple of times. Every summer in Nashville, they'd have the *Summer Lights Festival*. So I'd go out and make an appearance there and, you know, wear the suit. I ran into one affiliate one time, and I was in my uniform. I walked in, and all these people, I guess the ad execs, were on the second floor, on the stairway. When I walked in they all started singing "Zombio," the song I had written for the video we did when we were showing the movie *White Zombie*. So being serenaded out there, I think that was a highlight. (*singing a calypso melody*) "Oh my achin' head/I'm in love with a lady that's dead/She walks around with eyes open wide/But she doesn't see me, I feel empty inside." Chorus—"Ohhhhh, zombio/You drive me crazy when you walkin' so slow/Your touch is cold, but to me it's just right/ So be my zombie baby and bite me goodnight!" (*Laughs*)

So, anybody you met on the road, any fans that you really remember, any incidents? Did you ever get a sense on the road of, "Man, I'm really reaching people out here, people on the other side of the set?"

I didn't do a lot of public appearances. It was mostly industry kind of things. But I was always surprised when people would recognize me. When the show was on, it would happen a lot, just walking around the city. Yeah, it was amazing, of course, to be recognized and for people to know you. It does make you think how powerful the medium is, how big television is. I enjoyed it though. I enjoyed meeting the people. Most of the people I met were very friendly. They wouldn't come up to me, I guess, if they didn't at least enjoy the show.

What do you think about how people perceive people on TV as more personal than, like, a theater actor?

Right, right. Yeah, it's like we were talking about with radio, you're talking to one person basically. And I think people feel that. I do. I mean, when I meet somebody on TV, I'd think, sure, I know them. If I met Bob Barker, I'd think we met before.

Toy ad for The Comedian from *The Watchmen*, it does look like someone familiar!!1

You mentioned some films you appreciated. Can you think of any you would actually keep in a collection?

Actually, I do that once in a while. I have my own VHS tapes of, I think, every show that we did, with commercials and the movie and everything. So yeah, I'll take down one of the good zombie pictures once in a while. I have a look at it. Not too often.

I need to ask you about a comic book called The Watchmen *that came out right around the time you were on TV. There's a character in that called The Comedian who, swear to God, looks like you. The costume is a little harsher. But he's got the moustache, cigar, suspenders, red top. Military pants and boots. He was basically what Nixon sent over to Vietnam.*

Is that how we won? (*Laughs*) Oh my God! I was not aware of *The Watchmen* at all. No, never heard of it.

The last image of the guy is sitting in his chair with a drink, a tear rolling down his eye, watching television.

I can relate to that.

Was the Commander's love of John Wayne something that came out of you? Or was that something that grew organically from the character?

The Commander thought of John Wayne as a hero. He didn't watch a lot of Wayne's movies, but loved that portrait. You must have seen that portrait, John Wayne with the stagecoach and the sky ... and him standing there with the big neckerchief on. Now for the Commander, that's art. That's beautiful, pure art.

So what would the Commander be doing today?

The Commander, he moved back down to Florida, I believe. He's still looking for Lefty. Lefty made most of the money on that show, you see. Put it right in the pocket.

The right hand didn't know what the left hand was doing, huh?

If he could help it! Lefty was no slouch, I can tell you that. His father was a socialist, you know. That's how he got the name.

Hey Group! Take III
Son of Ghoul (Keven Scarpino)
Interviewed by Michael Monahan (2006)

Keven Scarpino was one of Ghoulardi's kids, held in thrall by the anarchistic antics of Ernie Anderson's popular horror movie host character. Two decades after Anderson left Cleveland for California, Scarpino was presented with the opportunity to host horror movies himself. The temptation to pull from childhood memory was too much to resist.

When The Son of Ghoul first arrived on the scene in 1986, some viewed him as an upstart and outsider. Though he appropriated familiar Ghoulardi catch phrases and music cues, he was the first of the post-Ghoulardi horror hosts not to have a direct connection to Ernie Anderson, and Anderson's inner circle at first viewed him with some suspicion. Anderson ultimately granted Scarpino a degree of indirect permission to carry on the phony beard hipster tradition in a phone call, but genuine acceptance from his peers was long in coming.

Keven Scarpino persevered, creating a multi-decade body of work (including a three-year stint hosting a live game show) and earning respect from many in the local hosting establishment for his appreciation of tradition. He survived a lawsuit, the death of a key cast member and a protracted period of being ostracized to become recognized as a semi-legitimate part of Cleveland's horror host legacy and "the last host standing" when the city's impressive broadcast history began to wind down.

As a living tribute to the Ghoulardi style of horror hosting, he became a popular attraction at the city's annual GhoulardiFest convention, sharing the floor with many local TV icons, including Ernie Anderson's old friend and colleague, Big Chuck Schodowski.

How old were you when you first discovered Ghoulardi? What was local TV like at the time, and what sort of effect did Ghoulardi have when he came on the scene?

Here in Cleveland we had three stations, and that was it. When Ghoulardi came on ... well, there's been a lot of misinformation about Ghoulardi. How he blew up live frogs and did this and that. He never did anything like that. It was just that he was wild. It was just things that he said, you know? He was just so free.

I do remember the only time I ever got to see him in person. He made an appearance at the Stark County Fair. They were having the horse races, and there was a little stage on the other side of the horse track. That's where he was going to be. I guess the race was running long and the grandstand was just packed and people were standing at the fences and stuff. Then Ghoulardi came out from underneath the grandstand. He walked out the door and suddenly people were jumping over the fence and he got mobbed. Some guy stole the phony beard off his face. He pulled his beard right off and stole his fright wig. So Ghoulardi just did the whole show standing there with a moustache ... only.

I had sent in for an original Ghoulardi postcard, which he autographed on the back and sent it back to me. I made a poster that said "Ghoulardi For Future Baby Sitter" for some reason. And I glued or taped that postcard on the corner of that poster. He was talking for a while and I held my poster up. I handed it to him and he said, "Hey! Ghoulardi for future babysitter! Hey! Hey!" And he tossed it into the air and there went my poster and postcard! It was gone.

When he left, he walked down these little steps behind the booth. And he went to a ... probably a limousine, I would think. And he got in the back seat and sat in the middle, between two guys with suits and ties. I saw these two older kids running for the car. So I ran after them. These two kids say, "Hey Ghoulardi, how about a handshake?" The one kid shoves his arm in the window and shakes his hand, and then the other one. And then they step aside and it's my turn. But when I stuck in my arm, the window starts going up. I pulled my arm back out and Ghoulardi gave me that, "Oh well..." look as they pulled away.

That was the only time I ever saw him. It was a Thursday when he made the appearance. So the next night when he was on the Friday show I distinctly remember he said, "Last night, I was at the Stark County Fairgrounds for a personal appearance. And I tell you, group, I'm never going there again. Because as soon as I walked out, somebody went like this..." Then he pulled his beard and wig off and they went to black and back into the movie.

Most people today have no idea what a unique experience live television was. Watching a show back then was almost

The Son of Ghoul (Keven Scarpino) at WOAC-TV 67 in the early days of his show, circa 1986

literally like looking through a window directly into the studio. As a kid, did you have any awareness that what you were seeing on television was live?

Absolutely. I don't know how many people knew that, but I knew it. I could watch my kid's show host, like Barnaby or something, and they would slip in adult humor sometimes. Or things would happen. Like something would fall over, and they would start cracking up. And as I kid, I was hip to that. I knew what they were doing. I knew something messed up, and I knew they were live.

I always had a bit of a Ghoulardi-type costume, even as a kid in grade school. I remember dressing up with a paper beard and moustache on at recess at grade school, out on the blacktop, trying to do Ghoulardi. And I remember doing it in the neighborhood too. I'd be at my mom's house, which had a big front window. I remember the neighbor kids standing out on the lawn and I was up in the window. That was my ozone (*a wavy electronic circle used by Ghoulardi on his show*).

Doing Ghoulardi?

Doing Ghoulardi.

Like live TV!

Exactly!

The studio side of the window…

Exactly, exactly! We would do that and then a couple of my buddies would come out and we'd pantomime Beatles songs, and then we'd come back and I'd be up in the window again. We had a big audience, about five neighbor kids, stretching anywhere from five to nine year olds.

That's great. That was you first horror hosting experience.

Yeah, you know, years after, I ran into a girl with whom I went to grade school. She came to me and she said, "You know, when I saw you on the air I couldn't believe it. I remember you doing that on the playground at school." So there was one person who actually remembered. So that was neat.

What about the transition from Ghoulardi to Hoolihan and Big Chuck? Were you still a regular viewer when that happened?

Oh, absolutely.

Do you remember anything about Ghoulardi leaving? Was there any sort of announcement?

Well, a couple things happened. There was a point where Ghoulardi was also doing an afternoon show, the *Laurel, Ghoulardi and Hardy* show. They showed Laurel and Hardy comedy shorts. The station might have been on strike or something, because Ghoulardi was off for a week. He wasn't gone for good at that point, but he was off for a week. And there were two guys that sat on his set with white beards and moustaches that did the show for a week. As a kid I didn't understand what that was about.

Ron Sweed (The Ghoul) had mentioned something about that on one of the Ghoulardi tribute shows they did on radio with Chris Quinn. He thought it was some news guy, the weatherman from WKBD, a Detroit station, who they brought down to cover Ernie during the strike. Big Chuck was talking about WJW going out on a writers and artists strike…

That must be it then. I know the guys wore white beards and moustaches.

And there was more than one guy?

Two guys. See, that's why I asked Chuck if it was he and Hoolie. He said no, it wasn't. But it was two guys, two guys in beards and moustaches.

Was that toward the end of Ghoulardi's run?
I think it was about around the middle.

So ... 1964, 1965?
He came back on for a good while.

What was the difference between the late-night Ghoulardi show, the early evening movie and the afternoon Laurel and Hardy show?

On the late-night show, he would sit in the ozone circle and do mail and stuff that way. The afternoon show was filled up mostly with the Laurel and Hardy comedies, which could run up to 28 minutes. But at that time, there weren't too many commercials. I remember the afternoon show would start with a bunch of clips. I know it showed the fat ballerina falling. Over that they played the song, "It's a mad, mad world ... I'm a real mad man ..." (*"Mad, Mad World" by Al Jones*) then cut right into "Papa Oo Mow Mow Mow" (*by The Rivingtons*). I don't know what it cut to after that. I asked Chuck about it, but he said there was never a regular opening. They would change it once in a while.

The late-night show would come directly out of the news and right into a skit. They'd run the "Friday Night at the Cheapies" intro and maybe have a Parma Place skit right at the top of the show. They'd go right into the movie from there and you wouldn't see Ghoulardi until maybe the second break. And for a while they showed the Flash Gordon serials. He would go, "Now we have chapter two of *Flash!*" They would show *Flash Gordon*, and then they'd start the movie. I can also remember he was bitching at one point because they started showing a Boris Karloff *Thriller* episode instead of movies. He just hated that. I remember him complaining about that. But I don't remember him announcing he was leaving. He might have announced it. But I was a kid and at the height of retardation.

Was this where your interest in broadcasting come from?

I was a TV kid from the very beginning. I watched the local hosts, I watched the kids' shows, I watched Ghoulardi and I watched Big Chuck. I always liked that stuff. About 1970, I was going with my dad to the mall. He had to go to JC Penney's to pay on their charge bill. And as we was walking up to the mall, there was this guy in front of Mr. Ted's Tux Shop, I think it was called. Here's a guy with belt -ength long hair doing an AM radio remote. He had two turntables and a phone, and he was talking back to the station. I told my dad, I said, "I'm going to watch this guy do this. I'll be right here."

I kind of strolled over. I was just fascinated by this guy's technique. His name is Charlie Cooper. His on-air name was "Super Duper Charlie Cooper." I was a teenager at the time, and he was much older. And that was my first influence in broadcasting. I thought, man, this guy's got it made. I used to actually go to other radio remotes that he did, and we used to do this ventriloquist and the dummy bit. I just stand there like this and he's put his arm up my back and I'd move my mouth. It was all an attempt to hustle women.

Hustle women for you or for him?

Both! At the same time, 1970-1971, Ron Sweed came on the air as The Ghoul. And that was as close to Ghoulardi as you could get. He was wild, man. It wasn't Big Chuck and Hoolihan! Here's a guy who looked like Ghoulardi and said the things Ghoulardi said. And you either liked him or you didn't like him. There was never an in between. People either hated him or they liked him. I was one the guys who thought he was great.

In that period, the early 1970s, he had more of a hippie/punk appeal. Same sort of radical Ghoulardi spirit, but for a new generation.

Absolutely, he had long hair and was kind of hip to what was going on. He loved the Beatles. He played a lot of Beatles on his show. I was always a Beatles nut, so that was a great tie-in. He was making personal appearances and I decided I was going to go to Hudson Haunted House to meet him. My ex-wife and I drove up and there he was. I stood in the line, and when I got up to get his autograph, I told him. hey, I got a costume just like yours! He says, "Yeah? I wanna see it!" So I drove back to Massillon, got the costume and drove back up to Hudson again for the nighttime appearance. He says, "Where's your stuff?" I go, I got it in the suitcase. "Well, get in here!"

So I climbed over this fence, got into the little building where his set was erected and started putting this stuff on in the dark. I jumped out with my stuff on, and that was actually the first appearance. I think it was that same night though that he said, "Hey, in a week or two I'm going to be at Geauga Lake. Why don't you bring your costume and come up there?" Yeah, wow, great, sure!

So up to Geauga Lake we went. He said two o'clock. Okay. So we get there about one. By the time we park the car and get into the park it's about a quarter to two. We get to the place he's supposed to be and the guy's already on stage. I sat there for a while and finally got his attention. He goes, "Where's your stuff?" I hold up my little suitcase and he says, "Put it on!" Okay, so I ran

The Son of Ghoul took over *Thriller Theater* in 1986, replacing The Cool Ghoul (George Cavender).

He took off. And I'm talking to the people until they shut the mic off. Then I got "detained" at the guard station, because they said I ran up on stage and they had guns pointed at me. I could have gotten shot. That's what they told me. Hey, if you're guarding Ron Sweed with guns, then something's definitely got to be wrong here. Soon after that he left the air, the show was over. By that time we probably had Chuck and John and Super Host left on the air. And I went on to have a baby, have a family, work and pay bills. And I started playing music.

Had you set aside any thoughts of broadcast by then?

I didn't even think about broadcasting. When I was younger, I thought it would be a great job. But I didn't think it would be a reality to me. In about 1981, Sweed landed a job at a local Cleveland radio station, WDMT, and they gave him a shift between midnight and six in the morning. That's a long stretch. Then he would play obscure Ghoulardi songs and take phone calls over the music. At that time Channel 61, Sweed's old station, had left the air. But now a new 61 had come back. So immediately he was saying, "I'm going to Channel 61, my old stomping grounds. I'm getting back on the air." And he literally started bugging their offices to get a new show.

Within a year, they finally gave him a show. But WCLQ (*Channel 61*), at that time, shared a broadcast band with almost a pay-per-view movie channel at night. At 7 p.m. they would switch over to this pay-per-view. "On Demand TV," I don't know what it was called. They would have regular broadcasting during the day and switch to this thing at night. When Sweed first came back, they put him on at noon on Saturdays. And I thought, cool, the guy's back on the air. But it just didn't have the punch that it did back in the 1970s. But it was still cool; it was all right. If you were a Ghoul fan at the time, you accepted it. It was okay.

That version of the show had more of a regular cast of characters: Blanche, Spike Who Rides a Bike...

A bunch of other people appeared. Shortly after he went on the air, he decided to have a look-a-like contest,

behind the stage and his wife, Barbara, watched me put the stuff on. I jumped up on stage and within a minute, he was wrapping up his show to leave. He told the people goodbye, "I'm going to leave this guy with you."

and I won it. And even when it was over, it was over. It was all fun. And when it was done, that was the end of it.

You did an appearance on his show, right?

Yeah. The winner got to win a segment on his show. That was the big, big prize.

That was your first on-air horror host experience.

Exactly. He let me decide want I wanted to do. I said, "I wanna sit on the stool." I remember he said, "You've got two minutes." That was it.

That was unscripted? You just ran with it?

Totally, it was totally unscripted. I had kind of an idea what I was going to say. If you listen to it, I even squeeze my son's name into it. But when that was over, again, that was it. The costume went into the closet and it was forgotten. It was just a moment of fun. Then about a year later, off the air he went again.

This was about 1982, 1983?

Gone in '83. In '82 a local television station in Canton, WOAC Channel 67, signed on. They were an independent. And they brought on a character called The Cool Ghoul. He was originally on another local station down here, Channel 17, back in 1971. The Cool Ghoul, George Cavender, actually beat Ron Sweed's first run on the air by three weeks. Not that it mattered. I don't think many people got to see the Channel 17 show. Their viewing range was kinda small.

How did you get onto Channel 67?

Labor Day weekend, they announced on the air that they were going to show Three Stooges movies on the side of the building at the television station during the evening hours of the (*Jerry Lewis Muscular Dystrophy*) Telethon. And they were inviting everybody to "Come on out, see the Stooges, throw some money in the fish bowl for Jerry's Kids, meet George Cavender. Meet the Cool Ghoul; he'll be out here hosting." I'm coming home from a gig and I'm still wide awake; it's two o'clock in the morning. So I pulled in and there's a lot of cars in the driveway and maybe 40 people out there watching. So I dropped my money in the tank, a whole dollar of it. Yeah, I'm a big spender. Next thing I see Cavender come out of the studio and I watch him do a live cut away for the break.

At that point, I moseyed over. He was just standing there and I introduced myself, told him what I did with Ron's show and local-like stuff, and he seemed real interested in all that. He said, "Well, next week you know, we're doing our regular taping. Why don't you stop in, check it out?" And I said, "Oh great, I'd love to." I showed up the next week and I watched them tape their show. He was real nice, and I thought it was kind of fun and interesting. Then out the door I went. So, the very next week, I must have grown big balls or something, because I just showed up at the TV station unannounced. I can remember them all looking up at the door like, "What's he doing here?"

I said, "Hi, I had so much fun, I thought I'd just come and watch you guys again." He said, "Ah, come on in." Things were so loose at the time and he would need different people to do things. Like he'd do a skit, and he'd need some one to hold a prop off at the side or something. I started doing that. Then I started appearing in the skits. I did a number of things. I did one Christmas show. I appeared dressed as one of the ZZ Top members. We played the Three Wise Guys. And I was in the Thanksgiving show; I played a pilgrim. But I'm getting ahead of myself.

I'd hanging around for about four months at this point. I could walk into the back door of the TV station during the day, and nobody would ask me what I was doing. So that was kind of cool. George was taping skits one Sunday night, and I was in to help. They had been training a board operator, and I found out that tonight was supposed to be his first solo on the board by himself. What they did is, they'd bring somebody in to run the commercials and all that stuff and they'd train you for two or three weeks. It was all manual at the time, it was really a task. And I guess the board-op sat down, and when it came to the first commercial break, he rolled countdowns over the air for the commercials. One jammed and he couldn't get back into the movie right. He went to the slide for a while. He went back and he finally went back in the movie. The guy just stood up, said, "Gee I am sure glad I'm not perfect," and walked right out — got in his car and left.

At that point I think, "Oh man, the board-op just quit?" There's a position open right now. Even before it's announced, I know it's open. So the next morning at nine o'clock I walk in the back door of the station. And right at that point down the hall comes the operations manager. I say, "Lee, I want to talk to you about possibly becoming a board op." He just got back from the general manager's office, telling him the guy quit. And he looked at me and said, "Then you're the man I need to talk to. Follow me." I followed him back to his office and he set me down and asked me what my experience was. And I said, "Well, I own a VCR, and I know 16 millimeter" And basically I just told him this is what I need to do. This is the work I need to do. This is what I'm cut out to do; this is what I *want* to do. Obviously he liked my attitude, and he was so frustrated after three weeks of training some guy that he said, "Okay, I'll think it over."

So I drove home, and about 45 minutes later the phone rang. He said, "You got the gig." So I went in for training on Christmas Eve of 1985. I was in Master Control with training that night, all night. And it was like me trying to learn to run the deck of the Enterprise. It was really tough. In two weeks of training I couldn't get it. My timing was just horrible. I knew if I couldn't do this, I was out. And … I did it. I don't know how.

About six months later, George came at odds with his personal life and the station. He went in and announced that he was leaving. So I went into the office and asked the general manager, what are you going to do with the time slot? You've got an audience here, and you don't have a host now. He told me a few people had expressed interest. So I expressed interest too. We shot a VHS tape, like, a year before that, as just a goof off, in the garage. I gave it to him, they looked at it, and he said, "Well, we'd like to see how you look on our equipment."

When you taped the "goof off" thing, what costume were you in? Was it the hat and cape?

No, I was in the Ghoulardi/Ghoul costume. I didn't really have any idea; I just thought it would be cool. Sweed was gone from the air. Nobody knew where he was and nobody heard a thing. So I thought it would be cool to bring the old feel of Ghoulardi back again, you know? I wanted to do that. I told them, though, that I wouldn't be looking like that. I told them I wanted to change the costume to be different. And he (*the General Manager*) agrees. He says, "Yeah, you'd almost have to."

Anyways, I give them a demo show. They take it in the office Monday. The operations manager and general manager both watched it. They took about 15 minutes. They called me into the office and told me I had 13 weeks. They whipped up a contract and I signed it. They told me, "You can tape on Thursday evenings, like George did. And yes, we'll allow you to bring some of your own crew in." They gave me a paid director. But they said for the first three shows, they wanted me to film during the day and use all station personnel as crewmembers, to make it go smooth. And they wanted me to tape the next morning at 10 o'clock.

So, I started preparing that night, and I was up all night long. I fell asleep about 5:30 a.m. About 10 I get a phone call from my one of my friends who was doing audio for me. He called me and says, "Kev, it's 10 till 10!" I was still in bed, totally out. I jumped up in a panic—no shower, greasy hair, got to the station late. We didn't get started till about 11. I remember the operations manager saying, "Keven, you're not getting off to a very good start." But I taped the first show. As I'm cleaning up, the general manager comes in and calls all the station employees into the studio. They premiered it right then and made me stand there while they all watched it. They all applauded and that was the beginning of the whole thing.

The first film you hosted was The Gong Show Movie *(1980).*

The Gong Show Movie … just because that's what happened to be scheduled. I started using the cape by the second show, and just kept it then. I think we taped two shows in the morning. By the third week we bumped it to Thursday night. I got my own crew to come in at that point; these people were all my close friends at the time. I still got the paid director, which happened to be Mark Williams. We never got along. He wanted to do it his way; I wanted to do it my way. Then Mark decided he didn't want to be part of it anymore. I went into the office and told them I refused to tape if I had Mark Williams as a director. They gave me John Case then, which was a very cool thing. We started rolling at that point. John was a good guy; he did a lot of pre-production work. He'd have everything ready.

Were you consciously trying to do something different than Ghoulardi or The Ghoul after those first couple of weeks?

No, I wasn't, not at all. I think I had it in my mind that to wear this little beard in the tradition of Ghoulardi, you had to act a certain way and say certain things. Maybe I thought that because that's what Sweed did. I thought what Sweed did was what Ghoulardi did. But I realized that it wasn't really what Ghoulardi did. Sweed added a few things of his own to it. But I thought in my mind that was the only way anybody would accept this character. I didn't think anybody would accept a third person trying to do it at all. I thought this isn't going to work. I thought I wouldn't go past 13 weeks. It took me a good couple of years to really start developing and really start to break out. It wasn't probably till the lawsuit actually happened that I really made a change, though I really didn't have to change anything. According to the lawsuit decision, I could continue to do whatever I wanted to do.

Could we get a little background on the lawsuit?

Yeah. Like I say, Sweed had been off the air, nobody's heard or seen him. About two years into my show, I was in an edit room at the station. The secretary buzzes me.

"Keven, you got a call on line three." Okay, thanks. It was a reporter from the *Akron Beacon-Journal*, and he said would I like to comment on the lawsuit that was filed against me by Ron Sweed? I said, "What? What are you talking about? Could you hold on for one minute? Somebody's gotta hear this." I ran up to the general manager's office and I had him take the call. My comment was that I won't comment because I didn't know anything about it prior to this. I mean, Sweed never attempted to get ahold of me and say, "What are you doing? I disagree with this." He just went after the dollar. So he tried to sue me for half a million dollars.

Based on what?

That's what the business is worth to him.

Was this tied in to another comeback attempt on Cleveland TV for him? Or was it just completely out of the blue?

He was completely off air at the time, no show. He was bitter. I was on; he was off. I was wearing that beard. He thought he was the *only* person with rights to wear that beard, because Ernie said he could do it. Right before the lawsuit was filed, my coordinator, Vince Scarpetti, called Ernie Anderson's secretary. Ernie was still very much healthy and doing voiceovers at ABC. He was still actively on the air. She told us on Tuesdays and Thursdays he was out at this one studio doing voiceovers. Call this number at this time and he'll answer the phone. She was hip to what was going on, so that's why she was friendly enough to us to give us the number.

So Vince Scarpetti called and actually talked to Ernie. He explained to him who I was and what I did. Once Vince told him I was doing the show, he said, "If you're doing it, do it. Go with it. Just leave me out of it." That's exactly what he said. He did not care. We wanted to interview him, that's why we had originally called. Ernie's answer was, "Look, I spend 12 hours a day in front of a microphone. I don't have time to do any of this shit. But what I will do is this, just send me what you want me to say, I'll record it and send it to you."

Three days after that phone conversation, before we had a chance to send that request to him, Sweed filed the lawsuit. At that point, the general manager of the station told me not to do anything with anybody. No contact, no letters, don't bother them. I missed my opportunity to get voiceovers from him. Just think, I could have Ernie going, "Carrying on a Cleveland tradition."

How did the lawsuit finally wrap up?

I think the court case went on for about a year and a half. At one point, Sweed and his attorney showed up at the TV station there in Canton. I was in the Master Control, and I remember the operation manager walking in. He told me Sweed and his attorney were out front and they were going to hold me in the back. They came in and demanded to see videotape. They wanted to search through our tapes. They wouldn't let him see any tapes and they sent him home.

Were they trying to deliver a cease and desist or something?

No, they just wanted to gather up as much evidence as they could gather. And now I realize why. He didn't have anything. The video of me that he showed in the courtroom was very minimal. I mean he hardly had anything.

He probably didn't have anything from Ernie in writing either, did he?

The popularity of the *Son of Ghoul Show* prompted the station to drop the *Thriller Theater* name.

Kevin Scarpino and Ron Huffman at the Talon studios in October of 2000

No, he had nothing in writing. And then I got a few threats from his wife. His wife threatened me at Nautica. I walked in for a concert and she walked up to me and said, "Do you know who I am?" Barbara Sweed, right? "Yeah! Well, you're going to get what's coming to you, you son of a bitch!" And I said, don't threaten me, Barbara. I just walked away. At that point, my attorney told me not to say anything, no matter what it was. So I did. I shut my mouth.

When we went to court, rumor had it that Ron and her had already split up. But the attorney got Big Chuck to come down in Ron's behalf, just to go into court and say, "Well yeah, I guess Ernie told Ron that he could do this." Chuck didn't want to be there, but he was there anyway. I remember Chuck commenting afterwards. "Man," he said, "they split up." Yet, in the courtroom, they acted like they were man and wife, to the point of even holding hands.

But they were split up. Was she seeing the attorney at the time?

I think she was. It was a big masquerade the whole time. I never knew what the whole thing was about. I don't know if she ended up marrying the attorney. She lives with him, I think.

But ultimately the court decided in your favor.

Ultimately, the only thing Ron owned was the name "The Ghoul." He had a service mark for it. That's the only thing he owned. He tried to say that I stole his camera angles, the music, the feel of his show. And he owned nothing. Now, my attorney brought in a big blackboard. And he wrote down nine or 10 things that Sweed said he owned and that I was copying. The only item from the list that I used was the name "The Ghoul," and I wasn't using that name. Just "Son of Ghoul," not "The Ghoul." So my attorney just kept on saying, "Do you own this music?" No. Scratch a line through it. "Do you own the idea of putting cameras in a certain position in the room?" No. Scratch a line through it. Sweed owns nothing.

He was trying to say I was ruining his business. But in fact I wasn't. My attorneys called all the Cleveland television stations and asked them if I was the reason they wouldn't hire Ron Sweed. And they said no, I had nothing to do with it. So they proved I wasn't the reason he couldn't get a job.

But by that point, you were starting to develop an individual personality anyway.

Yeah, I started developing my own kinds of characters, just as things grew and people come up with ideas. I started growing as my own character at that point.

When did you first discover you had a fan base?

Well, I knew that The Cool Ghoul had an audience. That's what the general manager said to me. He told me I was a hell of a salesman, since I went in and sold him on the idea that they had an audience and they should continue this. He said, "You're a hell of a salesman." I wish that was true. But I knew he was right when I started getting letters right away.

Now things are starting to wrap up at the station.

Well, the station was always for sale from day one. It was for sale before I worked there, and we were told that. Finally they came in and said the station was sold and there would be new owners. They'd drop money into the station, and everybody's jobs would be secure. Well, the new owners showed up that day. They walked into the office and told the general manager to leave. Then they went into the conference room and called in every employee one after the other and fired everybody.

The reason I didn't get fired, I had a contract that said they had to give me three weeks in writing. So they said, "Okay, we're giving you three weeks in writing. You've got three weeks. Go for it." They still had programming up on the station; it hadn't changed over to home shopping. The station still had contracts to run some stuff. So, the news department got fired, local sports got dropped. Everything ended, except me. When I went in to tape those last three weeks' shows, it was virtually an empty television station, with all the equipment sitting there.

And there was no management to say anything. You could go there any time of day. The doors were unlocked, the cameras sitting in there. Walk right in. In the meantime, I had this guy who was working for me named Cowboy Bob. He acted like he was a manager or executive or something, but he was just a con man. He was involved in some promotions and stuff. He was an all right guy. He moved along to the CAT (Channel 35 & 29 in Akron, Ohio) and he talked to them about me coming up there. Right away they were interested in the show because they were interested in a local identity.

I was losing the station and the production facilities, so I went to a local place called Talon Media. A couple of guys had gotten some equipment and were working out of a building in Massillon. They were trying to set up a little makeshift studio there. They came to me and said, don't worry, everything will be smooth. We know what you need for your production, we have it all covered.

So, they built me the set I'm still using now. They designed all that, I didn't do anything. I walked in the first day and they had it standing. And it was one big clusterfuck at that point. Everything they'd promised me, they weren't able to deliver. I almost threw in the towel right then. It was just too overwhelming. Everything I'd taken for granted, all the luxuries of the station. When I moved to Talon Media, I gave up half my money to production costs. Well, that wasn't working out. I was originally taping every week. Then I started taping every two weeks. I did two shows. Then I started taping three shows at once, trying to save time and money.

I stopped working at Talon and went over to Digital Illusions. And it was an illusion. I did that for about a year. It was a completely different building. I liked the studio. I liked how the set was staged. But workable it wasn't. Again, I'm taping three shows a week and not coming back for a month. And the owner was expecting me to be paying his rent by coming in every week. And when that didn't happen, he said, "That's it. I'm closing the studio." At that point, I had no choice but to buy the editing equipment off him, for a phenomenal amount of money. Way more than what it was worth. But I had no choice. That's when I took over all the editing myself, and I prefer it that way.

Did you find you began to shape the show differently?

Well, I thought it saved the show. By that time, we were into doing 12 years of the show. All the tricks we'd been able to do the first nine years, we weren't able to do anymore. I was working with guys who weren't getting paid, and believe me, it was showing up onscreen. So at that point, I was just tired of dealing with people and I'm sure they were tired of dealing with me. My attitude was really bad too. I had no patience. Everything was a pain in the ass.

I bought the editing equipment, but I couldn't shoot because I didn't have a camera. So, I had to take the set back over to Talon, put it back up again and keep shooting. We were there another two and a half years. Eventually the owner let the place go. So that was the end of that.

Once you took over the editing yourself, how much time did you start spending on a show?

It all depends. The way we used to do it, John Stone would load the sound carts and I would cue them in and out. We did it together. Sometimes we would go in and sound-effect the movie maybe 2 1/2 hours before we started taping. Sometimes we would tape and try to sound-effect the movie afterwards. You can really tell with some of the old shows, where the audio drops out or the soundtrack abruptly cuts out. We didn't even think about mixing it, because that's all the technology we had there.

When I moved the editing here, to my home, I figured I could do a better job with the sound effects. So then I started taking my time with it. I can work on a movie for two weeks; I can work on it for three days. I can't really put in quality time. What I do now is work on it some night for two hours, get burned out, and shut it down. And sometimes I won't go back to it for a couple of weeks. Then I'll go back in and do a couple of segments or something.

The author and his absurdly indulgent wife with Ron "Fidge" Huffman in October of 2000

Sometimes you load up the films pretty heavily with sound effects. How does that compare with the movies back on Ghoulardi's show?

Chuck Schodowski did the audio drops on the movies. They didn't put a lot in there since their idea was to catch you off guard. So the sound effect would be a surprise, rather than something you expected to happen. I didn't sound-effect all of my movies at Channel 67. When I went to the CAT, they wanted the sound effects. They said, "Oh yeah. Put 'em in. Go for it." So the first movie I did for them, *Godzilla vs. Megalon* (1973), I actually did on Channel 67's equipment.

That was the first one. We did it ourselves after that. I had more time to do it. Now, I'll be watching the movie, and I'll see something and think, "Wow, this one little sound drop from this one old movie or cartoon would be great right in here." So I hit the stop button … and it may take me two hours of digging through all my stuff to find that one cut.

It seems to me your love of cartoons and Three Stooges films make your choices particularly creative. You turn the films into live action cartoons.

Well, sure. There were so many sound effects in those old cartoons, and so much of it keyed off action. I loved all that. And all that stuff has became more available. You've got CDs of cartoon music and cartoon sound effects, *Little Rascals* music, what have you. You can get anything you want to. But if I had to do it all over again, I would have started in 1986 and never used one piece of recorded music by anybody. I would have done it all myself, all original. If I had any brains, I would have done it that way, because if someone decided to syndicate my show in a large market, they might run into problems with copyrights.

Another major change from the Channel 67 days was the character Fidge, played by Ron Huffman, a little person.

When I moved to the studio in Massillon, Fidge, a local guy who knew the owner of the studio, would come and hang out at Talon. Once word got out I was working there, he asked if he could come down to a taping. He showed up the next Tuesday, just as a spectator. And what the hell, there's one midget in the room. Please! Right away it was, "You, come here!" The word "fidge" came from the *Little Rascals*, and the name stuck.

Around 2000, Regis Philbin comes on with *Who Wants to Be a Millionaire* and suddenly game shows are all popular again. The Klauses (*Robert and William Klaus own and run The CAT, WAOH-LP Channel 29 and W35AX Channel 35 in Cleveland*) thought immediately, "Let's get on the game show band wagon." They called me in and said, "Look, the movie show has been steadily losing money. We have an idea. We want to produce a live game show to cash in on the popularity of this *Who Wants to Be a Millionaire*. It'll be a call-in show with contestants on the phone. And we want to do this two hours a night, five nights a week, live."

Five nights a week! Immediately the calculator starts going off in my head. Oh man, what a payday this is going to be! But they turned around and said, "We'll continue to give you your regular pay." I said, "Wait a minute. You're paying me for a two-hour slot, but you want me to do five nights for two hours for the same money? Can't do it."

Fortunately for me, within about a week or two of talking about this, they came to their senses and realized five nights a week was completely nuts. See, their perspective was, they had live deejays on their talk radio station that were doing four-hour shifts six days a week. Why couldn't some guy do TV two hours, five nights a week? That was their idea. In reality, that would have been the biggest burnout that ever happened.

But they still wanted to produce the show. What they said at that point was, "Why don't you drop the movie show? Because we feel it's not as important as it used to be. We want you to focus all your attention on the game show. In between games, you can still show your little skits and stuff." My answer was, "Without the movie show, why do you need me then? Why not get some guy in a suit and tie? The whole point of me is the movie show." They said, "We're not going to pay you for two shows." So instead of five nights a week, they decided to do it one night a week. They were unsure whether they wanted to make it an hour show or a two-hour show, but it was going to be called *The Son of Ghoul's House of Fun and Games*.

So we tried three trial nights. The first night (*August 30, 2000*), I did an hour. The second night, I did an hour and a half. The third night we did two hours, and I took Fidge with me just for the hell of it, just to break up the monotony. Having him there turned into the biggest goof, because not only could he not hear the answers, he had absolutely no idea what to write on the scoreboard. Now we were live, so we had contestants on the phone. And once I started goofing on him, you could hear these people laughing over the air. So I thought to myself, "This is kind of working. In some odd way, this is working."

So we did the three shows, and management said, "We think you should have the midget all the time. He was a scream." And compared to the first two shows, he was a scream. It was different, since now I had somebody to play off of. It wasn't just a straightforward game. It was better for me. That was my Abbott and Costello thing. I never really wanted to have a co-host, and I didn't consider him a co-host. I considered him a crewmember. But we got locked in on the game show and it made us seem like a team.

A sidekick…

Exactly. But I referred to him as a kickstand, rather than a sidekick. Boy, I used get so annoyed picking him up to go to the game show. There were many weeks during the 45-minute ride to the station where I wouldn't speak to him the whole time. I was so annoyed that he didn't have a license. I had to go pick him up and take him everywhere he went. Anyway, once they wanted him on the game show, then I negotiated for him to get paid. They said, "We're not going to pay him what we pay you." I said, well, I hope not. But you've got to give the guy something. Give him 50 bucks a week, anything.

There were a number of people who called in regularly to the show who became characters themselves, and they would keep you up to date on their lives, almost like a local television diary.

Yeah. And the funny thing about it was, I'd get people coming up to me saying, "I've been trying to call in for two months and I can't get a line to ring." And other people would call and get in every damn week. Every week! And yeah, we had regulars who called in for this dumb old game show. And for as crappy as it actually was there was something about it.

A community feel?
Yeah.

People did get to know each other on the air.

Exactly. So much TV is just mechanical now. Even with news crews. You've got these news crews come on who are so far removed from the public. You would never get a chance to talk to them. And they're so plastic with their presentation. We scripted nothing. I probably made more mistakes and flub-ups, and uttered mispronounced words, than any other host in the country … on a continuous basis.

The game show was on Wednesday night. Thursday and Friday night, the station played my movie show. So that was a total of six hours every week. My face probably had more screen time than all these people. It was a two-hour game show. And I would say all but maybe 15 minutes of those two hours was stuck on my mug.
And that was for three, three and a half years?
Yeah, yeah.

You did the game show as long as Ernie Anderson/Ghoulardi did his show back in the 1960s.

Exactly. Now, the game show was fun. But again, it was lack of revenue. The station, being a small, low-watt outfit, had a home shopping network that bought time on

A moment of peace in a decades-long feud—Keven Scarpino and Ron Sweed at a Parma Animal event, May 3, 2003. Another local celeb, "Jungle Bob" Tuma, stands to their right.

green blackboard in the hallway that went right back to his office. I glanced up, and right there in white chalk he wrote on his blackboard, "FIDGE RULES." So I thought, "Oh I got this gig." I didn't really know, but I went in and asked what he wanted. They wanted me to put on three stage shows a day: Friday, Saturday and Sunday for the entire month of October, including Halloween night, a total of 17 nights.

I had never really done a stage show at that point. But I figured this couldn't really be that hard, could it? They loved the idea of Fidge; they loved Fidge. The first show was on a Thursday night and was open only to the park employee's families. It was a real thin crowd that first night and it was real stiff. We didn't have it down yet. That whole first weekend, it was kind of weird, real half-assed crowds.

The second weekend, the weather was warming up, and the park's just packed, lots of people. And I'm wheeling through; I'm not in make-up or anything. I'm just wheeling through. And when I rounded that corner to where the theater was, it just stopped me in my tracks. There was at least 350 people standing in line for at least half an hour, waiting to get into this thing. And I was just, "Oh my God!"

We had two weeks of standing room only. We did 18 shows to standing room only. It went great. The manager of the park loved Fidge so much. Fidge wasn't really that big a part of the stage show. He came out and did a couple of things. He might have been on the stage for 10 minutes. Fidge did *Fidge's Fables* and sang "Monster Mash." That was about it.

When it was decided he would do "Monster Mash," we realized there would be no way he could do it live on stage. So we decided to record it, and just let him lip synch it. It took him 70 takes to get through the song, 70 takes. And believe me, I was ripping the rest of my hair out of my head over that.

The Six Flags shows were really nice for Fidge. Down here in Massillon, none of the locals saw my TV show. Nobody carried the station. So he had no idea of the

the weekends. And they had three different infomercial companies that bought big chunks of airtime, a lot of time and a year at a time. What I later found out was that the revenue from those infomercials and the home shopping on the weekends was actually paying my salary. That's how they could keep it afloat. All at once, all three of those accounts decided not to renew their contracts for the following year. They lost all that revenue. At that point, they put the brakes on everything! We had to stop the game show.

Weren't you were invited to produce a stage show at Six Flags for their October 2002 Halloween season?

We had a local amusement park in Aurora, Ohio called Geauga Lake Sea World, and they sold out to Six Flags, who closed down half the park and revamped the other half. I had a website up by that time, and I got an email from the general manager of the park. Aurora cable carried our show, and he watched. Loved Fidge ... loved him. He emailed me, about some possible Halloween appearances at the park. Would I be interested?

So I drove up for a meeting. When I went into the office, I see the guy there in charge of the park had this viewer response. But people up north saw it. And it was really cool when he finally got to go to Six Flags. People would stick around to get autographs, whole families.

One guy brought his kid in. He had a speech impediment. And Fidge talked a little funny. The guy said, "We brought him to meet you because he can relate to you." It was big thing for that kid to meet Fidge. I was so glad the little guy got to see the love from the people, and he got a feel for the effect he had on them. He had no clue up until then. So he did get to see that, and that was good.

When he died, I at first had no idea. We didn't hang out socially. It was a Monday afternoon when the phone rang. It was some guy from town here. "Keven, did you hear about Ronnie?" I said, what? What did he do now? "Well, he passed, man. He passed away." What! He's dead? What happened?! "He was at the bar, and some people were feeding him alcohol. It's all cloudy, we're still not sure."

This is Monday afternoon at four o'clock. We've got to hit the air Wednesday night with the game show. What am I going to do? I immediately called the Klaus family. I said, hey, man, Fidge died. What are you going to do? Well, obviously I've got to put together some kind of tribute for him. I mean, I've got to do something. We can't just go on with, here's the game! Here we go!

So I got virtually no sleep from that point on. I went downstairs and started pulling out tapes. I can remember getting all done with the editing, and I was just kind of numb from it all. It was Tuesday afternoon, and the show was going on the air Wednesday night. I had a moment there where it all caught up with me. I kind of broke down a little bit.

Goddamn! I felt really pissed because after all that time and effort, feeding him lines, getting his little act together ... everything was in vain. It was all flushed down the toilet. How do you start over now? How do you turn around and make it different? Then I had to sit back and think how I'd done 9 1/2 years without the guy. Let's just go back to the roots, you know? At that point, I had to become the buffoon again. I had to do Bud Abbott *and* Lou Costello at the same time.

I can see that. When you were partnered with Fidge, you assumed the role of the straight man, or the adult.

When Fidge passed away, we did the tribute show. At that point the Klaus family announced that they was going to get a replacement for Fidge. They put the show on hiatus, that's what they said. They had wanted me to stop the movie show once they started the game show. But I told them the only way I'd do the game show is if they kept the movie show on. Then when they decided to stop the game show, they assumed I would take the movie off to continue working. Because when the game show stopped, the money stopped. That's what they said.

But at that point, I was so close to 20 years on the air. And my goal was to go 20 years. I was doing a lot

T-shirt art for Son of Ghoul

of appearances, a lot of conventions and I was actually making a pretty good business selling DVDs. And they knew the viewers were still there. So the station managed to devalue the show, but they kept it on.

What do you feel is going to happen once the last connection to the Ghoulardi legacy disappears from the air? And how do you feel about your place in that legacy?

I think once it all comes to an end, in this day and age, the way television is today; it's all going to be down to dollars and cents. When the new management came into FOX 8, the first thing they wanted to do was "get rid of the old guy." The "old guy" was Dick Goddard, who was a staple around here for years, doing the weather. They had no idea of the impact he had in the area, no idea.

They were ready to shuck Chuck and John, too. I think that's another reason Chuck's kind of thinking about retiring. I don't really understand, but Chuck's my buddy now. It occurred quite suddenly. It took 20 years. It was a hard thing, man. I grew up watching my favorite local television idols, people you feel like you know because you seen them so long, Not being accepted by them was really a kick in the groin.

Chuck has over 40 years on the air. If there's anyone who's going to have an appreciation for the Cleveland host legacy, it's going to be him. I'm sure he sees the fondness you have for all of this.

You know, when Chuck says he's close to Ernie, I don't think they fully understand it. Chuck really loved Ernie as a person. I have to tell you, I once sat next to Chuck in a theater during a screening of some of the old Ghoulardi footage. A clip came on, and when Ernie laughed on-screen, Chuck literally wiped a tear out of his eye. It really meant something to Chuck; you know what I mean?

I've always been very respectful around him. And we've done enough appearances together now that I don't think there's going to be any problem now. Maybe it's good it took this long, since it made the 20th anniversary something that much more special. Maybe if we'd all been a happy family 10 years ago, it wouldn't have had the same impact.

The 20 years for me has been an intense roller coaster ride. You climb that hill, you get to the top and suddenly you're down in that dip, and you might be down in that dip for quite a while. And right when it seems like nothing's happening, and things are just stale and it's not fun anymore, I suddenly get a phone call saying, "Hey, would you like to come out to San Francisco for three days? We're going to fly you out, and put you up in a room, and pay you, and do appearances. We'll film some stuff." And you think, "God, life's pretty cool!"

Blood, Breasts and Beasts
Joe Bob Briggs (John Bloom)
Interviewed by Sandy Clark (2004)

Unlike most hosts of genre movies, the character of Joe Bob Briggs reflects less the people that inhabit the films he shows than the audience who watches them. *Dallas Times Herald* columnist John Bloom created Joe Bob Briggs in 1982 for the express purpose of giving critical respect to the exploitation movies ignored by the mainstream media. Though comically lowbrow and peppered with colorful cracker-isms, the goal, at least in part, was to raise the profile of filmmakers who dealt in the genuinely bizarre and often taboo subjects shunned by Hollywood.

In 1990, The Movie Channel secured Bloom's unique persona for *Joe Bob Briggs' Drive-In*. The show ran until 1996. The same year, Joe Bob was back on cable hosting *TNT's MonsterVision*, which ran until the year 2000.

A genuine expert on the extreme fringes of popular cinema, Bloom has contributed commentary tracks to several DVD releases, notably *Jesse James meets Frankenstein's Daughter* (1966), *The Incredibly Strange Creatures Who Stopped Living and Became Mixed-Up Zombies* (1964) and the notorious *I Spit on Your Grave* (1978).

John Bloom's extensive literary output includes *Iron Joe Bob* (1992), *Profoundly Disturbing: Shocking Movies That Changed History!* (2003) and *Profoundly Erotic: Sexy Movies That Changed History* (2005).

Even without a wealth of historical cinematic analysis to point to, Bloom's name would be forever enshrined in the Great Hall of Popular Culture for introducing the term "aardvarking" to the vast library of sexual intercourse synonyms.

What is a horror host? How would define it?

Actually, there are two different kinds of horror hosts. First there are those that make fun of the movie. You know, who use the movie to bounce off comedy sketches. And then there are those that love the movies. Now, I try to do both. I love the movies. We always start with the idea you got to respect the movies. We got to love the movies; we've got to respect the genre. But some of them are so bad; we've got to love them in a tongue-in-cheek sort of way. But I don't like a horror host that just puts down the movie, where every routine is just a way to put down the movie. Some of them don't even appear to have watched the movie and they don't celebrate the genre. I mean, we have to celebrate the genre; we have to love the horror movie itself. So I like the kind of hosting that can go either way, but is basically affirmative towards the movie.

How much an element of fun should a horror host have? Should they ever be serious, or should they always be fun and lighthearted?

It depends on what you mean by fun. Some very serious things are a lot of fun. Sometimes they're intense. I mean, I did a DVD hosting of *I Spit on Your Grave* (1978). There's a 25-minute rape sequence and I was speaking during the entire rape sequence. You have to do a little bit different take on how you talk about it, how you deal with it when you're doing a movie like that.

When did you first become aware of the genre? When did you start getting into it, and what was life like for young John Bloom, sneaking out to movies and what have you?

I actually was a newspaper reporter and I was trying to finish a book. I wasn't working at any particular publication. I was trying to finish a book I was working on, a true crime book. In order to have a job where I could just stay in one place for a long time while I finished this book, I took this film critic's job. The film critic job was open at the *Dallas Times-Herald*. And I didn't realize it was a sought-after job. Actually, my friend was the Features Editor. And I said, "Hey, can I just do this until I finish this book?" (*Laughs*) So I started. I liked films, but I didn't set out to be a film critic.

And so, as I started out watching films every week, there were basically two kinds that I liked. I liked the foreign films. And the reason for that is, by the time a foreign film gets to the US, it's just the top one percent of foreign product that comes over here. We always get the best ones. And then the other thing I like are the exploitation films. And the way I started getting interested in them is this. I would see the ads for the film. They would always be playing at the drive-in, and no one would review them. And no one would screen them, no one! You couldn't find a review. Maybe *Variety* would do a review. No one else would do a review. And so I started calling up the distributors and saying, "I want to see these movies in advance." And they'd say, "Are you kidding? We never screen these things for critics. No way!"

215

John Bloom assumes a culturally significant pose in the guise of drive-in critic, Joe Bob Briggs.

So I started going to the drive-in to watch the films. And at that time I created Joe Bob Briggs as a way to have a populist appreciation of that type of film. I mean, I'm talking about *Dr. Butcher M.D.* (*Zombi Holocaust*, 1980)*, Graveyard Tramps* (*Invasion of the Bee Girls*, 1973)—"They Bite, They Squeeze, They're Ready to Please!" Remember that poster? I think the first film I did was *The Grim Reaper* (*Anthropophagus*, 1980*)*, which was an Italian cannibal film. These films, when they were mentioned at all by film critics, were mentioned with a sneer or with a call for censorship. So, there were really only a couple of guys in the country that reviewed these movies, and the other two were fanzines. So I started reviewing them with love, you know, with celebration. And giving the ratings for what people want in these moves, the three Bs—"Blood, Breasts and Beasts."

The one guy who would screen the movies for me was Roger Corman, because I met Roger Corman at an early stage and I said, Roger, what do you put into your movies? And he says, "Oh, that's very interesting that you should ask me that, John." And then he goes into exactly what he puts into the movies. He was very scientific about it. He had a very specific idea of exactly how much nudity he wanted, exactly how much action he wanted, exactly what he wanted before the titles, exact rules about when the movie was over. And I sort of took those and I dressed them up, you know, as the three Bs—Blood, Breasts and Beasts. Because that's basically what he told me. Many of the elements I developed as the standard for the drive-in movie were sort of taken from the Roger Corman formula. I added to it over time. Roger's not a big kung fu guy, for example. He made a series of martial arts movies with Don Wilson. But he doesn't really gravitate towards martial arts. So I went elsewhere for my martial arts information.

At any rate, I developed it in that way, as a way to celebrate this movie genre that I genuinely loved. I loved the movies. They were never boring. It was a little like professional wrestling. They were always taking issues that were in the news and exaggerating them and doing them in an interesting way. And many of those movies that I saw early on as a critic were eventually stolen and made into A movies. *I Spit on Your Grave* became *The Accused* (1988), with Jodi Foster, and [she] won the Academy Award for Best Actress. The only difference between *I Spit on Your Grave* and *The Accused* is that in *The Accused*, the legal system takes the revenge. And the legal system doesn't work as well as the girl with the axe, in the original version. *The Great Texas Dynamite Chase* (1976) became *Thelma and Louise* (1991) and also won an Academy Award. Same exact plot, except in *The Great Texas Dynamite Case*, they don't drive of a cliff at the end. I mean, the examples are abundant and form an ongoing pattern.

So these movies, once despised, become classic plots that … well, it's like a reverse food chain. The ideas move *up* instead of down, as it's perceived to be. These guys are perceived to be rip-off artists. You know, that they take big popular ideas and rip them off. Sometimes they do. But also it works in the other direction.

What type of thinking went into your show then? What did you know you were going to have to include to take it from print to TV?

Well, really, the show happened more or less by accident. The Movie Channel had a show on Friday nights called *Drive-In Theater*, and they had guest hosts every week or month. And they invited me to be one of the guest hosts. I came back two or three times. I forget where they'd seen me. They'd seen me onstage, or seen some writing that I'd done. And so, after about the fourth month I just became permanent. It was almost like osmosis. I don't even remember making a big deal out of doing a contract or anything. I mean, I think I was on two years before there was any kind of formal (*laughs*) agreement.

And the show just grew organically. I mean, originally, it was just *me* talking straight to the camera for a minute and a half. Then it became me in a big chair talking straight to the camera for two minutes. Then it was me in a chair in a trailer house talking to the camera for three minutes. Then it was me in a chair with a trailer house and occasionally a bimbo would come on with me as a sidekick. And then occasionally we would have a guest. I mean, it was like the opposite of the way you normally do TV. It was like, hey, let's add this, let's add that. And so over time it just became a show.

The technical term for it in cable is "interstitial programming," for which there is no category. The writer's guild or the director's guild doesn't even have that category. It's like it doesn't exist, you know. We were nominated twice for a Cable Ace, but we were up against, like, a Discovery Channel five-minute short on cockroaches or something, you know? (*Laughs*) That was the closest form of programming to which we corresponded.

So how much control over the content did you have? Was it all you, anything you wanted to say you could pretty much get away with?

Yeah, pretty much I had total control over content. I had very few disagreements at The Movie Channel. I mean, it's premium cable, so they don't have the normal limitations you have on language and taste, although we did have a "Too Grisly for Cable" list. There were some movies they wouldn't show even on premium cable. *Texas Chain Saw Massacre* was on that list for along time. *Demons* (*Dèmoni*, 1985), I think, is still on that list; the Alberto Bava film from the mid-1980s. And *I Spit on Your Grave* was on that list.

But as far as what I said, we only had about three or four knock down, drag out fights. I remember one year. We always did a Christmas special where we made fun of Christmas. One year I had this ecumenical gathering in a bar, with a Baptist preacher and this Jewish rabbi and a Catholic priest and a Unitarian feminist, discussing the meaning of Christmas. And the Baptist preacher and the Jewish rabbi get into a fistfight when the Baptist preacher says they killed the Jews, that the Jews killed Jesus. And so we filmed the thing at great expense. I had written the whole thing. It got back to New York. We filmed it in Dallas and it got back to New York. They said, "We can't say that the Jews killed Jesus." I said we're not saying it. The redneck Baptist preacher is saying it. And they said, "Well, we can't say that." I said, it was in the script. You should have objected to it at script level. He said, "Well, since we should have objected to it at script level, we will actually pay for the whole re-shoot. So you can do your Christmas special if you just have the fist fight but don't say the Jews killed Jesus." So we had to re-shoot the whole thing. But it was that kind of thing. It wasn't any ongoing battle over language. That came later at TNT. They were much tighter about what you could say on TV.

How did you end up doing the show at TNT?

Well, I was on The Movie Channel for nine years, and then they changed formats and went in a different direction. So we parted ways. I was unemployed for four months, and then TNT called and said, "We want you to come over here and do something similar." And so I started … I essentially … took the same set. (*Laughs*) We didn't even build a new set. I said, here, I'll save you some money. I have this trailer; I have some chairs. I have all this stuff in a warehouse, you know? I mean, it was even the same La-Z-Boy recliner. I think we dressed it up a little bit.

We essentially just moved the show from The Movie Channel over to TNT. They were much better at tricking up the show with production elements, with graphic elements, shooting nice professional video and everything. It wasn't quite as on the fly as we'd done it at The Movie Channel. But as part of Turner Entertainment, they had a long list of things that you couldn't say on TV. They had an actual list of words you couldn't use. And I'm proud to say some of them of them were nonsense words that I invented that would end up on the list. (*Laughs*)

Such as?

I used to use the term "slope-head" to mean a stupid person, you know. And suddenly slope-head is on the list. I said, why would you put slope-head on the list? And it was like, "We think it's offensive to Asians." And I said, no, that's slant-eye! That's slant-eye. *That's* offensive to Asians. Slope-head is a completely different concept. But they were, like, "No, slope-head is an offensive Asian …" I said, no! You confuse slant-eye with slope-head. Now look it up in H.L. Mencken; he wrote these all down in the 1920s. But, please … They would never admit … I said, no, I invented slope-heads. Slope-heads is a new one. They said, "Well, you still can't say it."

Oh … the word lesbian. You couldn't say the word lesbian. First it was just lesbo. I would say lesbo, and they'd say, "You can't say lesbo." And I'd say, you know, the word lesbo comes from the Isle of Lesbos. It's very close to the origin of Sappho—Lesbos. They didn't buy that and they banned lesbo. So I just started saying lesbian. It would be in the script, lesbian. I'd say lesbian. So they banned lesbian. It turned up on the list! I said, lesbian, the word lesbian … what if you're talking about Melissa Etheridge, you know? What in the world?"

How can you ever talk about the whole concept, the whole sexual concept of lesbianism if you can't use the word lesbian? They actually banned the word lesbian. I noticed other people on the network using it. I think it was banned just for my show. (*Laughs*) They were very sensitive and I never knew why. I talked to their lawyers several times and at one time one of the lawyers said they were always in fear of Congressional legislation that would limit cable in some way. So they tried to keep it as clean as possible. I said, you know, it's like, we're always going to be behind HBO. It's like, as long as you don't get up to the level of *Def Comedy Jam*, what's the danger?

Did they have trouble with "aardvarking" as a phrase?

"Aardvarking" I always got away with, partly because no one was ever quite sure what I meant by it. We would continue to get mail. "What's aardvarking," you

Joe Bob Briggs presented the charmingly inept *Jesse James Meets Frankenstein's Daughter* (1966) on a 2003 DVD release.

know? And I would always just say, well, if your mother didn't tell you, I'm not going to be the first. Originally the reason I invented all those words is that there were a lot of things … the most restrictive environment of all is the daily newspaper. You know, you really just can't say anything in there. And so the reason I invented all the words, like "aardvarking," was to have a nonsense word that everybody gets but you don't get in trouble. So that's how I started out doing that in the first place.

Were you still doing anything in print while you were on the air?

Oh, yeah, I continued. I had a syndicated column for years, *Joe Bob Goes to the Drive-In*.

How much cross-pollination was there?

Oh, all the time. I was stealing all the time from myself. It's like, I was doing *MonsterVision* and I would be on four hours a night, every commercial break, 52 weeks a year. No breaks. I forget what it comes out to. There's something like nine commercial breaks in a movie, then there's space between the movies. You end up being on, like, 25 times in the night, then 52 times in the year. And these Weenie sit-com writers complain having to do 26 22-minute shows per year. It's, like, we did 22 minutes five times a week. And all the shows were scripted. Because the show devoured material, we couldn't keep up with it. I was always taking things from my columns and saying, "Okay, that's pretty funny. We'll convert that into a little monologue or a little rant. And then for the commercial breaks I'd get most of the information from the movie itself. I would watch the movies very closely.

Did you pretty much write everything yourself, or did you have a staff of writers?

I wrote everything myself at The Movie Channel. And I wrote everything for myself for the first year at TNT, until it got overwhelming. And then I got my writing assistant. But even the writing assistant was still using mostly my original material to put the scripts together. And I was watching every movie, because I still think the great thing about movie hosting, especially on a commercial station, is that it's one of the rare times—this is prior to DVDs—where you can watch the scene and then immediately talk about that specific scene. So I liked to take advantage of that and speak directly to what was going on in the film right then.

I love DVD commentaries for the same reason. I've been doing a lot of those. It's rare that you can get that close to what you want to talk about. So it made it more entertaining. Of course, it's very time consuming to go through a movie in that much detail, and study it in such a way that you pull out those gems. I mean, the greatest thing you can do is point out something in a movie that the person saw but didn't realize what they saw. Because people are always deceiving themselves about what they see in a movie.

For instance, a very common thing is somebody getting stabbed in a scene, but when they shot the scene, they have to shoot it several times. So if you look closely, they'll have a little residual blood *before* they get stabbed on their shirt. It was cleaned off from three previous stabbings. You know, things like that. People love those little details about the making of the movie and the background of the people in the movie.

Along the lines of the instantaneous comment, how do you feel about what Joel Hodgeson and the Mystery Science Theater 3000 *people do? Do you think that was stepping over the line in terms of mocking the movies?*

Well, they were set up specifically to mock the movies. So their show was more about the characters watching the movie than the movie. I like that, I appreciate it. It's not technically horror hosting, though. It's more like a whole new art form of itself that's a crossbreed. So yeah, I always enjoyed their show. And that's the sort of thing that I would do with some of the total turkeys we had. I'm sure when they were choosing their movies they were looking for turkeys. We were always *not* looking for turkeys. If we got stuck with turkeys we would go in that direction, but were trying to get the best possible cult movie that we could find.

Commander USA was pretty contemporary to what you were doing, over on the USA network. Did you ever notice that show at all?

No, I never watched it.

How about Elvira? Had you seen any of her hosted stuff?

Well, she was definitely iconic when she did my show. I don't recall how long she was on the air. But I think, like, three years, four years, something like that. She wasn't on the air that long, but seemed to get bigger after she was off the air. Elvira—Cassandra Peterson—is basically an actress. And she had done the let's-make-fun-of-the-movie kind of shtick, and also let's-make-fun-of-my-Mae-West-persona kind of shtick. So hers was a sort of self-contained act that she took to Knott's Berry Farm and other places where she performs as Elvira.

So it wasn't strictly horror hosting as I think of horror hosting, in the tradition of Zacherley. It was more like she was the event, Elvira herself, bigger than life. And then she went on to do movies as Elvira. So yeah, she was an icon. She was almost like a comic book heroine by the time she was on the show that I did with her. And I tried to write some stuff that played up to that.

Rhonda Shear was the same way. I later did a show where Rhonda Shear appeared. And I said, Rhonda, I'm going to write this stuff for you—like Mae West. And she said, "Yeah, that'd be good!" I said, okay, that's what I thought, a Mae West kind of thing. So, yeah, Rhonda sort of did the same thing—the sex bomb that's hanging around the movie, rather than be the explicator of the movie. You didn't really get the impression that Rhonda watched the movie. Who else...?

John Stanley...

Ah! John Stanley is probably the most knowledgeable of all horror hosts. In terms of what's in his head, and how many he's watched, and his sort of balanced view of them, he probably knows more about horror movies than any person alive. He's basically a writer, as opposed to a performer. But he's great. He should have a show somewhere, because he's sort of the intellectual of the group, just in terms of what he knows.

Do you have any sort of special affinity for him, since he did come from a writer's background – and you come from a writer's background?

Just that I love his book, *The Creature Feature (Movie) Guide* and *The Creature Feature (Movie) Guide Strikes Back*. I don't know how many versions of it he's had. Apparently—I've never quite understood—they're self-published or something and you can only buy them from this one place in Northern California or something.

Count Floyd.

Count Floyd. I had Count Floyd on the show, on *MonsterVision*. Actually, I had Rhonda Shear and Count Floyd at the same time. It was the first time Joe Flaherty had done Count Floyd in years and years and years. It was still funny as hell, because he gets the essence of being a horror host. He knows how kind of stupid it is on some level, you know? So his Count Floyd is really good. He's the most famous horror host who's never hosted a horror film.

At the two extremes, I think, you have John Stanley at one extreme as totally being about the movie. And at the other extreme you have Count Floyd, where there are no movies. (*Laughs*) And all the rest of us are on some spectrum in between. I tend to be closer to John Stanley, in terms of celebrating the movie, playing off the movie, making the material respond to the movie. All of this, of course, is deadly boring stuff, except to those of us creating the show. And as you get up closer to the Count Floyd level, you get your Elviras and Rhonda Shears, who are doing comedy.

Do you see a lineage of how horror hosting moved across the country, or any sense of the waves and how they may have influenced each other over time? You had hosts on your show from pretty much every generation.

Well, you can't really say there's any development in the art of horror hosting. The truth is that the only time hosts ever get hired, especially late-night hosts, is when the station or network wants to do something really cheap and has no other choice. It's the cheapest form of programming you can do. It's just one guy speaking straight to camera. Then you can get as elaborate as you want with what you put around the guy. Often, when you have a new cable channel that has no money, they'll frequently employ hosts, because it's the cheapest thing they can do.

I mean, if you look at the development of MTV, for example. Originally, all they had was vee-jays and videos. And people still think of MTV as videos, even though they don't run many videos at all any more. And they don't have many vee-jays anymore, in terms of the classic vee-jay. People think of them that way, because that's how they started. But they started that way 'cause the station was cheap! No programming. So you can't make any generalizations. A host can pop up anywhere. And it's usually on some place that's hurting financially. (*Laughs*)

Another angle of being the host is to build station identity. Did you ever get the sense of building station—or in your case, network— identity?

I think I did build up network identity at both places. But most local stations don't want to build up station identity. They'd rather be an affiliate, because there are all kinds of financial advantages to doing that—being middle-of-the-road, to not be too distinctive. I think that's what eventually ended Fritz the Nite Owl's show in Columbus. He was just too distinctive. Even though he still had a following, and he was still beloved there, the station wanted to be more standardized.

You know, all these things depend on who's the director of programming. Who's the vice-president in charge of development? It's going to be that one guy, or two guys or three guys. And they either like you or they don't. And if they don't like you, eventually you'll be fired. I've been fired many times. And if they like you, you'll have, like, a good time. (*Laughs*) We're not in charge. We the hosts; we're not in charge.

Let me continue on that thread. Do you think this change in programming has hurt local TV? Do you think we've lost something by losing the locality of local television?

Well, I'm not as sentimental about local TV as most people are, because I think it just reflects what's happening in the whole country. The whole idea of being local just doesn't exist anymore. It's just the United States. I mean,

I go to every city in the country. I would say 95% of those cities are exactly alike. The airport is exactly the same, the downtown is exactly same, the old slum that they turned into a tourist district is exactly the same—Courtyard on the Square Plaza or whatever they call it. River Place or whatever, they all have the same things. It's like there are three or four distinctive cities in America and everything else is homogenized.

Well, all these TV stations just represent the same concept as the mall. The mall in Minneapolis is the same as the mall in Atlanta, in the same way that TV stations are the same everywhere. We've become like Germany where, yes, they have some traditions—Bavaria is a little different from Hamburg and Hamburg is a little different from Frankfurt—but ... not really. The United States has become very federal, very homogeneous. And so, the TV stations are that way, too. Now having said that, if you do manage to slip something in that's really, really quirky, it almost always works. You'll eventually get fired doing it. That's what I've done my whole career. It's like I get the quirky unexpected thing onto the air or into the newspaper or whatever. It's very popular, and it eventually gets me fired.

So there is a longing for that time when there was more individuality in the places around the country. You see it in little doses, like, in places like Austin, which is just as homogenized as everywhere else. But the city keeps vestiges of the old Austin around, so that they can feel special. Madison, Wisconsin, you know, there's a similar kind of thing. Chapel Hill, North Carolina. You have these little pockets where locals try to keep their distinctive flavor. And those are places you can go and do a quirky character and be accepted as a celebrity. It's harder to do it in, like, Omaha.

There's one more area I'd like to cover. What were your childhood influences? When did you discover horror movies? What was the routine? Was there a certain theater that you went to regularly? Were there any horror films that stood out?

I didn't watch horror movies when I was a young kid. It wasn't a really big thing in our family, but we weren't really allowed to see anything that was scary. I tended to want to see the comedies and those were not controversial within the household. I didn't start watching horror movies till later. I remember one of the first ones that really scared me was a movie that's not the favorite of anyone except me, *Wolfen* (1981), which was the first movie to use the Steadicam. It's a movie about these supernatural wolves that roam around the Bronx, and the story is told

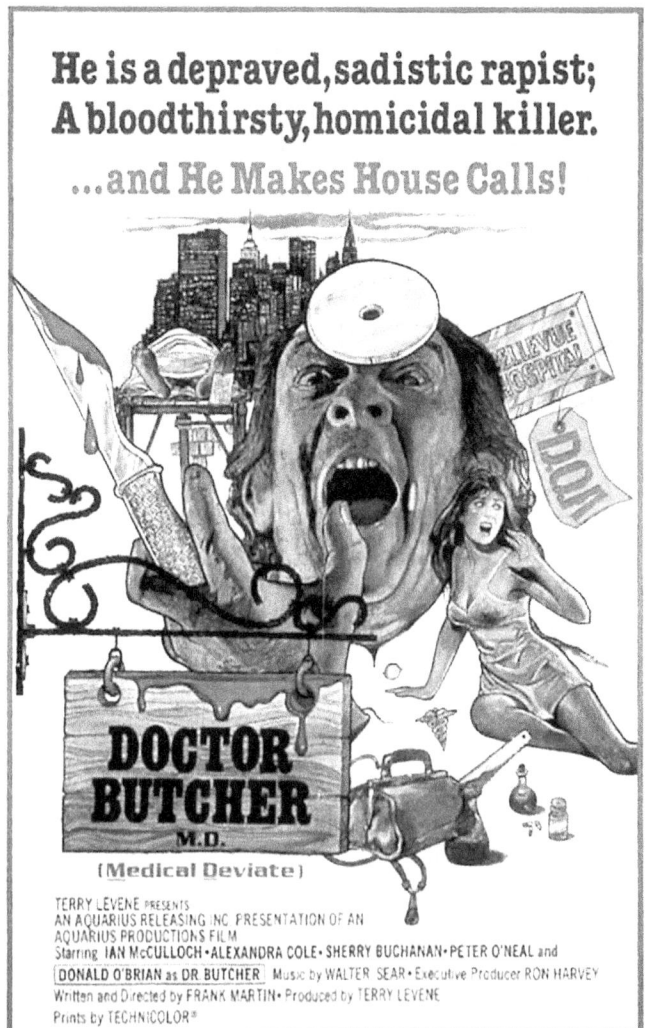

***Doctor Butcher—M.D.** (**Zombi Holocuast**, 1980), one of the films that inspired John Bloom to create his populist film critic, Joe Bob Briggs.*

from wolf eye level. There was something about that movie that just scared me to death. And part of it was the shock of never having seen the Steadicam. I didn't even know what the Steadicam was. That motion you get from the Steadicam. You know, we accept the Steadicam now as just a part of life. They use it all the time, just for people walking down the street having a conversation. It's not even considered a special effects camera anymore. But when it first came out it was a roller-coaster effect, and that scared me for some reason.

Did you review anything that you've come to love? Any films over the years that you would never have seen had you not been making the effort to review these films?

Oh yeah, there are a lot of films that I probably wouldn't have come across if I didn't seek them out as a reviewer, such as the Italian horror film. I probably

Joe Bob Briggs holds court over a gathering of TV hosts—Big Wilson and Zacherley (standing); Stella and Fritz the Nite Owl (sitting).

wouldn't have ventured deeply into Italian horror unless I had been looking for these titles—Dario Argento, Lucio Fulci and Mario Bava. Oddly enough, these Italian guys, they feel insecure about their place in the horror pantheon. Even though I think much of their work is superior to American work that was being done at the same time. But they don't look at it that way. They always wanted to be American filmmakers. They always wanted to have their movies accepted in America.

You'll notice in a lot of movies, like *House By the Cemetery* (*Quella Villa Accanto al Cimitero*, 1981), they'll put a carton of Kellogg's Corn Flakes on the table, so you'll know that it's in America, even though it's not in America. It's in Italy. They were always trying to aspire to be Americans, or to make American horror films, or at least to crack the American horror market. Meanwhile, Italian filmmakers were doing more interesting things in many ways than the guys in America were doing. So, that was pleasant. Are you talking about films that I particularly liked?

Films that you particularly liked, but mostly ones that you hosted, or ones that you came in contact with through the hosting or the reviewing, films that you wouldn't have hit otherwise.

I was at the world premiere of *Basket Case* (1982), which was at the Cannes Film Festival in … I want to say … 1982, something like that. I think the only two people who reviewed it were Rex Reed and me, and we both liked it. *Basket Case*, I think, is just a work of genius. It has that John Waters quality, but it also has genuine horror effects. It has that cheesy New-York-as-the-armpit-of-the-universe look that was popular in the 1970s. You know, where New York looks like the worst cesspool in the world. And the film's funny; it's genuinely funny. So that's a film that I discovered as Joe Bob.

I still think that *Hellraiser* (1987) is one of the greatest films, genre or otherwise, that's ever been conceived. When I watch a film that goes in places where I can't predict, but makes logical sense, I am impressed. In other words, I don't know where I'm going on this wild ride, but when I get to the end of it, I know where I've been. That's what *Hellraiser* was for me. It was a great, amazing, original work. I've never seen another work of his (*Clive Barker*) that I've liked as much. And I actually didn't like turning Pinhead into a celebrity and all that. I didn't think that Pinhead was the point of the movie. So, that's definitely one of those films I discovered. I mean, there are many more.

Do you think there's been anything that's been lost or gained in horror movies over the years? Do you think the films getting made are any worse or better now?

No, I think 95% of all movies made are failures, whether it's horror movies or any other kind of movies. But it depends on what you mean by horror movies. For example, do you include David Cronenberg as a great horror director? His movies have gotten more and more scary, more and more bizarre and more and more interesting over the years. But if you look at a filmmaker like George Romero, he's basically in the same place. If he made a horror movie today, the look would be pretty much like the film he made in 1967. So it depends on what level of horror you're talking about.

It seems there's been an influx of more mainstream movies that lean toward the slasher genre and away from the more cerebral stuff. The older hosts … well, they just don't identify with the movies that are getting made now.

"I did a DVD hosting of *I Spit On Your Grave* (1978). There's a 25-minute rape sequence in which I was speaking during the entire rape sequence. You have to do a little bit different take on how you talk about it, how you deal with it, when you're doing a movie like that."

Crematia Mortem, for instance, makes the point that one of the reasons her show went off the air was that was all they were left with.

Who?

Crematia Mortem, she was on in Kansas City. Kansas City is a place where you drive into town, there's all these billboards advertising churches. And she just felt she couldn't keep airing that stuff in town.

Well first of all, I would say I enjoy slasher films if they were well made. Just like I like any kind of film, if it's well made. The slasher film came about in 1978. The slasher film has been around a long time. People say, "Oh, everything is slasher now," as if it just came out yesterday. *Halloween*, that's the first slasher. You can even say 1974, for *The Texas Chain Saw Massacre* might be considered the first slasher film. You can find examples before then, but certainly you can in the 1970s.

The slasher is an established genre; it's been around for 25 years. What are they talking about, you know? That, oh, everything's slasher now? Where did they live the past 25 years? Slashers are *here*. There are good slasher films, and there are bad slasher films. There are extremely well made slasher films. There are slasher films so well made, they become A quality films, you know, and they win awards. So I don't think the existence or the non-existence of the slasher film means anything.

Now, starting in the 1990s, we had send-ups of the slasher films, starting with *Scream* (1996). So filmmakers couldn't make the sort of *Friday the 13th* (1980) slasher film any longer, because it was too much of a parody target. So we had this sort of self-referential period in horror that went on several years, and there wasn't anything new created. But everything is in cycles, and the special effects technology showing the classic crimes of men—meaning stabbing, knifing, shooting, maiming—will always be around. This idea that the slasher film is this unstylish thing that is going to pass, then we'll go back to some kind of classic film, is simply wrong.

The reason those classics films didn't have more gruesome horror is that the Hays Office existed in 1932. Otherwise, they would have had effects just as gruesome. It's just the fact that we can show those effects now. There will never be a time when we go back to the standards of *Frankenstein* and *Dracula*. I think that's crazy to think that we would. So, no, I don't think there's anything bad about the slasher film, or that it's ruined any kind of programming, or that it's somehow demeaned the horror hosting or anything else.

Your Old Pal, Zomboo!
Zomboo (Frank Leto)
Interviewed by Michael Monahan (2010)

Frank Leto returned from the first Gulf War with an appreciation for his own mortality and a renewed commitment to pursue his passions in life. One of these passions was television. While working at KOLO–TV 8 in Reno as a commercial producer, he had the opportunity to create a skit show for the station called *Coming Distractions* in 1997. This was popular enough for the management to suggest Leto as the star of a hosted horror show on Saturday nights.

In 1999, *Frank's House of Horror Movies* premiered, with Leto playing both "Frank," a floating head in a jar, and one of the castle occupants, Zomboo. Other characters involved with the various skits and blackout gags on the show were Miss Transylvania (*Maureen Allan*), Werewolfie (*a hand puppet styled after Soupy Sales' White Fang, created by Kathy Easly and controlled by Paul Dancer*), Quasi the Hunchback (*Oscar Alfaro*), and for a little added spice, The Rack Girl (*Bianca Paris*). Leto drew inspiration from his childhood heroes, Soupy Sales and John Zacherle, producing a program that was both macabre and blatantly silly.

Zomboo proved to be a breakout character, and with the second season, the character name replaced Frank's name in the show's title. Like most horror host shows still on the air, *Zomboo's House of Horror Movies* is forced to rely on public domain movies for content. But in the spirit of Soupy and Zach, he playfully tweaks the films by quickly cutting away for Zomboo one-liners or adding video and audio enhancements to a scene. In between the film, every sort of zany, corny, old-fashioned gag is pulled out, dusted off and delivered like a fresh crème pie to the face.

Frank Leto has used the show too as an opportunity to promote local charities, blood drives and organizations that provide support for children with special needs. For Leto, the most important lesson about living a life is giving back.

Can you talk a little about your background? What led you to broadcasting and why did you want to be a horror host. Did you grow up watching a horror host? What was so appealing about that specific genre?

I grew up on Long Island in New York. And at the time the big horror host program was Zacherley, John Zacherle, who did *Chiller Theater* for a year or two. That's where I became interested in the genre. I watched him for a couple of years. I loved horror movies and wanted to become a special effects technician when I graduated from college, something that never really happened. But I did go into film and television.

I started out in the aerospace business, and got a secret clearance. I was a suit. I did that for a couple of years. After getting shot at in the first Gulf War, I decided it was time to have some fun. When I came back, I just decided to get involved with local television. I followed that through and worked for the company that owned the *New York Times*.

I came out to Reno to work at KOLO, the ABC affiliate, and was a producer. I did commercials and special projects. I ended up running the department after being here for a couple of years. I like to think it was because I was good at what I did. You know, I'm the guy with the sense of humor and the East Coast work ethic. And everybody came to me because they knew that they could get the project done in a reasonable amount of time. So, one day the sales department approached me and said, "We have to compete with another hosted show." They didn't show horror movies, they basically showed *Matlock* and some other types of movies. But they said, "Come up with an idea." The three ideas we came up with at the time were Westerns, Charlie Chan and horror movies.

We couldn't do Charlie Chan, because that was copyrighted, and Turner had all of those films locked up. Westerns, you know, you can only watch those Gene Autry or Bob Steele movies so many times. And they're all the same. They go from point A to point B on their horse a couple of times and shoot a couple of people and go to jail, and that's about it. We decided there were a lot of horror movies out there. When we did the initial study we found that about 250 public domain movies exist. So we decided that, okay, this is what we're going to try. That was back in 1999. We started back then, and we've been every week since.

How many shows do you produce a year?

It depends. This year (2010) we kind of hit a brick wall, because I don't have the time. When we started out, we did 26 shows the first year. We did 26 shows the second year, and then it went down a little bit after that. We're in our 13th year now, and we've done about 160 shows. And they're all—amazingly and surprisingly—good quality. They all have some funny material in them, and they're all mostly entertaining. It's a good show. Some people who see it say it's the best one like it on TV, and we're very flattered by that. I love doing it, and it's what I look forward to doing. As the creative services production manager I have to do everyone else's stuff. But the caveat that lets me smile and get through all that is the opportunity to work on Zomboo at the end of the day or weekends, when I have the time.

The first season the program was titled Frank's House of Horror Movies. *What's the background there?*

I had a reputation in town. Any funny commercial that was done in Reno, pretty much, I did. And so they said, "Look, a lot of people know you because of the commercials and everything. So we're just going to call it *Frank's House of Horror Movies.* The original idea was that we had my head in a bell jar. The head nurse carried around this bell jar with the head in it, and I would come off with these one-liners. It was actually pretty neat. It was done with Photoshop and After-Effects, against a green screen. And it looked pretty good. But the problem was, it was just too much work. It took a long time to do all the jokes, and we couldn't do as many jokes as we wanted to.

We had other characters on the show. We had Miss Transylvania, we had the Rack Girl, we had Quasi and Werewolfie and Zomboo. Zomboo had a little role and he popped up a couple of times. After the first year, we just said, look, we don't have enough time to do this. We get the most comments for this guy, Zomboo. So let's incorporate him and make it *his* show. It took a little bit of persuasion. But finally everybody said okay, go with it. Because it was just too time-consuming to do the effects of my head in a bell jar, and it really wasn't that funny. Zomboo's like a clown when you see him. He's always getting beat up or taken advantage of. It was a wider range of a character that we could deal with and do a lot more with.

In designing the show, what influences did you draw on? Soupy Sales is pretty evident, but what about people like Zacherley? Ernie Kovacs?

Frank Leto as Reno's long-running horror host, Zomboo

We basically looked at what we could produce, and what we could do that would make people watch. We didn't try to mimic things. Yes, there was an influence from John Zacherle. And yes, there was an influence from Soupy Sales. There was an influence, possibly, from the Three Stooges and that kind of slapstick. But it was more, what do people want to see? What can we do with this vehicle? And we came up with audience participation. How do you do that? Well, you have people send in stuff. They send in pictures for the art gallery. And three-minute horror movies that they make themselves. We featured pretty girls, jokes, jokes that are innuendoes, double entendre. We included things like that. We figured if you combined all that stuff, you had a fighting chance to put on something that people would watch and enjoy.

It's clear you're reaching for a broad audience. The show is gently risqué, but definitely family friendly.

You've got to do that. I don't agree with these shows that have devil worship and Satanism. I just want to make people laugh and relax; let them be able to forget their problems at the end of the day. And if viewers need to have a bottle of beer, or a drink or something else to enjoy the show, that's great. It's there, and it is what it is. I think it's basically a formula that works. And I don't want to deviate from it because it *does* work.

In this way, with the regular cast of characters you have to shuffle around, it's unlike most other hosted programs that tend to have a single focal point. In that regard, it reminds me of Bullwinkle cartoons or maybe even a bit of Captain Kangaroo.

Zomboo puts the bite on Maureen Allan's Miss Transylvania. Allan also played The Head Nurse.

That was the other influence, *Rocky and Bullwinkle*—Jay Ward and Bill Scott. The double entendres there, I loved. I grew up with those and loved it.

To what extent was the design and structure of the show a personal or collaborative effort?

The same writers have written the show since the beginning. We've added some here and there, and we've lost some. But it's still the same core three people who write it. There's myself and there's Mel Hawes, who used to work with me over at Channel 8 and now works at IGT. And there's Lance Peterson, who also works at IGT as a writer. Those are the guys I write the show with. David Allen shoots the show; does all the effects. He does all the painting out of people in the real movie and creates the background so we can insert Zomboo in on the green screen. We have Paul Dancer, who plays the Angry Man Behind the Door; I can't say enough good things about. He's so funny and so talented, and that voice adds so much. You just laugh every time. You just know something stupid is going to happen. It sets you up, and it works. Paul is a terrific talent.

He's one of those classic Abbott and Costello type characters.

Right. He's like Stinky or Mike the Cop. Whenever they come in, you know there's going to be some kind of mayhem or problem or humor. It just works. We've been very lucky. I've been very thankful that I've been able to do this for as long as I have. We've been fortunate that everybody who's worked on the show since the beginning is basically still with us. I do get calls every now and then from people who want to get involved with the show, but we don't have time. We have regular jobs and responsibilities.

What elements were in place—in terms of character design and format—when you first rolled camera on the show and what's evolved over time?

In terms of evolution, I just think the production got better as we went along. It became easier to write the thing. I remember the first three or four shows we did, we had to crank them out in about a week, a week and a half. It was very difficult. When we got the first one, we went, oh, this is great! Now how are we gonna do the next one? It was a very ominous thing. But once you get in a groove with something, and surround yourself with talented people who are serious about the project, it just took off. It was easier to do every week.

And now, I go driving down the road and I come up with an idea. It just comes into my head and I get to work and write it down. And it's easy to write a skit around it. The set's the same, and everything else is the same. I think the biggest change has been that we've been able to take it from something that was very ominous—scary to do—to something that we were able to harness and produce most every week.

Who built the set?

We're lucky in Reno that we have a lot of casinos, and we have a local stage workers union. I asked the union for help. And basically what we did with them was that they built the set as part of the apprenticeship program. We bought the materials and they made the set. We were sanctioned by IATSE (*International Alliance of Theatrical Stage Employees*), so we are technically a union show. It just works out well. We traded services and everybody came together. The project was great, and it's a great set.

You have Elvira sitting in her beautiful little set there with the couch and the candelabra and it all looks very nice and perfect. Then you have ours, which is cheesy and looks like something from a sit-com in the 1950s. But that's what makes it work. My show would not work in a cathedral abbey or a real type haunted house, because it's basically slapstick humor.

I think you've touched on a quality of timelessness in the way the set looks and how you work in it.

You got the rack; you got the wall for a Frankenstein machine. You got the window where you can look up and see anything going on outside, and the wall where we put the pictures for the picture gallery. And you've got the door, where Paul Dancer comes! You've got everything you need!

How long does it take to put together a show? What is the general production schedule?

Basically, when we have time we do it. There are not a lot of movies left that I'd like to do. Stuff pops up now and again, but the quality of the pictures plays a big part. I mean, I won't do slasher films; I won't do a lot of sexually oriented stuff or devil worship. I try to keep away from that, because the show is basically slapstick, tongue-in-cheek humor. I don't want to mess with things I can't get away with in a family environment. I think that's one of the reasons the show works so well. The show contains pretty good humor. It's got some innuendoes in there, but it can be watched by all ages. A lot of families do watch the show. They write in and they say, like, "I watch the show with my son. I grew up in Cleveland and I remember Ghoulardi." Or, "I grew up in Tampa and I remember Dr. Paul Bearer. You're keeping the genre alive, and it's very funny."

And that's basically what I want to do. I won't do *Manos, Hands of Fate* (1966). I won't do a lot of this blood and guts stuff. You have to know the parameters that you're going to work within. Once you know that, you can come up with a good and interesting product that people will watch. But you go off into devil worship and Satanism, cutting off stuff and showing blood, some T&A, you're going limit yourself right away, because you're going to lose one segment of the population. Then when you show so much, you're going to lose something else. Why risk it? It's all a numbers game now, and you want to try to get as many people to watch as possible. Basically, that means you're going to try not to offend large numbers of people.

There's a genuine sort of innocence, a bubbly quality, in horror-hosted programming. The Universal films, the Hammer movies—those libraries were drying up. They were being bought up by cable. And the next wave of films that became available were the Friday the 13th *types, which are anathema to an atmosphere that's supposed to be playful. You can't go from some guy getting a hatchet in the face to a host saying, "Hey kids, welcome back!" It just doesn't work.*

Horror movies from Mexico were quality pictures. Anybody that knows film history knows it was Churubusco studios that wanted to make something like the Universal horror pictures. And they had to come up with something that didn't violate the copyright. They came up with their own werewolf characters, mummy characters and vampire characters. And then K. Gordon Murray, in this country, got the rights to them and dubbed them in English. Paul Frees did a lot of the voices—and of course he did a lot of voices on the Jay Ward–Bill Scott *Bullwinkle* show. It's amazing when you look at the whole big picture and see the interaction between so many big things at the time. They were very successful. I liked them, too.

The minute you put a wrestler together with a vampire, you know something's going to happen.

That's right.

You reuse the same clips over and over again in your set-ups, which make an audience laugh, because it's so obvious. It becomes a joke all by itself.

Yeah, because you know that something stupid is going to happen. It's a great set up because it does trigger some sort of emotional response, hopefully on your funny bone. I always loved the Three Stooges. When I write, I try to go from one gag, or one joke, to the next. You know

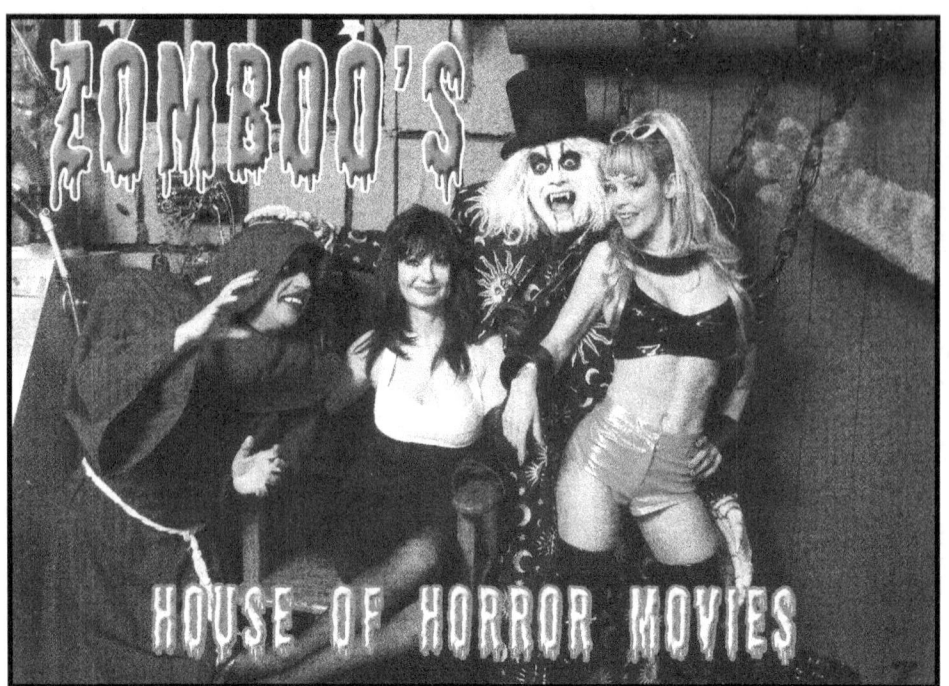

The cast of *Zomboo's House of Horror Movies*—Quasi, Miss Transylvania, Zomboo and The Rack Girl

everybody's not going to laugh at every joke. When you don't spend five minutes to set it up, and it falls flat on its face, you're able to do a little joke there and a little joke here. Some of them will be funny and you develop a rhythm, and people will enjoy it. You know, some stuff falls flat because it's too drawn out.

A lot of little jokes are like a string of firecrackers going off. They have a cumulative effect.

Right, right.

The first season was definitely designed as a local show. At what point did syndication seem to be a possibility? And how did it—if it did—change the production of the program?

I think we did about four or five years of shows, and the people we were licensing the movies from approached us. They said, "We'd like to try to sell the show in some other markets." I said, fine; go for it. But the show's always remained the same. We thought the formula was good, we felt it would work anywhere it went. We didn't deviate from that a great deal.

Did you have to go back and re-do segments from the earliest shows?

There were a couple of things we'd made local to Reno. We did go in and cut out the jokes and re-do the show. But that was basically in the first or second season.

When we put everything on DVD, we had a chance to go in and fix everything and take out all the local things, unless it was a funny joke or something we thought we could keep in there.

How has television changed since you started? What's been the effect of the Internet and the broadcasting transition to digital? Has the Internet helped with Zomboo?

I think the Internet does help a lot. You have venues like Facebook and YouTube and some other sites—such as Horror Host Graveyard, which is a favorite of mine. I'm amazed at how much material that the web master, Corpse Chris, has accumulated on that thing. He always seems to have something new every day or so. It's wonderful to see all that stuff, because you can see other people that have done this in the past. And you also see a lot of people out there doing it now. It's great, because people are following their dreams. They're out there and doing something fun. And whether they have the opportunity to do it like myself through a professional organization, or do it on their own public access or the Internet, they're doing it.

I always tell the younger people who come through the station to go out and do it. I'm a mentor to a lot of the people who come through the station. I do things in the community for a lot of causes. And I tell them it's never going to work unless you do it. You never want to say I would of, could of, should of. It's like, yeah, I tried and it didn't work or I tried it and it worked great and I had a lot of fun or I learned a lot by doing it. Don't be a couch potato. Go out and do it. As long as you have fun and enjoy doing it, you should try it.

There's no bad outlet for creativity...

That's right. Who knows what will happen? Someone might be the next Zacherley or Elvira. You never can tell. But the problem with the business now is that it's run by bean counters, not broadcasters. It's a constant numbers game. A classic example is I have a friend who distributes classic movies. And he called the station up and told the programmer, who was about 22 years old and got the job because he was either related to the owner or was cheap, "We've got some Alfred Hitchcock movies." The kid goes, "Who's Alfred Hitchcock?" Right there and then, that's what the business has turned into. They don't understand what's old again is new again. I think a lot of it too is that they don't want to give up a two-hour block of time in the middle of the night.

But people watch this stuff. And now, as local programming is becoming more important, a lot of those stations are losing viewers to the national cable channels. They need to re-group and concentrate on local programming. And this is a great way. If you have a horror host and some bad movies, you can throw them together. And you can get involved with charities, do a lot of appearances and be a viable entity to increase viewership on that station. That's where television has to go now, because so many people now are getting sucked into this national channel thing. Look at the news. A lot of people just watch CNN now. We get a lot of national news, but what about the local stuff? Again, it becomes a numbers game. The object is to create local programming to get local viewers.

Frank Leto prepares for a public appearance and dons his own make-up. The moment recalls the carnival roots of horror hosting.

There is a hunger for community, local community, for some portion of the population, and television is so reflective of that. It comes out in how people react to you as a local personality.

It never ceases to amaze me, the power of that little box in the corner of the room. It's funny, because it's a conscious choice. People invite you into their home. You're there, and I think you have to act respectfully. But then again, there are thousands of other channels out there. The choice is theirs if they want to watch you or not. You hope that you can produce something that people will continue to watch.

Distinctive personalities on a station are an important thing. It used to be that there were only three or four stations available in an area, and each was defined by the personalities they had on the air. And audiences would divvy up their loyalties based on the type of show. One station ruled kids' programming; the movie host on another station dominated that time slot. The whole concept of viewer loyalty has gone out the window.

Back where I grew up, you had Captain Jack and he had Popeye cartoons and a boat set. You had Officer Joe and The Three Stooges. On the other stations we had Sandy Becker or Uncle Fred Scott, Johnny Jellybean. All these guys had shows that hooked up with viewers. You don't get that sort of thing anymore, since I guess it's gotten too expensive. I just don't think a lot of people get it. I think if you had a station that had kid shows on from 4:30 to the 6 o'clock news or something, they'd do pretty well. Remember how long the waiting list was to get on *Bozo's Circus*? Larry Harmon made a career out of that.

What is it about a horror host that stands out? Why are audiences still attracted to something like that?

I don't know. On TV, he's a personality who introduces a movie. It's an added thing. But sometimes the host gets bigger than the movies. I have a lot of people who tell me, "We got hooked on your show, because we

want to see what dumb thing you're going to do next." I say thanks. If I made you smile and forget some of your problems, that's great. That's what I wanted to do. If the host gets out in the community and does a lot of charitable events, he becomes a physical person. When I do events, I limit them to four hours, because of my age. It's hard to stand and wear all that make-up and costume for any longer amount of time. But you end up taking one picture after another. People want their pictures taken with you. You're a person. I'm happy-go-lucky as I go through life. And it sure beats working for a living when I get to do the Zomboo thing. I'm very lucky. I never knew I wanted to do it until I had the opportunity.

What's in the future for Zomboo? What are you working on now?

We're looking at pay-per-view on the Internet. We'd like to get syndicated in a couple more cities. I like to go out and do personal appearances, do charitable work with people who are less fortunate than I am. I've had a lucky life. I've been pretty well for most of my life. I get to create things out of nothing. It's just wonderful to do that.

What I'd like to do is perpetuate the thing for a few more years. I can say I've done it for 13 years. I'd like to make it 20 years and make it into the Nevada Broadcasters Hall of Fame. And I'd like to make a little money with it. So many of us do it as a labor of love, for fun. Very few of us can make a living off it. It's a matter of timing—being at the right place at the right time with the right product. Anybody who wants to do it, or can do it, should give it a shot and see what happens. There's no set formula for creativity, and you don't know why some programs are popular and some aren't. I say again, I was very fortunate to have an idea that I could develop and turn into a moderate degree of success. You just have to throw that handful of spaghetti against the wall and see if any of it sticks.

Balrok and Roll
Balrok (Brian Hall)
Interviewed by Michael Monahan (2010)

Brian Hall grew up in the San Francisco Bay Area as part of the last generation raised on local TV. He was particularly fond of KTVU's *Creature Features* and *Captain Cosmic*, programs that satisfied his craving for bizarre horror and science fiction. These childhood experiences ultimately led him into the field of broadcasting, where Hall had an opportunity to work with John Stanley, the second *Creature Features* host, a meeting that energized his desire to revive the hosted horror genre in Northern California.

The opportunity presented itself in 1999 when KOFY-TV 20, eager to re-establish its independent station identity following a decade as a WB affiliate, jumped at the idea. Along with local shock jock, Mike "No Name" Nelson, Hall developed *Creepy KOFY Movie Time*, in which he played a guileless gray demon named Balrok.

Creepy KOFY mixed rock bands, local artists, strippers and dancing girls into a loud and often tasteless weekly monster party, something more akin to a biker bar than a cartoon crypt. The scandalous atmosphere quickly divided the local fans. Traditionalists who had been raised on hosts like Asmodeus, Bob Wilkins and The Ghoul were appalled at the boozy rudeness and hedonistic sexuality. For younger fans, these were the very elements that drew them to a movie schedule dominated by threadbare antiques like *Attack of the Giant Leeches* (1959) and *The Evil Brain from Outer Space* (1965).

The show's pungent formula was successful beyond expectations, and *Creepy KOFY Movie Time* soon became one of the top-rated shows on the station—a disreputable testament to Brian Hall's boyhood dreams.

Can you talk a little bit about your background? Did you grow up in this area? What were your tastes in horror, and did you have a horror host while growing up?

Yeah. I grew up in San Leandro, so I remember *Creature Features* being on. And I remember fighting with my folks and trying to stay awake. I tended towards the more comedic side of things. For me, the B movies were always tricky. You either wanted them to go all the way, to like really gory and scary, or, go all the way toward the totally comedic. So sometimes the ones that were funny because they were bad didn't always land well.

But as much as I liked *Creature Features*, *Captain Cosmic* was the one that really landed for me. I remember watching when they had scenes for *Star Wars* (1977), right when that was getting released, and that's still, to this day, burned into my head, running home and seeing that. Movies in general have always been a big thing. I tended more towards the John Stanley era (of *Creature Features*).

I always wanted to do something in films or TV. I knew that early on. And circumstances worked out that I ended up at Cal State Hayward. They had what formerly was a print and radio program. It was one program. So you kinda had to do everything. And through that I got an internship at Channel 36 (KCIU, San Jose). You never really realize how great these opportunities are until you look back. It was a phenomenal place to intern. At the time, this was before the duopoly rules (*The FCC regulations regarding multiple media outlet ownership in a given market*) changed.

So it was still a mom and pop operation. They featured *Movies Til' Dawn* and *Dialing for Dollars* in the afternoon. Only later did I realize that Brian Adams had been doing this stuff for years. And Steve Dini was there and all these great characters from an era of TV that was dying. I went in as a PA and eventually worked into being an editor/producer. And I had been pitching to bring back the horror movies forever. Every place I've ever been, that's the first thing I pitched.

With an actual host?

With a host, a scary movie, late-night thing. I remember what a big deal it was, and what a rock it became as a franchise. It was the thing on Saturday night, you know? And now, 30 years, 40 years later, the words *Creature Features*—boom! You have a distinct image in your head of what this was, what you thought about it and when you saw it. It's amazing, when you really think about it, that something has that kind of lasting power.

So the first thing I ever got to produce at Channel 36 was when the Matthew Broderick *Godzilla* (1998) movie was coming out. We were playing around with the idea in programming. They had bought a bunch of runs of the first six or seven Godzilla movies. The original idea

Brian Hall in full make-up as Balrok, a demon curious about the ways of the world. To learn about mankind, he watches cheesy, sleazy horror movies. Chuck Jarman, a local prop artist, created the Balrok mask. Photo courtesy Adam Marr

was we'll do some trivia bumps, make it like a theme day. That was given to me. "Here's your first project. We just want kind of a theme day." And of course, being an idealistic kid, I grew it into something much bigger. Because I started timing out the movies, and a lot of these movies, especially when they're cut for TV, have these weird lengths. So to make it to the top of the hour, some of these things were going to have to have, like, 10, 15 extra minutes of commercials. It's ridiculous; no one's going to watch that.

So I pitched them to run the movies all day. And if one of them starts at 47 minutes after the hour, we just trust that we're running this marathon. And then I started pitching maybe we should host this. We can do something more. Looking back, thank God it was a mom-and-pop-we'll-throw-anything-at-the-wall environment. So they were saying, "Well, what do you think?" And being, again, an idealistic kind of goober, I was like, you know what would be funny is, we'll get a Godzilla costume. The idea is that Godzilla is kind of annoyed that's he's not in the new movie. So he's shown up at the door with all his movies. And he's this angry, belligerent guy He doesn't get any residuals, he did all this work and now this movie's being made and he's not a part of it. He's embittered.

They liked the idea. Melissa Tench-Stevens, our program director, is married to a guy named John Stevens. He was one of the head photogs/engineers at Channel 2. So through him, we actually got John to host it.

John Stanley?

Yeah. So there's me, this little kid, sitting there. John came in, and he was just such a frickin' pro. We'd had a quick phone conversation. I explained my thought of what it was going to be, and he thought it was pretty funny. And he did the work on the side. I sent him some ideas of what we could do with bits and this and that. That guy's amazing. He came in, researched stuff, had all these monologues written. It was so much more than I could have even asked. It really saved my ass, because it was the first thing I had ever produced. You never do it right the first time, since there are 10 million things to coordinate. It's herding cats, trying to produce something. So I was blown away when he came in.

I thought I could phone a costume shop and say I need a Godzilla costume. And they'd be like, "Sure, come pick it up Tuesday." No. Turns out that nobody on earth has a Godzilla costume. The closest I was able to get was a dinosaur, and, you know, a kind of Barney type. So eventually, there was this one guy in Castro Valley who'd made a suit for himself, I guess. I forget how we found him, but I was able to get ahold of him and we rented the suit. And it was a pretty awesome suit, actually.

There was a guy at work named Alan Waterous, who does all the voiceover work at Channel 36. He just retired, actually. He's an old school radio guy. He has one of these perfect voices. He's older, kinda bald, with a beard and gray hair. In real life, he's this kind of cynic—"I've been in the business for a hundred years ..." So I pitched him the idea of him playing the human actor inside Godzilla.

And that took two weeks. Alan, you've got to do this. It's going to be funny. He fought it tooth and nail. Eventually he was like, "Fine, I'll do it."

The day came. The way it came together was just incredible. Instead of just graphic bumps, we put an intern in the Godzilla costume in front of the green screen. We just made him dance for 20 minutes. We had this Godzilla cutout on the side, and this animated facts thing. Then, when we actually sat down to do the bit; all these ideas were coming fast and furiously. We had Alan in one chair in the Godzilla costume, with the head under his arm, with this big cigar in his mouth. You know, "I did summer stock for 20 years! I get replaced by a goddamn computer?" And John in his bright red jacket says, "Who's really the monster here?" It was phenomenal. It was so much fun. The first big thing I'd ever done.

It was a one-and-done; it was just this one Saturday. And it drew pretty well. I mean, it didn't draw a gigantic number, but it held the number for nine hours. In 2000, the duopoly rules changed and Cox, who owns Channel 2, bought Channel 36. The "Let's pitch ideas" went away. It became corporate. It became horribly un-fun. You came in and had to justify your existence. They laid off a bunch of people. And then they moved us out of the building. For me, it was just an awful time. It was a clear illustration of this idea that I had of TV was completely gone. It was absolutely dead. It was the end of this fun little thing we had.

I was able to hang on for, like, a year or two. Then I quit. I didn't even think I was going to do TV anymore. It was an awful experience. But then I got a job doing commercials, which has that same kind of creative bent. You don't have the corporate layers. You sell a client on the idea and you get to do it, no matter how stupid. So I could pitch, we're going to rent a monkey. They'll hold your logo. And if they go for it, you get to do it. So I was a little recharged by that. Again, then the corporate world came and I got laid off. Luckily, I knew some people who were coming in here (*KOFY TV 20*). This was the Granite Broadcasting second change. They went into bankruptcy; a hedge fund group bought Granite and took it over. They were putting in a new general manager named Craig Coane, a new sales manager and all that. So I was able to come in here. Craig's mandate, right off the bat, was "We're going to go back to what used to be here."

I was very familiar with KOFY. I mean, *Dance Party*, of course, I remember that. I remember writing the 3x5 cards to try to get my eighth-grade class onto *Dance Party*, not realizing what an idiotic idea this was. But the thing that really stuck with me from the James Gabbert years—besides the dogs, the hosts and all that—was the Sunday night late-night movies. That was a genius idea.

The Sleazy Arms Bar and Grille *show.*

That was the greatest I idea I think I've ever seen. It was just one set. You didn't have to pay anybody, but you had this fun environment. So when I got here, we had a meeting with all the creative types. There was a big blackboard. Again, it was, "Let's throw everything up on the wall. Let's try whatever." We have nothing to lose was kind of the spirit. And of course the first thing I pitched again was late-night hosted movies. That was an idea that they liked.

There was a couple of other Internet-driven stuff that we pitched that we tried. But for whatever reason, they didn't get traction. But I kept being told by Sales that everything we got done, even if it didn't air, is a victory. Because we get that much closer to getting them to see what it takes to do stuff and what it's going to take to produce shows. Then they're much more open-minded about the *next* thing that we pitch.

So then I was told, "Pitch me an idea for the hosted late-night movie." I pitched two ideas. The first idea I pitched was this—The cave containing the demon with a human friend. The idea is he's using these movies to teach this demon about how people work. The other idea, which I didn't have as fleshed out, was that there was a kid who was left in a nuclear fallout shelter. All he has are these movies, and he's been there since the 1950s. He gets discovered underneath the studios here at KOFY. But that one didn't come together as easily. There was a third one that I honestly can't remember.

So we had three ideas. Craig said, "Well, since you spent 20 minutes talking about the demon idea, and five on the other two, I can see clearly which idea you want to pitch." I was like, yeah! Here's how we do it ... blah, blah, blah. He liked the idea. And he loved the idea of some kind of late-night franchise, because he was from this market, too. He remembered *Creature Features* and all that.

The next step was No Name. At the time, a lady named Robin Rockwell, promotions director at LIVE (*radio KITS 105.3 FM*), came over here. She knew Mike (*Mike Nelson, aka No Name*). Mike had a meeting with Craig. Same thing; he pitched a late-night horror hosted show.

Really? Completely separate?

Yeah. So Craig said, "You two should get in a room and talk about this." So Mike and I got together. I had known Mike previously from the *Alice and No Name* late-night show. I was part of the crew for that. I had known him a little, enough to say hi, you know. He came in. We went and had lunch and kicked around ideas. He said, "So, what's your vision?" In his mind he had an amped up Rob Zombie–Marilyn Manson fire-and-blood kind of late-night thing. We had been going through the archives here and found a bunch of the old *Sleazy Arms* things, so I grabbed one of those and I took Mike into the edit bay. We sat down and I put it in and hit play. It was Gabbert. He had these four strippers on, and one of them is flashing ... and so I elbowed Mike.

Balrok with his co-host No Name (Mike Nelson). In the show's fifth season, No Name abandoned his generic zombie look for a tribute to Mickey Hargitay's Crimson Executioner from *The Bloody Pit of Horror* (see the monitor). Photo courtesy Adam Marr

I'd forgotten Gabbert had gone that far; I remember the bands and the beer...

Oh yeah, they used to bring the strippers on. He had a trade deal with Showgirls, or whatever, in San Jose. And they would bring up four, five girls and they would kind of dance on the bar. So those are other images buried in my head. There's a guy here named Bob Twigg, who's been here for 25 years. He the director of our show and he used to direct *Sleazy Arms* and other shows.

So we went back to Craig and we sat down. His marching orders to me were: "What would that show have become if it never left the air?" Well, there's a couple ways it could have gone. The show was great, but 20 [years] later, with the way society changed, and the way TV changed, it would have morphed into something different.

It would have to. If you even look at the difference between the Bob Wilkins and John Stanley versions of the show, the flavor changed radically by the end of Stanley's first year. He had a new set, and really started to apply all of his ideas to create a separate entity from the Wilkins era.

And even if John had stayed, the show would have changed. Everything does. And that's when it hit me, if the show had been on Channel 20, it would eventually have become *Sleazy Arms Creature Features*, which is what we are. What it boils down to is that we're the offspring of those two parents. And this is why, when we first started, there was a lot of friction. There were people with distinct images in their head of what they wanted to see.

Something more traditional, right?

Right. They wanted to return to *Creature Features* from 20 years ago. But the thing is John Stanley already did it, and we certainly can't do it better. We're not going to sit here and try to ape his show ... because it was good.

And I felt you were reaching back to the earlier history of Channel 20, back when it was KEMO. They had a host called Asmodeus, who was a demon. San Francisco was home to the Church of Satan, so it made perfect sense that a demon would host a show. Shoot that through the Sleazy Arms Bar and Grille, *and that's San Francisco!*

Right, exactly! And that's when I got the green light. Yes. Go, go, go! Then it became, where are we getting the movies? And that was a whole other animal, because like any general manager, he wants to do it for no money. So then it turns into the Internet search of public domain movies. Where do you get public domain and which movies are public domain? What's the legal definition of public domain?

It's very shaky.

Dude, it was miserable! It took weeks and weeks. And I would find a place. "Yeah, we've got really great prints of these movies. It's 200 bucks a print." I'd go upstairs, and he'd be like, "Too much." Damn it. Then it's another week of finding another place that's cheaper. And then it would be like, "Maybe. Keep looking." So that took a while. Eventually we found a distributor who had a price we were able to work with. It was actually kind of convenient, because with many of the titles would get delivered on a hard drive. It just goes straight into Final Cut, which makes it easy.

At the time, when I was here working at KOFY full-time, I was producing and cutting the show. So it was a much more stressful situation than it is now. That part made it easy, because the movie is already in the machine, you don't have to dub it or anything.

So we launched that New Year's of 2009. The only thing that was on the set when we started was the *Dawson's Creek* poster. And I think we may have had a couple other little pieces. Everything else that's on has been given us all from guests. I think that's really cool. It builds a connection.

For better or for worse, Mike and I didn't want the show to be about us. It was important that our show was a place for local bands, local artists, stand ups. There's really nowhere else for these people to perform. The first show was really hard, because you have to explain the concept as well and get people to come down here for free and do their whatever. But I kept saying, once we do this once, it's going to be a whole different ballgame. And that's what happened.

We got a band to come in; we got a couple bands to come in, as a favor through other friends. "Oh, I know a band that'll come and do it." But the thing is, once you meet one band, everyone in that band plays in another band. Everyone they know is a musician. "I know this guy, and this guy and this guy," and then it turns into this organic web of people who want to come and do it. And that part became a lot easier.

They're hungry for an outlet.

Right. So one of the bands we had in the first season was The Deadlies. Our biggest problem was that, in our first season, we tried to do the bands the same day as the show, which took forever. It took an hour to set up, and you had to test everything. We were here all night, till 10 o'clock. It was awful. The thing is, these guys came in; they were super-easy, super-fast and flexible. Can you play this? Can you pay that? Sure. We had talked about having a house band to begin with.

Originally, the first shows we did—which is so weird now for me to go back and watch—is just Mike and me doing our bits. There's no audience, no nothing. It's a trip, because I'll admit I was a little hesitant about the audience to begin with. And now, going back to watch those old shows I'm like, good God, what was I thinking? There's no energy. So we started to let more people in. And we talked about adding the band for the next season, since we

had a little success with the bands. Once you got a little bit successful, then you can go back upstairs and say, "We want to do this, we want to do that." Once again, "Do it for free, but sure. Okay fine, here's a hundred bucks."

So we were able to spend a little bit and build the set further out. Now we can take a wider shot without worrying about filming beyond the set. And the set (*a cave*) is all papier-mâché. Another producer, four interns and I built the set. Just every day we came in here. It took forever to construct. This thing was all hand-built, little by little. It's cool now, because it's full. That's the part that I love. We get artists who come in and draw stuff. (*Pointing out a painting of No Name and Balrok*) There's my favorite. That thing is the coolest. And that was how I knew we had done something.

That was from one of the Scary Art Collective guys, John Hageman. He came back with it the second time they were on. They came and did their bit and we taped it. Then they came back just to hang out. Hagerman brings this and goes, "Here." It was awesome! It's funny, because Mike and me made a pact that when the show gets canceled, we're going to treat that like the Stanley cup. He gets it for six months. Then he sends it to me for six months, because we *both* want it. I ended up making some high-res photo copies and framing it. I gave one to Mike, and I have one hanging in my house.

Have the outside influences created any changes or growth in the show?

None of it's conscious. It's not like, oh, we have a band now, we can do this. It just kind of comes from what we're doing. So now, when we have the dancing, it can be like oh, we can just have the band play music, rimshots or getting them involved if we're asking questions or taking a poll or whatever. This probably is going to sound bad, but we had none of it planned. The idea was it would be cool to have a band in, to play us in and out to breaks. They come on down and they throw their stuff in.

Going back to the changing landscape of television, the other thing that happened between Wilkins, Stanley and now was *Mystery Science Theater 3000. Mystery Science Theater* was a complete game-changer. That completely changed not only the way you watched movies but also the way you talked about them. I was a fan. The first time I saw it on TV, I was like, holy shit! This is completely different. This is the most genius idea I've ever heard of. The great thing about ideas like that is it gives you a little bit of, "I'm so mad that I didn't think of that" frustration. Those, for me, are the best kind of ideas.

No Name shares a beer with bass player Bob St. Laurent (left) and James Patrick Regan (center) of *Creepy KOFY's* house band, The Deadlies. Photo courtesy Adam Marr

That started at an indie station....
Yeah, one in Minnesota.

Right. They had the movies and they had to figure out something to do with them.
Exactly. So that was the weird mixture. The thing about MST ... for one, those guys are talented. But the show is so production heavy. That would have been tough to replicate.

Not so much in the early days. Once they moved to Sci-Fi, the production values were really amped up. But I always felt part of the show's success was that it played like local TV, just the fact that they would read letters and hold up art work. Many kids never experienced local community television.
Which, sadly, is becoming a larger and larger number. Where I work now, I work in the sales department. And all of the assistants are 25 and under. A bunch of the A.E. staff is, like, under 30. And it is horribly depressing and weird to listen to their points of reference. These guys they don't remember any of it. They never saw *Dialing for Dollars*. They never saw anything.

It goes back to what you were saying earlier about television production itself—it used to be fun. Back in the '60s and '70s, it was the Wild West out there! These are guys who came home from the wars—basically your Mad Men *generation—full of male bonding, with a piss-and-vinegar attitude. They were smokers; they screwed around. You never see anyone in the hallways loosening their ties anymore, much less treat the station like a frat house. And the fun translated to your show...*
The thing is, this station has that. Part of it is necessity, since it's so small. If you're not all pulling in the same direction, you're not going to go anywhere. So when the show launched, there was a lot of involvement. People wanted to be in the promos, or "Hey, we need bodies for this..." You go to Sales, or you go upstairs to Traffic. "Sure. What do you need? What do you need?" Everyone's *committed*. That was huge. This show couldn't exist anywhere else in the market, nowhere.

Earlier, you talked about having nothing to lose. That was another component in the early days of television— advertising was cheap. Like you said, you pitch someone and it's a 25 dollar spot, and the announcer is screwing around and doesn't get the text right ...It doesn't matter, man. It's 25 bucks.
And that's completely changed. The time I spent here actually made me feel much better about it. But the spirit of the TV I wanted to work in is dead. It happened when Cox bought Channel 36. That was the end of it. We were the last little station. At that time, Channel 20 was a WB affiliate. Everybody was networked up. Channel 36 was still this little island, doing weird stuff. And once that went it away, it was palpable. You could feel it. I was walking around the building over there and it was, "Straighten up" and "Be careful what you say." There would be people in the building you didn't know, people that you've never spoken to that worked with you.

TV changed from being a community hub to a product delivery system. Rather than hundreds of shows being produced across the country, it was one show on everywhere at the same time.
Yes, absolutely. And the duopoly thing, again, is the real villain. You can run programming for multiple stations, all from the same master control room. And those

buildings are all empty now, except for a small little sales staff. This is the thing I've learned having now been in the corporate side for the last few years. Stations are driven by the bottom line. First and foremost, that's God—the financial sense of everything. I can clearly understand why on paper it works. You can go to a distributor who represents 10 different shows. And you can go to them and say, we want *Family Matters* and *Family Ties*, and we can guarantee they're going to air in five different markets. And we can negotiate. They're going to air between 6:00 p.m. and 8:00 p.m. everyday. And if you're the distributor, that makes sense. You don't have to go to Reno; you don't have to go to Seattle or anywhere else to have this meeting with some mom and pop station. So the independents, then, get priced out, because you can't compete with the deals that they're cutting with somebody who represents 10 markets.

So, your show specifically, is that viewed as counter-programming to those bigger packages?

In spirit, yes it is. But it's not the strategy, per say, in this building. You are basically fighting a guerrilla war, rather than a conventional one. So it's not necessarily a strategy of, oh, they're airing something aimed at women, so we're going to air something aimed at men. That goes with the bigger armies. These bigger folks, who don't even take notice of what Channel 20's doing, just because I don't think there's that luxury. In this building, I think, the idea is we're a niche station. I mean, we are what we are, and people are going to find us. And the ones who are, like sci-fi fans or horror fans, they're never going to garner the big numbers. But they're going to be the most committed. And they'll do what you ask them to, as long as you don't break that trust.

And again, that was one of the things we talked about early. Should we try to make the show, for lack of a better word, more accessible? Or maybe not be so geeky about stuff. My response to that is the Mr. Miyagi line (from *Karate Kid,* 1984): "You walk on one side of the road; you don't get hit. You walk on the other side of the road; you don't get hit. But if you walk in the middle of the road, you're gonna get run over." And that's the thing. If you water it down too much, or try to make it something else, you're going to lose *everybody*. The blanket is only so big. It is what it is, and we try to make that as good as it can be. And by that, of course, I mean as fast as we can produce it. The show is still really fun to me. And that's probably going to be the biggest determining factor in my decisions. There's a lot of love that comes back. It's great. I love that stuff.

Do people see you in line with traditional hosts, or do they see you as a standalone: This is a really cool show?

It's interesting. When the show first started, like I said, there were a lot of people who had a distinct image of what they wanted to see. And we were clearly not that. So there was a lot of hate mail for a while. But like I said, we can't do what's already been done. There's no reason to do it if you can't do it better. And we're certainly not stupid enough to think we could do it better. So it never really hurt when we got this hate, because I understood it. These people had these distinct ideas of what they liked. But we would just get emails that would say, "You guys suck! We hate you!" I'd be like, "Okay ... great."

Being out of the building, I don't see that daily email stuff anymore. But there's a Balrok MySpace page. So I get a lot of feedback from people: "Oh, I watched the show last night. I liked this, loved that, blah, blah, blah." And that stuff is great because we found a number of guests that way. We get people who say, "Hey, I'm a magician. I'd love to come on the show." "Our band loves your show; we'd love to come down." "I'm making a movie and we love your show." Great, come on down. You know, whatever we can do.

I went into this with the philosophy that this show doesn't win unless we all win. Going back to the very beginning, from the earliest moments Mike and I both agreed the show isn't about us. Neither one of us is hugely that personality driven, like, "Look at me, look at me!" I built a show where I wear a mask. You know what I mean? I'm not really looking for personal recognition.

I like the way you now take things away from the cave. People bring in film clips or when Mike interviews celebrities such as George Romero at the radio station. It really enhances the show to go outside the cave and come back in. Otherwise, it's just two guys sitting and talking.

That's actually something that we did talk about. We were saying, "There's only two ways we can go. We can go further inside the cave, where we would have to be producing bits—more sketch kind of stuff—or we venture outside. And that's the way we went. Here again is another avenue for people to get their short films seen. That's way more important.

And people are getting something out of it. And it's not exploitive at all. It's commercial time that they're otherwise never going to get. It's the best sort of community barter.

It's funny you bring that up. When I first started doing the breakdown for the show, the manager wanted 10 breaks, two minutes each, which is kind of the standard.

237

No Name and Balrok welcome Annie Cruz for a popular segment called "Ask An Adult Film Star." Photo courtesy Adam Marr

I went back and I was like, look, it's midnight. Originally we were on 12 to two. I was like, it's midnight, dude. You can't give people two minutes every 15 minutes to go somewhere else. What I wanted to do, and this is still the goal, I want to program a solid 120 minutes. And that's why we try to fold all the advertising into the show, like with the Kuvaro Law Firm, or the Sixty Seconds of Horny or the beer people. I want to go all the way back to the 1950s, you know? "Brought to you by Brillo."

Because of the station, and the kind of niche-y thing that it is, you can't go out with a one sheet and say, you need to buy us because of our ratings. It's not that kind of sell. It's a more emotional sell. You need to be a part of this. This thing has this following. You have to sell it that way.

So a 30-second spot doesn't have the same value here, to a sponsor, as it would at one of the bigger stations. It's a different kind of sell, selling the show. So that has way more value. You're not a Tivo fast-forward victim if you're just in the commercial break. It's starting to make more sense. The move to 11:00 p.m. helped. They've got some new account executives and things, and they apparently just closed a real big deal with The Exotic Erotic Ball.

Perfect!

That's what I said! When I got that email, I was like, that's perfect! Because we're going to be able to deliver them an audience they won't be able to reach anywhere else. And it's affordable enough that they get a lot out of it. They get to sponsor a segment, plus get mentions. It's value to them.

There are products so specific to San Francisco that wouldn't sell in Fresno or the Midwest. But San Francisco has always had that tie-in to the exotic. The Erotic Ball is part of the identity of the City in the same way that Mardi Gras defines New Orleans.

Yeah, I know. When I saw that email, I thought that makes absolute sense. I'd like to think that it's starting to click that way. And the good news is, I think there's only nine minutes, and there are only five or six breaks in the whole show. But eventually, that's the goal, to get down to a solid 120 minutes.

I thought it was really smart, too, the way the films were being broken up. You're coming back from the film fairly often. But it keeps that forward momentum going. And especially with the films you're dealing with, you need to have people going, "Jeez, this is crap ... Oh, look, those guys are back."

Right, because you could put up with a bad film for five minutes. We're not pretending it's anything other than what it is. But, hey, it's funny to watch. Plus we got cool guests. So stick around. We're not going to leave you there alone for 25 minutes.

It's almost like a circus atmosphere in which that is one of the rings. The movie is one ring. Then—boom— back to the clowns.

And that was one of the metaphors that Mike and I used when we had that first meeting. The circus thing's a great idea. That's kind of what it is. Here's all this madness going on. Let's take a second to look over here. Let's take a second to look back over there. Oh wait, there's some craziness over here. Hopefully, it's fun.

And that's what TV used to be.

I know. It makes me sad every day.

I'm old enough to remember waking up early enough on Saturday morning to see the test pattern with the Indian head.

I never got to see the Indian head in person, but I remember signing off. I remember when they used to sign off. Then there'd be the American flag. "We'll be back tomorrow." I remember that. It does come back to community. Because it makes it feel like your friend's going to sleep too. I'll see you in the morning, buddy. "Okay, thanks." Know what I mean?

If you enjoyed this book,
please visit our website
www.midmar.com
or call for a free catalog
410-665-1198

www.ingramcontent.com/pod-product-compliance
Lightning Source LLC
Chambersburg PA
CBHW081719100526
44591CB00016B/2429